About the Author

Noted author, scholar, educator, and librarian Jessie Carney Smith is Dean of the Library and William and Camille Cosby Professor in the Humanities at Fisk University, Nashville, Tennessee. She is a graduate of North Carolina A&T State University, Michigan State University, and Vanderbilt University, and she holds a Ph.D. from the University of Illinois.

In addition to the first and second editions of *Black Firsts,* her Visible Ink publications are *Black Heroes* and, with Linda T. Wynn, *Freedom Facts and Firsts: 400 Years of the African American Civil Rights Experience.* Other important works that she has written or edited include *Encyclopedia of African American Popular Culture* (3 volumes), *Notable Black American Women* (Books I, II, and III), *Notable Black American Men* (Books I and II), *Encyclopedia of African American Business* (2 volumes), *African American Almanac* (8th edition), *Ethnic Genealogy,* and *Black Academic Libraries and Research Collections.*

Dr. Smith has been honored widely with recognitions such as the National Women's Book Association Award; the Candace Award for excellence in education; the Anna J. Cooper Award for research on African American women from *Sage* magazine; the Academic/Research Librarian of the Year Award from the Association of College and Research Libraries; the Distinguished Alumni Award from the University of Illinois, Graduate School of Library and Information Science; and the Research Career Award from Fisk University.

Also from Visible Ink Press

African American Almanac: 400 Years of Triumph, Courage, and Excellence
by Lean'tin Bracks, Ph.D.
ISBN: 978-1-57859-323-1

Black Firsts: 4,000 Ground-breaking and Pioneering Events, 3rd edition
by Jessie Carnie Smith
ISBN: 978-1-57859-369-9

Black Heroes
by Jessie Carnie Smith
ISBN: 978-1-57859-136-7

Freedom Facts and Firsts: 400 Years of the African American Civil Rights Experience
by Jessie Carnie Smith
ISBN: 978-1-57859-192-3

More "Handy Answer" Books!

The Handy American History Answer Book
by David L. Hudson
ISBN: 978-1-57859-471-9

The Handy Civil War Answer Book
by Samuel Willard Crompton
ISBN: 978-1-57859-476-4

The Handy History Answer Book, 3rd edition
by David L Hudson, Jr.
ISBN: 9781578593729

The Handy Religion Answer Book
by John Renard, Ph.D.
ISBN: 978-1-57859-379-8

Please visit www.handyanswers.com for a complete list of "Handy Answer" titles and Visible Ink Press at www.visibleinkpress.com.

THE
HANDY
AFRICAN
AMERICAN
HISTORY
ANSWER
BOOK

THE HANDY AFRICAN AMERICAN HISTORY ANSWER BOOK

Jessie Carney Smith, PhD

VISIBLE INK PRESS

Detroit

THE HANDY AFRICAN AMERICAN HISTORY ANSWER BOOK

Visible Ink Press®
43311 Joy Rd., #414
Canton, MI 48187–2075

Visible Ink Press is a registered trademark of Visible Ink Press LLC.

Most Visible Ink Press books are available at special quantity discounts when purchased in bulk by corporations, organizations, or groups. Customized printings, special imprints, messages, and excerpts can be produced to meet your needs. For more information, contact Special Markets Director, Visible Ink Press, www.visibleinkpress.com, or 734-667-3211.

Managing Editor: Kevin S. Hile
Art Director: Mary Claire Krzewinski
Typesetting: Marco Di Vita
Proofreaders: Chrystal Rozsa, Sharon Gunton
Indexer: Larry Baker

Cover images: Front cover: Serena William–Shutterstock; Barak Obama–Library of Congress; Civil Rights March (background)–Library of Congress; Tuskegee Airmen–Library of Congress. Back cover: Tuskegee Airmen (U.S. Air Force); Alvin Ailey American Dance Theatre (Knight Foundation); Chicago American Giants (Library of Congress); Condoleezza Rice (U.S. government).

Library of Congress Cataloging–in–Publication Data
Smith, Jessie Carney, 1930–
Handy African American history answer book / Jessie Carney Smith.
    p. cm.
  ISBN 978-1-57859-452-8 (pbk.)
  1. African Americans–History–Miscellanea. 2. African Americans–Biography–Miscellanea. I. Title.
  E185.S5814 2013
  973'.0496073–dc23

2013031270

Printed in the United States of America.

10 9 8 7 6 5 4 3 2 1

Contents

Photo Credits

3dhardway: p. 242.

AgnosticPreachersKid: p. 105

anthony turducken: p. 116.

dbking from Washington, DC: p. 87

Fisk University: p. 341.

Huber, C. Rudolf: p. 340.

Infrogmation of New Orleans: p. 63.

Jean-Luc: p. 225.

John Morse: p. 295.

Karenfaye: p. 141.

Knight Foundation: p. 31

Library of Congress: pp. 19, 110, 170, 343.

Louis Panassié p. 230.

MDCarchives: p. 174.

Michael Rivera: 286.

Mrssisaithong: p. 55.

Sanfranman59: p. 8

Shutterstock: pp. 4, 5, 28, 29, 32, 38, 39, 40, 57, 98, 108, 124, 155, 156, 182, 213, 226 (top and bottom), 227, 234, 235, 269, 270, 275 (top and bottom), 280, 313, 318, 346, 352, 354 (bottom), 355, 358, 361, 362, 365.

TonyTheTiger: p. 140.

World Economic Forum: p. 59.

Published in the US before 1923 and public domain in the US: pp. 24 (left side of photo showing Billy Van), 73.

All other photos are in the public domain.

Timeline

Year	Event
1526	The first recorded slave revolt in North American occurs, after Spanish explorers bring Africans to what is now South Carolina.
1620	By this time, musical styles and forms of entertainment of the black enslaved begin to take various forms.
1700s	Free blacks are involved in the fashion industry, when Stephen Jackson makes hats of fur and leather. The industry carries over into slavery.
1701	The Society for the Propagation of the Gospel in Foreign Parts (SPG), headquartered in London, makes its first sustained effort to convert African Americans to Christianity. The SPG is a missionary movement that systematically seeks to evangelize and teach slaves.
1746	Lucy Terry (Prince), a slave and orator, writes the poem "Bars Fight" and becomes the first black American poet. It is not published until 1855.
1758	The independent black churches founded in Colonial America are Baptist. The first black Baptist church known to have begun during his period is the African Baptist or "Bluestone" Church. It is organized this year on William Byrd's plantation located near Bluestone River in Mecklenburg, Virginia.
1760	Poet and tract writer Jupiter Hammon is the first black to publish a poem as a separate work. He is also the first black American writer of prose.
1770	Crispus Attucks becomes the first black casualty in the American Revolution.
1770s	Negro spirituals, or religious songs that black Americans sang since their enslavement in America, emerge during this time.
1772	Congress excludes blacks from the military by law.
1773	Phillis Wheatley publishes the first book of poetry by a black person in America (and the second published by a woman). *Poems on Various Subjects, Religious and Moral* is published in London, England.
1775	On December 5, Salem Poor becomes the first black soldier to win a battle commendation.
1776	Congress proclaims on January 16 that "free Negro who have served faithfully in the Army at Cambridge may be reenlisted there," thus racially integrating the Continental Army by 1778.

1777	Vermont is the first state to abolish slavery and adopts a state constitution that prohibits slavery.
1781	The first known black Methodist preacher is Harry "Black Harry" Hosier (Hoosier, Hoshur, or Hossier), a circuit-riding preacher. His sermon "Barren Fig Tree" is delivered at Adams Chapel, Fairfax County, Virginia; it is the first preached by a black to a congregation of Methodists. His sermon in 1784 at Thomas Chapel in Chapeltown, Delaware, is the first preached by a black to a white congregation.
1784	Paul Cuffe is the first black to sail as master of his own ship.
1787	Established as a mutual aid society on April 12, the Free Africa Society is generally regarded as the first African American organization of note.
1787	Prince Hall and fourteen others are the first American black Masons and begin the Masonic movement among blacks. The Negro Masonic Order is the first African American self-help fraternal institution.
1787	The antislavery movement plays a vital part in creating schools for blacks; as a result, the Manumission Society founds the New York African Free School.
1789	The first critically important slave narrative is *The Interesting Narrative of the Life of Olaudah Equiano, or Gustavus Vassa, the African, Written by Himself.*
1794	Andrew Bryan begins to erect the first African Baptist Church building in Savannah, Georgia. The first building erected for the purpose of black worship in the city, it is finished in this year. Bryan formed his church on January 20, 1788.
1794	Richard Allen and Absalom Jones leave St. George's Methodist Episcopal Church, a white congregation in Philadelphia, and form the Free Africa Society. Allen organizes Philadelphia's Bethel African American Church on July 17, believing the Methodist practices are more compatible with black people. Today, the church is called Mother Bethel Church and is the first black Methodist church in America.
1798	James Forten Sr. establishes the first major black-owned sail-making shop; it is located in Philadelphia.
1798	The first slave narrative written by a black American is published as *A Narrative of the Life and Adventure of Venture, a Native of Africa but Resident above Sixty Years in the United States of America.*
1800s	Consumer cooperatives, or self-help programs, are established in the African American community late in this century.
1805	The first black American to become a prominent boxer in England is Bill (William) Richmond, a free-born man.
1807	The slave trade ends in Great Britain, when authorities agree with the growing number of abolitionists that slavery is immoral and violates Christian beliefs.
1808	An Act to Prohibit the Importation of Slaves becomes effective on January 1. It was passed in March 1807 and was the first law prohibiting the importation of slaves into the United States.
1810	The African Insurance Company of Philadelphia is founded, and becomes the first known black insurance company.
1816	At a general convention in Philadelphia, on April 9, ministers from several states meet and officially form the African Methodist Episcopal Church, the first black denomination in America. Richard Allen is elected the first black bishop in the denomination.
1817	Jarena Lee becomes the first woman to preach in the African Methodist Episcopal (AME) Church.
1817	John Caesar leads raids in the First Seminole War and convinces runaway slaves and free blacks to join his efforts. He is successful again in 1835.

1818	Ralph Waldo Tyler, reporter and government official, becomes the first and only black official war correspondent during World War I.
1821	James Henry Brown and James Hewlett found the American Grove Theater, the first known black theatrical company in the United States.
1822	The first black Americans arrive in Liberia as result of the American Colonization Society's efforts to transport freed slaves back to their homeland. Eventually, 11,000 freed black slaves from the United States make the transatlantic voyage to a secured freedom in Liberia.
1822	The first revolt leader of note is Denmark Vesey, who in May this year organizes a slave revolt in Charleston, South Carolina.
1826	The first black actor to attain international renown is Ira Frederick Aldridge, one of the leading Shakespearean actors of this century.
1827	David Walker publishes "Appeal. In four articles, together with a Preamble to the Coloured Citizens of the World, but in Particular, and Very Expressly to Those of the United States." The pamphlet calls for a slave revolt, which stirs the public in the South and North.
1827	The black press begins, and from this year until the Civil War, it is where many leaders against racial injustice find a voice.
1827	The first antislavery newspaper, *Freedom's Journal,* is published in New York on March 30. The newspaper advocates the abolition of slavery and attacks anti-black sentiment.
1829	George Moses Horton is the first Southern black to publish a collection of poetry, *The Hope of Liberty*.
1829	The first permanent order of black Catholic nuns, the Oblate Sisters of Providence, is founded in Baltimore, Maryland, on July 2. The order is founded through the efforts of French priest James Joubert, and four women of Caribbean origin: Elizabeth Lang, Rosine Boegues, May Frances Balas, and Mary Theresa Duchemin.
1830s	William Tyler Johnson becomes known as the "Barber of Natchez" and helps to popularize the black barbershop industry.
1831	In Southampton County, Virginia, Nat Turner, minister and slave, leads what is recognized as the first slave revolt of significant magnitude on August 21–22.
1831	The first slave narrative published by a black woman in the Americas is *The History of Mary Price, West Indian Slave.*
1832	The Salem Female Anti-Slavery Society is founded by African American women, sometimes called "females of color." This is the first women's antislavery society in the United States.
1833	The first college in the United States founded with a mission to educate blacks is Oberlin College in Ohio.
1833	The National Negro Congress passes a resolution that black businesses will only sell to, and black consumers will only buy from, those products that are slave-made.
1834	David Ruggles is the first known black bookseller and the first black to have an imprint in a book when he publishes *The "Extinguisher" Extinguished.*
1836	The first autobiography by an American black woman is *The Life and Religious Experiences of Jarena Lee, a Coloured Lady,* by religious leader Jarena Lee.
1841	Joseph Cinqué and two crew who are aboard the slave ship *Amistad* are awarded freedom after being captured off the coast of New York State. John Quincy Adams wins the case before the U.S. Supreme Court, and the men are allowed to return to Africa.
1843	After many religious visions, Sojourner Truth adopts that name on June 1. She is in great demand as a speaker.

1845	The best-known slave narrative is *Narrative of the Life of Frederick Douglass, an American Slave, Written by Himself* is published by Boston's Anti-Slavery Office.
1850s	Black minstrel troupes begin to appear, but it is not until after the Civil War that they are established on the American stage. Prevailing segregation laws prevent them from appearing in their natural faces.
1853	Elizabeth Taylor Greenfield, the nation's first black concert singer, becomes the first black singer to give a command performance before royalty when she appears before Queen Victoria on May 10.
1853	Mary Ann Shadd (Cary) becomes the first black editor of a newspaper in North America, when she edits and finances the *Provincial Freeman,* published in Windsor, Ontario, Canada.
1853	William Wells Brown becomes the first published black novelist with the work *Clotel; or, the President's Daughter: A Narrative of Slave Life in the United States,* published in England.
1854	Abolitionist and orator Frederick Douglass publishes the first of his three autobiographies, *Narrative of the Life of Frederick Douglass.* It was followed by *My Bondage and My Freedom* in 1855, and his third and final autobiography, *The Life and Times of Frederick Douglass* in 1881.
1854	Lincoln University (Pennsylvania) and Wilberforce University (Ohio), the oldest historically black colleges in America, are established.
1854	Patrick Francis Healy becomes the first African American president of Georgetown University in Washington, D.C.
1855	Blacks succeed in dismantling segregated school laws in Massachusetts.
1855	The first black history founded on written documentation is William Cooper Nell's *The Colored Patriots of the American Revolution.*
1857	Dred Scott, a Virginia slave, successfully sues for his freedom after living on free soil in Missouri. The decision in *Dred Scott v. Sandford,* issued on March 6, is the first decision by the U.S. Supreme Court denying blacks citizenship.
c.1857	Around this time, the earliest known manuscript of an unpublished novel by a black woman slave, *The Bondswoman's Narrative,* is written by Hannah Crafts.
1858	The first black pianist to win national fame is Thomas Greene Bethune, or "Blind Tom," who is also the first black to perform at the White House.
1859	Frances Ellen Watkins Harper writes "The Two Offers," the first short story published by a black woman in the United States.
1859	Harriet E. Adams Wilson published *Our Nig; or, Sketches from the Life of a Free Black, In a Two Story White House North, Showing That Slavery's Shadows Fall Even There,* on August 18, and becomes the first black woman to publish a novel.
1860s	Abolitionist and entrepreneur Christiana Carteaux Bannister, also known as Madame Carteaux Bannister, operates her "Shampooing and Hair Dyeing" business in Boston, Worcester, Massachusetts, and Providence, Rhode Island.
1860s	Elizabeth Mix (Mrs. Edward Mix), who has been healed of tuberculosis, becomes the nation's first black healing evangelist.
1861	Mary Smith Kelsick Peake, a free woman of color, becomes the first teacher for freed slaves on September 17. Supported by the American Missionary Association, she is appointed to teach children at Fort Monroe, Virginia.
1861	The American Missionary Association establishes Hampton Institute (now University) in Virginia, its first institution of higher learning specifically aimed at educating black people.

1862	*L'Union* is published and becomes Louisiana's first black newspaper and the first black biweekly.
1862	The New England Freedmen's Aid Society, organized in Boston on February 7, is founded to promote education among free African Americans.
1863	Harriet Ross "Moses" Tubman, conductor on the Underground Railroad and a Union spy, leads Union troops in a raid along the Combahee River in South Carolina in June, becoming the only woman during the Civil War to plan and carry out an armed expedition against enemy forces. Her work results in freeing 800 slaves.
1863	The first black commissioned officer, and the highest black officer in the segregated army, is Alexander T. Augusta.
1863	The first black in the Civil War to earn the Medal of Honor, which he does on July 18, is William Harvey Carter, sergeant of Company C, 54th Massachusetts Colored Infantry.
1863	The official Emancipation Proclamation is issued on January 1, freeing enslaved blacks. Emancipation is effected only in those states that are in rebellion (i.e., the South).
1863	The severe manpower shortage forces the War Department to approve the organization of additional black regiments led by white officers, in May, and the units are designated as the United States Colored Troops (USCT). The 54th and 55th Massachusetts regiments are excluded from this designation.
1864	The National Equal Rights League is founded with John Mercer Langston as its first president.
1864	Thomas Morris Chester becomes the first and only black correspondent for a major daily, the *Philadelphia Press,* during the Civil War.
1865	All southern states, except North Carolina, begin to seek substitutes for old codes (i.e., Black Codes) aimed at controlling slaves, and pass a number of new codes.
1865	Just over two years after the Emancipation Proclamation, Congress passes the Thirteenth Amendment, banning slavery throughout the United States, on January 31. The Confederate states did not free their four million slaves until after the Union was victorious on April 9 this year.
1865	President Abraham Lincoln orders the first black commissioned as a field officer with the rank of major in the regular army. Receiving that rank is Martin Robinson Delany.
1865	The Freedman's Bank, officially named the National Freedman's Savings Bank and Trust Company, is founded on March 3 to serve the financial needs of African Americans.
1865	The practice of setting aside "40 acres and a mule" for newly freed blacks is put in place after General William T. Sherman's military advancement from Atlanta to Savannah. This set aside involves a track of land for the exclusive settlement of 40,000 freed slaves in South Carolina, Georgia, and Florida.
1865	The Reconstruction, a twelve-year rebuilding of the South that followed the Civil War, begins.
1866	Born a slave, Biddy Mason is the first black woman property owner in Los Angeles.
1866	Congress passes the Civil Rights Act of 1866, which takes a first step toward enfranchising the black population by guaranteeing the legal rights of former slaves. It does not become law until March 1, 1875.
1867	Congress approves the first all-black units in the regular army. These soldiers are known as "Buffalo Soldiers," as well as the U.S. Colored Troops, and comprise the 9th and 10th Cavalry Regiments, as well as the 24th and 25th Infantry regiments.
1868	John Mercer Langston organizes and establishes the Law School at Howard University in October. This is the first law school in a black college.

1868	The Fourteenth Amendment, also known as one of the Reconstruction Amendments, is passed on July 28, granting black Americans citizenship and equal protection under the law for the first time.
1868	The University of South Carolina is first opened to all races on March 3.
1868	From his year to 1900, twelve institutions are established with a mission to provide medical education for African Americans.
1869	The first black woman to head a major educational institution for blacks is Fanny Jackson Coppin, who is named principal of the Institute for Colored Youth in Philadelphia.
1870	The Freedmen's Bureau operates over 2,600 schools for blacks in the South; almost 4,000 schools are in operation prior to the abolition of slavery.
1870	Richard Theodore Greener becomes the first black to graduate from Harvard University.
1874	The first black to attend Yale University is Edward Alexander Bouchet, who graduates this year and in 1876 becomes the first black to receive a doctorate from Yale. He is also the first to receive a doctorate from an American university.
1875	Congress creates the Freedmen's Bureau in March as the Bureau of Refugees, Freedmen, and Abandoned Lands.
1875	Congress passes the Civil Rights Bill of 1875, prohibiting discrimination in places of public accommodation.
1875	The first jockey of any race to win the Kentucky Derby is Oliver Lewis, who rides three-year-old Aristides in the first race in record time. Thirteen of the fourteen jockeys in the first Derby race are black.
1876	Nat Love, the only black claimant to the title Deadwood Dick, claims to be the first known black rodeo champion.
1877	Henry Ossian Flipper becomes the first black to graduate from the U.S. Military Academy at West Point. He suffers four years of exclusion and ostracism by white cadets. Later, he joins the Buffalo Soldiers.
1878	James Bland, composer and minstrel entertainer, is the first black to compose a song that becomes an official state song. "Carry Me Back to Old Virginny" is adopted by Virginia in April.
1878	The first black newspaper published in Chicago is *The Conservator*. Later this year, Richard H. De Baptiste, a minister, assumes editorial control of the paper.
1881	Booker T. Washington, with the assistance of his wife, Fanny Norton Smith Washington, founds Tuskegee Institute (now University) in Alabama on July 4.
1881	One of the first African Americans to play white intercollegiate baseball is Moses Fleetwood Walker, or "Fleet" Walker. He becomes a catcher on Oberlin College's varsity team. In1884 he joins the Toledo Blue Stockings and becomes the first African American major leaguer.
1882	George Washington Williams writes *History of the Negro Race in America from 1619 to 1880,* the first major history of blacks in America.
1882	The Fisk Jubilee Singers introduce the spiritual to the world as an American art form.
1883	The first black women's college in the country, Hartshorn Memorial College, opens in Richmond, Virginia, on November 7.
1884	Isaac Murphy (Isaac Burns) is considered one of the greatest race riders in American history. He is the first jockey of any race to win the Kentucky Derby three times, his first this year, the second in 1890, and the third in 1891.
1884	The Medico-Chirugical Society of the District of Columbia is the first established black medical society, formed on April 24, as the result of refusal of white medical society to admit blacks,

1885	Editor, journalist, and feminist Gertrude Bustill Mossell begins the first black woman's weekly column in the *New York Freeman,* in its first issue in December.
1885	The *Philadelphia Tribune* is first published and remains the oldest continually published non-church newspaper.
1888	By this year, Thomas Day, a free black, is the first widely recognized black furniture and cabinet maker in the Deep South.
1888	Robert Robinson Taylor is the first black admitted to the School of Architecture at Massachusetts Institute of Technology. Later he designs "The Oaks," the residence of Tuskegee Institute founder Booker T. Washington. In 1912 he prepares the first plans for the rural Negro schools that philanthropist Julius Rosenwald helps to fund.
1888	*The Freedman* is established in Indianapolis, Indiana, on July 14, and becomes the first black illustrated newspaper and the first to make a feature of portraits and cartoons. Journalist Edward Elder Cooper is the paper's founder and editor.
1888	The True Reformers' Bank of Richmond, Virginia, and the Capital Savings Bank of Washington, D.C., become the first black-created and black-run banks.
1890	George "Little Chocolate" Dixon becomes the first black world boxing champion, on June 27, when he defeats Nunc Wallace to win the bantamweight title.
1890	The Afro-American League is launched under the leadership of newspaper editor Timothy Thomas Fortune.
1890	Thomy Lafon of New Orleans is thought to be the first black millionaire and was recognized as such during his lifetime.
1890	Those Historically Black Colleges and Universities receiving land-grant status under the Second Morrill Act, or the Land Grant Act of 1890, are referred to as the 1890 schools.
1891	In New Orleans, Charles "Buddy" Bolden is the first black to form what may have been a real jazz band, incorporating blues and ragtime.
1891	Novelist and folklorist Zora Neale Hurston is born in Eatonville, Florida, an all-black town.
1891	*The Creole Show,* an all-black production in New York City with a white promoter, John Isham, is the first minstrel show to introduce black women in the cast.
1892	Black colleges build powerful football teams and play in contests of their own. In this year, Biddle University (now Johnson C. Smith University) plays Livingstone College on Thanksgiving Day in the first recorded black college football game.
1893	Former slave Nancy Green becomes the first Aunt Jemina and the world's first living trademark.
1893	Paul Laurence Dunbar is the first black poet to gain national fame.
1894	The first newspaper written for and by black women is the *Woman's Era,* with Josephine St. Pierre Ruffin and Florida Ruffin Ridley as editors.
1894	On May 20, Julia A. J. Foote becomes the first woman to be ordained a deacon in the African Methodist Episcopal Zion church.
1895	The first black to receive a doctorate from Harvard University is William Edward Burghardt Du Bois, a writer, educator, and Pan Africanist. He is also the first black to obtain a Ph.D. in history.
1895	The National Medical Association is organized in Atlanta, Georgia, in October, during the Cotton States and International Exhibition. It is formed in reaction to the racial practices of predominantly white associations.
1896	The National Conference of Colored Women meets in Boston. The meeting leads to the formation of the National Federation of Afro-American Women, which merges into the

National Association of Colored Women on July 21. The new organization is founded as a national coalition of black women's clubs.

1896   The *Plessy v. Ferguson* decision is reached. It is commonly referred to in "separate but equal" provisions for blacks that held for nearly sixty years as the legal foundation and justification for separating the races.

1897   Founded in Washington, D.C., on March 5, the American Negro Academy (ANA) is the first major African American learned society.

1897   John A. Lankford opens one of the first black architectural offices in Washington, D.C. In the 1930s, he helps to establish the School of Architecture at Howard University.

1897   The first black show to play on Broadway and the first to break away from playing in burlesque theaters is *Oriental American.*

1898   *A Trip to Coontown,* which plays for the first time on Broadway, is the first full-length black musical comedy and the first black show to draw a large white audience.

1898   Henry McNeal Turner is the first prominent black churchman to declare that God is black.

1898   Marshall W. "Major" Taylor, originally a trick rider for a cycling shop, is the first native-born black American to win a major bicycle race.

1898   The first Methodist woman to be ordained an elder is Mary J. Small.

1899   When the distance of the Kentucky Derby is trimmed from one and one-half miles to one and one-quarter miles in 1896, Willie (Willy) Sims is the first winner of the race at this distance three years later. Later, he also wins many of the best-known horse races in America, such as the Preakness Stakes, Belmont Stakes, and Champagne Stakes at Belmont.

1900s   Twentieth-century icons of the early beauty shop and manufacturing industry are Madam C. J. Walker, Sarah Spencer Washington, and Annie Turnbo Malone. By around 1910, Walker and Malone had become millionaires

1900s   Early in this decade, "Black Wall Street" begins as an example of enterprise and economic resilience in Durham, North Carolina, and Tulsa, Oklahoma.

1900   The first meeting of the National Negro Business League is held in Boston, with 300 delegates present.

1901   The National Training School for Women and Girls opens in Washington, D.C. Its founding president is Nannie Helen Burroughs, whose name the school later bears.

1902   Ma Rainey (Gertrude Pridgett) of the Rabbit Foot Minstrels is the first black to sing the blues in a professional show.

1902   Poet, novelist and playwright Langston Hughes is born in Joplin, Missouri.

1903   Maggie Lena Walker becomes the first black woman bank president on July 28.

1904   Charles W. Follis becomes the first black professional football player, playing for the Blues of Shelby, Ohio.

1904   Mary McLeod Bethune becomes the founder and president of Daytona Normal and Industrial Institute in Daytona Beach, Florida. The school later becomes Bethune Cookman College (now University).

1904   Sigma Pi Phi, known as the Boulé, is formed in Philadelphia and becomes the first black Greek letter organization on May 4,

1904   The first black architect at Horace Trumbauer and Associates in Philadelphia is Julian Frances Abele. He becomes the firm's senior designer and designs over 200 buildings. Later he is credited as being the first black American architect to make major contributions to how large buildings are designed.

1905	Robert Sengstacke Abbott, newspaper editor and publisher, founds the *Chicago Defender* and develops it into one of the most successful black business enterprises.
1905	The *Chicago Defender* begins publication on May 6. Founder Robert Sengstacke Abbott calls it "The World's Greatest Weekly."
1905	W. E. B. Du Bois and William Monroe Trotter organize the first American civil rights organization of the twentieth century, the Niagara Movement, paving the way for the creation of the NAACP.
1906	The Alpha Phi Alpha fraternity is founded at Cornell University and becomes the oldest Greek letter organization for blacks on a college campus.
1906	Pentecostalism bursts on the American scene and becomes a major religious force within the black community. Later, the Church of God in Christ, a Pentecostal denomination, becomes the second largest black denomination in the United States.
1908	African American women join sororities, beginning with the Alpha Kappa Alpha Sorority founded at Howard University.
1908	Rebecca Cox Jackson establishes the first largely black Shaker family in Philadelphia. A religious visionary, Jackson becomes an itinerant preacher and spiritual autobiographer.
1908	The first black bandmasters are appointed to the U.S. Army 9th and 10th Cavalry regiments and the 24th and 25th Infantry regiments.
1908	The first black heavyweight champion is Jack Johnson, whose skill as an unrepentant black who dominated white boxers is cause for much concern among white boxing fans. He knocks out Tommy Burns on December 26 in Australia to win his title.
1908	The Anna T. Jeanes Foundation establishes the teaching program to support black schools in the South. The first black Jeanes teacher is Virginia Estelle Randolph.
1908	The founding meeting of the National Association of Colored Graduate Nurses (NACGN) is held at St. Mark's Methodist Church in New York City. It is the first national organization for black nurses.
1908	Vertner W. Tandy Sr. is the first black architect registered in New York State. In 1917 he designs the country mansion Villa Lewaro in Irvington-on-Hudson, New York, for hair care magnate Madam C. J. Walker.
1909	Composer, cornetist, band leader, and publisher W. C. Handy writes "Memphis Blues," the first written blues composition and the first popular song to use a jazz break.
1909	The Knights of Peter Claver is founded in Mobile and becomes the first national Catholic black fraternal order.
1909	The NAACP, the first racially integrated institution of its kind, is founded. It is a partial response to the Springfield race riot held in 1908.
1909	W. E. B. Du Bois becomes founder and editor of the NAACP's official publication, *The Crisis* magazine, published in October, as the vehicle for the dissemination of information on educational and social programs for black people.
1911	Philanthropist and organization founder Julius Rosenwald, and Booker T. Washington, founder of the Tuskegee Institute in Alabama, develop a program that builds schools, teachers' homes, shops, and other buildings for blacks in sixteen southern and border states until 1932.
1911	Scott Joplin's opera *Treemonisha* is the first black folk opera written by a black composer.
1911	The National Urban League is founded in October, when the Committee for Improving the Industrial Conditions of Negroes in New York, the National League for the Protec-

tion of Colored Women, and the Committee on Urban Conditions among Negroes merge. George Edmund Haynes and Eugene Kinckle Jones are cofounders.

1911   The Negro Society for Historical Research is founded in Yonkers, New York, on April 8.

1912   Charlotta Bass buys the *California Owl* and runs it for about forty years. She is thought to be the first woman to own and publish a newspaper in this country.

1912   James Reese Europe and his Clef Club Orchestra, the leading black orchestra in the country, holds a concert on May 2 for a largely white audience at Carnegie Hall in New York City. It is a historic first "Concert of Black Music" by black singers and instrumentalists.

1913   The National Dental Association (NDA) is formed as a forum for practicing African American dentists who are denied membership in other oral health organizations.

1913   The New Negro Alliance (NNA) is established in Washington, D.C.

1914   Marcus (Mozian Manaseth) Garvey, black nationalist and orator, founds the Universal Negro Improvement Association (UNIA), the first black mass movement organization.

1914   M. J. "Father" Divine (George Baker) proclaims himself God as he establishes his movement, Father Divine's "Kingdom" and Peace Mission. His initials stand for Major Jealous.

1915   D. W. Griffith's controversial *The Birth of a Nation* is produced; the film bolsters highly stereotypical black images and spurs blacks to respond with "race movies" to bolster positive black images.

1915   Dancer and actress Anita Bush organizes the Anita Bush Players and becomes the first black woman to run a professional black stock dramatic company in the United States on November 15.

1915   Frederick Douglas Patterson is the first black to manufacture cars: the Greenfield-Patterson car.

1915   The Association for the Study of Negro Life and History is co-organized by Carter G. Woodson; it is the first learned society specifically devoted to the professional study of black history. Since 1972 the organization is known as the Association for the Study of African American Life and History

1916   Methodist minister Charles Tindley publishes many of the hymns that he writes during his ministry. In this year he publishes *New Songs of Paradise,* which is intended for informal worship. Included in this collection is a song that would be known fifty years later as the signature piece of the Civil Rights Movement: "I'll Overcome Someday."

1916   The Lincoln Motion Picture Company is founded and becomes the first movie company organized by black filmmakers.

1917   Singer Roland Hayes becomes the first black to sing in Symphony Hall in Boston.

1917   The NAACP holds a Silent Protest Parade, also known as the Silent March, in New York City on July 28. It is spurred by violence toward African Americans and race riots in various cities.

1918   Henry Johnson and Needham Roberts are the first black soldiers to be awarded the French *Croix de Guerre* as individuals. They are privates with the 369th Infantry.

1918   Marcus Garvey established his Negro Factories Corporation and later employs over 1,000 blacks in his various enterprises.

1919   Lucie (Lucy) Campbell (Williams) publishes "Something Within" and becomes the first black woman composer to have a gospel song published.

1919   Red Summer occurs, as race riots explode in over twenty-five cities across the nation, ushering in one of the greatest periods of interracial discord in U.S. history.

1919	Solomon Lightfoot Michaux of the Gospel Spreading Church in Washington, D.C., and known as the "Happy Am I Evangelist," begins radio broadcasts. Later he becomes the first black to have a national and international audience on a regular basis.
c.1919	S. B. Fuller, known as the "Fuller Brush Man," builds a multi-million-dollar industry through door-to-door sales in the black community.
1920	Andrew "Rube" Foster develops baseball's National Association of Professional Baseball Clubs, also known as the Negro National League, in Kansas City, Missouri, on February 13. Blacks play in their own leagues and showcase the extremely talented and dedicated minority ball players. When the Negro American League is organized in 1937, the two leagues have the most sustained success among the Negro Leagues. Foster also organizes the National Association of Professional Baseball Clubs, usually called the Negro National League.
1920	Black actor Sherman H. Dudley and white theater owner Milton Starr found the Theater Owners' Booking Association, known simply as T.O.B.A.
1920	The first black to star in a major American play, Eugene O'Neill's *The Emperor Jones,* is Charles Sidney Gilpin. He is called "the first modern American Negro to establish himself as a serious actor of first quality."
1920s	Thomas "Daddy" Rice and George Washington Dixon begin to popularize the blackface character.
1920s	Jack Cooper, once a vaudeville performer, is successful as a pioneer and entrepreneur in black radio from the 1920s through the 1950s.
1920s	The Harlem Renaissance, variously identified as the Negro Renaissance and the New Negro Movement, is founded. Some claim that the date of the renaissance is fluid; it may have begun in the early 1900s and may have extended to the mid-1930s.
1921	Eva Beatrice Dykes, Sadie Tanner Mossell Alexander, and Georgiana R. Simpson are the first three black women to earn a doctoral degree.
1921	In January the Pace Phonograph Company, which uses the Black Swan label, becomes the first record company owned and operated by a black person.
1922	Outfielder for the old Negro Leagues, James Thomas Bell, known as "Cool Papa Bell," and one of the most important figures in black baseball, signs with the St. Louis Stars in May, placing himself with a major powerhouse in the National Negro League.
1922	Students at Florida Agricultural and Mechanical University protest the governor's requirement that the school shift emphasis from teacher-training to training tradesmen. This agitation is one of a growing racial consciousness, a demand for change in emphasis on vocational programs to higher-level curricula, and leads college students at several black colleges to publicly protest.
1923	Singer Bessie Smith, one of the most important women in the history of American music, records "Downhearted Blues/Gulf Blues," which is the first record by a black to sell more than one million copies.
1923	The New York Rens, or the New York Renaissance, baseball team is organized and becomes what many believe is the greatest baseball team of its time. It ranks alongside the Harlem Globetrotters.
1924	The first black musician to perform on the Grand Ole Opera in Nashville, Tennessee, is DeFord Bailey Sr. He is perhaps the first black musician heard on nationwide radio.
1924	Florence Mills headlines at the Plantation Club on Broadway and becomes the first black woman to do so at a Broadway venue. She is successful in *Shuffle Along* (1921) and *From Dixie to Broadway* (1924).

1925	Asa Philip Randolph founds the Brotherhood of Sleeping Car Porters on August 25. The Brotherhood is the first major nationwide black union.
1925	Legendary singer, guitarist, and bandleader B. B. (Riley B.) King is born. By the 1960s he becomes a successful performer.
1926	Composer, musician, choral director, educator, writer, and actress Eva Jessye becomes the first black woman to achieve acclaim as director of a professional choral group.
1928	Grocer A. B. Brown founds the Colored Merchants' Association (CMA) and fosters black economic development.
1929	The "Don't Buy Where You Can't Work" movement, also known by other titles, begins in Chicago when blacks organize a boycott of Chicago's white merchants who refuse to hire blacks. The movement quickly spreads to other cities across the nation. The campaign forces America to take a look at the economic potential of the black race.
1929	The Atlanta University System is the first and only black college consortium. John Hope becomes the first president of the system.
1930	W. D. Fard organizes the group that later became Temple No. 1 of the Nation of Islam in Detroit.
1930s	Popular among the dances of the Harlem Renaissance era are the Lindy Hop, Big Apple, Twist, and Tap.
1930s	A religious movement known as Rastafarianism is founded in Jamaica.
1930s	David Augustus Williston becomes the first black landscape artist to establish his own practice.
1930s	During the middle of this decade, the Works Progress Administration (WPA) sponsors one of the greatest organized efforts to assist and encourage American actors, especially African American actors.
1931	Thomas Dorsey, the "Father of Gospel Music," founds the first gospel choir in the world with Theodore Frye at Chicago's Ebenezer Baptist Church. The next year, Dorsey establishes the first music publishing firm, Dorsey Music, dedicated to only gospel music.
1931	William Grant Still is the first black to have a symphony he wrote performed by a major orchestra. The Rochester Philharmonic Orchestra presents his first work, *The Afro-American Symphony,* on October 29.
1932	Rudolph Fisher is the first black writer to publish a detective novel in book form, *The Conjure Man Dies,* which reveals his medical and scientific knowledge within the story line.
1932	The *Atlanta Daily World* becomes the first daily black newspaper published in twentieth-century America.
1933	Margaret Allison Bonds becomes the first black American guest soloist with the Chicago Symphony Orchestra, performing Price's *Piano Concerto in F minor* at the World's Fair.
1933	Oliver Harrington creates the first cartoon to focus on black American life. His first comic strip, *Boop,* later renamed "Scoop," is featured in the *Pittsburgh Courier* on March 11.
1933	The first black cartoonist to work for national publications is Elmer Simms Campbell. He contributes cartoons and other artwork to *Esquire, Cosmopolitan, Redbook, New Yorker, Opportunity,* and many newspapers.
1934	A group of young black cooks and waiters, including George Ellington Brown Jr., organizes the Dining Car Employees Local 370 in New York City. Brown becomes president of the union the next year and the first black to head a labor union for dining car employees nationwide.

1934	Henrietta Vinton Davis is the only woman to serve as president of the Universal Negro Improvement Association.
1934	Reverdy C. Ransom, bishop in the African Methodist Episcopal Church, organizes the Fraternal Council of Negro Churches, the first black ecumenical organization.
1935	Educator Mary McLeod Bethune is instrumental in founding the National Council of Negro Women on December 5. This is the first black organization of organizations and the first national coalition of black women's organizations established in the twentieth century.
1936	Legendary athlete Jesse Owens becomes an icon in track and field at the Berlin Olympics, winning four gold medals. Adolf Hitler refuses to acknowledge his superiority or that of fellow black athletes.
1937	Hugh Morris Gloster founds and becomes first president of the College Language Association.
1938	"Sister" Rosetta Tharpe (Rosetta Nubin) sings on a Cab Calloway show from the Cotton Club and becomes the first black to take gospel music into a secular setting.
1938	Heavyweight boxer Joe Louis (Joseph Louis Barrow) becomes the first black of his weight class to score a first-round knockout when he defeats Max Schmeling on June 22. This feat immediately makes him the first black national sports hero.
1939	Edward Bancroft Henderson publishes *The Negro in Sports,* the survey on the African American in sports.
1939	Hattie McDaniel wins an Academy Award for a supporting role, becoming the first black actress so honored.
1939	The Daughters of the American Revolution refuses to allow Marian Anderson to appear at its Constitution Hall on Easter Sunday because of her race. She gives what is perhaps her most remarkable concert, singing on the steps of the Lincoln Memorial in Washington, D.C., and makes national news.
1940	Benjamin Oliver Davis Sr. becomes the first black American general in the U.S. Army and the highest-ranking black in the armed forces when he is promoted to brigadier general on October 25.
1940	In the wake of the Federal Theater Project, the American Negro Theater is established in Harlem, by Abram Hill, Austin Briggs-Hall, Frederick O'Neal, and Hattie King-Reeves.
1940	Sue Bailey Thurman becomes founder-editor of *Aframerica Women's Journal,* the first published organ of the National Council of Negro Women. Later, the title is changed to *Women United.*
1941	Doris (Dorie) Miller becomes the first national black hero during World War II. He is a U.S. Navy messman first class on the battleship *Arizona* at Pearl Harbor when the Japanese attack on December 7.
1941	The first black conduct the New York Philharmonic and the first black American recognized as a symphonic conductor of international stature is Dean Charles Dixon.
1942	Bernard Whitfield Robinson becomes the first black commissioned officer in the U.S. Naval Reserve on June 18.
1942	President Franklin D. Roosevelt signs the act that creates the Women's Auxiliary Army Corps (WAAC) on May 14, making it possible for more African American women to serve in the military than previously.
1942	The 100th Squadron of four fighter squadrons comprised solely of black men is activated on October 13 at the Tuskegee Army Air Field in Alabama, becoming the first black American military aviation group. Later, three other black fighter squadrons are combined and become known as the Tuskegee Airmen.

1942	The Coast Guard's Women's Reserve is created on November 23, when President Franklin D. Roosevelt signs Public Law 772. The Women's Reserves becomes known as SPAR.
1943	Harriet M. Waddy (West) becomes the first black woman major in the Women's Army Auxiliary Corps (WAAC) on August 21. The corps is later renamed the Women's Army Corps (WAC).
1943	Muddy Waters (McKinley Morganfield) is the first person to combine blues and amplified guitar to create urban blues.
1943	The Army Ground Forces Headquarters calls for the activation of the 555th Parachute Infantry Battalion, an all-black volunteer united. It is officially activated on December 30. On November 25, 1944, the unit moves to North Carolina and is reorganized as Company A, 555th Parachute Infantry Battalion, formally becoming the world's first black paratroopers. The unit becomes popularly known as the Triple Nickels.
1944	Alice Dunnigan of the Associated Negro Press becomes the first black woman accredited to the White House and the State Department, and the first to gain access to the House of Representative and Senate press galleries.
1944	By this time, black America has credit unions in churches, especially the larger ones. The credit movement in America began in 1908 and later touched African Americans, who used cooperative credit unions to save and borrow money.
1944	The first black correspondent to be admitted to a White House press conference, on February 8, is Harry S. McAlpin, correspondent for the National Negro Press Association and the *Atlanta Daily World*.
1944	The United Negro College Fund (UNCF) begins on April 24 in response to the need to address economic conditions on private black college campuses. Frederick D. Patterson is its founder.
1944	Twelve black ensigns and one warrant officer are commissioned in the U.S. Navy in March. They break the color barrier in the navy and later dub themselves the "Golden Thirteen."
1945	John H. Johnson founds *Ebony* magazine on November 1, modeling it after *Life* magazine. In 1951 he publishes the first issue of *Jet,* a weekly magazine.
1945	Tuskegee University in Alabama establishes a School of Veterinary Medicine for African Americans who lack opportunity to study veterinary medicine in the South because of racial restrictions.
1946	The Links, incorporated, is founded on November 9 and later becomes the largest black volunteer service organization.
1947	Brooklyn Dodger second baseman Jackie (John Roosevelt) Robinson breaks the color barrier in modern-day professional baseball when he joins the Brooklyn Dodgers. He plays his first game in Brooklyn against the Boston Braves on April 15. In 1948 he shifts to third baseman. In 1949 he becomes the first black batting champion and the first black to receive the National League's Most Valuable Player Award.
1947	The Journey of Reconciliation is put to the test by the Congress of Racial Equality (CORE). It tests the South's compliance with the U.S. Supreme Court's ruling that outlaws segregation on interstate buses.
1948	President Harry S. Truman issues Executive Order 9981 on July 26, signaling an end to legal segregation in the U.S. military.
1948	The Churches of Christ establishes Southwestern Christian College in Terrell, Texas. It is the denomination's first institution for higher learning for blacks established during the period of racial segregation in education.

1948	The first black member of the Regular Army Nurse Corps in March of this year is Nancy Leftenant-Colon.
1948	The first black pitcher in the American League and the first black to actually pitch in a World Series game is Satchel (Leroy Robert) Paige.
1948	The first black woman to win an Olympic gold medal is high jumper Alice Coachman Davis at the London Olympics. She paves the way for generations of American athletes to come.
1949	Gordon A. Parks becomes the first black photojournalist on the staff of *Life* magazine.
1949	(Daniel) Louis "Satchmo" Armstrong, jazz trumpeter, is selected Mardi Gras King of the Zulu Social Aid and becomes the first black to preside over the New Orleans Mardi Gras.
1950s	Highlander Folk School in Monteagle, Tennessee, becomes the educational center of the Civil Rights Movement. Rosa Parks and Martin Luther King Jr. are among those who attend workshops there before participating in the Montgomery demonstrations.
1950	Gwendolyn Brooks, poet and novelist, is the first black to win a Pulitzer Prize for poetry, with *Annie Allen,* on May 1, and becomes established as a major American poet.
1951	Park's Sausage Company is founded and brings a fortune to entrepreneur Henry Green Parks Jr. His company is the first owned by an African American to be traded publicly.
1952	Five different cases, all dealing with segregation in public schools but with different facts and from different places, reach the U.S. Supreme Court.
1952	Journalist Simeon S. Booker is the first full-time black reporter for the *Washington Post.*
1952	Ralph Waldo Ellison becomes the first black to win the National Book Award for a novel, *Invisible Man.*
1952	The Chicago-based Harlem Globetrotters basketball team is founded, owned, and coached by Abe Saperstein.
1953	The first chapter of Phi Beta Kappa at a black university is established at Fisk University on April 4. Four days later, a chapter is formed at Howard University.
1954	Benjamin Oliver Davis Jr. becomes the first black U.S. Air Force general on October 27.
1954	The U.S. Supreme Court rules unconstitutional racial segregation in public schools on May 17. The landmark ruling is known as *Brown v. Board of Education of Topeka,* and declares unconstitutional the "separate but equal" doctrine of the *Plessy v. Ferguson* case of 1896, which denied black children their basic rights.
1955	Clotilde Dent Bowen is commissioned in the U.S. Army with the rank of captain, becoming the first black woman medical officer in the army.
1955	Martin Luther King Jr. begins a campaign of nonviolence as part of the modern Civil Rights Movement, rising to prominence as a leader during the Montgomery Bus Boycott.
1955	The Montgomery Bus Boycott begins on December 1, marking the beginning of mass protest among African Americans. When Rosa M. Parks is arrested for refusing to surrender her seat to a white man, the thirteen-month boycott ensues.
1955	When Marian Anderson make her debut as Ulrica in Verdi's *Un Ballo in Maschera* on January 7, she becomes the first black to sing a principal role with the Metropolitan Opera.
1956	After three and a half years of legal efforts on the part of the NAACP, Autherine Juanita Lucy (Foster) becomes the first black student admitted to the University of Alabama. A riot follows, and she is suspended that evening.
1956	Althea Gibson wins her first tennis title when she wins the French championship, and goes on to triumph in 1957 and 1958 in the women's singles at Wimbledon.

1957	Congress establishes the Civil Rights Commission as a temporary independent bipartisan agency to investigate complaints of citizens who claim that their voting rights are violated because of race, color, religion, national origin, or other discriminatory reasons.
1957	The Southern Christian Leadership Conference (SCLC) is formed and becomes a network of nonviolent civil rights activists from black churches on February 14. Martin Luther King Jr. is founding president.
1958	The Alvin Ailey American Dance Theater is founded.
1958	The first black newscaster for WNTA-TV in New York City is Louis Emanuel Lomax, who is also a civil rights activist.
1958	The first sit-in movement to win concessions in a Southern state in modern times occurs on August 19 in Oklahoma City.
1959	Playwright and activist Lorraine Hansberry is the first black woman to premiere a play on Broadway. Her play *A Raisin in the Sun* opens at the Barrymore Theatre on March 11.
1960s	During the last part of this decade, war protest efforts of black students emerge, and activist black students join those of other races on college campuses. Violence erupts on some campuses and some students are killed, particularly at South Carolina State University on February 6 and Kent State University in May 1970.
1960s	A new wave of black women entrepreneurs emerges with the civil rights era.
1960s	The Black Arts Movement begins early in this decade and becomes the first major African Americans artistic movement since the Harlem Renaissance.
1960s	The Black Power Movement of the mid 1960s is an outgrowth of the modern Civil Rights Movement. Stokely Carmichael, known later as Kwame Turé, uses the expression "Black Power" to galvanize African Americans and promote positive racial identity.
1960s	This decade ushers in a period called the Black Aesthetic, which is used to define African American literature and history.
1960	The first sit-in movement to achieve major results occurs on February 1, when four students from North Carolina A&T College (now University) in Greensboro seek service at F. W. Woolworth's counter and receive widespread public attention. Twelve days later, on February 13, Nashville Tennessee's African American college students launches its first full-scale sit-ins. On May 10, Nashville becomes the first major city to begin desegregating is public facilities.
1960	The Student Nonviolent Coordinating Committee (SNCC) is founded on April 15 at Shaw University in Raleigh, North Carolina. One of its leading founders is Ella Josephine Baker.
1961	President John F. Kennedy signs Executive Order 10925 on March 6, establishing the President's Commission on Equal Employment Opportunity and requiring contractors doing business with the federal government to hire without regard to race, creed, color, or national origin.
1961	The most well known of the "freedom rides" occurs on May 4, when the Congress of Racial Equality (CORE) tests the enforcement of the federal law by initiating a protest against local segregation laws. The Freedom Riders board a bus from Washington, D.C., headed south, and are met with violence in Montgomery, Alabama, on May 20.
1962	Mal (Malvin) Russell Goode becomes the first black network news correspondent for any major television network when ABC hires him.
1962	Samuel R. Delany becomes the first black American to earn acclaim as a science fiction writer. His science fiction novel *The Jewels of Aptor* is published this year.
1963	Martin Luther King Jr. writes a letter from his jail cell in Birmingham, Alabama, on April 16, explaining why he is in Birmingham. The long letter is smuggled out of jail and published in various newspapers and magazines across the nation. It became known as

King's "Letter from the Birmingham Jail" and one of the most significant statements of the modern and nonviolent Civil Rights Movement.

1963   The Sixteenth Street Baptist Church in Birmingham, Alabama, is bombed and four little black girls are killed, marking one of the most tragic periods of the Civil Rights Movement. The church is the first constructed as the First Colored Baptist Church of Birmingham, Alabama, in 1873.

1963   Wendell Oliver Scott becomes the first and only black driver to win a NASCAR Winston Cup (called the Grand National race).

1963   When the historic March on Washington occurs on August 28, and a quarter of a million people gather at the Lincoln Memorial to hear speakers, Martin Luther King Jr. delivers his famous "I Have a Dream Speech" in words that define the movement and continue to inspire those who work for reforms. The march is a peaceful demonstration to advance civil rights and economic equality. Although women play vital roles in the Civil Rights Movement, they are thrust into the background during this march.

1964   Freedom Summer is held to draw the nation's attention to the violent oppressions that African Americans in Mississippi face as they attempt to exercise their constitutional rights. By August 4, however, four people are killed, many beaten, thousands arrested, and homes and businesses burned. Over a thousand volunteers, most from affluent white northern colleges, join the summer activities. Freedom Summer marks one of the last key interracial civil rights efforts of the 1960s.

1964   Congress passes the Civil Rights Act of 1964, which is the most comprehensive American civil rights legislation since the Reconstruction. (The Civil Rights Act of 1957 is only a modest statute that created the Civil Rights Commission with the authority to investigate civil rights violations.) The 1964 act is among the Civil Rights Movement's most enduring legacies, and is directed at removing barriers to equal access and opportunity that affect blacks.

1964   The Delta Ministry is organized in September to reconcile the black and white communities in Mississippi, and to address the conditions of Mississippi's black residents.

1964   The first black professional woman golfer is Althea Gibson, who plays on the Ladies' Professional Golf Association tour. She is best known, however, for her achievements in professional tennis.

1964   The first freedom school for blacks begins during Freedom Summer in Mississippi as an effort that leads to voter registration drives.

1964   The Mississippi Freedom Democratic Party is founded as an alternative to the state Democratic Party that prevents African Americans from voting.

1965   "Bloody Sunday" is the moniker given to the date March 5 because of the violence directed toward civil rights demonstrators during an attempted march from Selma to Montgomery in Alabama.

1965   The Higher Education Act is passed and becomes a component of President Lyndon B. Johnson's "War on Poverty." It supports educational, economic, and social mobility among diverse groups, and it makes postsecondary education possible for students from low-income families and underrepresented groups.

c. 1966   Black Studies programs emerge, beginning with black course offerings and later undergraduate and graduate degree programs, including doctoral degrees.

1967   Charley Pride, singer and guitarist, is the first black singer to join the Grand Ole Opry in Nashville, Tennessee. In 2000 he is first black voted into the Country Music Hall of Fame.

1967	Clarence Edward "Bighouse" Gaines leads the Winston-Salem Rams of Winston-Salem State University to national prominence, and they become the first black college team and the first in the entire South to win the NCAA College Division Basketball championship.
1967	The Negro Ensemble Company is founded in New York and is perhaps most beneficial to black actors. It is the brainchild of playwright/actor Douglas Turner Ward.
1968	After the Public Education Act (Public Law 89-791) is enacted in 1966, Federal City College and Washington Technical Institute are established in Washington, D.C., and are given land-grant status, becoming the first black colleges to receive such status by that law.
1968	Gordon A. Parks Sr. produces *The Learning Tree* and helps to break down racial barriers in Hollywood when he becomes the first black to produce, direct, and score a film for a major studio.
1968	The nation's first black-owned McDonald's opens in Chicago.
1968	The Poor People's March on Washington is held in an attempt to broaden the Civil Rights Movement to include an economic plank for all poor people, regardless of race.
1969	Photographer Moneta J. Sleet Jr., who covered many historical moments of the Civil Rights Movement, wins a Pulitzer Prize for his image of Coretta Scott King and her daughter at the funeral of Martin Luther King Jr.
1969	The Studio Museum of Harlem begins for artists who need working space.
1970	Earl G. Graves becomes editor and publisher of the first African American business journal, *Black Enterprise,* in November.
1970	Playwright Charles Gordone wins a Pulitzer Prize for drama for his work *No Place to Be Somebody.* Others who follow are Charles Fuller, *A Soldier's Play* (1982); August Wilson, *Fences* (1987) and *The Piano Lesson* (1990); and Suzan-Lori Parks, *Topdog/Underdog* (2002).
1970	Tony Brown becomes host of the first and longest-running minority affairs show on television, *Black Journal,* and a leading voice on black issues.
1970	Vernon D. Jarrett, journalist, radio, and television moderator and fiery journalist, becomes the first black syndicated columnist when he joins the *Chicago Tribune*.
1970s	The Afrocentric Movement emerges as result of the work of such scholars as Molefi Asante and Maulana Karenga.
1971	Johnson Products, founded by George Ellis Johnson Sr. in 1954, is the first black firm to be listed on a major stock exchange, the American Stock Exchange.
1973	The *Adams v. Richardson* case is heard on June 12, well after the passage of the Civil Rights Act of 1964. It breaks down barriers that prevents African Americans and other minorities from claiming their rights as U.S. Citizens, and it has a positive impact on private black colleges in several areas, underscoring the need for their existence.
1973	The National Black Network begins broadcasting to forty affiliates across the nation.
1974	Hazel B. Garland is named editor-in-chief of the *Pittsburgh Courier,* becoming the first woman to head a nationally circulated black newspaper in the United States.
1975	Daniel H. "Chappie" James Jr. becomes the first black four-star general in the U.S. Air Force.
1975	Arthur Ashe becomes a pioneering sports hero and one of the most passionate and articulate sportsmen for minority athletes. He is the first black man to win Wimbledon, the U.S. Open, and the Grand Slam of tennis.
1975	Wally "Famous" Amos is the first black to open a cookie-only retail store; his was the first black-owned gourmet cookie company to build a national following.

1976	Addie L. Wyatt, a member of the national executive board of the Amalgamated Meat Cutters and Butcher Workmen, becomes the first black woman labor executive.
1976	The first black woman science-fiction writer to be published is Octavia Butler.
1977	Federal mandates for minority business set-asides begin as affirmative action programs aimed for minority businesses.
1977	Randall S. Robinson founds TransAfrica, an organization concerned with human rights of people of African descent throughout the world.
1977	Reginald "Reggie" Martinez Jackson becomes a cultural phenomenon as a New York Yankee player against the Los Angeles Dodgers in the World Series on October 18. In three consecutive times at bat, he hits three home runs; he also bats a .450 average and afterward becomes affectionately known at "Mr. October."
1978	Charlayne Hunter-Gault is the first black woman to anchor a national newscast, *The MacNeil/Lehrer Report*.
1978	When Muhammad Ali wins a unanimous decision over Leon Spinks in New Orleans to win the heavyweight title, it is his third such title, making him the first prizefighter to win the title three times. Ali's fights continue as events with enormous popular appeal until his retirement in 1981.
1979	Hazel Winifred Johnson climbs the ranks in the military and becomes the first black woman general in the U.S. Amy.
1980	President Jimmy Carter signs Executive Order 12232 and establishes the White House Initiative on Historically Black Colleges and Universities to help these colleges benefit from federally funded programs.
1980	The first black anchor at Cable News Network is Bernard Shaw, who is appointed its chief Washington correspondent.
1981	Ed (Edward R.) Bradley becomes he first black co-editor of *Sixty Minutes,* a CBS television network weekly news program.
1981	The *Guinness Book of Records* certifies Michael Jackson's album *Thriller,* for which he wins eight Grammy Awards, as the best-selling album to date. The enormous record sales of the singer, songwriter, dancer, and choreographer later lead to his being called the "King of Pop."
1981	The National Coalition of 100 Black Women is founded on October 4 in response to a nationwide call to develop a leadership forum for professional black women representing the public and private sector.
1982	*The Today Show* names Bryant Charles Gumbel its first black co-host, after seven years as co-host of NBC's Rose Bowl Parade.
1983	Alice Walker is the first black woman writer to win a Pulitzer Prize for a work of fiction on April 18. Her novel *The Color Purple* is popular but controversial, and it establishes her as a major American writer.
1984	Leontine Turpeau Current Kelly becomes the first woman bishop of a major denomination, the United Methodist Church. She is consecrated on July 20.
1984	The black sitcom *The Cosby Show* begins and runs from this year until 1992.
1984	The first black to enter the high-stakes world of billion-dollar business takeovers is Reginald F. Lewis.
1985	Sherian Grace Cadoria becomes the first black woman brigadier general in the regular U.S. Army and the first black woman to command a male battalion.
1986	Nigerian playwright, poet, and novelist Wole Soyinka becomes the first African and the first black writer of any nation to win a Nobel Prize for literature.

1986	*The Oprah Winfrey Show* debuts on February 8, making Winfrey the first black woman to host a nationally syndicated weekday talk show. After twenty-five seasons, the show ends on May 25, 2011.
1987	Colin L. Powell becomes the first black National Security Advisor.
1987	The first National Black Arts Festival in the United States is held in Atlanta, Georgia.
1988	Eugene Antonio Marino becomes the first black Catholic archbishop in the United States and only the second ordinary bishop (a bishop who heads a diocese).
1989	The first black columnist to be awarded a Pulitzer Prize is Clarence Page of the *Chicago Tribune*.
1989	The first black head coach in modern NFL history is Arthur "Art" Shell, coach of the Los Angeles Raiders.
1989	The world's first woman Anglican bishop is Barbara Clementine Harris. She is elected on September 24, 1988, and takes office the next year. On February 12 of this year, she is consecrated suffragan bishop in the Diocese of Massachusetts.
1990	The first black woman brigadier general in the U.S. Air Force is Marcelite Jordan Harris. In 1995 she becomes the first black woman major general.
1990s	Playwright, actor, and film director Tyler Perry begins writing plays and focuses on an untapped audience to rocket himself to enormous success. He introduces the character "Madea."
1991	The first black president of the World Council of Churches is Vinton Randolph Anderson.
1992	The first African-Caribbean to be honored with the Nobel Prize in literature is Derek Walcott.
1993	Historian and educator David Levering Lewis wins a Pulitzer Prize for his biography *W. E. B. Du Bois: Biography of a Race: 1868–1919,* and in 2001 published the second volume of the Du Bois biography, *W. E. B. Du Bois: The Fight for Equality and the American Century, 1919–1963,* and again wins a Pulitzer Prize, becoming the first biographer to win twice for back-to-back books on the same subject.
1993	Novelist, educator, and editor Toni Morrison becomes the first black American and the second American woman to win the Nobel Prize in literature on October 7.
1994	Corporate executive Ann M. Fudge is the first African American woman to head a major company, when she becomes president of the Maxwell House Coffee division of Kraft General Foods.
1994	Michael Jeffrey Jordan earns $30.1 million in endorsements of commercial products, becoming the highest paid athlete. His exploits on the basketball court with the Chicago Bulls make him a household name throughout the world.
1994	Tom Joyner launches *The Tom Joyner Show,* featuring rhythm and blues, celebrities, comedy, news, and political commentary.
1994	Whoopie Goldberg hosts the sixty-sixth annual Academy Awards telecast on March 21 and becomes the first black and the first solo woman ever to host the event.
1995	Lonnie R. Bristow becomes the first black president of the American Medical Association.
1995	The nation's first Million Man March and Day of Absence takes place in Washington, D.C., on October 16. It occurs with parallel activities in cities and towns across the country. Louis Farrakhan of the Nation of Islam proposes the march earlier this year to bring whites and blacks together to spotlight national inactivity toward racial inequality.

1996	An HBO movie titled *Tuskegee Airmen,* starring Laurence Fishburne, is released, followed by a movie titled *Redtails* in 2012, which also tells the story of the legendary airmen.
1997	Eldrick "Tiger" Woods wins the crown jewel of golf matches, the Masters, becoming the youngest ever to win the prestigious event. He wins the Masters for a second time in April 2001, and a third time in April 2002. By March 2012 he becomes the first golfer to win over $100 million. In 2013 he regains his ranking of the world's No. 1 in golf.
1997	President Bill Clinton establishes the Initiative on Race, Executive Order No. 13050, as an effort to move the country closer to the stronger, unified, and more just America. All Americans are to become a part of a national effort to speak openly and fairly about race. Historian John Hope Franklin chairs the advisory board to the initiative.
1997	The first Million Woman March is held in Philadelphia on October 27. Its purpose is to strengthen the bond between African American women from all elements of society and to bring about positive change.
1998	Jonathan Lee Iverson signs with Ringling Brothers/Barnum and Bailey's "The Greatest Show on Earth," as ringmaster of the Red Unit and becomes the first black and youngest ringmaster in the history of Ringling Brothers.
1998	Mark Whitaker becomes the first black editor of a major news weekly in the United States, *Newsweek*.
1999	Gwen Ifill is hired as moderator of Public Broadcast System's *Washington Week in Review,* making her the first black woman to host a prominent political talk show on national television.
1999	Serena Williams and sister Venus Ebone Star Williams become the first black women's team to succeed at the U.S. Open. In this year, as well, Serena becomes the first black woman to win the U.S. Open since 1958, and in 2001 Venus wins both the Wimbledon and the U.S. Open. The sisters continue to triumph, and in February 2013 Serena recaptures the number-one ranking in women's tennis, now holding this rank for the sixth time in her storied career; then, in September 2013, she wins her fifth U.S. Open title.
2000	Business executive and lawyer Kenneth I. Chenault is the president and chief operating officer of American Express, the first black to hold either position.
2000	Vashi Murphy McKenzie becomes the first woman elected bishop in the African Methodist Episcopal (AME) Church.
2001	Laili Ali scores a major decision in a fight with Jacqui Frazier-Lyde on June 8. This is the first pay-for-view boxing match between two black women.
2001	Richard Dean Parsons takes office as chief executive officer of AOL-Time Warner on May 16, becoming the first black to head the world's largest media conglomerate.
2002	President George W. Bush signs into law the No Child Left Behind Act on January 8. The Act is designed to close the achievement gap between whites and nonwhites and represents a reauthorization of the Elementary and Secondary Act of 1965.
2003	LeBron James emerges as a high school basketball phenomenon and later is called the best basketball player in the world. When he leaves the Cleveland Cavaliers in 2012 to join the Miami Heat, he angers his Cleveland fans and some respond by burning his jersey.
2003	The National Museum of African American History and Culture is established on December 19; its goal is to showcase the work of African Americans.
2005	The U.S. Senate passes Resolution 39 on February 7, which apologizes for the practice of lynching in the United States.

2006	Urban Prep Academy, founded on Chicago's South Side, is the first all-boys public charter high school in the country.
2007	President George W. Bush awards the legendary Tuskegee Airmen the Congressional Gold Medal, the highest honor Congress can give to a civilian.
2007	When Super Bowl XLI is held in Miami, Anthony Kevin "Tony" Dungy led the Indianapolis Colts, the AFT champions, to the win on February 4. His opponent is Lovie Smith, black coach of the Chicago Bears. They are the first two black coaches to lead their teams to a Super Bowl.
2008	Former frontman with the rock band Hootie & the Blowfish, Darius Rucker, makes his debut in country music, producing his debut disc in the genre, *Learn to Live*.
2010	The first black woman and the fifty-ninth bishop in the Christian Methodist Episcopal (CME) Church is Teresa Elaine Snorton.
2011	Kenneth C. Frazier is the first black chief executive officer and president of Merck & Co., the nation's second largest pharmaceutical company. The appointment makes him also the first black CEO of any major pharmaceutical company.
2012	Sixteen-year-old gymnastic phenomenon Gabrielle "Gabby" Christina Victoria Douglas becomes the first African American to win a gold medal in the women's all-around final competition in the London Olympics. She wins two gold medals at the Olympics, the other being with her U.S. Women's Gymnastics teammates.
2012	President Barack Obama signs Executive Order 13621, the White House Initiative on Educational Excellence for African Americans on July 26. The order provides every child greater access to a complete education for a career.
2012	Singer, songwriter, pianist, and singer of soul, R&B, and Pop rock Lionel B. Richie Jr. crosses over into country music.
2013	There are 106 Historically Black Colleges and Universities located in twenty states, the District of Columbia, and the U.S. Virgin Islands.

Foreword

Writing African American history is as much a glorious uncovering of information as it is an opportunity to use the power of the pen—or in this technological age, the computer—to shape a story. There are countless ways to document our story. Perhaps one of the most widely known ways is the publication of a multivolume set that recounts in some detail the events that mold African American history from beginning until now. Our history has been told also in chronologies, documentaries, regional accounts, periods in history, political works, by professions, stories for dummies, and even "cute" ways, such as day-by-day stories, which is also a type of chronology. The focus of this work is on convenience of access to facts; hence, *The Handy African American History Book*. As easy as it may be to glean a cursory view of our history from this work, the aim is also to highlight many of the significant developments in the formation of an African American culture.

As I compiled this work, I remained deliberate in my coverage of information on women. Some call it "herstory." I did so because women, particularly African American women, are still underrepresented in too many published works; sometimes what is included is in scattered sources. There are, of course, many works with a singular focus, such as those in music, religion, civil rights, sports, and so on, that tell "herstory," but I continue to find a need to include our women in general accounts of African America. Like our general accounts, African American history is old as well as current. Here I trace our development from Africa to America and show how our people have been greatly influenced by African developments in sports, medicine, music, the arts, religion, and in other areas. But the shaping affects general American culture as well, for what has impacted African American culture has helped also to shape American culture.

Although the timeline that appears early in this work gives a cursory view of the book's contents and of the historical development of African Americans, we must piece together the story that the timeline tells, for, as intended, it is merely a skeleton. Still, skeletons are important, for they sketch the information covered throughout the work and help the writer know early on where there are important gaps that need to be filled. Timelines tell us also that history repeats itself, sometimes continuously, sometimes sporadically, as we will see, for example, in the civil rights struggles that appear over and over again.

Beginning with a summary chapter called "Upon America's Shores," *The Handy African American History Book* is further arranged into fourteen chapters, each devoted to a different subject: Arts & Entertainment; Business & Commerce; Civil Rights & Protest; Education; Journalism; Literature; Military; Music; Organizations; Politics & Government, Religion; Science, Medicine & Inventions; and Sports. Readers will find the references used to compile this work, which concludes the text, especially helpful for additional information on African American history and culture.

While it is impossible to fully cover the scope of African American history in a single volume, what is given here is a quick study of our history written in an engaging question-and-answer style that immediately catches one's attention. It should be the first, good place to start learning about African American history. Its aim also is to attract the interest of anyone who wants a quick introductory or refresher course on this subject.

Protocol prevents me from taking full credit for this work, nor do I want to do so. At the outset I lift up and thank wholeheartedly my good friend of long standing, and the former academic dean of Fisk University who once was my supervisor, Dr. Carrell Peterson Horton, who read the entire manuscript and gave insightful comments, criticisms, and suggestions. She is a scholar with a passion for exactness and clarity, and both this book and I have benefited immensely from her careful oversight.

Thank you Cheryl Hamberg, my next-in-charge person in the John Hope and Aurelia Elizabeth Franklin Library at Fisk University, for exploring leads for me, clearing up some ambiguities, and helping to fill in the blanks, thus adding to the quality and accuracy of this work. And to my other library staff members at Fisk University, who always show support and an interest in what I am writing, and who aided my work in various ways, thank you for being there and for your uplift. And to all of my friends out there, thank you for your continued inquiry in what I do, as you ask, "What are you working on now?" Thank you for asking. This work had also some familial involvement. Thank you, my niece, Dr. Duane Patrice Lambeth, for your helpful suggestions for the sports chapter. Thanks to my brother Ray Carney, my perpetual #1 fan. My son Ricky remains my mainstay in whatever use I make of the computer. Thank you, computer wizard and my very own computer nerd.

To Visible Ink Press and its leader, Roger Jänecke, thank you for extending an offer to me to compile this work and for saying "yes" when I said "no," for showing me that I did have time for this fascinating work when I said that I did not, and for your long and abiding faith in my work. Managing Editor Kevin Hile, I continue to appreciate your guidance and the work of your editorial staff as we continue to produce works in African American history and culture.

UPON AMERICA'S SHORES: BEGINNING THE BLACK EXPERIENCE

The historical voices of people of color are those of an oppressed people who were forced from Africa to the Western Hemisphere, constituting a massive population shift. Beginning in 1619, they "came in chains" on their journey across the Atlantic Ocean, on a route referred to as the Middle Passage. Some claim that as many as twenty-five million came, several generations of people ripped from their homelands. From the seventeenth century to the mid-nineteenth century they added to the riches of their European and American captors and owners.

It was not until 1807 that Great Britain, deeply entrenched in the African slave trade, ended such commerce in that country. The trade was outlawed only as a result of the growing number of abolitionists who argued that slavery was immoral and violated Christian beliefs. Yet, slavery throughout the British Empire continued until 1833, when the great anti-slavery movement was finally successful. In the United States, however, the slave trade was prohibited, but slave ownership was allowed to exist. In 1808 the slave trade as it had been known officially ended and was outlawed throughout the Americas.

Throughout the period of slavery, many anti-slavery efforts took place. Leading journalists, merchants, and influential men and women, black and white, slave and free, joined in the efforts. Many belonged to groups such as the American Anti-Slavery Society, the American and Foreign Anti-Slavery Society, and similar organizations. Women also had their own groups, such as the Salem Female Anti-Slavery Society. Great orators, like abolitionist and escaped slave Frederick Douglass (1818–1895), were quite vocal in the movement at home and abroad.

Equally well known among the efforts to end "the peculiar institution" called slavery was the Underground Railroad, a network to emancipate slaves. Its most ardent leader was abolitionist, nurse, Union spy, and feminist Harriet Tubman (c. 1820–1913), sometimes called "the Moses of her people." Tubman made at least fifteen trips from North to South and led over three hundred of her people from bondage to freedom. Of

Artist Charles T. Weber's painting *The Underground Railroad* (1893) depicts his friends Hannah Haddock and Levi and Catharine Coffin leading slaves to freedom. The painting was done on commission for the World's Columbian Exposition and celebrates the work of abolitionists.

equal importance was Sojourner Truth (1797–1883), abolitionist, women's rights activist, lecturer, and religious leader, who was also an uneducated slave known for her rigid opposition to slavery. She had an articulate and a fearless voice in the promotion of liberal reform in race and gender.

So determined were some slaves to crush the "peculiar institution" that they tried to force change by engaging in insurrections. Some historians believe that these efforts were far more widespread than records show, yet they acknowledge leading efforts of such men as Nat Turner (1800–1831) in Southampton, Virginia; Denmark Vesey (1767–1822) in Charleston, South Carolina; and the efforts of ardent white abolitionist John Brown (1800–1859), who led a violent raid in Kansas on May 14, 1856.

From 1861 to 1865, a bloody war raged between the Confederacy and the Union, known as the Civil War, which, among other issues, prompted President Abraham Lincoln to make a proclamation to emancipate slaves. On January 1, 1863, the official Emancipation Proclamation was issued, and on January 31, 1865, Congress passed the Thirteenth Amendment, banning slavery throughout the states. Even so, the Confederate states refused to free their four million slaves until April 9 of that year. The news reached some states much later, meaning that former slaves, particularly those in Texas in 1865, had no idea that they were legally free. In June of 1865, Union General Gordon Granger, along with two thousand Union troops, arrived in Galveston, Texas, to take possession of the state and force compliance with the Emancipation Proclamation. African Americans began to celebrate the date of their freedom, or what they call Juneteenth; they honored June 19, the date on which they learned of their new status. Juneteenth has since become a day of celebration among many black Americans throughout the nation.

The Reconstruction period—a twelve-year period from 1865 to 1877—followed the Civil War and was a time to rebuild the South. The South lay in ruins and food and supplies were scarce. Blacks were homeless, cities destroyed, and government was nonexistent. Slowly, efforts followed to aid in the rebuilding, such as the passage of the Civil Rights Act of 1866 to enfranchise blacks, although it was not until 1875 that the act became law. In 1883, however, the U.S. Supreme Court overturned the law. Meanwhile, efforts of agencies such as the Freedmen's Bureau, or the Bureau of Refugees, Freedmen, and Abandoned Lands, created in 1865, aided in uniting black families, built over forty hospitals, distributed food to the needy, and established 4,239 schools for blacks, including several historically black colleges. Even so, the bureau ceased to exist in 1868, because of Congress' feeble efforts and a lack of a national commitment to provide equal citizenship for blacks.

Among other laws that addressed the civil rights of black people was the *Plessy v. Ferguson* decision—often equated with "separate but equal" provisions—that for almost sixty years served as the legal foundation and justification for keeping the races separated. This law existed until 1954, when it was overturned with the *Brown v. Board of Education of Topeka, Kansas* decision, which denied legal and unequal segregation in schools and public places.

Race relations left much to be desired, however, and a number of protests preceded the modern Civil Rights Movement. Protests were seen in Memphis (1866); Hamburg, South Carolina (1873); New Orleans (1874); Atlanta (1906); Springfield, Illinois (1908); Houston (1917); Tulsa (1921); Harlem (1935 and 1943); Detroit (1943); and elsewhere. Freedom's call extended from the work of the abolitionist crusaders to the work of civil rights activists and leaders throughout the centuries. Such crusaders have included W.E.B. Du Bois, A. Philip Randolph, Martin Luther King Jr., and Ida Wells-Barnett. Then came the modern Civil Rights Movement, which represented a time when African Americans had had enough and new protests swung into action. Led by the Reverend Martin Luther King Jr., the movement followed a policy of peaceful protest and included boycotts, marches, sit-ins, and other demonstrations. Included were the Montgomery Bus Boycott of 1955, the Albany, Georgia, movement, and the sit-in movement, including those of national prominence—the Greensboro, North Carolina, sit-ins and the Nashville, Tennessee, sit-ins. There were protests such as Freedom Summer (an intensive voter registration project in Mississippi), Freedom Rides, the famous March on Washington in 1963, and the Poor People's March on Washington in 1968. The period saw the rise of the black power movement and greater racial pride, both stimulated by the work of activist Stokely Carmichael (later known as Kwame Turè).

In addition to King, the various movements catapulted others into prominence, including Hosea Williams, John Lewis, Diane Nash (Bevel), Rosa Parks, Ella Baker, Stokely

President Bill Clinton tried to unify Americans with his Initiative on Race.

Carmichael (later known as Kwame Turé), James Farmer, and a number of other sung—and unsung—heroes. These actions helped to spur on the passage of the Civil Rights Act of 1964, which helped to remove barriers to equal access and opportunity affecting blacks, and the Voting Rights Act of 1965, which guaranteed the voting rights of black Americans.

Organizations such as the Niagara Movement, the NAACP, and the National Urban League, helped to dismantle segregation, support education of blacks, address issues of housing, promote jobs and economic development, address issues of health in the black community, and promote black leadership. The federal government had taken some steps to promote racial justice, as seen, for example, in the work of the United States Commission on Civil Rights, a bipartisan agency established in 1957 as a temporary, independent agency. It continues to investigate citizens' complaints about violations of voting rights and other fraudulent practices. In 1997 President Bill Clinton established the Initiative on Race in an effort to move the nation closer to a stronger, unified, and more just America. Black America has not forgotten the ills that their ancestors endured, many calling for the federal government and white America to pay reparations, or compensation, for being wronged. The idea has been discussed many times; for example, near the end of the nineteenth century former Tennessee slave Callie House became a leader in a movement to petition the U.S. government for pensions and reparations for African Americans held in involuntary servitude. During the Civil Rights Movement, leaders of the Student Nonviolent Coordinating Committee issued a "Black Manifesto," insisting on reparations for African Americans. In 1990 the idea of reparations gained currency with some of the American public.

OUR CULTURAL STRIVINGS

The hold that America had on enslaved black Americans failed to thwart blacks from seeking their own cultural agenda. They came from Africa with musical and artistic talents, giving full expression to their creativity on the slave plantation. Dance, music, and song were entrenched in African societies and used in religious ceremonies and rites.

Now in America, these cultural expressions enabled slaves to shape the black community by entertaining themselves as well as their masters. Their shout, or ring shout, was an example of an artistic form from their African background. In music as well, talented slaves demonstrated their skills. Slave musicians played violin, flute, piano, and sang; some gave public concerts. For example, in 1858 Thomas Greene Bethune, also known as "Blind Tom," performed before President James Buchanan at the White House and received national fame as a pianist.

African Americans are also known for their religious songs, or spirituals, and began to sing them from the time they were first enslaved. Sometimes called sorrow songs, some also call them the most prominent style of Southern slave music. The development of the spiritual is difficult to trace, for the music was not recorded at first, but preserved and passed on orally; it probably emerged in the late 1770s and became prominent between 1830 and the 1860s. The spiritual represented a shield against the inhumanity of slavery, as slaves endured the pain of work on the plantation and sought routes to freedom either through an unknown being that would carry them out of slavery or through a more earthly method of escape. Slave songs often had hidden messages, such as use of the Jordan River as a "river of escape." Beginning in 1882 the Fisk Jubilee Singers from Nashville's Fisk University began to popularize spirituals by singing them during their tours across America and in England.

One of the things that African American culture is known for is its spiritual songs, which came into being in the form of Southern slave music. Today, that tradition remains strong in the form of gospel choirs that perform all across the country.

The music of African Americans was presented later on through big bands, in concert halls, through their own compositions, and in musical forms such as jazz, the blues, gospel, and soul. Certain eras in history saw the effects of African Americans and their music on cultural developments. For example, during the modern Civil Rights Movement, songs of protest and progresses re-emerged or were written, and were sung in marches and rallies to inspire protesters and to send messages to others. The song "We Shall Overcome" became the theme song of the movement, yet this spiritual was actually a song from the early anti-slavery movement. From Bessie Smith to B. B. King, the soul of black America has been presented in song.

Slave artisans were also skilled in their work as painters, silversmiths, cabinet-makers, and sculptors. Some worked in iron and others with metals during the eighteenth century, and their work was seen in Southern mansions, churches, and public buildings. Names of many of these artisans remain unknown. Leading painters from the eighteenth through the twentieth centuries include Edward Mitchell Bannister, Meta Warrick Fuller, Edmonia Lewis, and Henry Ossawa Tanner.

Perhaps no other era in African-American history has been preserved and studied more than the Harlem Renaissance period, also known as the Negro Renaissance and the New Negro Movement. This literary, artistic, and cultural revolution was centered in the Harlem section of New York City, particularly during the 1920s. There were precursors of the movement as well as intense cultural developments after that time. James Weldon Johnson is an example of a precursor as well as a Harlem Renaissance luminary. Among the leading writers of this period are Arna Bontemps, Langston Hughes, Nella Larsen, Jessie Redmon Fauset, Zora Neale Hurston, Claude McKay, and Jean Toomer. Visual artists were also important, including Aaron Douglas, Meta Warrick Fuller, and Augusta Savage. Actors like Charles Gilpin, independent filmmakers such as Oscar Micheaux, and dancer and actor Florence Mills helped to round out this group of luminaries. After World War II, and into the modern Civil Rights Movement, some artists depicted black migration from the South to urban areas in the North in their works. Such artists included Romare Bearden, Beauford Delaney, and Jacob Lawrence. As well, Walter Williams, Sam Gilliam, David Driskell, Faith Ringgold, and Elizabeth Catlett Mora often embodied their personal stories into their work. Some artists moved their works to the streets of the ghetto, as graffiti became popular and developed a market value. Photographers Gordon Parks and Moneta Sleet chronicled black history through the camera.

By the 1930s organized efforts of the federal government helped to encourage and support black artistic talent. The Works Progress Administration and the Federal Theater Project employed many African Americans to work in plays, contemporary comedies, circuses, and in films. Katherine Dunham, Rex Ingram, and Butterfly McQueen were among the dancers and actors who benefitted. Two major black theater projects emerged in the wake of the Federal Theater Project: the American Negro Theater and the Negro Ensemble Company. Later, playwrights Lorraine Hansberry and August Wilson became prominent. By the late 1990s, Tyler Perry reached an untapped audience and was rocketed to enormous success. During the last century, African Americans also emerged as cartoonists and radio show hosts. Much of black America's culture is showcased at national black theater and art festivals.

BUSINESS AND ECONOMIC DEVELOPMENT

Although not all African Americans were enslaved, much of the information about African Americans as entrepreneurs has been handed down through slave narratives. The talents of both free and enslaved blacks, however, were legion. Free blacks had many more opportunities to develop businesses than those enslaved and maintained many businesses outside the South. As early as the 1700s, records show that Stephen Jackson of Virginia made hats of fur and leather. Before the Civil War, there were landowners, brokers and merchants, a tailor, a grocer, and a lumber and coal merchant. One prominent name among the wealthy African Americans was William Alexander Leidesdorff (c. 1811–1848), a trader, rancher, landholder, hotelier, ship captain, and steamboat innovator. The leading black antebellum entrepreneurs included cotton planters, a sail maker, a barber, a sugar planter, and a commission broker. By the Civil War period, the combined wealth of free blacks exceeded $100,000, a respectable amount at that time.

Notable among slave-born entrepreneurs is William Tiler Johnson (1809–1851), who became known as the "Barber of Natchez"; he was especially popular among white Americans. Until the late nineteenth century black barbershops with large white clientele fared well. During the lifetime of the African-American community, both barber shops and beauty shops have been successful industries. Those shops that survived in the racially segregated South, however, often catered to whites. Icons of the black beauty industry are Madam C. J. Walker (1867–1919), Sarah Spencer Washington (1889–1953), and Annie Turnbo Malone (1869–1957). In addition to manufacturing companies that these women founded and owned, they established beauty schools and revolutionized the care of black hair. In later years, the Cardozo sisters, Rose Morgan (1912–2008), and Joe L. Dudley (1937–) became prominent salon owners, stylists, and/or owners of manufacturing companies. Barber shops and beauty shops became vital to the Civil Rights Movement of the 1960s and were political incubators for politicians and civil rights workers who needed a safe haven in which to plan and promote their work.

The Universal Negro Improvement Association (UNIA), founded by journalist and activist Marcus Garvey (1887–1940), was well known for promoting economic development in the black community. Garvey also launched a shipping company and established other business organizations that employed many blacks. He also founded a tailoring business, grocery stores, restaurants, a doll factory, and other ventures that brought him phenomenal success.

The Oakland, California, headquarters of the Universal Negro Improvement Association was located in Liberty Hall, which is now on the list of the National Register of Historic Places. The UNIA promoted economic activity in the black community.

Among other businesses that supported economic development in the African-American community is the funeral business. Following the Civil War, the funeral business emerged as a one-person operation and later grew into a family business. This industry was highly successful up to the 1980s, when inflation took its toll, and many firms closed their doors. Others, however, merged and remained successful. Some funeral establishments owned burial associations, insurance companies, cemeteries, and other services.

Black business districts in two cities became known as "Black Wall Street." In the first decades of the twentieth century, Durham (North Carolina) and Tulsa (Oklahoma) each had a number of flourishing businesses owned and operated by blacks. In Durham, these included the well-known North Carolina Mutual Life Insurance Company as well as cafes, movie houses, barber shops, boarding houses, grocery stores, funeral homes, and other traditional services. Tulsa offered hospitals, libraries, churches, grocery stores, a bus line, construction companies, and other ventures. The golden age of black business development came during the first half of the twentieth century, as blacks in many areas served a segregated market with businesses such as real estate, hotels, homes, theaters, railroad lines and other transportation systems, automobile repair shops, banks, and loan associations.

Not to be overlooked is the banking business and the leadership that African Americans provided in that area. While the federally founded Freedman's Bank (or the National Freedman's Savings Bank and Trust Company), established in 1865, aimed to serve the financial needs of African Americans, it was privately owned by whites. In 1888 the nation saw the first black-created and black-run banks: the True Reformers' Bank of Richmond, Virginia, and the Capital Savings Bank of Washington, D.C. In 1903 Maggie Lena Walker (1865–1934) founded the Saint Luke Penny Savings Bank in Richmond, Virginia, and became the first black woman bank president in the nation. Her bank survived the Great Depression and continues to function today.

The African-American community has been the source of many self-help programs, such as consumer cooperatives. Spurred by union leader A. Philip Randolph in Harlem and the Housewives League of Detroit, they began to evolve after World War I. The Colored Merchants Association was a notable example of a consumer cooperative. Founded in 1928, the cooperative was a voluntary chain consisting at first of twelve members who operated their grocery stores as "C.M.A." stores. Soon the organization spread to other states, with its national headquarters in New York City. The organization began to decline in the 1930s.

Economic boycotts and protests have a long history in black America and date back to 1933, when the National Negro Congress resolved that black business should not buy or sell products that were slave-made. Between 1900 and 1906, blacks in over twenty-five Southern cities protested against segregated seats on street cars. Similar economic protests and economic withdrawals continued and became more widely known during the sit-ins and freedom rides of the modern Civil Rights Movement. Jobs for blacks, promoted through the "Don't Buy Where You Can't Work" campaign that began in 1929, were a forerunner of the economic protests of the Civil Rights Movement.

The food service industry (including soul-food restaurants), insurance companies, manufacturing, publishing, and other ventures have brought prominence to the black community. To protect the rights of workers in segregated work situations, black union leaders such as A. Philip Randolph, George Ellington Brown, and Addie L. Wyatt emerged. Black women have prospered as entrepreneurs as far back as the 1860s. Some leaders include Christiana Carteaux Bannister (1819–1902), who operated a "Shampooing and Hair Dyeing" business in Massachusetts and Rhode Island; slave-born nurse and midwife Biddy Mason (1818–1891), the first known black woman property owner in Los Angeles; and women of the hair-care industry, such as Madam C. J. Walker and Annie Turnbo Malone, who both became millionaires.

ORGANIZED FOR PROGRESS

The educational, economic, social, and cultural needs of the African-American community have been addressed by a number of organizations focused on meeting these needs.

Since many of these organizations were founded during the time of widespread racial segregation, they addressed issues that advanced the black race. While the exact year in which black organizations were first founded is unknown, it has been established that in 1787 the Free African Society was founded, becoming the first black organization of note in this country. Grouped by type, these organizations include abolitionist, business, civil and human rights, educational, financial, funeral, journalism, medical, political, social, religious, and women's groups. The National Negro Business League, organized by educator and school-founder Booker T. Washington in 1900, had various initiatives, among them to help black people establish new ventures and to bring about black economic independence. In the 1920s many African Americans worked wherever they could to meet financial needs; thus, they took jobs with companies such as the Pullman Palace Car Company. They endured numerous injustices in employment, which led them to unite in protest. In 1925 A. Philip Randolph organized the Brotherhood of Sleeping Car Porters, the first major nationwide black union, but many years would pass before the Pullman Company actually accepted their collective bargaining plan. In time, other unions were established to ensure equal benefits in employment between white and black workers.

While not a black organization, the American Missionary Association was established in 1846 with an aim to form overseas missions for freed slaves. Soon the AMA turned its efforts to abolitionist and educational activities within the United States. From 1850 until the end of the Civil War, the AMA established over five hundred schools for blacks and whites in the South. Later the AMA founded several black colleges. The need to promote the civil rights of African Americans led to the establishment of such organizations as the National Equal Rights League in 1864, the National Afro-American League in 1890, and the Niagara Movement in 1905, which was the forerunner of the NAACP (founded in 1909). In 1910 the Committee on Urban Conditions Among Negroes was founded and, in 1911, became the National Urban League. Its purpose was to secure civil and economic opportunities for black people. When the modern Civil Rights Movement began in the 1950s, blacks saw a need to establish organizations to promote nonviolent and direct-action attacks on segregated America. Thus, the Southern Christian Leadership Conference grew out of the 1955–1956 Montgomery Bus Boycott and worked to appeal to the moral conscience

A Pullman porter assists a white woman onto a train. The racist injustices the porters faced led to their organizing the Brotherhood of Sleeping Car Porters.

of those who supported racial segregation. A youth political organization was also organized in 1960 and became known as the Student Nonviolent Coordinating Committee, which helped students to become involved in the fight for equal rights.

Those organizations formed as learned societies to promote professional study of black history and culture included the Association for the Study of Negro Life and History, co-founded in 1915 by Carter G. Woodson; in 1976 it was renamed the Association for the Study of African American Life and History. The organization sponsored the first Negro History Week in 1926; since 1976, the week-long celebration has been renamed Black History Month. In the educational arena, the United Negro College Fund began in 1944 in response to the need to address economic conditions of private black colleges. It continues to exist, with support from various philanthropic organizations. A few black colleges have been recognized for their academic excellence and granted chapters of Phi Beta Kappa, a prestigious honorary society for undergraduate achievement in the humanities. The first chapter was established at Fisk University on April 4, 1953, followed by a chapter at Howard University four days later.

There are also black fraternal, social service, and religious organizations founded for blacks. Among these is Sigma Pi Phi (or the Boulé) for men who have made a place for themselves in the community and black fraternities and sororities (or Greek-letter organizations), once social organizations and now service-oriented. These include the oldest—Alpha Phi Alpha—established in 1906; Omega Psi Phi, Kappa Alpha Psi, and Phi Beta Sigma. Black women's sororities include Alpha Kappa Alpha (the oldest, founded in 1908), Delta Sigma Theta, and Zeta Phi Beta. Undergraduate chapters exist on college campuses, while graduate chapters are within many communities. In addition to these organizations, the medical community organized the National Medical Association in 1895 and the National Dental Association, which was founded in 1932 with the merger of several dental associations. Among those organizations founded for black women are the National Council of Negro Women, which educator Mary McLeod Bethune helped to form in 1935; from 1957 to 1998 the organization was headed by nationally known community servant Dorothy Irene Height. The Links, Inc. was established in 1946 as an international not-for-profit corporation for women. It is one of the largest and oldest volunteer organizations in the country.

A POLITICAL AGENDA

African Americans have long seen a need to create their own political agenda, primarily as a means of securing their equal rights. While a few blacks, such as Henry Highland Garnet, Charles B. Ray, Samuel Ringgold Ward, and Frederick Douglass, had been involved in national political gatherings as early as 1843 and 1866, and one (Douglass) was nominated as a vice presidential candidate at the Republican Convention in 1872, much more political action came during the Reconstruction (the twelve-year period following the Civil War). During this period, black Americans were represented at every level of government, at the local, state, and federal levels. The nation saw blacks as postmaster, deputy U.S. marshal, treasury agent, federal office clerks, on county governing boards, police juries, and boards of supervisors. In 1868 John Willis Menard (1839–1893) was the first black elected to Congress. Between 1879 and 1901, more than one thousand African Americans were elected to local and state office. There were six lieutenant governors and one governor. In Louisiana, P.B.S. Pinchback (1837–1921), became the first African-American governor; he was appointed to the post but defeated in elections in 1871. He remained the nation's only black governor until 1989, when L. Douglas Wilder was elected governor of Virginia.

The Great Migration, which occurred from about 1880 to 1970 (with a break between 1930 and 1940), saw blacks move from the South to urban centers in the North, to Kansas, and other Midwestern states. They also settled in major cities, such as New York, Cleveland, Detroit, Chicago, and Los Angeles. They migrated because of economic desperation, racism, and difficult living conditions. The Republican Party was the party of choice by most African Americans until the 1930s, when blacks became alienated from that party and U.S. President Herbert Hoover. After Franklin D. Roosevelt took office, certainly by his second run in 1936, blacks switched their support in his favor and toward the Democratic Party.

President Roosevelt established a network of African-American advisors who became an informal body known as the "Black Cabinet." This group represented black interests and concerns during the Great Depression and the New Deal economic recovery programs of the 1930s. Members included journalist Robert L. Vann, law school administrator William H. Hastie, National Urban League executive Eugene Kinckle Jones, educator Mary McLeod Bethune, and Ralph Bunche (later of United Nations fame). Blacks also gained considerable political clout during the Roosevelt administration, becoming specialists and advisors in a number of governmental departments. During President Bill Clinton's administration, a record number of African Americans joined his cabinet. These included secretary of commerce Ron Brown, energy secretary Hazel R. O'Leary, U.S. surgeon general Joycelyn Elders, secretary of agriculture Michael Espy, and secretary of transportation Rodney Slater.

President George W. Bush appointed fewer African Americans to top positions than Clinton. His appointees include Colin Powell (as chairman of the Joint Chiefs of Staff and later secretary of state), secretary of education Rodney Paige, secretary of housing and urban development Alphonso Jackson, and secretary of state Condoleezza Rice.

African Americans have made inroads in the federal courts; for example, Thurgood Marshall (1908–1993) became the first black associate justice of the U.S. Supreme Court in 1967. Clarence Thomas was named to the court in 1991, becoming only the second black associate justice of that court. Black women have made their mark on the political scene as well. In 1996 Constance Baker Motley (1921–2005) was the first black woman federal judge, serving on the U.S. District Court, the Southern District of New York. Women have served as mayors of cities and in the U.S. Congress.

Most historic among the political accomplishments of African Americans was the election of Barack Obama to the U.S. Presidency in 2008, and his reelection in 2012, making him the first of his race elected to the highest office in the nation. He was catapulted onto the national political scene in 2004, after giving a stirring keynote address before the Democratic National Convention. During his campaign for the presidency, he garnered financial support from small donations solicited over the Internet and used blogs and other nontraditional media avenues to change the way political campaigns are conducted. His campaign for reelection was characterized by smart political moves by his advisors, such as door-to-door voter solicitations in unexpected neighborhoods and a demonstrated record of uplifting the national community, particularly its economic conditions.

AMEN, BROTHER!

Religion has been an important part of the African-American experience. From the beginning, Colonial America saw some slaves Christianized but soon questioned this practice because a number of Christian slaves successfully sued for their freedom. John Wesley and others became sympathetic to their cause and needs. Others who brought the gospel to slaves included Harry Hosier, also known as "Black Harry"; he was the first known black Methodist preacher. The African influence was seen early in the family structure, funeral practices, and church organizations of black Americans. As early churches during slavery were segregated, informal black churches, called "hush harbors" or "bush arbors," were gradually established. These were hollows or remote and inconspicuous places in the slave community where slaves, led by slave preachers, worshipped God as they pleased and in a tradition that their masters never knew they had.

Independent black churches were founded by various religious denominations. The first black Baptist church was organized in 1758, in Mecklenburg, Virginia. Some say that such a church existed in Lunenburg in 1756, but this is unsubstantiated. The first black Baptist church under black leadership was formed in Silver Bluff, South Carolina, with David George, a slave, as its first black pastor. Andrew Bryan built the First African American Baptist Church in Savannah, Georgia, in 1794. Methodist societies also held revivals and some churches had racially mixed memberships. Many early black Baptist and Methodist preachers were unable to read or write, and some of the earliest preachers and exhorters were former African priests who had leadership and persuasive abilities. Their services were emotionally charged and filled with imagery.

Leaders of the African American Episcopal Church included Richard Allen and Absalom Jones, who left a white congregation in Philadelphia and formed the Free African Society. Then Allen organized Bethel Methodist Church in Philadelphia in 1794. Allen later became the first black bishop in the African Methodist Episcopal Church; he sanctioned the inclusion of women in the ministry and authorized Jarena Lee to be an ex-

13

The first African Baptist church, seen here, was established in Savannah, Georgia, in 1794.

horter in the church. His church, and many other black churches of that period, was a forum for abolitionists and anti-lynching campaigns. As blacks protested their ill-treatment, Henry McNeal Turner, a bishop in the African Methodist Episcopal Church, became the first black churchman to declare that God is black.

The black church has continued to believe in the importance of music, especially singing, in the worship service, saying that it is a magnet of attraction and serves as a vehicle of spiritual transport for the congregation. This is a carry-over from the West African diaspora where the music is vocal or instrumental. Some use African drums, while the use of spirituals in the black church has been perpetuated. Music in black churches popularly includes performances of groups of liturgical dancers. Gospel music has been promoted in the black church as well, and was greatly influenced by the work of Charles Tindley, at first an itinerant preacher who preached and sang at camp meetings in Maryland. Later he became one of the most powerful leaders in Philadelphia's black community, speaking before black and white audiences. His Temple United Methodist Church became famous for concerts and new music, much of it written by Tindley himself. Other gospel composers of that period and later times include Sallie Martin, Roberta Martin, Lucie Campbell, Thomas Dorsey, and Mahalia Jackson.

A key to the success of the modern Civil Rights Movement was the black church and its leadership. Many remained at the forefront of the movement and were also leaders of such civil rights organizations as the Southern Christian Leadership Conference. Most prominent among these church leaders was Martin Luther King Jr. His "Letter from the Birmingham Jail" as well as his "I Have a Dream" speech, delivered at the 1963 March on Washington, became well studied and well quoted in many arenas. As well, his leadership of various protest marches in which he literally put his life on the line before staunch segregationists attested to his full support of equal rights for all people, but particularly blacks.

Black megachurches have emerged during the last two decades of the twentieth century. Their leaders—many of them charismatic preachers and speakers—include T. D. Jakes, Creflo Dollar, Eddie Long, and Frederick K. C. Price. Jakes is said to be the best known among the megapreachers and now has celebrity status as well as material success. In addition to these churches and the various religious denominations of note, some blacks have joined the Jewish faith. In 1906 Pentecostalism began to spread in the black community. Some black church leaders advocated Black Nationalism; for example, men like Bishop Henry McNeal Turner, Marcus Garvey, Elijah Muhammad, and Malcolm X popularized the movement. It was about 1914 that M. J. "Father" Divine, or George Baker, and William J. Seymour promoted the traditions of the Pentecostal movement. The Rastafarianism movement began in the early 1930s; it was founded in Jamaica and is based on interpretations of the Bible and repatriation to Africa. Muslims in America follow the traditions of Wallace Fard, who in 1930 organized the group that became Temple No. 1 of the Nation of Islam in Detroit.

Women of righteous discontent emerged early on and were vital leaders of the community, sometimes serving as traveling evangelists. After being denied access to the pulpit for many years, women finally emerged as leaders. These included Sojourner Truth, Zilpha Elaw, and Jarena Lee. The first largely black Shaker family in Philadelphia was founded by Rebecca Cox Jackson. Since 1984 the nation has seen black women bishops—Leontine T. C. Kelly in the United Methodist Church, Barbara Clementine Harris in the Anglican Church, Vashti McKenzie in the African Methodist Episcopal Church, and Teresa Elaine Snorton of the Christian Methodist Episcopal Church. Since the 1970s, as women sought equality and many joined the feminist movement, there began a trend called woman's theology. The term was derived from the "Womanist" theory of writer Alice Walker, who believes that the experiences of black women and white women are vastly different. Some say that it is similar to black theology, or the hope and liberation of women or of black people.

SCIENCE AND SCIENTIFIC CREATIVITY

African Americans have changed the world through their contributions to science, medicine, inventions, and aviation. Names such as Benjamin Banneker, who issued almanacs and helped to survey the national capital, and George Washington Carver, who derived hundreds of products from peanuts, sweet potatoes, and pecans, are commonly and rightfully known. What are perhaps less well-known are the inventions of slaves and free blacks who lived much earlier. Since slaves were forbidden from receiving patents, their inventions went unrecorded, and patents were assigned to their masters instead. Free blacks were able to record some of their inventions; for example Henry Blair patented a corn or seed planter, Thomas Jennings invented a dry-cleaning process, and Augustus Jackson improved the process for making ice cream ice cream (his work was not patented). In 1781 Peter Hill became America's first known black clockmaker. Published works often promote the work of Norbert Rillieux, whose inventions were of great value to sugar-refining; Elijah McCoy, who patented several lubricators for steam engines; Lewis Howard Latimer, who patented the first cost-efficient method for producing carbon filaments for electric lights; and Garrett A. Morgan, the first black to receive a patent for a safety hood and smoke protector. The implantable heart pacemaker that Otis F. Boykin invented has

This photo shows George Washington Carver working in his laboratory at the Tuskegee Institute. Carver is most often remembered for his many discoveries that advanced agricultural science.

helped to save and lengthen the lives of thousands of men and women worldwide. Black women have achieved as inventors as well; for example, Marjorie Stewart Joyner patented a permanent waving machine and, in more recent years, Patricia E. Bath discovered and invented the laserphaco probe, a new device for cataract surgery.

The history of African Americans in medicine shows that slaves, who lived in unsanitary conditions, were concerned about their health and used their homeland knowledge of herbs, barks, and other items found in everyday life to create cures. Herb or root healers dispensed medicine for the treatment of slaves and their masters as well. In addition to the self-trained practitioners during the slavery period, early black physicians, some of them self-taught and others trained by apprenticeship, included David Ruggles, William Wells Brown, John Sweat Rock (also a lawyer), and Martin Robison Delany. Those professionally trained included James McCune Smith and Alexander Thomas Augusta. Some physicians graduated from what was known as the Eclectic Medical College in Philadelphia, which was composed of physicians in pre-Civil War America who believed in native remedies such as plants and herbs. The nation continues to acknowledge Daniel Hale Williams, who performed the world's first successful heart operation in 1893, as well as Charles Richard Drew, the first person to set up a blood bank, in 1940. Benjamin Solomon Carson gained international acclaim in 1987 when he and a seventy-member surgical team successfully separated seven-month-old West German twins who were conjoined at the back of the head. A number of black medical schools were established, soon after the Civil War. Howard University was the first historically black institution to establish a medical school, in 1868. During the next four decades, at least thirteen other black institutions followed. Notable among these is Meharry Medical College, founded in 1876 and thus the oldest surviving black medical school in the South.

In aviation and space, one of the early black pilots in America was Eugene J. Bullard, who in 1917 flew for the French. Black women drew attention in aviation in 1921, when Bessie Coleman became the first African American woman to gain an international pilot's license. She was also the first black woman "barnstormer," or stunt pilot. The first black astronaut was Robert H. Lawrence Jr., in 1963. America's first black astronaut to make a space flight was Guion (Guy) Bluford Jr. In 1986 Ronald McNair became the first black astronaut to lose his life during a space mission, when the space shuttle *Challenger* met disaster, exploding shortly after liftoff. Black women made their mark in space as well, notably Mae C. Jemison, who was named the first black woman astronaut in 1987. The world saw the first black commander to lead the National Aeronautics and Space Administration's shuttle *Discovery* mission in Charles Frank Bolden Jr., who also became America's leading voice on space exploration when he was appointed to lead the NASA space program in 2009.

A SPORTS AGENDA

As Africans came to the New World, many brought with them athletic prowess. In Africa they had enjoyed many athletic contests, often connected to religious ceremonies, rites of passage, or simply entertainment for onlookers. They also had been taught general fitness to develop speed, endurance, and flexibility. They were taught economic survival (made possible, for example, through hunting and fishing), cooperative values (as seen in team work), and military skills (used to train warriors). As their bond servants' sporting activities threatened to disrupt the daily life of the slaveholders, they made efforts to control and limit the slaves' sports activities. Slaves were allowed to train gamecocks and horses, and to work in taverns. Then they were allowed to run races, swim, wrestle, box, and play ball games.

Before the Civil War, free blacks and slaves engaged in numerous sports, some of which drew large crowds of black and white spectators. Blacks were especially involved in horse racing, and the best jockeys and horse trainers were black. Slaves had grown up caring for horses and knew how to handle them. In the North, however, jockeys were imported from England or were local whites. The first jockey of any race to win the Kentucky Derby was Oliver Lewis, who won in record time in 1875. Thirteen of the fifteen jockeys in that race were black. The first jockey of any race to win the Kentucky Derby three times was Isaac Murphy (or Isaac Burns), who won 44 percent of all the races that he rode and was considered one of the greatest race riders in American history. When the Derby distance was trimmed from one and one-half miles to one and one-quarter miles in 1896, Willie (or Willy) Simms was the first winner at that distance.

Another sport that brought world fame to black sports figures was cycling. Marshall W. "Major" Taylor (1878–1932) was the first native-born black American to win a bicycle race, in 1898. Boxing has long been a popular sport and is said to have had a more profound effect on the lives of African Americans than any other sport. During slavery, masters often matched one strong black man against a peer from a nearby plantation. An example was seen in the boxing feats of Tom Molineaux (1784–1818). Although he defeated white boxer Tom Cribb to become the first black American boxing champion in England in 1910, his victory was never acknowledged because Londoners did not want the public to know that a black boxer had beaten a white. Other boxing greats included Bill (William) Richmond (1763–1829), who became prominent in England in 1805; George "Little Chocolate" Dixon (1870–1909), who won the bantamweight title in 1898 (and later the featherweight title) to become the first black world champion; Peter Jackson (1861–1901), known as the "black prince" and the "Black Prince of the Ring," was called "the most marvelous fighting man of his time"; Jack Johnson, who became the first black heavyweight champion in 1908; Joe Louis (1914–1981), the "Brown Bomber" who became the first black national sports hero and the first black heavyweight champion since Jack Johnson; and colorful character Muhammad Ali (1942–), the first black prizefighter to gross more than a five-million-dollar gate and the first to win the heavyweight title three times. Others included Joe Lashley, Ezzard Charles, Sugar Ray Robinson Jr., Joe Frazier, Thomas "Hitman" Hearns, and George Edward Foreman. Black women boxers emerged as well, and included Laila Ali and Jacqui Frazier-Lyde, daughters of two boxing greats—Ali and Frazier.

Negro Leagues Baseball was popular prior to 1947, when the sport was racially integrated. Andrew "Rube" Foster, who played with, managed, and owned the Chicago American Giants, developed the Negro National League in 1920 in Kansas City, Missouri, and became known as the father of the Negro Leagues. The Negro National League, along with the Negro American League, had the most sustained success among black baseball leagues. During the heyday of the Negro Leagues, the best teams included the Kansas City Monarchs and the Homestead Grays. Players Leroy "Satchel" Paige, John Gibson, and James Thomas Bell (known as "Cool Papa"), became legendary. The Brooklyn Dodgers broke the color line in baseball, in 1947, when the team signed Jackie Robinson from the Monarchs. Other players of this era included Larry Doby, Don Newcombe, and Roy Campanella. The move to integrated baseball signaled the demise of the Negro Leagues. Later, other star players of the sport included Henry "Hank" Aaron, Willie Mays, Reggie Jackson, and Barry Bonds.

Major league sports were slow to integrate. Professional basketball was not integrated until 1951, when the Boston Celtics drafted Chuck Cooper and the New York Knicks hired Nat "Sweetwater" Clifton. Among the big stars of a later period were Bill Russell, Wilt "Wilt the Stilt" Chamberlain, Kareem Abdul-Jabbar, Elvin Hayes, and Willis Reed. Then came Julius "Dr. J." Erving, Moses Malone, Wes Unseld, Earvin "Magic" Johnson, Patrick Ewing, Charles Barkley, Shaquille O'Neal, Allen Iverson, Kobe Bryant, and LeBron James. The Harlem Globetrotters, founded in 1952, continues its show-stopping basketball games in national and worldwide events. Women's basketball has become a popular

A 1911 photo of Chicago's American Giants baseball team, the most successful team in the Negro Leagues from the 1910s through the 1930s. The team disbanded in 1952.

attraction as well, through the work of legendary college coaches C. Vivian Stringer (1948–) and Carolyn Peck (1966–), and other women sports leaders.

Unlike other major sports, professional football began as an integrated activity and continued until 1930, when it changed to a segregated entertainment. A few black players were recruited in 1945; these included Woodrow Wilson "Woody" Strode, Kenny Washington, and Ben Willis. The number increased in the 1950s, with Jim Brown becoming a superstar for the Cleveland Indians in 1957. The Washington Redskins were the last NFL team to integrate. Other black football icons include Jim Brown, Alan Cedric Page, Herschel Walker, Walter Jerry Payton, Warren Moon, Jerry Lee Rice, Barry Sanders, and Marcus Allen. In the new millennium, the sport has seen Emmitt J. Smith III, Donovan McNabb, and the emerging icon Robert Griffin III (RG3). Professional football also began to hire black coaches. In 1989 Arthur "Art" Shell Jr. headed the Los Angeles Raiders, and in 2007 Anthony Kevin "Tony" Dungy led the Indianapolis Colts to the championship in Super Bowl XLI, defeating the Chicago Bears and his coaching friend Lovie Smith in the contest.

Pioneers in golf who won major professional championships have included Charlie Sifford, Lee Elder, and Calvin Peete. The most popular and accomplished black golfer is Eldrick "Tiger" Woods, who won the crown jewel of golf matches—the Masters, in Augusta, Georgia, in 1996—the first of his race to do so. He went on to become the first golfer ever to hold four major golf titles simultaneously—the U.S. Open, the British Open, the PGA championship, and the Masters again in 2001. Althea Gibson became the first black professional woman golfer in 1964.

African-American icons in other sports include Dominique Margaux Dawes, the first black woman gymnast to compete on a U.S. Olympic team; in 1996 she helped the U.S. women's team win its first Olympic gold. The world rejoiced during the 2012 Summer Olympics, when Gabrielle "Gabby" Douglas, then only sixteen years old, became the first African American to win gold in the women's all-around final competition. In tennis, several black athletes became legends. Ora Washington pioneered in the sport and was the first black woman to win seven consecutive titles in the American Tennis Association. Other tennis luminaries include Althea Gibson, Arthur Ashe, and Venus and Serena Williams. Black stars have dominated in track and field, including sprints, relays, long jump, broad jump, and triple jump. Perhaps best known among the icons is Jesse Owens, who in 1936 won four gold medals at the Berlin Olympics. Other icons include Ralph Boston, Carl Lewis, Rafer Lewis Johnson, Edwin Corley Moses, Michael Duane Johnson, and Maurice Greene. Alice Coachman Davis was the pacesetter among black women track stars, becoming the first to win Olympic gold at the 1948 Olympics in London. Wilma Rudolph overcame a serious disability to win three gold medals in the 1960 Olympics. The late Florence Griffith Joyner and her sister-in-law Jackie Joyner-Kersee are among the remaining women track stars. In other sports, Wendell Oliver Scott became a legendary race car driver; Willie Eldon O'Ree and Grant Fuhr excelled in hockey; Debi Thomas and Shani Davis were winners in ice skating; James "Bubba" Stewart dominated in motocross; and Phil Ivey became one of the world's best all-round poker players. In rodeo, former slave Nat Love, known as "Deadwood Dick," became the first known black champion; Bill Pickett developed bulldogging; and Fred Whitfield excelled in calf roping.

The voices of African Americans continue to tell the story that they have lived on America's shores. They have spoken, and continue to speak, through their gifts and talents and have preserved much of the rich heritage that they brought with them from their motherland. The history of a people often cursed and despised has blossomed into the culture of a people of immense talent, determination, and endurance.

ARCHITECTURE

What **early African-American architect** of acclaim helped to **build Tuskegee Institute**?

Among America's early African-American architects is Robert Robinson Taylor (1868–1942). He was the first black admitted to the School of Architecture at Massachusetts Institute of Technology in 1888 and the only black in the first-year class. After Taylor graduated, educator Booker T. Washington hired him as a teacher in the Mechanical Industries Department and as campus architect, planner, and construction supervisor for Tuskegee Institute in Alabama. Taylor designed twenty-eight buildings for Tuskegee, including Booker T. Washington's residence, known as "The Oaks," and a laundry that later became the George Washington Carver Museum. In 1912 he prepared the first plans for the rural schools that philanthropist Julius Rosenwald funded under Washington's request. Two years later he prepared plans for an industrial building and a teachers' home for the rural schools project. Taylor also chaired the Tuskegee, Alabama, chapter of the American Red Cross—the only black chapter in the nation.

Who was **John A. Lankford**?

John A. Lankford (1874–1946) opened one of the first black architectural offices in Washington, D.C., in 1897. A year later he designed and supervised construction of a cotton mill in Concord, North Carolina. He served as an instructor of architecture at several black colleges and as superintendent of the Department of Mechanical Industries at Shaw University in Raleigh, North Carolina. As national supervising architect for the African Methodist Episcopal Church, he designed "Big Bethel," the landmark located in Atlanta's historic Auburn Avenue district. His other designs included churches in South

John A. Lankford was the first African American to open an architectural office in Washington, D.C.

and West Africa. Lankford was commissioned to design the national office for the Grand Fountain United Order of the True Reformers, which organized one of the first black-owned banks. In the 1930s, Lankford helped to establish the School of Architecture at Howard University.

What African American was a **prolific architect** of the **Gilded Age**?

Julian Francis Abele (1881–1950) was one of America's most prolific architects of the Gilded Age. He became the first black architect at Horace Trumbauer and Associates in Philadelphia in 1904 and, as senior designer for that firm, designed over two hundred buildings. That same year, Abele became the first black to graduate from the Pennsylvania School of Fine Arts and Architecture. Trumbauer sent Abele to study at École des Beaux-Arts in Paris, from which Abele received a diploma in 1906. He became chief designer for the Trumbauer firm in 1908. During his career with the firm he designed a number of major buildings, including Philadelphia's Free Library and Museum of Art; the Widener Library at Harvard University; and the chapel, the Allen Building, and much of the campus at Trinity College in Durham, North Carolina (now Duke University). Abele's work on the Duke campus gained him membership in the American Institute of Architects. He is credited as being the "first black American architect to have an impact on the design of large buildings" and was known for modernizing classical forms when designing structures.

Other early black architects of renown included Albert Irvin Cassell (1895–1969), who was long associated with Howard University in Washington, D.C., as campus planner and architect; and Moses McKissack III (1879–1952), who in 1905 founded the first African-American-owned architectural firm in Tennessee.

Who designed what became known as a **historic mansion** for Madam C. J. Walker?

In 1908 Vertner W. Tandy Sr. (1885–1949) became the first black architect registered in New York State. Tandy is also known as a founder of Alpha Phi Alpha fraternity at Cornell University. In 1909 he established a partnership with architect George Washington Foster that lasted until 1915. Through the partnership the men received several significant commissions, including St. Philips Episcopal Church and its Queen Anne-style parish house (1910–11) and the Harlem townhouse of black hair-care magnate Madam C. J. Walker. Later, after the partnership ended, in 1917 he designed the country mansion Villa Lewaro, in Irvington-on-Hudson, for Madame Walker. His other works include Small's Paradise, the Harlem Elks Lodge, and, in the 1940s, the Abraham Lincoln Houses in the Bronx.

Who was the **first black landscape artist**?

In the 1930s, David Augustus Williston (1868–1962) became the first black landscape artist to establish his own practice. Although the date is uncertain, by 1934 he was living and practicing in Washington, D.C. Williston was born in Fayetteville, North Carolina. He studied at Howard University's Normal School from 1893 to 1895 and went on to Cornell University. In 1898 he became the first black to graduate from Cornell with a bachelor's degree in agriculture. Williston taught agriculture and horticulture at several black colleges, including Tuskegee Institute and Fisk University. By 1910 he was in charge of landscape planning and construction at Tuskegee. He did planting designs for The Oaks—the home of Booker T. Washington—as well as the George Washington Carver Museum and other facilities at Tuskegee. While there he established a lifelong friendship with George Washington Carver. He was also landscape architect for the homes of President John Hope of Atlanta University and U.N. Secretary General Ralph Bunche. Williston opened his business in Washington, D.C, the first African-American-owned landscaping firm in the country.

From 1900 to 1932 Williston worked almost exclusively with the leading black land-grant colleges, as landscape designer and consultant, and was virtually the only black teaching horticulture and site planning. While in Washington, he was landscape artist for five buildings at Howard University. He and architect Hilyard R. Robinson did the site planning and landscape design for the Langston Terrace housing project, the nation's first federal housing project. Among his other landscape projects were those for Fisk University's campus, Roberts Airfield, and the presidents' residences at Atlanta University and The Catholic University of America.

PERFORMING ARTS

How were slaves involved in **entertainment during colonial America**?

Talented slaves were among the earliest black entertainers in colonial and antebellum America. On plantations throughout the South slave performers—using clappers, jawbones, and blacksmith rasps—danced, sang, and told jokes for the entertainment of their fellow slaves as well as their masters, who often showcased their talents at local gatherings. Some masters hired out talented slaves to perform in traveling troupes.

Two famous blackface performers of their day were Billy Van (left) and George Washington Dixon (right).

What dominated the presentation of **early blackface minstrels**?

White performers such as Thomas "Daddy" Rice and George Washington Dixon popularized blackface characters as early as the 1820s and 1830s. In 1843 Dan Emmett and his Virginia Minstrels appeared on stage, and blackface characters became a vital part of shows later dubbed minstrels. These popular early minstrel shows were those that showcased whites with burnt-cork-darkened faces to achieve the visible image that they desired. The shows intended to imitate Southern blacks as whites saw them, not by black realities. The performers combined acting, singing, dancing, and other forms of entertainment. They depicted blacks as lazy, stupid, and happy, and their speech patterns and behavior ridiculed them more. Shows with whites in blackface lost their popularity during the Civil War and were replaced by black minstrels who perpetuated the negative images already seen on the stage.

When did **black minstrel troupes** appear?

Black minstrel troupes began to appear in the 1850s, but it was not until after the Civil War that they became established on the American stage. Prevailing segregation laws prevented them from appearing in their natural faces, thus they blackened their faces as well. Although black minstrels inherited the negative stereotypes of blacks that white minstrels had established, the African-American performer won a permanent place on the American stage, providing a training ground for the many black dancers, comedians, singers, and composers to come. Notable among these stage personalities were: dancer-comedians Billy Kersands, Bert Williams, Bob Height, Dewey "Pigmeat" Markham, and Ernest Hogan; singers Gertrude "Ma" Rainey and Bessie Smith; and composers James Bland and William Christopher Handy.

When were **black women introduced** in the **minstrel show cast?**

In 1891 *The Creole Show,* an all-black production in New York City with a white promoter, John Isham, became the first minstrel show to introduce black women into the cast. In the finale Dora Dean and Charles Johnson introduced the first theatrical cakewalk, derived from the old plantation chalk-line walk. It is also one of the first shows in which black performers did not wear blackface.

When did black shows **break away** from the **burlesque theater?**

In 1897 *Oriental America* became the first show to play on Broadway and the first to break away from playing in burlesque theaters. The production followed the minstrel pattern, but the afterpiece was a medley of operatic selections. It had only a short run.

Who was the **first black actor** to attain **international renown?**

In 1826 the first black actor to attain international renown was Ira Frederick Aldridge (1805–1867), one of the leading Shakespearean actors of the century. Born in New York City, he attended the local African Free School No. 2 until age sixteen and then left home. From 1821 to 1824, Aldridge worked with the African Theater Company in New York City, and later moved to Europe, where he studied briefly at the University of Glasgow in Scotland. His first professional engagement in London was in October 1825 with the Coburg Theater. For three decades his fame in Europe exceeded his high standing in England. Aldridge won acclaim for his portrayal of tragic, melodramatic, and comic roles, but was best known for his portrayal of Othello.

What was the influence of the **Works Progress Administration** on **African-American actors?**

In the mid-1930s, the Works Progress Administration (WPA) sponsored one of the

Ira Frederick Aldridge gained international attention in the 1800s as a Shakespearean actor and was most acclaimed for his portrayal of Othello.

greatest organized efforts to assist and encourage American actors, especially African-American actors. The Federal Theater Project employed a total of 851 black actors to work in sixteen segregated units of the project in Chicago, New York, and other cities from 1935 to 1939, when Congress ended the project. When the project was in operation, black actors appeared in seventy-five plays, including classics, vaudeville contemporary comedies, children's shows, circuses, and "living newspaper" performances. Notable among the black actors who worked in the project, and later became stars on Broadway and in film, were Butterfly McQueen, Canada Lee, Rex Ingram, Katherine Dunham, Edna Thomas, Thomas Anderson, and Arthur "Dooley" Wilson.

MUSICALS

What was the **first full-length black musical comedy**?

A Trip to Coontown (1898) was the first full-length black musical comedy. It was also the first black show to draw a large white audience, and it played for the first time on Broadway in 1898. In a break with the minstrel tradition, it had a cast of characters involved in a story from beginning to end. The show was written and produced by Robert "Bob" Cole (c. 1863–1911), a composer, dancer, singer, musician, and actor. The first black show to be organized, produced, and managed by blacks, it ran for three seasons after its April 1898 debut in New York.

What **black woman** ran a **professional stock dramatic company** in the early 1900s?

Anita Bush (1883–1974), dancer and actress, organized the Anita Bush Players in 1915 and became the first black woman to run a professional black stock dramatic company in the United States. Her company was also the first stock company in New York since the African Players of 1821. The players opened at New York City's Lincoln Theater on November 15, 1915, with *The Girl at the Fort*. They had a short but successful run, and by December 27, 1915, had transferred to the larger Lafayette Theatre, where they became the Lafayette Players. Bush grew up in Brooklyn and began to appear on stage when she and her sister had roles as extras in *Antony and Cleopatra*. She joined Williams and Walker Company when she was sixteen and toured England with them in the smash hit *In Dahomey*. She formed her own dance group about 1909 and toured with the four or five other women members until she was injured in a serious accident in 1913. After the Anita Bush Players ended its short life, Bush continued to perform.

What **two major theater production companies** promoted black theater?

In the wake of the Federal Theater Project, the American Negro Theater was established in Harlem, in 1940, by Abram Hill, Austin Briggs-Hall, Frederick O'Neal, and Hattie King-Reeves. Its objective was to authentically portray black life and give black actors and play-

> ## What early and popular black musical introduced several singers and musicians?
>
> **W**hen Noble Sissle and Eubie Blake opened the all-black historical musical *Shuffle Along* in 1921, at the 63rd Street Theater in New York City, the performance introduced to the audience singers Josephine Baker, Florence Mills, and Caterina Jarboro. Composer William Grant Still and choral director and composer (Francis) Hall Johnson were introduced as well.

wrights a forum for their talents. It provided a training ground for many black actors who later became stars on Broadway and in Hollywood, including Ruby Dee, Ossie Davis, Harry Belafonte, and Sidney Poitier. In 1959 Lorraine Hansberry's *A Raisin in the Sun* opened in March and became one of the most successful all-black plays to appear on Broadway. Its director, Lloyd Richards, was the first black to appear on Broadway in over fifty years.

Perhaps most beneficial to black actors was the founding of the Negro Ensemble Company in New York in 1967. It was the brainchild of playwright/actor Douglas Turner Ward. Its continuing objective is to develop African-American managers, playwrights, actors, and technicians. The company has staged more than one hundred productions, including the work of forty black playwrights, and has provided work for countless aspiring and seasoned black actors.

Who was **Charles Sidney Gilpin**?

In 1920 Charles Sidney Gilpin (1878–1930) became the first black to star in a major American play, Eugene O'Neill's *The Emperor Jones*. He has been called "the first modern American Negro to establish himself as a serious actor of first quality." Born in Richmond, Virginia, he received little education. In 1896 Gilpin began traveling with vaudeville troupes, a practice which he followed for two years. In 1907 he joined the Pekin Stock Company of Chicago as a dramatic actor, and in 1916 the Lafayette Theater Company in Harlem. Gilpin played the lead in *The Emperor Jones* from 1920 to 1924, winning the Spingarn Medal in 1921 for his theatrical accomplishments.

What **black playwright** was the first to open her work on **Broadway**?

In 1959 playwright and activist Lorraine Hansberry (1930–1965) was the first black woman to premiere a play on Broadway; it opened at the Barrymore Theatre on March 11. The play tells the story of a black family's struggle to have a better life on the south side of Chicago. Hansberry took the title of her play, *A Raisin in the Sun,* from Langston Hughes' poem "Harlem"; it was the first serious black drama to impact the dominant culture. New York's most influential critics gave the play positive reviews, and both black and white audiences were overwhelming in their favorable reaction to the play.

27

What **black playwrights** have won **Pulitzer Prizes** for their work?

Winners of a Pulitzer Prize for drama are Charles Gordone, *No Place to Be Somebody,* 1970; Charles Fuller, *A Soldier's Play,* 1982; August Wilson, *Fences,* 1987, and *The Piano Lesson,* 1990; and Suzan-Lori Parks, *Topdog/Underdog,* 2002.

What **playwright** had **two shows playing concurrently** on Broadway?

In 1985 August Wilson (1945–2005) became the first black American to have two concurrent plays on Broadway. His play *Fences,* written in 1983, opened at the Forty-sixth Street Theater on Broadway in April 1985. It depicts the personal and economic problems of black families. The play grossed $11 million in one year and broke the record of earnings for nonmusical plays. In 1987 Wilson won a Pulitzer Prize and a Tony Award for the play. While *Fences* was still running on Broadway, Wilson's *Joe Turner's Come and Gone,* written in 1984, opened at the Ethel Barrymore Theater. The play explores the after-effects of slavery in 1911 in Pittsburgh and the Southern black migration to the urban North.

What **current black playwright** created the character **Madea**?

Playwright, actor, and film director Tyler Perry (1969–) began writing plays in the late 1990s; his actions rocketed him to enormous success. Perry revitalized urban theater and redefined gospel theater, drawing upon churchgoers and black audiences as role models for his characters. He created the beloved figure, Madea, who is a tall, matronly, no-nonsense black woman; Perry plays the role of Madea himself. Although some criticize him for creating stereotypical characters, Perry has been highly successful in film and television productions.

Well known for his creation of the no-nonsense character Madea, Tyler Perry is also a film director and playwright.

BLACK DANCE

How was **black dance** used on the **slave plantation**?

Dance forms and characteristics have been influenced greatly by West African dance traditions. Not only were dance, music, and song entrenched in African societies, but they were used in religious ceremonies and rites. From its beginning in Africa, dance helped to shape the black community by providing a way for slaves to entertain themselves as well as their masters. Slaves performed social as well as religious dance forms, yet sometimes whites considered slave religious dances as social dances. The shout, or ring shout, came to slaves from their African background. Slaves developed a number of social dances and used them for recreation, during special days, or to entertain their white masters. The Cakewalk, the Charleston, the Black Bottom, and the Itch are examples of their creations. White minstrels in blackface used many of the slave dances in their own shows. "Master Juba," performed by William Henry Lane, entertained audiences as a black minstrel dancer. The legendary black dancer, who did not work in blackface, toured in 1845. Later he and three white showmen toured together as the Ethiopian Minstrels.

Why was **Florence Mills** important?

In 1925 the first black woman to headline at a Broadway venue was Florence Mills (1896–1927). She became the preeminent woman jazz dancer during the Harlem Renaissance. Born in Washington, D.C., she demonstrated her talent as a singer and dancer early and was called a child prodigy. By age eight, she was a stage phenomenon, having been guided by the accomplished performer Aida Overton Walker, who sang "Miss Hannah from Savannah" in the musical comedy *Sons of Ham.* That led to her work with a vaudeville company beginning in 1905. In 1921 Mills joined Noble Sissle and Eubie Blake's production of *Shuffle Along.* Her success in the musical led Lew Leslie to hire her to perform at the Plantation Club on Broadway. When the musical comedy *Dixie to Broadway* opened in New York in October 1924, Mills sang "I'm a Little Blackbird Looking for a Bluebird" and was a showstopper. The revue, along with the work of Mills and other black performers, helped eradicate the racial stereotypes that up to this time char-

acterized blacks. Mills' heavy workload contributed to her declining health and eventual death on November 1, 1927. During her grand funeral in Harlem, it has been said that a flock of blackbirds flew over her funeral procession as it made its way up Seventh Avenue to Woodlawn Cemetery in the Bronx.

What **social dances** became **popular** among blacks in later years?

As blacks migrated from the South to major cities, black dance culture became popular there as well. They modernized slave dances, such as the Cakewalk and the Charleston, and helped to popularize them in their new homes. Popular among dances of the Harlem Renaissance in the 1930s were the Lindy Hop, Big Apple, Twist, and Tap. Much later, television programs helped

The athletic and daring form of modern dance called break dancing originated in the gritty urban streets of the American East Coast, where gang members created it in the 1970s.

29

to spread interest in these dances as well. American pop icons, such as Michael Jackson, Cab Calloway, and James Brown, helped to influence black dance. Break dancing, also called b-boying or breaking, was developed on the East Coast by gang members in the early 1970s, and by 1980 had popular appeal. It is a form of hip hop dancing that emerged around the same time, which is usually performed on the street and performed to hip hop music. Hip hop dancing is an energetic form of dancing that includes cool moves, quick spins, and allows freedom of movement that reflects the dancer's personality.

What is **stepping**?

African-American Greek-letter organizations, or fraternities and sororities, on college campuses developed a complex dance performance called stepping, as one of their rituals of group identity. The ritual of "marching on line," or marching in a line across the college campus, may have helped stimulate the stepping, as it became known. This tradition has been passed on for generations, making step shows a part of many black festivals and celebrations. The step show itself has gained worldwide popularity. Terms often associated with stepping include demonstrating, stomping, bopping, and marching. Stepping may also include synchronized movement of high steps, and clapping, arm crossing, and shoulder tapping (all mixed with speaking), and chanting. The routines are composed and transmitted orally, with a step master who leads the group. Some of the Greek-letter organizations have trade or signature steps which help to identify the organization. Stepping demonstrates the influences of break dancing, hip hop, and early elements of slave dances.

What is the **Alvin Ailey American Dance Theater**?

One of the leading dance companies in the United States is the Alvin Ailey American Dance Theater. Black dancers largely comprise the company. Founded in 1958, the Alvin Ailey troupes have been especially renowned and have performed in forty-eight states, on all continents, and in seventy-one countries throughout the world. The organization is composed of the Alvin Ailey American Dance Theater, the Alvin Ailey Repertory Ensemble, and the Alvin Ailey American Dance Center.

What is the importance of the **Dance Theater of Harlem**?

The Dance Theater of Harlem, the first world-renowned African-American ballet company, was founded by Arthur Mitchell (1934–), a principal dancer with the New York City Ballet, along with Karel Shook (1920–1985), a dance teacher and former director of the Netherlands Ballet. The impetus for the creation of the company came on April 4, 1968, while Mitchell was waiting to board a plane from New York City to Brazil (where he was establishing the country's first national ballet company) and he heard that Martin Luther King Jr. (1929–1968) had been assassinated. Mitchell later questioned the work that he was doing abroad rather than at home. He had spent his youth in Harlem, and he felt he should return there to establish a school to pass on his knowledge to others and to give black dancers the opportunity to perform. The primary purpose of the

The Alvin Ailey Dance Theater is shown here performing *Revelations,* a work by their founder, in a 2011 production.

school was "to promote interest in teaching and teach young black people the art of classical ballet, and modern and ethnic dance, thereby creating a much-needed self-awareness and better self-image of the students themselves."

Where are some places where the **Dance Theater of Harlem** has performed?

Arthur Mitchell's idea of a dance theater for young blacks was a success. During the 1970s and 1980s the company toured nationally and internationally, often performing to sell-out crowds and participating in prestigious events, including international art festivals, a state dinner at the White House, and the closing ceremonies of the 1984 Olympic Games. The Dance Theater of Harlem became acknowledged as one of the world's finest ballet companies. Not only did Mitchell succeed in giving black dancers the opportunity to learn and to perform, he effectively erased color barriers in the world of dance, a testimony to the universality of classical ballet.

THEATER

What was the **African Grove Theater**?

The African Grove Theater was the first known black theatrical company in the United States. It grew out of African Americans' lack of opportunity to participate in mainstream theater productions. After a number of gatherings were held in Brown's backyard around 1816, James Henry Brown and James Hewlett (fl. 1820s) founded the theater in 1821. Brown was a former steward of a Liverpool liner and hired Hewlett as an entertainer in his tea garden on Thames Street. Hewlett, from a New York family of mixed descent, tried to make his way as an actor and musician, beginning in the 1920s, and he became the principal actor in the African Grove. The theater led a precarious existence in New York City at the corner of Beeker and Mercer streets. A portion of the theater was reserved for whites, yet the audience often became unruly and police closed it down from time to time. Finally, the building burned down in 1823. Shortly before it closed, however, in June 1823 the theater produced *The Drama of King Shotaway*, a play written by a black author, the theater's cofounder and manager James Henry Brown. This was the first time that a play by a black author was produced in the United States.

What was the work of the **Theater Owners Booking Association**?

The Theater Owners Booking Association, known simply as T.O.B.A., was founded in 1920 by black actor S. H. Dudley and white theater owner Milton Starr. It grew out of their concern for the increasing number of theaters that catered to blacks and booking problems that they faced. By 1921 there were some ninety-four such theaters nationwide owned and managed by blacks. The T.O.B.A. worked in support of underpaid entertainers on the black musical stage, dealing with issues such as long travel days, demanding audiences, and similar difficulties. It is probable that most of the T.O.B.A. performers were Southerners; those from other regions associated Jim Crow and lynchings with traveling in the South. Joining the circuit were Ma Rainey and Bessie Smith and Mamie Smith. T.O.B.A. came to its demise because of the Great Depression and the impact of sound films on vaudeville.

What is the significance of the **Apollo Theater**?

The Apollo Theater, located at 235 West 125th Street in the Harlem section of New York City, is significant to African Americans for the opportunities that it gave black artists to showcase their talents. It was one of the first theaters in the nation to feature black artists and to be available to other minorities. Built in 1913, the classical revival structure was designed by architect George Keister. It served as a burlesque theater before it became a movie theater. It was sold in 1934 and reopened as the 125th Street Apollo. In 1934 radio host Ralph Cooper started the popular

The Apollo Theater in Harlem became one of the first American theaters to showcase black and other minority talent when radio host Ralph Cooper began an amateur night there in 1934.

Apollo Theater Amateur Night; it launched the careers of several successful participants, such as Ella Fitzgerald, Sarah Vaughn, and much later the Jackson 5. The Apollo's audiences declined in the 1950s and 1960s. In 1981 Percy E. Sutton, then Manhattan Borough president, bought the theater; it was placed on the National Register of Historic Places in 1983 and reopened in 1985. Once again the theater hosted the popular nationally syndicated program, *Showtime at the Apollo*. In 1991 New York State purchased the building. The Apollo Theater Foundation, a nonprofit, is aiding in its restoration.

A CULTURAL REVOLUTION

What was the **Harlem Renaissance**?

The Harlem Renaissance, variously identified as the Negro Renaissance and the New Negro Movement, was a literary, artistic, and cultural movement centered in the Harlem section of New York, but apparent in urban areas in other sections of the United States as well. The date of the renaissance is fluid. Some claim that it flourished from the mid-1910s to the mid-1930s. Others claim that it occurred during the 1920s. Clearly, there were precursors to the renaissance, beginning with the early 1900s and extending up to the date popularly assigned. The Harlem Renaissance represented a shift from a conciliatory stance to black intellectualism and embraced literature, poetry, and visual and performing arts, as well as the social and economic problems that black America faced.

Who were some of the **leading participants** in the **Harlem Renaissance**?

The Harlem Renaissance reflects the work of many black leaders as well as white patrons of the arts. Black luminaries of this period included patrons and supporters W.E.B. Du Bois and James Weldon Johnson, who contributed as writers as well; scholar and critic Alain Locke, who has been called the leading intellectual of this period; literary artists such as Arna Bontemps, Langston Hughes, Zora Neale Hurston, Nella Larsen, Jessie Redmon Fauset, Claude McKay, and Jean Toomer; actors Charles Gilpin and Florence Mills; musicians Cab Calloway, Duke Ellington, Fletcher Henderson, Jelly Roll Morton (Ferdinand Joseph LaMothe), and King Oliver; visual artists Aaron Douglas, Meta Warrick Fuller, and Augusta Savage; independent filmmakers such as Oscar Micheaux; and many others.

Who became the **"philosophical midwife"** of **Harlem** during the renaissance?

Alain Leroy Locke (1886–1954) frequented Harlem, especially after 1924 when he was on sabbatical from Howard University, and was welcomed into the company who met regularly in the cafes and nightclubs. He established himself as the "philosophical midwife" of Harlem's literary and artistic talent. He also became spokesperson for the New Negro Movement. He secured backing for many of the artists and writers, helped to establish the Harlem Museum of African Art, and became the interpreter of Harlem's cultural expressions there and nationwide.

33

What was the **lasting effect** of the **Harlem Renaissance** on African-American culture?

Leaders of the period, including Langston Hughes and Zora Neale Hurston, achieved great distinction in American letters well after the renaissance ended. Along with other writers, artists, and musicians, they produced works that are still studied in schools, colleges, and universities across the nation. Numerous books, theses, and other publications emanated from the works of these artists. Some of the participants, such as W.E.B. Du Bois, Arna Bontemps, and Aaron Douglas, and precursor James Weldon Johnson, joined black college faculties at Fisk, Howard, Atlanta Universities, and elsewhere—as mainstream institutions were not yet accepting black faculty members. Philosopher, arts patron, educator, and writer Alain Leroy Locke (1886–1954) carried the enthusiasm for Harlem's cultural reawakening to Howard University, where he chaired the philosophy department. In 1922 he proposed Howard as "the center for a national Negro theater."

RADIO SHOWS

What is the **importance of radio** in African-American popular culture?

Since the 1920s, radio has become one of black America's most popular and powerful mediums, serving as a source of information and culture in the community. It has helped to shape black communities at the local and national levels. The development of radio in the black community was gradual, however, and the 1930s and 1940s brought more black radio shows that were broadcast alongside mainstream radio; it also helped to erase many of the stereotypical and derogatory images that mainstream radio broadcasts perpetuated. Those who lived in major cities, such as New York, Chicago, or Pittsburgh, found little that they liked on white-run radio; therefore, it was important that black radio shows would take root and flourish in areas where more blacks lived.

Who were the **pioneers** in **black radio**?

From the 1920s through the 1950s, Jack Cooper, once a vaudeville performer, was a successful pioneer and entrepreneur in black radio. He hosted *The All Negro Hour,* which originated on WSBC in Chicago in 1929, and featured music and comedy routines by blacks. He also produced gospel and news programs such as the *Defender Newsreel* and *Search for Missing Persons.* He was the first black sportscaster, newscaster, and radio executive. Cooper was inducted into the Radio Hall of Fame in 2012. The 1930s brought such hosts as Eddie Honesty, who broadcast *Rockin-In-Rhythm* from Hammond, Indiana; Bass Harris, who brought swing band music from Seattle; and Hal Jackson, who started the first regular black-hosted radio program in Washington, D.C., which showcased black men and women luminaries.

What **changes** occurred in black radio of the **1940s and 1950s**?

The 1940s and 1950s brought a change in black radio shows, and reached the fast-growing, Southern-black-consumer market. Of popular appeal were *The Nat King Cole Show,* singer Mahalia Jackson's gospel show, and *Destination Freedom,* a Chicago-based show that highlighted historical figures. As popular as Nat King Cole's show was, it was short-lived because of lack of sponsors. Black disk jockeys also emerged during this time and abandoned standard English in favor of black vernacular language, slang, and catchy phases. Pioneer disk jockeys included Al Benson (called the "Godfather of Black Radio in Chicago"), Jack the Rapper Gibson, Jocko Henderson, and Dr. Hepcat.

Nat King Cole poses for a publicity shot for his television show, which premiered in 1956. Cole also had a popular radio show before that.

What was the impact of the **Civil Rights Movement on black radio**?

During the 1960s and 1970s, black radio both influenced— and was influenced by—the Civil Rights Movement. Jack the Rapper Gibson became one of the first to broadcast the social activists of this period, as well as Motown and hip-hop music, from WERD in Atlanta. Along with other black radio hosts, Gibson kept the black community apprised of daily events during the movement and also helped to coordinate various protests and demonstrations. Radio hosts also broadcast protest songs and helped restore calm during race riots in the black community.

Who are the **leading black radio hosts** from the late twentieth century into the new millennium?

Popular black radio show hosts of this era include a number of successful broadcasters, among them Tom Joyner, who began in Dallas in the 1980s. He later moved to Chicago and, in 1994, launched the *The Tom Joyner Morning Show,* featuring rhythm and blues, celebrities, comedy, news, and political commentary. Joyner also promotes education by raising money for black colleges. Beginning in the early 1990s, Steve Harvey has had a highly successful career in radio, film, comedy, and television. On his program, *The Steve Harvey Morning Show,* Harvey offers advice to callers. He also hosts the well-known *Family Feud* game show. His popular book, *Act Like a Lady, Think Like a Man,* published in 2009, has brought him even more acclaim. Among these hosts there is also Wendy Williams, who in the late 1980s launched a morning show on KISS FM. Her show was syndicated in 2001 and broadcast in several cities. She moved to television in 2009 and began her television feature, *The Wendy Williams Show*.

TELEVISION

What are some **stereotypical images of blacks** in the film and television industry?

Black images in film and television were carryovers from those seen in literature, the musical stage, and other forms of entertainment for white audiences. Those commonly known were tom, coon, mammy, happy slave, devoted servant, petty thief, sexual superman, promiscuous woman, superstitious churchgoer, lazy, shiftless, and many more. D. W. Griffith's film, *The Birth of a Nation,* is said to have created the most virulent stereotypes of blacks and was the most controversial Civil War-based film ever released in this nation. Released in 1915, the highly racist film covered the Civil War and Reconstruction era and served as a recruiting tool for the Ku Klux Klan.

What was the **early impact of television** on black America?

The rise of television in the 1950s generally had an adverse effect on the American theater. Employment for all actors fell sharply, but especially for blacks. Television had limited access for blacks as segregation was still the law of the land. Actors such as Lena Horne and Sammy Davis Jr. were occasional guests on television, but overall images of blacks were often derogatory. Shows like *The Beulah Show, Amos 'n Andy,* and *The Little Rascals,* which were on the air between 1950 and 1953, offered no lasting opportunities for blacks.

When did blacks **enter television**?

When the modern Civil Rights Movement in the 1960s became a continuous part of the airways, blacks broke new ground in lead roles such as Diahann Carroll in the television sitcom *Julia*. By the 1970s situation comedies were the top shows for blacks. Although there were some dramas, comedies thrived. Comedians such as Flip Wilson and Redd Foxx had their own shows, while family comedies included *The Jeffersons* and *Good Times*. Family comedies depicted black life as well as the challenges, successes, and creativity of black urban culture.

White actors Freeman Gosden (left) and Charles Correll played Amos and Andy, respectively, in a radio and then television show that was popular from the 1920s through the 1950s. By today's standards, however, the show is clearly racist and derogatory.

Clockwise from left, Isabel Sanford, Mike Evans, and Sherman Hemsley portrayed the Jeffersons in the successful 1970s and '80s television sitcom show about a black man with a successful business.

What was one of the **most popular early television sitcoms** in which blacks starred?

The most acclaimed black sitcom of the 1980s was *The Cosby Show,* which ran from 1984 to 1992. This show was popular for all American viewers and its success remains undeniable yet controversial. Many believed it portrayed the assumed idealized sense of the black upper-middle class family, while others saw it as a colorized version of the stock American family. In spite of these viewpoints, the show brought a new perspective of the black family. Another show that offered a view into black culture was *A Different World,* which aired from 1987 to 1993, and featured college students at a historically black college.

What are some of the **popular African-American television shows** of the **new millennium**?

Among the popular shows of this period are *Everybody Hates Chris,* which aired from 2005–2006; *Tyler Perry's House of Payne,* 2007 to present, and *Meet the Browns,* 2009 to present.

What is **Oprah Winfrey**'s contribution to television?

Oprah Winfrey (1954–) became the first black woman to host a nationally syndicated weekday talk show, *The Oprah Winfrey Show,* on February 8, 1986. The show, often called simply *Oprah,* garnered forty-seven Daytime Emmy Awards between 1986 and 2000, when Winfrey stopped submitting it for consideration. After twenty-five seasons, she ended the show with the 2011 "farewell season," with the final show on May 25. She started her career at WTVF, a CBS local affiliate in Nashville, Tennessee (where in 1971 she was the first woman co-anchor), and later moved to Chicago. In 1984 Winfrey took over *A.M. Chicago,* which aired opposite Phil Donahue, and later expanded to a one-hour television show. She formed Harpo Productions, which enabled her to develop her own projects, and in 1989 bought her own television and movie production studio. She is the first black woman in television and film to own her own production company. Oprah's Book Club, an

Running from 1986 to 2011, *The Oprah Winfrey Show* was one of the most successful daytime talk shows in television history and made its star one of the richest and most powerful women in the American media.

on-air reading club that ran from 1996 to 2002, aided in promoting reading nationwide. In 1997 Winfrey launched Oprah's Angel Network that encourages people to help others who are in need. On January 1, 2011, Winfrey launched the series premier of her network called OWN (Oprah Winfrey's Network), a joint venture with Discovery Communications.

What African **American woman** became an **executive in public broadcasting**?

Jennifer Karen Lawson (1946–) became executive vice president of programming for the Public Broadcasting Service in Washington, D.C., in 1989. As the highest-ranking black woman to serve in public television, she oversees the creation, promotion, and scheduling of national programming for 330 stations. For the first time, her appointment centralized national program decision-making in one executive. *The Civil War,* which was aired in 1990 under her administration, drew more than fifty million viewers and became the most-watched show in PBS history. Lawson was born in Fairfield, Alabama, and graduated from Columbia University.

FILM

Who was the **first African American** to **host** the **Academy Awards**?

When Whoopi Goldberg (1950–) hosted the Sixty-sixth Annual Academy Awards telecast on March 21, 1994, she became the first black and the first solo woman ever to host the event. More than one billion people watched the Oscars that year. She followed a long line of comedians, including Bob Hope, Billy Crystal, Johnny Carson, and others who had previously hosted the show, and went on to serve as host three additional times. Born Caryn Johnson in New York City, Goldberg lived with her mother in a housing project in the Chelsea section of Manhattan. She started acting at age eight, having been influenced by established actresses including Gracie Allen, Carole Lombard, and Claudette Colbert. She dropped out of school at age seventeen. During the 1960s, Goldberg was a hippie and participated in civil rights marches and student protests at Columbia University. Goldberg moved to the West Coast in 1974 to begin a new life with her daughter and to pursue an acting career. She made her film

Award-winning actress and comedienne Whoopi Goldberg first made a name for herself with her portrayal of Celie in the 1985 movie *The Color Purple*.

debut in *The Color Purple* (1985). For her lead role as Celie, Goldberg won a Golden Globe Award, the NAACP Image Award, and an Academy Award nomination. She won an Academy Award as best supporting actress in the film *Ghost* in 1991, the second black actress to win the award (Hattie McDaniel was the first in 1939). She is also on the television show *The View*.

How did early filmmakers depict blacks in films?

Since 1896 blacks have been involved in films, beginning with the short *Watermelon Contest*; however, these films depicted stereotypical images of blacks in American society. When D. W. Griffith's controversial film *The Birth of a Nation* was produced in 1915, it bolstered the highly stereotypical black image and spurred blacks to produce "race movies" or those that bolstered the black image. Black filmmaker Oscar Micheaux (1884–1951) became one of the film industry's most successful black filmmakers of that era, producing films such as *Within Our Gates* in 1920, *Body and Soul* in 1925, and *Swing* in 1935. Race movies declined by the late 1940s due to Hollywood's lessening of aggressively racist portrayals of blacks in films, the use of black actors in the Hollywood system, and the move toward postwar racial desegregation.

Why was Stepin Fetchit important?

Lincoln Theodore Monroe Andrew Perry (1902–1985), better known as Stepin Fetchit, was an actor and comedian billed in early films of the 1920s and 1930s. He took his   39 stage name from a race horse. He was a pioneer black actor who played stereotypical and degrading roles, yet was the first black to receive feature billing in movies and the first black to appear in films with stars like Will Rogers and Shirley Temple.

What was the **Lincoln Motion Picture Company**?

The Lincoln Motion Picture Company, founded on May 24, 1916, was the first movie company organized by black filmmakers. On January 20, 1917, the state of California formally incorporated the company and on April 30, 1917, Lincoln issued twenty-five thousand shares of common stock. Actor Noble Johnson was the company's founding president. Other officers included actor Clarence A. Brooks; James T. Smith, a druggist; and Dudley A. Brooks, treasurer and assistant secretary.

The film company's first production was *The Realization of a Negro's Ambition,* released in mid-1916. Other films were *Trooper of Troop K* (known also as *Trooper of Company K;* 1916), *The Law of Nature* (1917), *Lincoln Pictorial* (1918), *A Man's Duty* (1919), *By Right of Birth* (1921), and *A Day with the Tenth Calvary at Fort Huachuca* (1922). White cameraman Harry Gant handled the cinematography and directed most of the company's productions; blacks, however, still managed Lincoln. Publicity materials noted that the company expected to reach millions of people, and it booked its films in theaters and arranged for showings in churches, halls, schools, and small towns without theaters. Nevertheless, Lincoln closed in 1921.

Who was Hollywood's **first black film producer**?

In 1968 Gordon A. Parks Sr. (1912–2006) produced *The Learning Tree,* and helped to break down racial barriers in Hollywood when he became the first black to produce, direct, and score a film for a major studio, Warner Bros. The film *Seven Arts* was based on his autobiographical novel published in 1963. On September 19, 1989, the film became one of the first registered in the Library of Congress's national film registry. Other highly commercial films directed by Parks included *Shaft* (1971), *Shaft's Big Score* (1972), and *The Super Cops* (1974), all for MGM. After it had been struggling for some time, the *Shaft* films enabled MGM to become financially sound again.

Who are some of the **most successful black independent filmmakers**?

Among the popular and successful black independent filmmakers are Melvin Van Peebles, whose popular work *Sweet Sweetback's Baadasssss Song* was released in 1971, and

Movie director and producer Spike Lee gained acclaim with films like 1989's *Do the Right Thing* and 1992's *Malcolm X.*

Robert Townsend, whose satire, *Hollywood Shuffle,* appeared in1987. Such movies were labeled "blaxploitation films" and took a leading role in the film industry. Other notable black filmmakers include Spike Lee, who produced films such as *Do the Right Thing* (1989), *Malcolm X* (1992), and *When the Levees Broke* (2006); John Singleton, whose works include *Boyz n the Hood* (1991); Julie Dash, who created *Daughters of the Dust* (1991); and Tyler Perry, whose dramatic and comedic works include *Diary of a Mad Black Woman* (2005), *Madea's Family Reunion* (2006), *For Colored Girls* (2010), and *Madea's Witness Protection* (2012).

MUSEUMS

Where are **African-American museums** located?

African-American museums are located across the United States. They include the Studio Museum in Harlem, which began in 1969, initially for artists who needed working space. The Schomburg Center for Research in Black Culture, of the New York Public Library, also located in Harlem, is another. It is one of the most widely used research facilities in the world devoted to the preservation of materials on black life. The DuSable Museum in Chicago, established in 1961, grew out of an art center that was established under the Works Progress Administration during the Great Depression. Other notable museums are located on the campuses of the Historically Black Colleges and Universities, such as Hampton University in Virginia, Howard University in Washington, D.C., and Tuskegee University in Alabama.

Where is the **first national museum** of **African American history and culture**?

The first national museum founded to showcase the work of African Americans, the National Museum of African American History and Culture, was established on December 19, 2003; it is the nineteenth museum to open as a part of the Smithsonian Institution. Architect David Adjaye designed the building, which features a crown motif from Yoruban sculpture. Construction at the National Mall in Washington, D.C., is expected to be completed in July 2015.

VISUAL ARTS

What **African-American artists** in **colonial America** left a **historical record**?

The only African-American artist in colonial America to have left a historical record was Scipio Moorhead. Moorhead's artistic endeavors appear to have been aided by two prominent women who lived in Boston, where he was a slave: the wife of his clergyman master, the Reverend John Moorhead, who was a patron of arts; and poet Phillis Wheatley, who was herself a slave. Moorhead's style is in keeping with the period—classical allegorical, resembling the works of George Romney and Joshua Reynolds, British masters of the era. Although no major work is known to have survived, the small extant portrait of Phillis Wheatley is believed to be Moorhead's work.

What were the **crafts** from black artists and craftspeople of the **eighteenth century**?

There were many talented black artists and craftspeople in the eighteenth century who failed to achieve historical recognition. Records indicate that skilled blacks interested in buying their freedom worked as painters, silversmiths, cabinet and coach makers, ornamentalists, and shipwrights. One of them was Eugene Warburg, a black sculptor from New Orleans, who became well known for his ornamental gravestones and eventually went to study in Europe. Another, William Day, a celebrated carpenter who owned slaves in his shop, has gained recognition for his interior design as well as his furniture.

Much of the colonial ironwork and metalwork on eighteenth-century mansions, churches, and public buildings was created and executed by blacks, and occasionally reached heights that can be classified as fine art. The artists and artisans, however, remain unknown.

In what **tradition** did the **early black pioneers paint**?

Some African-American artists attempted to escape the classical tradition into which they were confined and painted themes closer to their heritage and existence. Some fine portraits of black freedmen were painted by talented but obscure black artists in the rural South during the period from 1870 through the early part of the twentieth century. Henry Ossawa Tanner's paintings in the 1880s of poor blacks, for example, belong to this little-known school of African-American art. His work *The Thankful Poor* (1894) is one such painting. The location of the painting was unknown for many years; it was rediscovered in 1970 and then acquired by a private collector.

Who are some of the **pioneering** and **highly acclaimed African-American artists**?

To become professionals, emerging African-American artists of the eighteenth and

Artist Henry Ossawa Tanner created works in the late-nineteenth century portraying the lives of poor black people. His paintings were lost for many years until they were rediscovered in 1970.

What black artists during the early 1900s demonstrated ethnic awareness?

During the period of transition, from 1900 to the 1920s, many black artists continued to express themselves in imitative styles. They studied in Europe where they felt that the interest in African-American culture was sincere. Among such artists of this period were Palmer Hayden, Archibald Scott, Malvin Gray Johnson, William Edouard Scott, Meta Warrick Fuller, and Laura Wheeler Waring.

nineteenth centuries were trained by white artists and traveled to Europe to study and receive validation, since their cultural roots were not recognized or appreciated in America. They also simulated European artistic styles. Although their works received some popular acceptance, racism kept them out of the mainstream. Most continued to work in the United States in spite of their status, and some overcame immense obstacles and won recognition for their work. These included Edward Mitchell Bannister, Robert Scott Duncanson, Meta Warrick Fuller, Joshua Johnston, Edmonia Lewis, and Henry Ossawa Tanner.

Who was the **leading painter** of the **Harlem Renaissance**?

At the urging of Alain Locke, W.E.B. Du Bois, and other influential leaders of the first three decades of the twentieth century, black creative artists began collaborating in literature, music, theater, and art to increase awareness of their culture. By the 1920s, this era became known as the Harlem Renaissance, named for the section of New York City where the transformation was based.

Aaron Douglas (1899–1979) became the leading painter of the Harlem Renaissance era. Active in New York from 1923 to 1925, he was the first of his generation to depict visual symbols—stylized African figures with overlays of geometric forms—that created a sense of movement and rhythm. The idea spread from Harlem, where many black intellectuals and artists from the Caribbean and elsewhere had settled, throughout the United States. This concept, while promoting ethnic awareness and pride, also counteracted the stereotypes and shallow interpretations prevalent in the popular culture of the time. Douglas's works include murals on the walls of Cravath Hall (the former library building) at Fisk University, the Countee Cullen Branch of the New York Public Library (now incorporated into the Schomburg Center in Harlem), and the College Inn Room of the Sherman Hotel in Chicago. He designed bookplates and also painted portraits of Mary McLeod Bethune, Charles Spurgeon Johnson, and other black luminaries. Douglas promoted African art in America through his murals and other illustrations. The Topeka, Kansas, native became an eminent muralist, illustrator, and educator. In 1939, he went to Fisk University in Nashville, where he established the art department.

How was the **migration of blacks** depicted in **artists' works**?

After World War II, blacks felt a sense of urgency to search for racial equality. The armed forces were integrated and offered hope for equality in other aspects of black life. As they sought greater cultural and professional opportunities, and looked for communities where other African-American intellectuals and artists lived, many blacks migrated from the South to urban areas in the North. Artists such as Romare Bearden, Beauford Delaney, and Jacob Lawrence documented this trend in their works.

What artists painted **exterior murals** during the **Harlem Renaissance** and **beyond**?

Artists Charles Alston, John T. Biggers, Jacob Lawrence, and Charles W. White used exterior murals to document the African architectural traditions. They were inspired by Mexican artists and were especially drawn to the themes, bold forms, and bright colors of Diego Rivera, David Alfaro Siqueiros, and José Clemente Orozco.

What were the **effects** of the **Great Depression** on **black artists**?

The 1930s brought the Great Depression and the Works Progress Administration. Black artists, now abandoned by white philanthropists of the 1920s, were rescued by the WPA. Harlem Renaissance artists Aaron Douglas, Augusta Savage, Charles Alston, Hale Woodruff, and Charles White were in this group. With WPA support, they created murals and other works for public buildings. In 1939 the Baltimore Museum show, the first exhibition of African-American artists to be held in a southern region, presented the works of Richmond Barthé, Malvin Gray Johnson, Hale Woodruff, Dox Thrash, Archibald Motley, and others.

What **philanthropic organizations** supported black artists early on?

Some white institutions, such as the Julius Rosenwald Fund, subsidized black artists in the early twentieth century. Later, such support came from other private institutions such as the Harmon, Guggenheim, and Whitney Foundations. Grant programs have come from governmental agencies that also supported these artists, with provisions from the Works Progress Administration, the National Endowment for the Arts, and state arts councils.

How did **historically black colleges respond** to the developments in the visual arts?

African-American artists felt a need to study the history, aesthetics, and formal qualities of art. Some continued to go abroad while others remained in the United States and studied at white colleges and universities and art academies and institutes. Historically Black Colleges and Universities (HBCUs) such as Fisk, Hampton, Howard, Morehouse, and Tuskegee responded by emphasizing art education as a viable career, as well as the basis for continuing a future cultural aesthetic in the visual arts. Fisk, for example, hired Aaron Douglas to establish its art department. He also adorned the walls of Fisk's then-new library with colorful murals that told the story of black people's move from Africa to America, the move into industrial areas, and their work as musicians, poets, and scientists.

Who were **America's primitive (untrained) artists** of acclaim?

After World War II, Jim Crow and segregation laws in the South began to slowly dismantle. Some black artists believed that art should be separate from race and politics that had dominated the subjects that black artists used in the 1940s and 1950s. Horace Pippin, William Edmondson, Clementine Hunter, and cartoonist E. Simms Campbell, who were self-taught, are in this group and went on to achieve widespread acclaim.

How did **black artists respond** to the modern **Civil Rights Movement**?

The Civil Rights Movement of the 1950s and 1960s was the most significant realignment of American democracy since the American Civil War of the 1860s. The movement asserted a rebirth and a reinvention of black identity and black consciousness as African Americans redefined themselves, while also forcing a reappraisal of white identity and America's democratic values.

Where was the **struggle to understand black art** during the **Civil Rights Movement** waged?

The art that grew out of the Civil Rights Movement is critical to understanding this tumultuous time. The struggle was waged on two fronts: in the streets and in the realm of images and ideas that proclaimed the awakening of a people in search of self-discovery, self-determination, and self-legitimization. Black artists asked themselves, "What kind of art should a black artist make in these times?"

Who were the **black artists** engaged in the **cultural revolution** of the **Civil Rights Movement**?

Culturally as well as aesthetically important works were produced during the Civil Rights Movement by black artists who are well known today. They included Romare Bearden,

45

Jacob Lawrence, Walter Williams, Charles White, Sam Gilliam, Jeff Donaldson, and others. Women artists, such as Betye Saar, Faith Ringgold, and Elizabeth Catlett Mora were included as well; they also celebrated heroes and heroines who embodied in their personal stories the struggle for social justice, as did Catlett Mora, in her iconic print *Malcolm Speaks for Us* (1969). As a visual record of the era, photographers Gordon Parks and Moneta Sleet used the camera to chronicle the times.

Why was artist **Romare Bearden** important?

Romare Bearden (1911–1988), painter and collagist, was one of the most original visual artists of the twentieth century. He experimented with different styles and mediums but is best known for his col-

Artist Romare Bearden is best remembered for his collages and photomontages.

lages and photomontages. Bearden had spent nearly two decades using abstract subjects when, in the 1960s, he departed from this focus and moved to collages. He joined twelve other African-American artists who called themselves "Spiral." Inspired by the Civil Rights Movement, these artists sought to explore the identity and images of African Americans through the use of art. Bearden's works are at the Museum of Modern Art, Pennsylvania Academy of the Fine Arts, and the Library of Congress. Bearden was born in Charlotte, North Carolina, on September 2, 1911, later moving to Pittsburgh and then to Harlem.

When did **black art move** to the streets of the **ghetto**?

Black art literally took to the streets of the ghetto in the 1960s and did so to meet with, appeal to, and celebrate the people, as was richly illustrated in Chicago and Detroit murals. In 1972 African-American and Hispanic teenagers in New York City created a colorful art form, "wall graffiti," to express their racial loyalty and pride. The content of wall graffiti is often merely the name of a street gang, the nickname of the painter, or the name of the street where the painter lives. Some of the paintings, however, depict extravagant scenes with cartoon characters and flamboyant lettering. Toward the end of the 1970s and well into the 1980s, this graffiti style became very popular and acquired value in the art market. Several of the young street artists, particularly Jean-Michel Basquiat, were welcomed into the mainstream art world and made into superstars.

CARTOONISTS

When did African Americans begin to **receive recognition as cartoonists**?

George Herriman (1880–1944), in 1910, was the first black to achieve fame as a syndicated cartoonist. On July 26, 1910, the prototype of Ignatz Mouse hit the prototype of Krazy Kat with a brick. The strip "Krazy Kat" was extremely popular, especially among intellectuals in the 1920s, and continued with somewhat diminished success until July 25, 1944. Herriman was born in New Orleans in a family classified as black; the family moved to Los Angeles to escape racial labeling. Some of his friends called him "The Greek," but he never openly divulged his background.

Who was **E. Simms Campbell**?

E(lmer) Simms Campbell (1906–1971) became, in 1933, the first black cartoonist to work for national publications. Born in St. Louis, he lived in Chicago while completing his high school education. He studied at the Art Institute of Chicago for three years. After returning to St. Louis, he was discouraged from becoming a commercial artist because the field was not a viable one for blacks. After working with a local commercial art studio for one year, he moved to New York City where he hoped to become a freelance cartoonist. There he worked for a local advertising studio and sold some of his work to other artists. He enrolled in the Academy of Design and also studied at the Art Students League under printmaker George Grosz. After publishing his well-known "A Night-Club Map of Harlem," which included such sites as the Lafayette Theater, Small's Paradise, and the Cotton Club, Campbell began to receive a number of commissions.

Campbell contributed cartoons and other art work to *Esquire* (he was in nearly every issue from 1933 to 1958), *Cosmopolitan, Redbook, New Yorker, Opportunity,* and syndicated features in 145 newspapers. He created the character "Esky," the pop-eyed mascot who appeared on the cover of *Esquire.* He worked tirelessly and became one of the highest paid commercial artists, often creating three hundred full-page drawings a year. In 1957 Campbell and his family moved to Switzerland. Fourteen years later, after his wife died, he returned to the United States and died a year later.

What cartoonist became popular as a **social satirist**?

In 1933 artist and cartoonist Oliver Harrington (1912–1995), one of America's most popular social satirists, created the first cartoon to focus on black American life. His early characters portrayed life during the Harlem Renaissance. His first comic strip, "Boop," was featured in the *Pittsburgh Courier* on March 11, 1933 (it was renamed "Scoop" on March 18). On May 25, 1935, Harrington published a panel in New York's *Amsterdam News* entitled "Dark Laughter." On December 28 of that same year he introduced the Bootsie character to the panel; this character continued in the newspaper for several years and was published later in the *Courier.* For forty years, Bootsie appeared in black newspapers. Harrington was born in the Valhalla community of Westchester County near New York City. He arrived in Harlem toward the end of the Harlem Renaissance and supported himself by working as a freelance artist. In 1940 he graduated from Yale University and started work on a master of fine arts degree.

Harrington illustrated Ellen F. Tarry's *The Runaway Elephant,* published in 1950. The American Institute of Graphic Arts selected both the book's cover and illustrations as one of the Fifty Best American Books that year—the first time the institute had so recognized a black artist. His book *Bootsie and Others,* an anthology of cartoons, was published in 1958.

Who was the **first** black cartoonist to deal with **social issues** through **comic books**?

In 1992, Alonzo Lavert Washington (1967–) created the first black comic book to deal with social issues and established the largest black comic book publishing firm. Born in Kansas City, Kansas, he studied at Kansas City Community College, Pioneer Community College, and Kansas City Media Project Communications. He developed an interest in comic books while growing up in the inner city; however, he was unable to relate to the characters. Whenever black characters appeared in books, they were either criminals or athletes, or they played a subordinate role to white characters. Washington first created his own black superheroes by painting the white action figures black and giving them Afro hairstyles. He later began to produce comics of his own—all dealing with social issues—and sold them to his classmates. In 1992 Washington promoted his first comic, "Original Man," by targeting churches, bookstores, and organizations in the community; he collected $1,000 in advance orders. That printing quickly sold out, prompting him to print ten thousand more. He made $30,000 in sales from his first issue.

By 1998 the firm Omega 7, which Washington founded, had become the largest black-owned comic-book company in the nation. Washington created a cast of action figure characters that included, among others, Omega Man, Lady Ace, and Original Woman, all with black features. His company was the first to offer black action figures on the market. He secured a deal with Toys "R" Us to distribute his toy characters, but generally marketed them in minority areas.

CIRCUS

When were **all-black circuses** first known to exist?

Ephraim Williams, a former shoeshine boy, formed a black traveling show in the 1880s. He was soon given the moniker of the "Black P. T. Barnum." His costume consisted of a tuxedo, top hat, and cane. Williams performed before lumberjacks as he traveled with his show to northern Wisconsin in 1885. His entertainment business grew to three circuses, which enabled him to expand his staff to one hundred people. To move his wild

> ## Who was Ringling Brothers' first black woman clown?
>
> **B**ernice Collins (1957–) became the first black woman clown with Ringling Brothers in 1977. The Kansas City native decided to become a clown when she was fourteen years old.

animals, equipment, and performers, he used fifteen railroad cars, which he owned. His entertainment business closed in 1902 because of bad weather and financial difficulties.

Who was **Ringling Brothers' first black ringmaster**?

In 1998, Johnathan Lee Iverson (1976–) signed on with Ringling Brothers/Barnum and Bailey's "The Greatest Show on Earth" as ringmaster of the Red Unit, one of the troupe's two traveling shows. He was the first black—and the youngest ringmaster—in the history of the Ringling Brothers Circus. The son of a postal worker and a firefighter, Iverson was born in New York City. At age eleven he joined the Boys Choir of Harlem and won several awards. He also sang on the soap opera *As the World Turns*. He graduated from Hartt School of Music in Connecticut and won a role in "The Fireside Christmas Show" held in Fort Atkinson, Wisconsin. It was there that Iverson's vocal talent captured the attention of the director of the show, who had also directed the circus. Iverson was encouraged to audition for the ringmaster's role, winning it after the first rehearsal.

What was the **first all-black circus** act in America?

In 1968, promoter Irving Field signed up the King Charles Troupe, the first all-black circus act in America. The troupe of basketball-playing unicycle riders, discovered auditioning on the sidewalk outside Madison Square Garden, also performed on television, appearing on such shows as *The Tonight Show*. Field introduced the troupe to the circus, billing them as "the first all-black circus act in America." Jerry King, architect of the act, first saw a unicycle act used in a small circus in Florida in 1916. Forty-two years later he taught his son, Charles King, and others in their Bronx, New York, neighborhood to ride the unicycle. To this the young riders added their basketball skills, created a special act, and became something like the Harlem Globetrotters on wheels. Charles King became the group's leader.

FESTIVALS

What is the **importance of festivals** in the black community?

African-American life has been celebrated in many ways, one of them being festivals of all kinds. They are a means of developing cultural awareness and celebrating with pride the talents and achievements within a group or a community. Some festivals have a long, historical significance, such as those originally held in colonial days, but most of this type are no longer preserved. Some represent religious observances, some are African-based, and others focus on artistic expression. Still others honor African-American leaders. Festivals in the black community aim to provide a positive venue for people to join in a joyful demonstration of unity and culture. Many current celebrations have been initiated to reclaim the past and connect it to the present and may be held to share African-American culture with the larger community. Whatever their purpose, festivals clearly honor the heritage of African Americans.

Who became the **first African American** to **preside** over the **New Orleans Mardi Gras**?

In 1949, (Daniel) Louis "Satchmo" Armstrong (1901–1971), jazz trumpeter, became the first black to preside over the New Orleans Mardi Gras. His lifelong dream came true when he was selected Mardi Gras King of the Zulu Social Aid and Pleasure Club; that led to his appearance on the cover of *Time* magazine for February 21, 1949.

When was the **first National Black Arts Festival** held in the United States?

The first National Black Arts Festival in the United States was held in Atlanta in 1987. Patron of the arts and educator Michael L. Lomax (1947–) founded the world-class celebration. Its mission is "to engage, cultivate and educate diverse audiences about the arts and culture of the African Diaspora and provide opportunities for artistic and creative expression."

EARLY DEVELOPMENT

What skills did **slaves bring** to **American culture**?

Free blacks gave evidence of a fashion industry as early as the 1700s, when Virginian Stephen Jackson made hats of fur and leather. The industry carried over into slavery, however, as slave women worked as seamstresses and embroiderers on large plantations. Some became widely known later on.

The economics of slavery required black labor that went beyond field work and house work and sought craftsmen who were artisans, dressmakers, musicians, barbers, furniture-makers, and brick masons. Once freed, these talented people developed skills that were immediately economically beneficial to them.

Slave narratives, or stories that slaves told about themselves, were the source of much of the early information about African-American businesses during that period. Although the American slave system restricted the life and times of the slave, some were able to operate businesses on the plantation of their master or were hired out for such purposes. When they were able to earn money for their labor, slaves often bought their freedom as well as that of their families and sometimes friends.

BLACK–OWNED BUSINESSES

Where were **early black businesses located**?

Most black businesses that operated during slavery were maintained outside the South. These businesses engaged in such skilled trades as catering, barbering, blacksmithing, shoemaking, and painting. During slavery, black fashionable dressmakers, fine caterers, and hairdressers worked primarily outside the South.

What is the **historical role** of the **barbershop** in the African-American community?

African Americans dominated the barbering business in the antebellum South and some enjoyed economic advantages. For example, in the 1830s William Tiler Johnson (1809–1851), who became known as the "Barber of Natchez," was born a slave and went on to become a popular barber in white America. He owned three barbershops and a bathhouse in Natchez, frequently hiring slaves to work as apprentices in his businesses. Until the late nineteenth century, black barbershops with large white clientele fared well. Barbershops have long been an important business as well as a center of cultural exchange in the African-American community. Some call them a repository of African-American folk culture and a place where various strata of the black community can come together. The 2002 comedy film *Barbershop* highlighted the black barbering business and its role in the community.

What is the **historical role** of the **beauty shop** in the African-American community?

Much like barbershops, beauty shops played an important role in black economic development. For the most part, the fine black artisans in the beauty shop industry worked outside the South. The beauty industry was one of the most popular black businesses of this period. Although some of these shops had black clientele, they catered to whites in order to survive in the racially segregated South, and began to thrive in their own communities when self-help activities for blacks were stressed to promote black economic development. Still-celebrated icons in the early industry are Madam C. J. Walker (1867–1919), Sarah Spencer Washington (1889–1953), and Annie Turnbo Malone (1869–1957), who owned manufacturing companies and established beauty schools, thus revolutionizing the care of black hair. Leading salon owners and stylists who emerged after the 1920s were the Cardozo sisters in Washington, D.C., Christine Moore Howell (1889–1972), Rose Morgan (1912–2008), and Joe L. Dudley (1939–). Black barber and beauty shops, which represented a cross-section of the community, were vital to the Civil Rights Movement of the 1960s and became political incubators for politicians and civil rights workers. In 2005 the comedy film *Beauty Parlor* was released; it highlighted the black beauty shop industry.

What was the importance of the **National Negro Doll Company**?

Racial stereotyping found its way into cultural artifacts that were produced in the nineteenth and early twentieth centuries, as can be seen in artifacts for amusement, such as dolls and other toys. The National Negro Doll Company was founded to introduce African-American children to dolls that looked like them, as opposed to the white dolls or stereotypical black dolls that were on the market. The company was founded in Nashville, Tennessee, as a part of the National Baptist Publishing Board, and managed by Henry Allen Boyd, son of the founder, Reverend Richard Henry Boyd. The company also supported the "buy black" campaign then in practice. The dolls were imported from Europe, advertised in the black press, and displayed and sold at bazaars and fairs nationwide. In the early 1900s, attempts were made to discredit the National Negro Doll Company and reduce the sale and distribution of black dolls that portrayed positive images. This came after the sale of white dolls in the black community declined and was as an effort to minimize the economic benefits that the African-American doll company reaped.

What **key areas** of **early black business development continue** to play an **important role** in the African-American business community?

Historically, African-American businesses have been restricted to the narrow range of service enterprises. African Americans have tended to establish businesses that require relatively limited capital and technical expertise, such as personal services and small-scale retailing. These firms have had to rely heavily on the African-American community as their market for goods and services. In 2002 four out of ten black-owned firms provided health care and social assistance, personal services, and repair and maintenance. These services remain a key base for African-American businesses.

When was the **golden age of black business** development?

What was called the golden age of black business development came during the first half of the twentieth century. Although they offered new lines of business, black enterprises continued to serve a segregated market. Emerging markets included real estate and structures such as hotels, homes, theaters, office buildings, and other facilities. There were also black-owned railroad lines, municipal transportation systems, automobile repair shops, and automobile manufacturing companies. Black banks and loan associations were their primary source of finance.

ADVERTISING

Who was the **first living trademark**?

Nancy Green (1831–1998), a former slave from Montgomery County, Kentucky, was the first Aunt Jemima and the world's first living trademark. In 1893, she made her debut at age fifty-nine at the Columbian Exposition in Chicago, where she dressed in costume and served pancakes in a booth. The Aunt Jemima Mills Company distributed a souvenir lapel button that bore her image and the caption, "I'se in town, honey." The caption later became the slogan on the company's promotional campaign. Green was the official trademark for three decades, touring the country and promoting Aunt Jemima products. The Aunt Jemima character, a variant of the mammy image, has perpetuated racial and gender stereotyping. Characteristically, the mammy icon in American culture is that of a plump black woman—a soft-witted, comical, and headstrong household servant who nurtures the children of her white master. Many people see these mammy characteristics in Aunt Jemima, a polite, indulgent, plump African-American cook who is closely associated with pancakes and kitchen products. Her image has been used on products that bore the Aunt Jemima label while the mammy and Jemima images have been seen in housewares, dolls and other toys, household decorations, in literature, films, radio, and elsewhere. Both images are now generally considered derogatory.

AUTOMOBILE INDUSTRY

Who was the first to build an **automobile manufacturing company**?

Frederick Douglas Patterson (1871–1932) was the first black to manufacture cars, starting in 1915. Between 1915 and 1919 Patterson built some thirty Greenfield-Patterson cars in Greenfield, Ohio. He was the youngest of four children born to former slaves Charles "Rich" and Josephine Patterson. The family was already successful when Frederick was born; the father had bought out his white partner and owned C. R. Patterson and Sons Carriage Company in Greenfield, which made the most popular carriages of the day. Frederick Patterson was the first black American to graduate from the local high school; he then entered Ohio State University where he was the first black to play on the football team. He left three years later and taught school in Kentucky for two years, before returning to Greenfield to work in the family's carriage business. Frederick's father died shortly after his return home, leaving him and other relatives to operate the business. While traveling with his sales manager, he made note of some "funny-looking horseless" carriages. When he returned, he persuaded his company's board to build these horseless carriages, or cars, and his bold plan resulted in the automobile known as the Patterson-Greenfield. Patterson's first car—a two-door coupe—rolled off the line on September 23, 1915. The car reportedly had a forty-horsepower Continental four-cylinder engine and reached a top speed of fifty mph. The company's two models—a roadster and a big four-door touring car—each sold for $850. Insufficient capital and slow car sales led to the car company's demise. Patterson went on to produce school bus bodies that were in great demand. The bus business closed in 1939.

BANKING

What purpose did the **Freedman's Bank** serve?

On March 3, 1865, the Freedman's Savings Trust and Company was incorporated by a congressional act. The bank became popularly known as the Freedman's Bank. It was, however, not a federal bank but a private white-owned and managed financial entity that many believed was a government institution. Few blacks were hired in the branch banks that were established in thirty-five cities across the South, and in St. Louis, Philadelphia, New York, and Washington, D.C. When the bank began to fail, Frederick Douglass was named president in January 1875, only six months before it closed. The bank was never a financial success; it also provided little benefit to blacks, so its title was actually a misnomer.

What **banks** were the **first created and run** by **African Americans**?

In 1888 the True Reformers Bank of Richmond, Virginia, and the Capital Savings Bank of Washington, D.C., became the first black-created and black-run banks. The True Re-

formers Bank, or the Savings Bank of the Grand Fountain, United Order of True Reformers, was chartered on March 2 and opened for business on April 3. The Capital Savings Bank was organized on October 17, and it was the first black bank to have no fraternal connections.

Who was the **first black woman bank president**?

In 1903, Maggie Lena Walker (1865–1934) became the first black woman bank president on July 28, when she founded the St. Luke Penny Savings Bank in Richmond, Virginia. The bank began as an insurance society in which Walker became active in 1886. When she retired in 1933, the bank was strong enough to survive the Great Depression, and continues to exist. The bank had a marked effect on black life in Richmond. Walker urged blacks to save their nickels and dimes, turning them into

The home of Maggie L. Walker in Richmond, Virginia, is an historic site. She founded the St. Luke Penny Savings Bank, which survived the Great Depression and still exists today.

55

dollars, and to finance their own homes since white-owned banks would not do so. An ardent feminist, she also urged women to improve themselves educationally and economically. She fought for women's suffrage and also worked in voter registration campaigns. She was instrumental in the formation of the Virginia Lily Black Republican Party. In March 1902 Walker founded *The St. Luke Herald,* a newspaper that illuminated black concerns and strengthened communication between the community and the Order of St. Luke, a black organization that dealt with the concerns of the race. The daughter of a former slave washerwoman, she became one of the wealthiest and most influential black women of the early twentieth century. Her spacious home in Richmond has been declared a National Historic Landmark.

CONSUMER COOPERATIVES

What was the function of **consumer cooperatives** in the black community?

Consumer cooperatives have functioned as examples of self-help and demonstrate how people within the same community may work together for the common good. Evidence of cooperatives in the African-American community working with other nationalities was seen as early as the late 1800s. There were farmers in the Grange movement in the 1860s and 1870s; however, the economic conditions of the members made it difficult for the cooperatives to flourish. As early as 1917, W.E.B. Du Bois and the National Association for the Advancement of Colored People (NAACP) encouraged blacks to form cooperatives. After World War I, consumer cooperatives in urban areas began to evolve. Union leader A. Philip Randolph also encouraged blacks in Harlem and elsewhere to form cooperatives, as did the Housewives League of Detroit. The latter organization also encouraged its members to buy from black-owned businesses. By 1935, in Gary, Indiana, there were 450 families in buying clubs. In the 1960s and 1970s, the idea of consumer cooperatives was revived and blacks in the Bedford-Stuyvesant neighborhood in Brooklyn established a buying cooperative and used the profits to build social service programs, to bolster education, and to support health care in the African-American community.

How did the **Colored Merchants' Association** function?

A movement in early twentieth century black America that fostered black economic development included a number of cooperatives such as shoe stores, department stores, grocery stores, and various retail establishments. Notable among these cooperatives was the Colored Merchants' Association (CMA), founded by grocer A. B. Brown in Montgomery, Alabama, on August 10, 1928. The cooperative comprised a voluntary chain of twelve members who operated their grocery stores as "C.M.A." stores. Soon the organization spread to other states; the members relied on cooperative buying and intensive selling. They did cooperative advertising, promoted quick selling to move their merchandise, and from time to time offered special bargain prices. In November 1928, Albon L. Holsey, a key staff member at nearby Tuskegee Institute, and a leader of the National Negro Business League (NNBL), was named national secretary of the CMA. Under Holsey's leadership, ties to the NNBL were strengthened and more stores were quickly added in major cities throughout the country. One successful experiment was seen in Winston-Salem, North Carolina, where the local black college, Winston-Salem Teachers College (as it was called then), aided in the development of a local store and set up a model store. In October 1929, the organization established its national quarters in New York City and Holsey continued his leadership. The organization declined in the 1930s, partially because of the Great Depression, internal dissention, and a desire to advertise or sell brands other than those of the CMA. Before long, the rapidity with which the stores were developed was seen also in their demise. However, for many years the CMA was a successful experiment in black self-help.

CORPORATE AMERICA

Who are some **successful black leaders** in **corporate America**?

Business executive and lawyer Kenneth I. Chenault (1952–) became president and chief operating officer of American Express in 2000, the first black to hold either position. In April 1999 his predecessor, Harvey Golub, declared Chenault as his CEO-designee, having tapped him two years early as president of the company. The appointment made him one of the most visible and highest-ranking blacks in corporate America. Since 1981, when he joined the company, Chenault has held a number of high positions with American Express. These include vice president of merchandise services and then senior vice president and general manager of the division, along with top positions in the Platinum/Gold Card Division, the Personal Care Division, the Consumer Card and Financial Services Group, and American Express Travel Related Services.

Reginald F. Lewis (1942–1993) became one of the four hundred wealthiest entrepreneurs in the United States. Born in Baltimore, Maryland, Lewis graduated from Virginia State College (now Virginia State University) in Petersburg and received his law degree from Harvard Law

Kenneth I. Chenault became president of American Express in 2000.

School. After graduating in 1968, he joined one of New York City's blue chip law firms, Paul, Weiss, Rifkind, Wharton & Garrison. Two years later he became a partner with Murphy, Thorp and Lewis, one of Wall Street's first black law firms. Later he bought out two of his partners and renamed the firm Lewis and Clarkson. Within a few years the firm had among its major clients General Foods, the Ford Foundation, Aetna Life, and Equitable Life. In 1983 Lewis created TLC Pattern and took over McCall Pattern Company, closing the deal on January 29, 1984, without using any of his personal funds. He sold the company in 1984 for a ninety-to-one gain.

Harvey Clarence Russell Jr. (1918–1998) became the first black vice president of a leading national corporation, PepsiCo, in 1962. Born in Louisville, Russell served in the U.S. Coast Guard during World War II and, though advised that he would not receive the position, became one of the coast guard's first black deck officers. He joined a Manhattan advertising firm where he was placed in charge of marketing. At PepsiCo Russell was put in charge of "Negro sales" and by 1958 managed its ethnic marketing department. In 1962 he was appointed vice president in charge of special markets for the company, in 1965 he was appointed vice president in charge of planning, and vice president for community affairs in 1969, where he remained until his retirement in 1983.

African Americans moved into corporate America's media industry as major leaders. Lawyer, political advisor, and corporate executive Richard Dean Parsons (1948–) was named chief executive officer of AOL-Time Warner and became the first black to head the world's largest media conglomerate. He took office on May 16, 2001. Parsons grew up in Queens, New York, and graduated from the University of Hawaii and Union University's Albany Law School. In 1971 he joined New York governor Nelson Rockefeller as assistant counsel. During Rockefeller's term as vice president, Parsons served as general counsel and associate director of the White House Domestic Council. In 1977 he joined the law firm Patterson, Belknap, Webb & Tyler and two years later was named a managing partner. He was one of New York mayor Rudolph W. Giuliani's first-term campaign team members, and in 2001 became a member of Mayor-elect Michael R. Bloomberg's transition team. Earlier in 2001 President George W. Bush appointed Parsons to co-chair, with former U.S. senator Daniel Patrick Moynihan, a commission to recommend changes in the country's Social Security program.

What **African-American entrepreneur** first became involved in **corporate takeovers**?

African Americans also made their mark in the area of corporate takeovers. In 1984, the first black to enter the high-stakes world of billion-dollar business takeovers was Reginald F. Lewis (1942–1993). Lewis created TLC Pattern (the Lewis Company) on July 29, 1983, with the intention of taking over McCall Pattern Company. His holding company was known as TLC Group. On January 29, 1984, he acquired McCall, doubled the company's profits, engaged in other maneuvers, and then sold the company, in 1987, for a ninety-to-one gain. In 1987 as well, he acquired Beatrice International and now headed the largest black-owned business in the country and the only black-owned company with over $1 million in revenues. Beatrice International comprised sixty-four companies in thirty-one countries; its parent company was Beatrice Foods, then the thirty-fifth largest industrial corporation in the United States.

Who was the **first African American woman** to **head a major corporation**?

Corporate executive Ann M. Fudge (1951–) became the first African-American woman to head a major company, when she was appointed president of the Maxwell House Coffee division of Kraft General Foods in 1994. Her success in corporate America began in 1977 when Fudge joined Minneapolis-based General Mills Company and, in 1978, was named assistant product

Kenneth C. Frazier, president and CEO of pharmaceutical giant Merck & Co., is seen here at the 2012 World Economic Forum on Africa in Addis Ababa, Ethiopia.

manager. Four years later she was made product manager with responsibility for four brands. Honey Nut Cheerios was developed under her leadership and became one of the division's top performers.

Who was the first African-American **major officer** in a **pharmaceutical company**?

In 2011, Kenneth C. Frazier (1954–) became the first black chief executive officer and president of Merck & Co., the nation's second largest pharmaceutical company. The appointment made him also the first black CEO of any major pharmaceutical company. He joined Merck in 1992, in its public affairs division, and moved up the corporate ladder. Now he sits on the company's board. The Philadelphia native holds degrees from Pennsylvania State University and Harvard Law School. He volunteers for organizations that serve the underprivileged.

ECONOMIC BOYCOTTS AND PROTESTS

What forms of **black economic protests** occurred early in the community?

The economic boycotts and protests that African Americans practiced in mid-twentieth-century America were not a new strategy aimed at securing equal rights guaranteed by the U.S. constitution. For example, in the period 1900 to 1906 blacks in over

Student Nonviolent Coordinating Committee leader John Lewis with minister James Zwerg after they were both beaten during one of the Freedom Rides. Groups like the SNCC and others put economic and other pressures against white businesses and institutions.

twenty-five Southern cities protested against segregated seats on street cars and boycotted them. Black organizations, such as the National Association for the Advancement of Colored People (NAACP), the Congress of Racial Equality (CORE), the Southern Christian Leadership Conference (SCLC), and the Student Nonviolent Coordinating Committee (SNCC) brought economic pressures on segregated businesses in protest of their exclusionary practices. It was CORE that used these practices during the sit-ins and freedom rides, beginning as early as 1942 in Jack Spratt's coffeehouse. One of the first cities to employ economic pressure where needed was Montgomery, Alabama, where a year-long boycott of segregated buses caused the city, downtown businesses, and the bus company to lose nearly $1 million. Such boycotts and economic withdrawals spread throughout the South. In 1960, Nashville, Tennessee, followed with its economic withdrawals by boycotting downtown merchants at Easter time—a time normally quite profitable to merchants. They used the motto "No Fashions for Easter" and deprived white merchants of incalculable profits. Blacks as well as whites joined in the protest. Similarly, economic withdrawals were applied to lunch counters, movie theaters, and elsewhere, sometimes causing whites to avoid these places in fear of physical disturbances. The results of such actions at times translated into significant losses of revenue.

What was the **"Don't Buy Where You Can't Work"** campaign?

This campaign forced America to take a look at the economic potential of the black race and to help determine the effects of employment and unemployment of people. In a sense, it functioned as a consumer cooperative. The campaign began in Chicago in 1929, when blacks organized a boycott of Chicago's white merchants who refused to hire blacks. It is known variously as "Don't Spend Your Money Where You Can't Work," "Jobs for Negroes," and "Don't Buy Where You Can't Work." It promoted what was known as the "Double Duty Dollar" that churches in Chicago promoted to encourage blacks to make their dollars help businesses financially as well as advance race-related goals. The campaign was the forerunner of the economic boycotts and protests that were practiced during the modern Civil Rights Movement. It spread from Chicago to other major cities, with branches in still more urban areas. Finally, it reached smaller towns, such as Richmond, Virginia, and Alliance, Ohio. The campaign was slow to take hold in Harlem, where it was launched around 1930; it took ten years for jobs for blacks to become a reality on a widespread basis. Organizations such as the Harlem Housewives League and the Colored Merchants' Association joined in the protest. These efforts in Harlem ended around World War II, when blacks had many other compelling issues to address.

FOOD AND FOOD SERVICE INDUSTRIES

What were some **early success stories** for African Americans in the **food service industry**?

During the eighteenth and nineteenth centuries, the work of African Americans in the food service industry was largely in catering and hotel restaurants. Some who operated catering businesses, particularly in the North, became quite wealthy, such as Thomas Downing and his son George; they also had a restaurant business. The most successful nineteenth-century black food service businesses were in Philadelphia. In the South, however, few hotel and restaurant businesses were successful because of social and legal barriers. One successful entrepreneur was Jehu Jones Sr., who, in 1816, established a hotel and restaurant business in Charleston, South Carolina.

One of the most highly successful food service industries run by African Americans in the nineteenth century was operated in Washington, D.C., by James Wormley (1819–1884). His hotel and restaurant business made him a comfortable fortune; later he added a catering business that was renowned in local black and white communities.

When did blacks become **owners of McDonald's franchises**?

The nation's first black-owned McDonald's opened in Chicago in 1968, with pioneering businessman Herman Petty as owner. In 2008 this historic building was rebuilt and reopened on its original site, at 65th Street and Stony Island Avenue, and had a grand reopening. Yolanda Travis, owner and operator of the rebuilt structure, said, "Breathing new life into this historic landmark franchise demonstrates McDonald's commitment to education and employment in our community."

Who is **"Famous" Amos**?

In 1975, Wally "Famous" Amos (1936–) was the first black to open a cookie-only retail store; his was the first black-owned gourmet cookie company to build a national following. The Tallahassee, Florida, native relocated to New York City where he lived with his Aunt Della, who loved to cook, often preparing her special chocolate chip cookie for him. Amos held a variety of jobs, including mail clerk for the William Morris Company in New York. In 1967 he moved to Los Angeles where he worked on his own as a talent agent. To supplement his income, he used his Aunt Della's recipe and began baking chocolate chip cookies that he distributed. He opened a small shop on Sunset Boulevard in Hollywood, which became the first of its kind dedi-

Entrepreneur Wally "Famous" Amos opened his own gourmet cookie company in 1975. Kellogg's now owns Famous Amos cookies, and Amos started a new company called The Cookie Man Cookies.

cated to gourmet chocolate chip cookies. Two years after he founded Famous Amos Chocolate Chip Cookies, his profits grew and his cookies were nationally distributed. Although he made millions in his business, by 1985 the company began to report a loss in revenue. Rather than lose the company, Amos sold the controlling share to the Bass Brothers of Fort Worth, Texas. He remained on the company's board as vice chairman, but later was no more than a company spokesman. He left the company in 1989. In 1992 he started another company, The Uncle Noname Cookie Company and offered five varieties of gourmet cookies. He was prevented from using the Famous Amos name.

What are some **well-known brand names** in the food industry that are owned by African Americans?

Parks Sausage Company, founded in Baltimore in 1951, brought a fortune to entrepreneur Henry Green Parks Jr. (1916–1989). His company became the first owned by an African American to be traded publicly. Another, Glory Foods, located in Columbus, Ohio, was founded in 1989 by Bill Williams, Iris McCord, and Daniel A. Charna. Among the canned items in the Glory Food line are cornbread mixes, sweet potatoes, and okra, while the fresh line includes packaged turnip and collard greens. The line enjoys a national market.

What is the **importance of barbecue** in the African-American community?

Barbecue establishments, particularly in the South, are traditionally an important part of the black community. Most of the businesses have been small and range from roadside stands to simple shacks to sit-down restaurants. Barbecue, or the open braising of meat, is a part of the African influence on American foods. In addition to being a source of income for black people, barbecuing became a part of festivals, church activities, and private and community celebrations throughout the country.

When did **soul food restaurants** become popular?

As segregation declined during the twentieth century and restaurants brought down racial barriers, many African-American businesses saw a decline in customers. African-American economic ventures in the food service industry of the twentieth century included two popular trends—soul food based on traditional black cooking and served in African-American-owned restaurants, and black ownership of fast-food franchises such as McDonald's and Wendy's.

What are some of black America's **well-known restaurants**?

Among the successful black-owned restaurants before, during, and after the Civil Rights era were Dooky Chase's in New Orleans, Paschal's in Atlanta, and Sylvia's in Harlem. They gained national and international fame. As well, many smaller businesses opened throughout the country and specialized in soul food.

Barbara "B" Smith (1949–) became highly recognized as a restaurateur and opened restaurants in the New York Theater district and in Washington, D.C.'s Union Station.

Dooky Chase's restaurant in New Orleans was a famous black-owned establishment during the civil rights era.

Black celebrities, such as singer Gladys Knight and Sean "Diddy" Combs, either purchased restaurants or allowed one to be named for them.

INSURANCE COMPANIES

What was the **first black-owned insurance company** in the United States?

The African Insurance Company of Philadelphia, founded in 1810, is the first known black insurance company. It was not incorporated, but had capital stock in the amount of $5,000. Its president was Joseph Randolph; treasurer, Carey Porter; and secretary, William Coleman. In 1931, Alexander and Company General Insurance Agency of Atlanta, Georgia, established by Theodore Martin Alexander Sr. (1909–2001), was the first black-owned and black-controlled general insurance brokerage and risk management agency in the South. It eventually grew to be the largest.

What **black-owned insurance company** was the **first to have $100 million** in assets?

The North Carolina Mutual Life Insurance Company, founded in Durham, North Carolina, in 1893, was the first black insurance company to attain $100 million in assets. The success of the company was largely due to the work of Charles Clinton Spaulding (1874–1952), who became general manager of the company in 1900 and was president from 1923 until his death. Born in Columbus County, North Carolina, he later moved to Durham and spent most of his life building the insurance company. He became one of black America's most influential leaders.

LABOR UNIONS

What was the **Brotherhood of Sleeping Car Porters**?

A. Philip Randolph (1889–1979) founded the Brotherhood of Sleeping Car Porters on August 25, 1925, the first major nationwide black union. It would take ten years of struggle and new federal labor legislation before the union established a collective bargaining agreement with the Pullman Palace Car Company. Thus the union became the first official bargaining agent for black Pullman workers on October 1, 1935. Randolph became active in civil rights as well. He used the power and reputation gained from his work with the Brotherhood of Sleeping Car Porters to call for a March on Washington in 1942. This planned protest against the government's indifference to the war efforts and black rights led to advances in civil and economic rights for blacks. In 1957 Randolph became a vice president of the American Federation of Labor and Congress of Industrial Organizations (AFL-CIO), representing the Pullman porters; he served until

1968. Randolph was born in Crescent City, Florida. He graduated from Cookman Insti-

A. Philip Randolph, founder of the Brotherhood of Sleeping Car Porters, is seen in this photo from the 1963 March on Washington in the center, front row. At far left of the front row is Whitney M. Young Jr., executive director of the National Urban League, and Roy Wilkins, executive secretary of the NAACP. On the right are Walter P. Reuther, President of the UAW, and Arnold Aronson, the secretary of the Leadership Conference on Civil Rights.

tute (now Bethune Cookman University) in Jacksonville in 1907 and held several short-lived jobs. In 1912 he enrolled in City College in New York where he associated with student radicals and adopted a belief in socialism. From 1918 until 1927 Randolph served as editor of the *Messenger,* a magazine geared to radical groups. He is regarded as one of the most important labor leaders of his time.

Why was the **Dining Car Employees Union** organized?

A group of young black cooks and waiters, including George Ellington Brown Jr. (1906–1951), organized the Dining Car Employees Local 370 in New York City in 1934 and the next year elected Brown president. As head of the union, Brown, then thirty-five years old, became the first black to head a labor union for dining car employees nationwide. Among other issues, the waiters and cooks protested the requirement that they sleep on small cots in the dining car when on overnight runs. They also protested the low wages that they were paid. After unsuccessful attempts to address the workers' demands, Brown took the matter to Pennsylvania's state representatives. In 1937, the Pure Food Law was amended and railroads in that state were forced to abolish the practive of sleeping in the dining car. Large railroads elsewhere followed suit. Top leaders of the Hotel, Restaurant and Bartenders International Union, with which Local 370 was affiliated, recognized Brown's potential as a leader. In August of 1938 Brown became the first black and the youngest person elected as a vice president of the American Federation of Labor (AFL), representing the Dining Car Workers and Hotel and Restaurant Employees. At the same time he became president-at-large of the railroad division and held that office until he died. Brown was born in Hoboken, New Jersey, the son of a steamship porter and former horse trainer. His mother was of Senegalese and German origin. He became a dining car cook for the Pennsylvania Railroad in 1925 and later served as a waiter.

When did **African-American women** become **union leaders**?

African-American women became involved in labor union leadership by the last quarter of the twentieth century. As a member of the national executive board of the Amalgamated Meat Cutters and Butcher Workmen, Addie L. Wyatt (1924–2012) became the first black woman labor executive, in 1976. That year she also became an international vice president of the union and was the first black woman to hold this leadership role in an international union.

MANUFACTURING

Who established the **first major black-owned sail-making shop**?

In 1798, James Forten Sr. (1766–1842) established the first major black-owned sail-making shop in Philadelphia. His financial worth soon reached $100,000. Forten was a leader in the radical abolitionist movement. An organizer of the American Anti-Slavery Society (1833), he also supported women's suffrage and temperance.

What was the importance of furniture-maker **Thomas Day**?

By 1818, Thomas Day (c. 1800–1861), a free black, was the first widely recognized black furniture and cabinet maker in the Deep South. Between 1827 and 1859, he operated one of the North Carolina's largest furniture enterprises, making sofas, chairs, chests, tables, and bedsteads from walnut, mahogany, and oak. He also built coffins and did fine interior work, such as stairways and trims. He was a slave owner and hired two of his slaves in his early furniture shop. He also apprenticed white bondservants in his business. Day sold directly to clients, and his ornately carved work was represented in homes of distinguished families throughout the state, including the home of the governor. One of his prime clients was also the University of North Carolina at Chapel Hill. Day was recognized as one of the finest artisans of the day. He worked in Milton, North Carolina, and his workshop, the Yellow Tavern, is a National Historic Landmark. He was born in Halifax County, Virginia, and moved to Milton in 1823, where he opened his shop. Evidence of his fine work may be seen in furniture scattered across North Carolina, but especially in Chapel Hill, Durham, Raleigh, Fayetteville, Greensboro, Winston-Salem, and Charlotte.

PUBLISHING

Who are some **successful black leaders** of the **publishing industry?**

Robert Sengstacke Abbott (1870–1940), newspaper editor and publisher, founded the *Chicago Defender* in 1905 and developed it into one of the most successful black business enterprises. His paper has been called one of the leading, if not the leading, black newspapers. His power was recognized as early as 1917, when he promoted the great migration of blacks from the rural South to areas in the North. Abbott was born in Savannah and was educated at Claflin University in Orangeburg, South Carolina, and Hampton Institute in Virginia. His move to Chicago in 1897 came as he planned to earn a law degree; he graduated from Kent College of Law in 1899. When he published his first issue of the *Chicago Defender* in 1905 it faced competition from the other three black newspapers published there as well. His hard work, business acumen, and understanding of the people's needs enabled him to succeed as a black publisher. Prior to his death on February 24, 1940, he prepared his nephew John H. Sengstacke to succeed him at the *Defender*.

Earl G. Graves (1935–) founded a new publishing venture, Earl Graves Ltd., located in New York City, and in November became editor and publisher of the first African-American business journal, *Black Enterprise*. The magazine turned a profit by its tenth issue. Graves established BCI Marketing, a development and market research firm to examine the buying patterns of potential readers; he then used this information to entice general and black businesses to subscribe to and advertise in his journal. *Black Enterprise* publishes articles on a variety of issues including economics, science, technology, health, and politics.

In 1968 he founded Earl G. Graves Associates, a management consulting firm specializing in urban affairs and economic development. The experiences of his company propelled him to study black-owned businesses in Caribbean countries and to develop a business plan and editorial prospectus for the business periodical that he envisioned. In 1970, with a $150,000 loan from the Manhattan Capital Corporation of Chase Manhattan Bank, he began his publishing venture. Graves was born in Brooklyn and graduated from Morgan State University.

John H. Johnson (1918–2005), the founder of *Ebony* (1945) and *Jet* (1951), was born poor in Arkansas City, Arkansas, and moved to Chicago during the Great Depression. He attended the University of Chicago part time while he worked at Supreme Life Insurance Company. Between 1943 and 1957, however, he had little contact with Supreme Life. The new black consciousness of the World War II era stimulated Johnson to begin a publication to inform the public about the achievements of blacks; he founded the Negro Digest Publishing Company and began issuing *Negro Digest* in November 1942. The magazine grew and established new records as a black journal. Johnson saw a market for another magazine—one modeled after *Life* magazine. On November 1, 1945, he founded *Ebony;* the magazine's first run of twenty-five thousand copies quickly sold out. In 1949 Negro Digest Publishing Company became Johnson Publishing Company. Johnson's company published a number of other magazines, including *Jet*, which was launched on November 1, 1951, and also had a book-publishing arm. The company later diversified and established Fashion Fair Cosmetics, a subsidiary, and entered the television market, sponsoring such programs as "Ebony Music Awards," "American Black Achievement Award," and "Ebony/Jet Showcase." Johnson rose from poverty to become a wealthy entrepreneur with an international reputation.

WOMEN ENTREPRENEURS

Who were some of the **early black women entrepreneurs**?

African-American women prospered as entrepreneurs as early as the 1860s, when Christiana Carteaux Bannister (1819–1902), also known as Madame Carteaux Bannister, operated her Shampooing and Hair Dyeing business in Boston and Worcester, Massachusetts, and in Providence, Rhode Island. William Lloyd Garrison's abolitionist newspaper, the *Liberator,* often carried advertisements for her enterprise. Bannister closed her business in the 1890s. She was also an activist in the abolitionist movement and raised funds to aid families of black soldiers in the Civil War.

Sarah Breedlove McWilliams Walker (1867–1919), known as Madam C. J. Walker, was born in Louisiana to indigent former slaves. She became interested in the hair problems of black women and, after moving to Denver, she began to manufacture hair products, including her Wonderful Hair Grower. She eventually produced five hair-care products. Her company began with door-to-door selling techniques; she eventually established a chain of beauty parlors across the country, the Caribbean, and South America. In 1910 Walker selected Indianapolis as her headquarters. She employed five thousand black commissioned agents, who demonstrated her techniques and sold her products. She became wealthy and built a palatial mansion, Villa Lewaro, on the Hudson River in Irvington, New York. Enrico Caruso gave the home its name. It became a gathering place for black leaders and entertainers. Walker lived there barely a year before she died. In 1993 investment banker Harold Doley bought the house and in 1958 turned it into a temporary decorators' museum to attract black designers and raise money for charity. The mansion has since changed ownership.

Annie Minerva Turnbo Pope Malone (1869–1957) was born in Metropolis, Illinois, and was orphaned at an early age. By 1900 she had developed successful straighteners, hair growers, special oils, and other products. Malone also manufactured and sold Wonderful Hair Grower and, with her assistants, sold products door-to-door. She opened Poro College in St. Louis in 1902, where she trained women as agents for the Poro system. Students were also taught how to properly walk, speak, and eat. By 1905 Madam C. J. Walker was one of Malone's first students. Poro claimed to employ seventy-five thousand agents throughout the United States, the Caribbean, and other parts of the world. In 1930, Malone relocated the college and the business to Chicago. Her business was poorly managed and also fell victim to several lawsuits. By 1950 most of the Poro property was sold.

REAL ESTATE

Who was **Biddy Mason**?

In 1866, Biddy Mason (1818–1891) was the first known black woman property owner in Los Angeles, California. Born into slavery in Georgia or Mississippi and named Bridget, she and her master, Robert Smith, took the strenuous journey first to the Utah Territory and then to California, where Mason legally gained her freedom on January 21, 1856. All members of her family were freed as well. Mason worked as a nurse and midwife—as she had done en route to the West—and saved her money. Her earnings and careful investment became the foundation that enabled her grandson Robert to be called the richest black in Los Angeles around 1900. A very religious and charitable woman, Mason opened her house for the establishment of the first African Methodist Episcopal Church in the city in 1872. She is also said to have opened the first day care nursery for homeless community children.

RETAIL

Who was an **early bookseller** of importance?

David Ruggles (1810–1849) was the first known black bookseller and the first black to have an imprint in a book, when he published *The "Extinguisher" Extinguished* in 1834. From 1829 to 1833 Ruggles was a grocer and butter merchant in New York. He opened his bookstore the next year, selling anti-slavery works and stationery and engaging in a variety of publishing tasks, including the composition of letters for those who were unable to write. His New York City shop was unfortunately burned out by a white mob in September 1835, fueled no doubt by his activities as an active abolitionist and worker on the Underground Railroad. The destruction did not stop Ruggles. He continued to live at the same address and to maintain his status as an anti-slavery advocate and agent for abolitionist papers. He was a secretary of the New York Vigilance Committee and was noteworthy for his aggressive and daring activities on behalf of former slaves. When his health began to fail, Ruggles spent his last years as a hydrotherapist and is believed to have been the first black hydrotherapist. He was arrested twice, once for assault and later in connection with a case in which a former slave was accused of theft. In the latter case, which occurred during 1839, he stood accused of a major crime for seventeen months before he was discharged without a trial.

STOCK EXCHANGE

What was the first **black company** on the **stock exchange**?

In 1971 Johnson Products became the first black firm to be listed on a major stock exchange when it was listed on the American Stock Exchange. The firm was founded by

Who was black America's first millionaire?

In 1890 Thomy Lafon (1810–1893) was thought to be the first black millionaire. He was a New Orleans real estate speculator and moneylender. He was recognized as a community activist and philanthropist before the Civil War, when he was still a young man. He was listed as a merchant in the New Orleans City Directory in 1842; in 1868 the directory listed him as a broker, and he was considered the city's second leading black broker until 1870. As his wealth grew, he gave freely to those less fortunate, including religious and anti-slavery causes; he also supported the Lafon Orphan Boys' Asylum and the Home for Aged Colored Men and Women, both of which he founded. The Thomy Lafon School, dedicated in 1898, made him the first black man and the second black person in New Orleans to have a school named for him. The Wall of Fame at the 1939–1940 New York World's Fair listed his name along with those of other blacks, Native Americans, and foreign-born Americans who were notable contributors to American progress and culture. He lived frugally, and despite his philanthropic gifts, his estate was valued at nearly half a million dollars. Lafon's will provided for his relatives and friends, but he left the bulk of his estate to charity.

Madam C. J. Walker, or Sarah Breedlove McWilliams Walker (1867–1919), is believed by some to be the first black woman to become a millionaire. Supporters of Annie Turnbo Malone (1869–1957) dispute this. Both women produced hair-care products for black women during the period; it is asserted that Walker worked as a salesperson for Malone products. Both became very wealthy by around 1910, but by 1927 Malone's business began to run into difficulties because of poor management.

George Ellis Johnson Sr. (1927–) in 1954. Johnson was the first black elected a director of the board of Commonwealth Edison, in 1971. Johnson was born in Richton, Mississippi, to sharecroppers. He relocated to Chicago with his mother, and attended Wendell Phillips Academy High School until he was forced to drop out to help support his family. He joined Fuller Products and later became a production chemist, developing a hair relaxer for men. In 1954 Johnson borrowed $250 from a finance company to establish Johnson Products. Later he and his wife turned the company into a multimillion-dollar enterprise known for innovations in the beauty-care products industry. In the mid-1980s he lost the company in a divorce settlement.

TRANSPORTATION

Who mastered his own ship?

In 1783 Paul Cuffee (1759–1817) was the first black to sail as master of his own ship. His father was an Ashanti slave who was brought from Africa. His father's second owner was a Quaker, who freed the senior Cuffee three years after purchasing him. The freedman married a Native American woman, and Paul Cuffee was thus born free. He went to sea at age fourteen, working as a sailor. By 1777 he was involved with maritime trade as a blockade-runner. During the Revolutionary War, he was plagued by issues of taxation and was once imprisoned by the British for three months after they seized an American vessel. When the war ended, Cuffee broadened his seafaring activities and bought property from which he operated his business. By 1800 his investment in ships, a waterfront farm, and a windmill resulted in assets of nearly $10,000, which may have made him the wealthiest African American in the U.S. at the time. Cuffee launched his ship *Alpha* in 1806 and served as its captain. An American-imposed embargo on international trade with Europe led to his interest in Africa and abolition of the slave trade. His Quaker heritage facilitated this interest as he worked with white Quaker abolitionist James Pemberton. Cuffee later developed trade with Sierra Leone, where he encouraged missionary work and colonization. His plans included carrying emigrants to Sierra Leone, and he launched the first black-led return to Africa in 1815. Although the voyage was successful, financial problems doomed his hope of making a yearly voyage. He tried to work with the newly formed white American Colonization Society. The organization seemed to attract persons who supported colonization for racist reasons and was condemned by black leaders in 1817, a few months before Cuffee's death. His name is sometimes given as Cuffe.

CIVIL RIGHTS AND PROTESTS

SLAVERY AND ANTI-SLAVERY

What was the *Amistad* incident and why was it important to slavery and the anti-slavery movement?

Joseph Cinqué (1811–1879) was born in Sierra Leone and in 1839 Spaniards purchased him and put him aboard the slave ship *Amistad* headed for Puerto Principe. A raging storm exhausted the crew who tried to control the ship during the turbulence. Then Cinqué led an uprising with the slaves aboard, seized the ship, and killed all crew members except two who were saved to sail the ship back to Africa. Instead, the ship, with about fifty Africans and Mende warrior Cinqué, headed to the northwest and landed off the coast of New York state where the insurrectionists were captured. When abolitionists learned of the event, they worked in support of the captives and enabled Cinqué to raise funds to appeal their case. Cinqué was an excellent speaker and his Mende language was translated into English as he joined the abolitionists' lecture circuit. John Quincy Adams won the case for the slaves before

While on the slave ship *Amistad* bound for Puerto Principe, Joseph Cinqué led a rebellion that killed most of the crew. Back in the U.S.A., he was put on trial, where he was successfully defended by John Quincy Adams.

73

the U.S. Supreme Court, in 1841, and they were awarded their freedom and allowed to return to Africa. The case caused further controversy between the North and South. It also documents an early slave revolt, the successful work of abolitionists, and shows how a group of Africans survived the litigation process and returned to their homeland.

When was **slavery outlawed** in **Europe**?

The slave trade ended in Britain in 1807, when authorities agreed with the growing number of abolitionists (those who argued that slavery is immoral and violates Christian beliefs) and outlawed the trade. In 1833 slavery was abolished throughout the British colonies as the culmination of the great anti-slavery movement in Great Britain. Still, trade on the black market continued until Britain stepped up its enforcement of its anti-slavery law by conducting naval blockades and surprise raids off the African coast, effectively closing the trade. The slave trade as it had been known officially came to an end after 1870, when it was outlawed throughout the Americas. Throughout the world today, the United Nations works to abolish slavery and other systems of forced labor.

When was the **importation of slaves** to the **U.S. prohibited**?

An Act Prohibiting Importation of Slaves became effective on January 1, 1808. It was passed in March 1807 and was the first law prohibiting the importation of slaves into the United States. First the Treasury Department, then the Secretary of the Navy, and at times the Secretary of State were responsible for enforcing the law. Although it was poorly enforced, the law helped to end slavery in the United States by prohibiting the transportation of slaves from Africa to the United States and its territories. It prompted some Southern states to pass similar laws, while other states refused to act.

Which **U.S. state** was the **first to abolish slavery**?

Vermont was the first state to abolish slavery, in 1777. On July 8 of that year Vermont adopted a state constitution that prohibited slavery. The first document in the United States to outlaw slavery, it read in part: "No male person, born in this country, or brought from over sea, ought to be holden by law, to serve any person, as a servant, slave, or apprentice, after he arrives to the age of eighteen years, unless they are bound by their own consent, after they arrive to such age, or bound by law, for the payment of debts, damages, fines, costs, or the like." Vermont's constitution also gave suffrage to all men, regardless of race. Vermonters were the first to put a black legislator in the state house: Alexander Twilight (1795–1857) was elected as a representative in 1836. Twilight also earned another first: in 1823 he graduated from Vermont's Middlebury College to become the first black person in the nation to earn a college degree.

When did the **anti-slavery movement begin**?

In the United States, the campaign to prohibit slavery strengthened in the early 1800s. Across the Atlantic, abolitionists had successfully lobbied for the outlawing of the slave trade in Great Britain by 1807. The following year the U.S. government also outlawed the trade, but possession of slaves remained legal and profitable. In the 1830s the call to abolish slavery and emancipate slaves became an active movement in the United States, precipitated by a revival of evangelical religion in the North. Abolitionists, believing slavery was morally wrong and violated Christian beliefs, called for an end to the system, which had become critical to the agrarian economy of the Southern states, where plantations produced cotton, tobacco, and other crops for domestic and international markets.

Who were the **leaders of abolition**?

Leaders of the anti-slavery movement included journalist William Lloyd Garrison (1805–1879), founder of the influential anti-slavery journal *The Liberator* and of the American Anti-Slavery Society (established 1833); brothers Arthur (1786–1865) and Lewis (1788–1873) Tappan, prominent New York merchants who were also founders of the American Anti-Slavery Society; and Theodore Dwight Weld (1803–1895), leader of student protests, organizer of the American and Foreign Anti-Slavery Society, and author of *The Bible Against Slavery* (1837) and other abolitionist works.

Underground Railroad conductor Harriet Tubman (c. 1820–1913) worked against slavery by helping to free hundreds of blacks who escaped slavery in the South and were heading for Northern states and Canada. Writers such as Harriet Beecher Stowe (1811–1896), author of *Uncle Tom's Cabin* (1852), helped strengthen the abolitionist cause and sway public sentiment. In the hands of some activists the movement became violent: in 1859 ardent abolitionist John Brown (1800–1859) led a raid on the armory at Harpers Ferry (in present-day West Virginia), in a failed attempt to emancipate slaves by force.

Who were the **leading blacks** involved in **abolition**?

Although the abolition movement was dominated by whites, numerous black leaders played a major role in the movement, among them Frederick Douglass (1818–1895), Alexander Crummell (1819–1898), Henry Highland Garnet (1815–1882), Samuel Ringgold Ward (1817-1866), David Walker (c. 1796–1830), Daniel Coker (1780–1846), David Ruggles (1810–1849), and Martin Robison Delany (1812–1885). Douglass, an escaped slave from Maryland, became one of the best-known black abolitionists in the country. He lectured extensively throughout the United States and England. In 1845 he published the first of his three autobiographies, *Narrative of the Life of Frederick Douglass*, followed by *My Bondage and My Freedom* in 1855, and his third and final autobiography, *The Life and Times of Frederick Douglass* in 1881.

Who was the **most successful agent** on the **Underground Railroad**?

American abolitionist, lecturer, and nurse Harriet Tubman (c. 1820–1913) set up a network to emancipate slaves. Tubman was motivated to do so after she had made her way to freedom in 1849, and then wished the same for her family: "I had crossed the line of

Harriet Tubman was a former slave who led about three hundred fellow slaves to freedom using the Underground Railroad, and she was also a Union spy during the American Civil War.

which I had so long been dreaming. I was free; but there was no one to welcome me to the land of freedom," she wrote.

For the next ten years Tubman acted as a conductor on the Underground Railroad, making at least fifteen trips into Southern slave states, and guiding not only her parents and siblings, but more than three hundred slaves to freedom in the North. She was called "the Moses of her people" for her emancipation efforts. These journeys to freedom were demanding and often dangerous missions. Though Tubman was small in stature, she possessed extraordinary leadership qualities. Author, clergyman, and army officer Thomas Wentworth Higginson (1823–1911) called her "the greatest heroine of the age."

Were any **anti-slavery societies** founded by **women**?

The Salem Female Anti-Slavery Society is an example of an anti-slavery society founded by African-American women, sometimes called "females of color," in 1832. This was the first women's anti-slavery society in the United States. It was established in Salem, Massachusetts, and, although its constitution made no specific reference to slavery, it called for mutual improvement and the promotion of the welfare of colored people. In 1834 the society dropped its founding name—the Female Anti-Slavery Society of Salem—and became the Salem Female Anti-Slavery Society. Membership was racially mixed and the constitution declared slavery a sin, called for its abolishment, declared that people of color had a right to a home in America, and noted the duty of its members to elevate the slaves' condition and become their friends and equals.

What did the **founding of Liberia** have to do with the **anti-slavery movement**?

With the goal of transporting freed slaves back to their homeland, members of the American Colonization Society (organized 1816–17) made land purchases on the west African coast. The holdings were named *Liberia,* a Latin word meaning "freedom." The first black Americans arrived there in 1822. The society's plan was controversial—even some abolitionists and blacks opposed it, as they believed the only answer to the question of slavery was to eradicate it from the United States and extend the full rights of citizenship to the freed black slaves in their new American home. Nevertheless, by 1860 eleven thousand black slaves from the United States had been settled there; eventually a total of fifteen thousand made the transatlantic voyage to a secured freedom in Liberia. The country was established as an independent republic on July 26, 1847.

What did **lawmakers do** to resolve the **slavery question before the Civil War**?

The mid-1800s were a trying time for the nation—the divide widened between the Northern free states and the Southern slave states, which were growing increasingly dependent on agricultural slave labor. Government tried but was unable to bring resolution to the conflict over slavery. Instead, its efforts seemed geared toward maintaining the delicate North-South political balance in the nation.

After the Mexican War (1846–1948), the issue was front and center as congressmen considered whether slavery should be extended into Texas and the western territories gained in the peace treaty of Guadalupe Hildago, which officially ended the war. Lawmakers arrived at the Compromise of 1850, which proved a poor attempt to assuage mounting tensions: the legislation allowed for Texas to be admitted to the Union as a slave state, California to be admitted as a free state (slavery was prohibited), voters in New Mexico and Utah to decide the slavery question themselves (a method called popular sovereignty), the slave trade to be prohibited in Washington, D.C., and for passage of a strict fugitive slave law to be enforced nationwide.

Four years later, as it considered how to admit Kansas and Nebraska to the Union, Congress reversed an earlier decision (part of the Missouri Compromise of 1820) that had declared territories north of the Louisiana Purchase to be free, and set up a dangerous situation in the new states: The slavery status of Kansas and Nebraska would be decided by popular sovereignty (the voters in each state). Nebraska was settled mostly by people opposing slavery, but settlers from both the North and the South poured into Kansas, which became the setting for violent conflicts between pro-slavery and anti-slavery forces. Both sides became determined to swing the vote by sending "squatters" to settle the land. Conflicts resulted, with most of them clustered around the Kansas border with Missouri, where slavery was legal. In one incident, on May 24, 1856, ardent abolitionist John

Abolitionist John Brown, who advocated armed conflict against those who were for slavery, led his followers into two battles against government forces in Kansas in 1856, killed five people in Pottawatomie, and was captured trying to raid an armory at Harpers Ferry, West Virginia. He was convicted and hanged in 1859.

Brown (1800–1859) led a massacre in which five pro-slavery men were brutally murdered as they slept. The act had been carried out in retribution for earlier killings of freedmen at Lawrence, Kansas: Brown claimed his was a mission of God. Newspapers dubbed the series of deadly conflicts, which eventually claimed more than fifty lives, "Bleeding Kansas." The situation proved that neither congressional compromises nor the doctrine of popular sovereignty would solve the nation's deep ideological differences regarding slavery.

SLAVE REVOLTS

When was the **first recorded slave revolt** in North America?

The first recorded slave revolt in North America occurred in 1526, after Spanish explorers brought Africans to land which would be known later as South Carolina. The escaped Africans settled with American Indians.

Who was the **first revolt leader** of acclaim?

The first revolt leader of note was Denmark (Telemaque) Vesey (1767–1822), who in May 1822 organized a slave revolt in Charleston, South Carolina. Vesey and nearly fifty others were executed after the revolt, one of the most elaborate on record. Vesey, a sailor and a prosperous merchant carpenter, had been free since 1800. While still in his teens, he opened his own master carpenter shop in Charleston. He found himself, however, in a strange position as a free man in a slave society in which many free blacks owned slaves and participated in slave trading. He viewed this as moral corruption in the free black community, and he became determined to uproot slavery. State laws preventing children from being free if their mother was a slave, difficulties arising when Charleston blacks left the white-dominated Methodist Church for the new African Methodist Episcopal Church (AME), and fines and taxes aimed at restricting the mobility of free blacks also contributed to his determination. Vesey had a revolutionary perspective and actively recruited followers for his cause, planning the uprising for several years. Five thousand blacks were prepared to participate in the revolt that was originally set for July of that year but moved up to June when Vesey learned that authorities had learned of his plans from traitorous insiders. Subsequently, he tried to postpone the revolt once more, but it was too late for word to reach everyone and the uprising proceeded. Vesey was arrested and tried the day after his arrest. Throughout the days following his arrest, however, Vesey and his co-leaders who had remained faithful refused to disclose any information; they are considered martyrs. Vesey was hanged two weeks after his arrest. On one July morning twenty-two men were killed in a mass execution. After the insurrection occurred, South Carolina and other states passed laws to control free blacks, to tighten the reins on slaves, and to keep watch for possible revolts.

When did the **first slave revolt of magnitude** occur?

In Southampton County, Virginia, on August 21 and 22, 1831, Nat Turner (1800–1831), minister and slave, led what has been recognized as the first slave revolt of magnitude.

The revolt was crushed, but only after Turner and his band had killed some sixty whites and threw the South into panic. After hiding out, Turner was captured on October 30, 1831, and hanged in Jerusalem, Virginia, on November 11. Thirty other blacks were also implicated and executed. It was not until John Brown's 1859 raid on Harpers Ferry, Virginia, that another slave revolt or conspiracy became known. Turner was born to African-born slaves of Benjamin Tucker, in the Tidewater region of southeast Virginia, near North Carolina. After several attempts to escape slavery, his father finally succeeded and emigrated to Liberia. Although slaves were forbidden to read or write, Turner did so with ease and became a wonder to the slave community. He became an itinerate preacher, using his travel to learn the terrain of Southampton, Virginia. He also identified slave and free blacks who would attend his sessions and prepare for what he called the great "migration" that God envisioned for them. Turner also claimed to have received signs that it was time for him to lead his rebellion. Finally, on the night of August 21, when whites had left their churches and settled in for the night, Turner and his insurrectionists moved swiftly in a surprise attack on plantations in the Southampton countryside. After he lost his tactical advantage, Turner grew concerned for his own survival and hid underground for six weeks. He was captured on October 30; he offered no testimony in court, nor did he allow defense on his behalf. His famous deposition became known as *The Confessions of Nat Turner;* it was later published, and copies sold out quickly.

A wood engraving depicting the capture of slave revolt leader Nat Turner in 1831.

EMANCIPATION

Why did President **Lincoln** issue the **Emancipation Proclamation before** the **end** of the **Civil War**?

As the war raged between the Confederacy and the Union, it looked like victory would be a long time in the making: in the summer of 1862 things seemed grim for the federal troops when they were defeated at the Second Battle of Bull Run (which took place in northeastern Virginia on August 29 to 30). But on September 17, with the Battle of Antietam (in Maryland), the Union finally forced the Confederates to withdraw across the Potomac into Virginia. That September day was the bloodiest of the war. President Abraham Lincoln (1809–1865) decided that this withdrawal was success enough for him to make his proclamation, and on September 22, he called a cabinet meeting. That day he presented to his advisers the Preliminary Emancipation Proclamation.

The official Emancipation Proclamation was issued later, on January 1, 1863. This final version differed from the preliminary one in that it specified emancipation was to be effected only in those states that were in rebellion (i.e., the South). This key change had been made because the president's proclamation was based on congressional acts giving him authority to confiscate rebel property and forbidding the military from returning slaves of rebels to their owners.

Abolitionists in the North criticized the president for limiting the scope of the edict to those states in rebellion, for it left open the question of how slaves and slave owners in the loyal (Northern) states should be dealt with. Nevertheless, Lincoln had made a stand, which served to change the scope of the Civil War (1861–1865) to a war against slavery.

On January 31, 1865, just over two years after the Emancipation Proclamation, Congress passed the Thirteenth Amendment, banning slavery throughout the United States. Lincoln, who had lobbied hard for this amendment, was pleased with its passage. The Confederate states did not free their four million slaves until after the Union was victorious on April 9, 1865.

What was the **Dred Scott decision** and why was it important?

Dred Scott (1795–1858), a Virginia slave, sued for his freedom after living on free soil in Missouri. The decision in *Dred Scott v. Sandford* rendered on March 6, 1857, was the first decision by the U.S. Supreme Court denying blacks citizenship. The ruling stated that

Virginia slave Dred Scott tried unsuccessfully to purchase his freedom, and then sued for it in Missouri, but his victory in that state was overturned at the state and then U.S. Supreme Court levels.

blacks could not be citizens of the United States, even though they might be citizens of their states. Prior to this decision, Scott had many times attempted to purchase his freedom with no success. He had also been denied freedom after suing in the lower courts. A county court first denied his suit for freedom and damages, but set a new trial date for December 1847. Scott then filed suit in the state circuit court in St. Louis. He actually won this suit, based on the fact that he had lived for five years with one of his owners in two areas that did not support slavery—the territory of Wisconsin and the state of Illinois. The Missouri Supreme Court overturned this decision, and the U.S. Supreme Court agreed in its 1857 ruling. The doctrine of dual citizenship remained important and resurfaced in the post-Civil War attack on black rights. In 1853 the Supreme Court again affirmed the doctrine of dual citizenship, federal and state, and suggested that most civil rights fell under state citizenship, and so were not protected under the Fourteenth Amendment.

What were **Black Codes**?

During 1865 and 1866, all Southern states except North Carolina sought substitutes for old codes aimed at controlling slaves and passed a number of new codes. The purpose of these Black Codes was to protect the states' agricultural interests by rendering immobile the dependent black labor force. The codes aimed to immobilize the penniless, unemployed, and powerless laborers, but were worded so that whites were exempt and only blacks were restricted by the new laws. Those in violation were arrested and hired out for one year. The Black Codes were made illegal when Reconstruction ended; however, many Southern practices ensuring some form of forced labor continued well into the twentieth century.

What was the importance of the **Fourteenth Amendment** to African Americans?

African Americans were granted citizenship and equal protection under the law for the first time with the passage of the Fourteenth Amendment on July 28, 1868. The Fourteenth Amendment, also known as one of the Reconstruction Amendments, was proposed on June 13, 1866, and ratified by the necessary number of states on July 9, 1868. It provided a broad definition of U.S. citizenship and superseded the 1857 *Dred Scott v. Sandford* decision, which excluded slaves and their descendants as citizens. It declared that all persons born or naturalized in the United States and subject to its jurisdiction are citizens thereof. It forbade the states to abridge the privileges or immunities of citizens of the United States, or to deprive any person of the life, liberty, or property without due process of law. It was used in the mid-1950s to dismantle racial segregation in the United States.

What was the **Reconstruction**?

The Reconstruction was the twelve-year period (1865–1877) of rebuilding that followed the Civil War. The last battle over, the South lay in ruins: food and other supplies were scarce, people were homeless, city centers had been destroyed, schools were demolished, railways torn up, and government was nonexistent. Furthermore, the nation had new citizens to enfranchise—and protect—the freed slaves. There was also the question of how to readmit each Southern state to the Union (they had seceded from the Union before the Civil War ended).

In short, the nation's wounds needed to heal. But the long years of the Reconstruction brought only more divisiveness and quarrels. This time the battlefield was not Gettysburg or Chattanooga, but Washington, D.C. President Andrew Johnson (1808–1875), a Southern Democrat and former slave owner, squared off with Congress, led by a radical Republican faction. The two branches of government fought over who should guide Reconstruction policy. Johnson favored a more tolerant and swifter approach to reuniting the nation, but his measures failed to protect the country's black citizens. Congress proceeded more cautiously, setting up military administrators in the South as

What does "forty acres and a mule" mean?

The term originated with General William T. Sherman (1820–1891) toward the end of the Civil War. On January 16, 1865, in his "March to the Sea," a military advancement he led from Atlanta to Savannah, Sherman issued Special Field Order No. 15, which set aside a tract of land along the South Carolina, Georgia, and Florida coasts for the exclusive settlement of forty thousand freed slaves. According to the order, each black family was to be given "a plot of not more than (40) forty acres of tillable ground … in the possession of which land the military authorities will afford them protection, until such time as they can protect themselves, or until Congress shall regulate their title." All of the lands were former plantations that had been confiscated during the war; they became the jurisdiction of the Freedmen's Bureau. Though there was a provision for "one or more of the captured steamers to ply between the settlements and one or more of the commercial points … to sell the products of their land and labor," there was no mention of providing a mule, or any other animal, to each freedman. The mules, tired army work animals, were distributed to the landholders. News of "40 acres and a mule" spread among the freed slaves.

Soon after the war ended in April 1865, this promise to materially assist the freedmen was abandoned when President Andrew Johnson (1808–1875) issued pardons for the ex-Confederates and ordered their lands returned to them. The somewhat obscure term "40 acres and a mule" resurfaced in the 1990s and early 2000s as the issue of reparations came to the fore in the United States.

an interim form of government until readmission of the states could be effected. In the end, Congress won out by overriding President Johnson's vetoes again and again.

What was the **Civil Rights Act of 1866**?

Congress passed the Civil Rights Act of 1866, which took a first step toward enfranchising the black population by guaranteeing the legal rights of former slaves. It did not become law until March 1, 1875. The act declared that everyone, regardless of race, color, or previous condition, was entitled to "make and enforce contracts, to sue, be parties, and give evidence, to inherit, purchase, lease, sell, hold, and convey real and personal property, and to full and equal benefit of all laws and proceedings for the security of person and property, as is enjoyed by white citizens." No citizen could be denied the right to serve on grand or petit juries. No provisions were made for access to public education. As blacks sought the provisions that the law dictated, the federal and district courts that were responsible for enforcing the law were indifferent to their claims of racial discrimination. The U.S. Supreme Court struck down the law in 1883, declaring that Congress lacked the power to regulate peoples' conduct and transactions.

What were the provisions of the **Civil Rights Bill of 1875**?

The U.S. Congress passed the Civil Rights Bill of 1875, prohibiting for the first time discrimination in places of public accommodation. The accommodations included theaters, public conveyances, and places of public recreation. The bill declared that every person in the United States was entitled to enjoy public accommodations whether or not he or she was ever in servitude. In 1883, the U.S. Supreme Court overturned the law.

What was the **Freedmen's Bureau**, or the **Bureau of Refugees, Freedmen, and Abandoned Lands**?

The U.S. Congress created the Freedmen's Bureau in March 1865 as the Bureau of Refugees, Freedmen, and Abandoned Lands. Initially it catered to whites as it fed, clothed, sheltered, and provided medical care to more whites than blacks. It was only after Congress directed it to promote the general welfare of blacks that it became identified with freedmen. Between 1867 and 1869 the bureau helped to locate missing persons and reunite families separated by slavery, established over forty hospitals, and distributed twenty-one million meals. By 1870 the bureau had established 4,239 schools and provided them 9,307 teachers to serve 247,333 students. A number of the Historically Black Colleges and Universities established around the 1860s and 1870s were impacted by the bureau. The bureau ceased to exist after 1868 because of feeble efforts of Congress and the lack of a national commitment to full and equal citizenship for blacks.

THE CIVIL RIGHTS MOVEMENT

What were the effects of the *Plessy v. Ferguson* decision on civil rights?

The term commonly used, "separate but equal," refers to the provisions of the *Plessy v. Ferguson* decision of 1896, which for almost sixty years served as the legal foundation and justification for separating the races. Homer Adolph Plessy, a mulatto who was one-eighth black, seated himself in a white compartment on the East Louisiana Railroad. The conductor challenged his seating. Plessy was arrested and charged with violating the state law. Attorney Albion W. Tourgée argued in the Criminal District Court for the Parish of New Orleans that the law requiring separate but equal accommodations was un-

Attorney Albion W. Tourgée argued in *Plessy v. Ferguson* that the "separate but equal" standard in New Orleans was unconstitutional.

constitutional. Judge John H. Ferguson ruled against him, prompting Plessy to apply to the Louisiana State Supreme Court to review the lower court's decision. Plessy was granted a petition for a writ of error that enabled him to petition the case to the U.S. Supreme Court. On May 18, 1896, the U.S. Supreme Court ruled against Plessy. The law was not overturned until 1954, with the *Brown v. Board of Education* decision denying legal and unequal segregation in restrooms, schools, and other places.

What were the **precursors** to **direct nonviolent protest activities**?

In 1941 A. Philip Randolph (1889–1979), civil rights leader and founder of the Brotherhood of Sleeping Car Porters (the first major nationwide black union for Pullman porters), threatened to publicly protest the struggle for black equality by staging an all-black March on Washington, D.C. He wanted President Franklin D. Roosevelt to bring an end to discrimination in employment and in the armed services. Roosevelt agreed and established a Fair Employment Practices Committee (FEPC) to address these issues, thereby preventing the public protest. A large-scale example of direct-action protest occurred the next year when the Congress of Racial Equality (CORE) was formed. The interracial group supported the Gandhian philosophy of direct nonviolent protest. The group initiated its 1947 Journey of Reconciliation to test the South's compliance with the U.S. Supreme Court's outlawing of segregation on interstate buses. Further examples of direct-action protest occurred during the war years, when large numbers of black Americans migrated from the rural South to the North and West in search of jobs.

Why did the NAACP hold a **Silent Protest Parade**?

The NAACP's Silent Protest Parade, also known as the Silent March, was held on 5th Avenue in New York City on Saturday, July 28, 1917, and was spurred by violence toward African Americans and race riots and outrages in Waco, Texas; Memphis, Tennessee; and East St. Louis, Illinois. Typical of this unrest was the East St. Louis Race Riot, also called the East St. Louis Massacre, which drove almost six thousand blacks from their burning homes, and left hundreds of blacks dead. A large, local committee composed of pastors of leading churches and influential men and women was formed to address the parade issue. The NAACP and the local group rejected the idea of mass protest in favor of a Silent Protest Parade. The parade down 57th Street to Madison Square brought out nine to ten thousand blacks who marched silently to what was called "the sound only of muffled drums." Children, some younger than six years old and dressed in white, led the procession. Women—some of them aged—dressed in white followed, and men—some also aged—in dark suits brought up the rear. The marchers carried protest banners and posters proclaiming the purpose of the demonstration. They distributed circulars explaining why they marched. "We march because we are thoroughly opposed to Jim Crow cars, …segregation, discrimination, disfranchisement, lynching, and the host of evils that are forced on us" is an example of what their circulars displayed. The parade moved in silence and was watched in silence.

RACE RIOTS

What was **Red Summer**?

The summer of 1919 was given the moniker Red Summer by activist and writer James Weldon Johnson (1871–1938) because it ushered in one of the greatest periods of interracial discord in U.S. history. Referring to the summer and fall of 1919, race riots exploded in more than twenty-five cities across the nation, regardless of region. Some were large and others were small. All the race riots were indicative of a complete meltdown in American race relations. Incited by racism, unemployment, and inflation, indigenous terrorist organizations such as the Ku Klux Klan urged the riots on by terrorizing African Americans into submission. Competition for employment also helped to inflame relations between the races. White Americans did not want to compete for jobs with African Americans. Additionally, the rise of communism fueled racial unrest, and African Americans who saw equality as a constitutional right were branded as radicals.

Among the riots that took place in 1919, the most violent incidents occurred in Chicago, Washington, D.C., and Elaine, Arkansas. The Red Summer of 1919 galvanized the NAACP and its supporters to lobby for the passage of a federal law against lynching. Although the Dyer Anti-Lynching bill ultimately failed in Congress, its supporters succeeded in bringing attention to and generating greater condemnation of lynching. On June 13, 2005, Congress officially apologized for failing to pass anti-lynching legislation early in the twentieth century, when it passed a non-binding resolution introduced by two senators from the South: Democratic Louisiana Senator Mary Landrieu and Republican Senator George Allen of Virginia.

Where did some of the **notorious race riots** occur?

Race riots occurred throughout the United States, preceding those of the modern Civil Rights Movement. These included the Memphis, Tennessee, Race Riot (1866), Hamburg, South Carolina, Race Riot (1873), New Orleans Race Riot (1874), New Orleans Race Riot (1900), Boston Race Riot (1903), Atlanta Race Riot (1906), Springfield, Illinois, Race Riot (1908), East St. Louis, Illinois, Race Riot (1917), Houston, Texas, Race Riot (1917), Longview, Texas, Race Riot (1919), Elaine, Arkansas, Race Riot (1919), Tulsa, Oklahoma, Race Riot (1921), Harlem Race Riot (1935), Harlem Race Riot (1943), and the Detroit Race Riot (1943).

How did the modern **Civil Rights Movement begin**?

On Thursday, December 1, 1955, Rosa McCauley Parks (1913–2005), a seamstress who worked for a downtown department store in Montgomery, Alabama, made her way home on the Cleveland Avenue bus. Parks was seated in the first row that was designated for blacks. The white rows in the front of the bus soon filled up. When Parks was asked to give up her seat so that a white man could sit down, she refused. She was arrested and sent to jail.

Montgomery's black leaders had discussed staging a protest against racial segregation on city buses. They soon organized, with Baptist minister Martin Luther King Jr. (1929–1968) as their leader. Beginning on December 5, 1955, thousands of black people refused to ride the city bus: The Montgomery Bus Boycott had begun. It lasted more than a year—382 days—and ended only when the U.S. Supreme Court ruled that segregation on the buses was unconstitutional. The protesters and civil rights activists had emerged the victors in this—their first and momentous effort to end segregation and discrimination in the United States.

Parks, who lost her job as a result of the arrest, later explained that she had acted on her own beliefs that she was being unfairly treated. But in so doing Parks had taken a stand and had given rise to a powerful, effective, and historic movement.

What was the **nonviolence movement**?

The Reverend Martin Luther King Jr. (1929–1968) was committed to bringing about change by staging peaceful protests; he led a campaign of nonviolence as part of the modern Civil Rights Movement. King rose to prominence as a leader during the Montgomery Bus Boycott in 1955, when he delivered a speech that embodied his Christian beliefs and set the tone for the nonviolence movement, saying, "We are not here advocating violence.… The only weapon we have … is the weapon of protest." Throughout his life, King staunchly adhered to these beliefs—even after terrorists bombed his family's home. King's democratic "protest arsenal" included boycotts, marches, the words of his stirring speeches (comprising an impressive body of oratory), and sit-ins. With other African-American ministers, King established the Southern Christian Leadership Conference (1957), which assumed a leadership role during the Civil Rights Movement. The nonviolent protest of black Americans proved a powerful weapon against segregation and discrimination and motivated lawmakers in Washington to pass civil rights legislation for equality and justice for African Americans.

When did the **sit-in movement** begin?

African Americans, particularly the young, became impatient with the slow pace that the federal government made toward dismantling racial segregation in America and disenchanted with what they labeled the legalistic and traditionalist practices of the NAACP in its efforts to secure the rights of black people. Students in black colleges decided to apply pressure on local and federal governments, thus beginning the sit-in movement. The first such movement to win concessions in a Southern state in modern times occurred on August 19, 1958, when NAACP Youth Council members sat at lunch counters in Oklahoma City; they were served without incident or publicity. However, on February 1, 1960, when four students from North Carolina Agricultural and Technical College (now University) in Greensboro sought service at an F. W. Woolworth store's lunch counter, they were refused service, and launched the first sit-in movement to achieve major results. They also attracted widespread public attention. The students—Ezell Blair, Franklin McCain, David Richmond, and Joseph McNeil—patterned their actions after the passive resistance techniques of Mahatma Gandhi. By February 10 the movement had spread to fifteen Southern cities in five states. The original site is now a Civil Rights museum.

What is the significance of the **Albany, Georgia, movement**?

Albany, Georgia, became a focal point for one of the first large-scale community protests against segregation after the Montgomery Bus Boycott. These efforts involved a coalition of organizations, including the NAACP youth chapter at Albany State College, the Baptist Ministers' Alliance, the Federation of Women's Clubs, the Student Nonviolent Coordinating Committee (SNCC), and the Southern Christian Leadership Conference (SCLC) led by Martin Luther King Jr. The coalition tested the Interstate Commerce Commission's outlawing of segregation in public transportation facilities. The protest was begun at the Albany bus terminal on November 11, 1961, by local activists. Dr. King and the SCLC joined the protest in December of 1961. Although King and the other protesters were arrested, they learned important strategic lessons from the protests.

What is the significance of the **Nashville, Tennessee, sit-ins**?

In 1958, following the formation of the Nashville Christian Leadership Conference (NCLC) by the Reverend Kelly Miller Smith Sr. and others, African-American leaders and students launched an attack on Jim Crow segregation. The NCLC utilized the concept of Christian nonviolence to stage the Nashville movement and combat racial seg-

This is the F. W. Woolworth store in Greensboro, North Carolina, that was the site of the famous 1960 sit-in protest by four black students upset that they were refused service at a lunch counter.

regation. The Reverend James Lawson, a devoted adherent of the Gandhi philosophy of direct nonviolent protest, trained local residents in the techniques of nonviolence. In November and December of 1959 NCLC leaders and college students staged unsuccessful "test sit-ins" in an attempt to desegregate the downtown lunch counters. Twelve days after the Greensboro, North Carolina, sit-ins, Nashville's African-American students launched their first full-scale sit-ins, on February 13, 1960. Shortly before Easter, African Americans boycotted downtown stores, creating an estimated 20 percent loss in business revenues. On May 10, 1960, Nashville became the first major city to begin desegregating its public facilities. One of the best-organized and disciplined movements in the South, the Nashville sit-in movement served as a model for future demonstrations against other violations of African-American civil rights. Many of the student participants, including Diane Nash (Bevel) and John Lewis, later a prominent U.S. congressman, became leaders in the national struggle for civil rights.

What was **Bloody Sunday** and when did it occur?

"Bloody Sunday" was the name given to the date March 5, 1965, because of the violence directed toward civil rights demonstrators during an attempted march from Selma to Montgomery, Alabama. The purpose of the march was to protest against police brutality and the denial of voting rights; it was a continuation of earlier civil rights efforts in the Selma area that began in 1963. Participants included key leaders of the Civil Rights Movement, such as John Lewis and Hosea Williams, as well as many unsung heroes from the local community and outside supporters. Martin Luther King Jr. had been in the Selma area on several previous occasions, enduring arrest and physical as well as verbal attacks, including death threats; he decided not to participate in the march. Alabama's white leaders, including Governor George Wallace, were committed to preventing the march from being successful. Wallace issued an injunction in support of efforts to stop the march.

When the approximately six hundred marchers left Brown Chapel African Methodist Episcopal (AME) Church, they were met at the foot of the Edmund Pettus Bridge by a large group of Alabama state troopers, many on horseback and wearing gas masks. They were joined by other groups of white men whom Sheriff Jim Clark had "deputized," some bearing large clubs and waving Confederate flags. News reporters, photographers, and cameramen, as well as a small group of blacks, were present to observe the event.

Alabama police officers confront demonstrators during 1965's Bloody Sunday.

Before Hosea Williams and John Lewis could stop the marchers, they were attacked with clubs and tear gas. Lewis was among the many who were wounded as a result of the attack, which continued as the marchers retreated in the direction of the church. The violence was recorded by the media and received international news coverage.

What were the **Freedom Rides**?

The "freedom rides" were a series of bus rides designed to test the U.S. Supreme Court's prohibition of segregation in interstate travel. In 1960, in the case of *Boynton v. Virginia,* the Supreme Court ruled in favor of a Howard University student who charged that segregation laws at the Richmond, Virginia, bus station violated federal antisegregation laws. The Congress of Racial Equality (CORE) decided to test the enforcement of the federal law by initiating the freedom rides. On May 4, 1961, thirteen people, black and white, boarded a bus for the South. Meant as a nonviolent means of protest against local segregation laws, the riders were nevertheless met with violence. When the bus reached Montgomery, Alabama, on May 20, a white mob was waiting; the freedom riders were beaten. Rioting broke out in the city, and U.S. marshals were sent to restore order. The interracial campaign to desegregate transportation was ultimately successful, but government intervention was required to enforce the laws, as numerous Southern whites had demonstrated that they would not comply voluntarily.

What was the significance of **Martin Luther King's "Letter from the Birmingham Jail"**?

Martin Luther King Jr. was arrested and jailed for leading a protest march in Birmingham, Alabama. Eight local Christian and Jewish clergymen condemned King and other blacks for what they deemed "unwise and untimely" activities and accused King of agitating citizenry by addressing the subject of direct action. They advised King to "wait" and be patient for justice to come to the city. King responded on April 16, 1963, by writing a letter from his jail cell explaining why he was in Birmingham, enumerating various injustices against black people, and explaining what nonviolent protest for social change meant. After King smuggled the long letter out of jail, the American Friends Service Committee, a group always sympathetic to blacks and their plight, published it. Various magazines and newspapers across the nation published the letter as well. Some claim that the letter—along with King's "I Have a Dream Speech"—became one of the most significant statements of the modern and nonviolent Civil Rights Movement.

What was the significance of **Martin Luther King Jr.'s "I Have a Dream" speech**?

The historic occasion was the March on Washington on August 28, 1963. That summer day more than a quarter million people—lobbying for congressional passage of a civil rights bill—gathered at the Lincoln Memorial to hear speakers, including the charismatic and influential King. His eloquent words defined the movement and still inspire those who continue to work for reforms. Among his words were: "I have a dream that one day this nation will rise up and live out the true meaning of its creed, 'We hold these truths to be self-evident; that all men are created equal.'"

On August 28, 1963, the Rev. Martin Luther King Jr. gave his iconic "I Have a Dream" speech at the Lincoln Memorial in Washington, D.C.

Congress did pass the Civil Rights Act, in 1964. The most comprehensive American civil rights legislation since the Reconstruction (the twelve-year period that followed the Civil War), the act outlawed racial discrimination in public places, assured equal voting standards for all citizens, prohibited employer and union racial discrimination, and called for equality in education.

What was **Freedom Summer**?

Freedom Summer 1964 was an intensive voter registration project in the state of Mississippi, initially started by the Student Nonviolent Coordinating Committee (SNCC) activist Robert Moses in 1961.

As a part of a larger effort launched by the Congress of Racial Equality (CORE) and SNCC, the goal was to increase the number of African-American voters in the South. The project was designed to draw the nation's attention to the violent oppression faced by African Americans in Mississippi when they attempted to exercise their constitutional rights and develop a grass-roots freedom movement that could be sustained after student activists departed the state.

By August 4, 1964, however, four people were killed, eighty were beaten, and thousands had been arrested; in addition, sixty-seven churches, homes, and businesses were set ablaze or bombed. Freedom Summer attracted more than a thousand volunteers, the majority of whom were affluent white Northern college students. Training sessions attempted to prepare them to register African-American voters, teach literacy and civics at Freedom Schools, and promote the Mississippi Freedom Democratic Party's challenge to the all-white Democratic delegation at the Democratic National Convention in Atlantic City that August. The efforts of the volunteers and subsequent refusal of local registrars to accept registrants' applications created momentum for the Voting Rights Act of 1965. Freedom Summer marked one of the last key interracial civil rights efforts of the 1960s.

What was the work of the **Delta Ministry** in the Civil Rights Movement?

Following the Freedom Summer of 1964, the Delta Ministry was organized in September of that year in an effort to reconcile the black and white communities in Mississippi and to address the economic, health, and social conditions of Mississippi's black residents. It was an effort brought about by the National Council of Churches' concern for mobilizing the liberal church in civil rights activities. The ministry established programs to address literacy, recreation, education, health care, politics, and other issues of concern. It fought racial discrimination in employment practices, supported plantation workers' strikes, and exposed cases of noncompliance with antidiscrimination clauses among plants that held federal government contracts.

Why was **Fannie Lou Hamer** important in the Civil Rights Movement?

Fannie Lou Hamer (1917–1977), of Ruleville, Mississippi, was a voting rights activist and civil rights leader. She was known for singing hymns and believed that the fight for civil rights was a deeply spiritual struggle; this belief no doubt helped her endure attacks, such as being falsely arrested, jailed, and beaten in 1963. In addition, she attempted to vote, but met with immediate opposition and was fired from her plantation job. Her deep commitment had become known to the Student Nonviolent Coordinating Committee (SNCC), who recruited her to join the group. She became a registered voter in 1963, when she was a field secretary for SNCC. Hamer led voter registration drives and worked with programs to aid deprived black families in the state. In that year, as well, she was instrumental in establishing the Delta Ministry. She then helped to found the Mississippi Freedom Democratic Party and became one of its delegates to the Democratic National Convention that gained national press for challenging the seating of the existing all-white, anti-civil rights delegation from Mississippi. Hamer's address before the national convention was broadcast nationwide. Later, she founded the Freedom Farms Corporation (FFC) to help the needy raise food and livestock, provide social services, support business opportunities, and aid education.

What was the **March on Washington**?

An estimated quarter of a million people participated in the March on Washington on August 28, 1963, a peaceful demonstration to advance civil rights and economic equality. This was one of the largest demonstrations ever witnessed in Washington, D.C., and it was the first to have extensive coverage by the electronic media. Successful in pressuring the administration of President John F. Kennedy to initiate a strong civil rights bill in Congress, the marchers gathered at the Lincoln Memorial one hundred years after the signing of the Emancipation Proclamation. The March on Washington influenced the passage of the Civil Rights Act of 1965 and galvanized public opinion. Bayard Rustin (1910–1987), organizer of CORE's 1947 Journey of Reconciliation freedom ride, coordinated and administered the particulars of the march. During this peaceful demonstration, Martin Luther King Jr. delivered his famous "I Have a Dream" speech, a speech that has become a classic and powerful document in American history and culture.

Crowds gather by the Reflecting Pool in Washington, D.C., during the 1963 March on Washington.

What **role** did **black women** play in the **March on Washington**?

Women played vital roles in the Civil Rights Movement; nevertheless, they were thrust into the background of the August 28, 1963, march. No woman marched down Constitution Avenue with Martin Luther King Jr., A. Philip Randolph, Roy Wilkins, and other male civil rights leaders. No woman went to the White House afterward to meet with President John F. Kennedy. However, because of Anna Arnold Hedgeman (1899–1990), the only woman on the march's planning committee and a major architect of the march, as a last-minute tribute at the event the Negro Women Fighters for Freedom Award was given to Daisy Bates, Diane Nash, Rosa Parks, Gloria Richardson, Myrlie Evers, and Mrs. Herbert Lee, the wife of a murdered farmer in Amite County, Mississippi.

How was the **Highlander Folk School** involved in civil rights activities?

In 1932 Myles Horton and Don West established the Highlander Folk School in Monteagle, Tennessee, as a community school with a Danish tradition. The school worked with trade unions but changed its focus in the 1950s when it shifted its efforts to the civil rights struggle. In 1952 Septima Poinsette Clark (1898–1987), known for her untiring efforts to promote her race, began her affiliation with the school by attending interracial institutes during two summers. Highlander became the educational center of the Civil Rights Movement during the 1950s and early 1960s. Both Rosa Parks and Martin Luther King Jr. attended the Highlander workshops before participating in the Montgomery demonstrations. Clark took over the school's literacy work in 1959, after Tennessee began its efforts to close the school. After repeated harassment from state and federal agents who claimed it had Communist affiliations and alleged other violations, in 1962 the state of Tennessee revoked the school's charter and confiscated its property. Then a new institution with essentially the same goals was chartered: The Highlander Research and Education Center. The center was briefly located in Knoxville and later moved to New Market, Tennessee, where it continues to support civil rights.

What was the importance of the **Civil Rights Act of 1964**?

The Civil Rights Act of 1964 was one of the most important pieces of domestic legislation of the post-World War II era. Congressional concern for civil rights lessened after Reconstruction and the U.S. Supreme Court's decision in 1883 to nullify the constitutionality of the Civil Rights Act of 1875. The U.S. Congress did not address the issue again until 1957, when it was under pressure from the modern Civil Rights Movement, and then it was only a feeble attempt to redress civil wrongs. The passage of the Civil Rights Act of 1957 was a modest statute that created the Civil Rights Commission with the authority to investigate civil rights violations; however, it lacked enforcement provisions and it was a weak corrective for voting rights violations. The Civil Rights Act of 1960 only slightly reinforced the voting rights provisions. The 1964 act had eleven main provisions or titles. Several strengthened the Civil Rights Commission and the voting rights provisions in the 1957 and 1960 acts. The Civil Rights Act of 1964 is among the Civil Rights Movement's most enduring legacies. It was directed specifically at removing barriers to equal access and opportunity that affected blacks. It greatly extended the reach of federal protection and led to a major restructuring of the nation's sense of justice; it also expanded legal protections to other minority groups. Beneficiaries of blacks' struggle for freedom included women, the disabled, gays and lesbians, the elderly, and other groups who experienced discrimination.

Who were the **leading black women** in the **modern Civil Rights Movement**?

Historically, black women have played pivotal roles in the critical battles for racial justice in this country. Their efforts predate the modern Civil Rights Movement and can be seen as far back as slave resistance in the antebellum South. Voices of women like Sojourner Truth (1797–1883), Maria Stewart (1803–1879), Sarah Parker Remond (1826–1894), and Sarah Mapps Douglass (1806–1882) were heard in their work as abolitionists, political writers, teachers, and orators.

Many black women were icons in the movement, whether or not their voices reached national audiences. Such women included Gloria Blackwell (1927–2010), a fearless warrior in the fight to desegregate Orangeburg, South Carolina, schools; and Clara Luper (c. 1923–2011), who staged one of the first publicized sit-ins in downtown Oklahoma City. Voices of women in the modern movement include trailblazing women like Pauli Murray (1910–1985), Modjeska Simkins (1899–1992), Septima Clark (1898–1987), Rosa Parks (1913–2005), NAACP lawyer Constance Baker Motley (1921–2005), Jo Ann Gibson

Did sit-ins or protest demonstrations exist prior to those of the modern Civil Rights Movement?

American blacks protested unequal treatment in public accommodations as early as 1866, when blacks in Tennessee boarded street cars in Nashville and refused to sit in the section designated for them. In 1942 the Congress of Racial Equality (CORE) organized sit-ins and pickets to protest racial accommodations in public accommodations. Sit-ins occurred in 1950, 1958, and 1959 in Washington, D.C.; Wichita, Kansas; and St. Louis, Missouri.

Robinson (1912–1992), journalist Daisy Lee Gaston Bates (1914–1999), SNCC worker Ruby Doris Smith Robinson (1942–1967), sit-in leader Diane Nash (1938–), Fannie Lou Hamer (1917–1977), a founder of the Student Nonviolent Coordinating Committee (SNCC) and community organizer Ella Baker (1903–1986), and Gloria Richardson (1922–), leader of the Cambridge (Maryland) Movement.

What was the **Black Power Movement**?

The Black Power Movement of the mid 1960s was an outgrowth from the modern Civil Rights Movement. However, the failure of legal and political decisions, and the failure of the nonviolent movement for African-American equality and justice in the American South to bring about significant transformation, resulted in a more militant posture against the prevailing white system of belief, and the development of a distinctly African-American ideology known as Black Power. Although the phrase had been used by African-American writers and politicians for years, the expression gained currency in the civil rights vocabulary during the James Meredith March Against Fear in the summer of 1966. At that time, Stokely Carmichael (1941–1998; later Kwame Turé), head of the Student Nonviolent Coordinating Committee (SNCC), used the expression as a means to galvanize African Americans. While the movement essentially disappeared after 1970, the concept of positive racial identity remained embedded in the African-American consciousness.

What was **Resurrection City**?

When the Poor People's March on Washington was held in 1968, blacks constructed a temporary shantytown at the National Mall and called it Resurrection City. The area housed citizens of the march who sought to place the problems of the poor at the seat of the federal government. The campaign was the Southern Christian Leadership Conference's (SCLC) last major initiative as it attempted to broaden the Civil Rights Movement to include an economic platform for all poor people, regardless of race. Approximately five weeks after the death of Martin Luther King Jr., Resurrection City was constructed for a multitude of protesters. The protest march for the poor departed from the Lorraine Motel in Memphis, Tennessee, the site of King's assassination, on May 2, 1968, and proceeded

Who popularized the term "Black Power"

Civil rights activist Stokely Carmichael (1941–1998; later Kwame Turé) was the first person to popularize the phrase "Black Power" as a slogan during James Meredith's voter registration drive in Mississippi. As Carmichael conceptualized the term, it was intended to develop black consciousness in Mississippi by stressing separation along with black power. In 1966 he became head of the Student Nonviolent Coordinating Committee (SNCC) and altered its orientation from nonviolent protest to black liberation. Carmichael was born in Trinidad and came to the United States when he was eleven. He later graduated from Howard University. During the turbulent atmosphere of the 1960s he was considered a radical. He was a member of the second group of Mississippi Freedom Riders, which originated in Washington, D.C. Carmichael left SNCC in 1967 to join the more militant Black Panthers. By 1968 he was prime minister of the Panthers' most militant group, but in 1969 he left to join the Pan-African movement, which emphasized cultural nationalism. Carmichael's activities often placed him at odds with other well-known African Americans. He moved to Guinea to escape police harassment and continued to espouse his revolutionary ideas.

to the nation's capital. Along the way teams of mules demonstrating the desperate plight of the rural poor pulled wagons of people through Mississippi, Georgia, and Alabama. President Lyndon B. Johnson ignored Resurrection City and Congress closed its governmental coffers to the people's demands for economic justice. While the campaign secured a few concessions from federal agencies, it cannot be considered successful.

AFRICAN–AMERICAN PROTESTS OF THE POST–CIVIL RIGHTS MOVEMENT

What were the **Million Man March** and **Day of Absence**?

The nation's first Million Man March and Day of Absence took place in Washington, D.C., on October 16, 1995. It occurred with parallel activities in cities and towns throughout the country; families were asked to stay at home from school and work during that "day of atonement" and to pray and fast. It provided an opportunity for black men to bear responsibility for their lives, families, and communities. They also were to show repentance for the ill treatment of black women. In the area of civil rights, the march aimed to bring whites and blacks together and spotlight national inactivity toward racial inequality. Louis Farrakhan (1933–) of the Nation of Islam proposed the march early in 1995. Planners garnered support from religious, political, and business-oriented groups and leaders. Historically Black Colleges and Universities (HBCUs) of-fered their support, excused students from classes, and chartered buses to take them to Washington for the event. While the number of participants is disputed, leaders of the march claim that a million people did, in fact, assemble at the Lincoln Memorial—the site of the historic 1963 March on Washington.

What are **reparations**?

Reparations are payments or other compensations made to a group of people who have been wronged or injured. The issue was in the news in the 1990s and early 2000s as law-makers, academicians, and other leaders pressed for a redress for slavery, which some scholars called the American, or black, holocaust. The concept is not a twentieth-century phenomenon for African Americans. Near the end of the nineteenth century, Callie House (1861–1928), a former slave from Tennessee, emerged as a leader in the movement to pe-tition the U.S. government for pensions and reparations for African Americans formally held in involuntary servitude. She also organized the National Ex-Slave Mutual Relief, Bounty and Pension Association to build a reparation movement among former slaves. The precedents for making reparations were several: The German government made reparations to survivors and families of victims of the Nazi holocaust. The American gov-ernment also made reparations to Japanese Americans who had been interned during World War II (1939–1945), as well as to Native Americans, for damages done to them.

In 1989 U.S. representative John Conyers (D-Michigan) introduced a bill in Con-gress to "establish a commission to examine the institution of slavery" and "to make recommendations to the Congress on appropriate remedies." The idea of reparations gained some currency with the American public in the 1990s. Critics of reparations said that compensating the descendants of slaves was unrealistic; determining those who would be paid would alone constitute an expensive government program. They ques-tioned why these descendants should be paid a century after the end of the brutal sys-tem, and that other programs, born of the Civil Rights Movement, have strived to bring equity to African Americans. Despite the criticisms, Conyers resolved to reintroduce the bill as often as necessary until Congress would act on it.

What was the importance of the **United States Commission on Civil Rights**?

The Civil Rights Commission was established by Congress in 1957 as a temporary, in-dependent bipartisan agency. Its purpose is to investigate complaints by citizens who claim that their voting rights were violated because of their race, color, religion, na-tional origin, or other fraudulent practices. The commission also studies and collects in-formation on cases denying equal protection under the law and examines federal laws and policies that relate to such protection. Often called a "Civil Rights Watch Dog," the commission plays "a vital role in advancing civil rights through objective and compre-hensive investigation, research, and analysis on issues of fundamental concern to the federal government and the public." Findings and recommendations of the commission are reported to the President and Congress. Congress and the President appoint the

What was the Million Woman March?

On October 25, 1997, over 300,000 African-American women from across the nation met in Philadelphia and held the first Million Woman March. The purpose was to strengthen the bonds between African-American women from all elements of society and to bring about positive change. They came to show solidarity and to address various issues confronting them, such as women in prison, independent schools for African-American women, crime, teen pregnancy, and the need to increase the number of black women in business and politics. Modeled after the Million Man March, women from all walks of life organized the campaign. Cofounders were retired Chicago police officers Phile Chionesu and Cheryl Thomas-Porter. Estimates are that 2.5 million people participated in various activities associated with the three-day march.

eight members who compose the commission. Since it was created, Congress has reauthorized or extended the legislation creating the commission several times, the last time by the Civil Rights Commission Amendments Act of 1994. In 1972 Juanita Goggins became the first black woman appointed to the commission. The first black chair of the commission was Clarence M. Pendleton Jr.

THE POST–CIVIL RIGHTS ERA

Has the **U.S. government passed legislation** to **investigate lynching** and **murders** during the Civil Rights era?

On February 7, 2005, the U.S. Senate passed Resolution 39 which apologized for lynching in the United States. The lack of prior action by the Senate, which rejected three anti-lynching measures presented by the U.S. House of Representatives between 1920 and 1940, resulted in denied civil rights and the deaths of numerous African Americans. The Resolution acknowledges lynching as the ultimate act of racism and apologizes to the victims as well as to the families. As a result of Resolution 39, the Emmett Till Unsolved Civil Rights Crime Act was made into law. This legislation established, within the U.S. Department of Justice, an office to investigate and prosecute Civil Rights era murders.

Why was the **President's Initiative on Race** established?

In 1997 President Bill Clinton established the President's Initiative on Race (Executive Order No. 13050) as an effort to move the country closer to a stronger, unified, and more just America. He asked all Americans to become a part of a national effort to speak openly and fairly about race. President Clinton appointed historian John Hope Franklin (1915–2009) to chair a seven-member President's Advisory Board to the initiative. It would counsel the president on ways to improve the quality of race relations in America. The board held dialogues on race across the nation and then counseled the president on improving race relations. The board's report, "One America in the 21st Century: Forging a New Future" (1998), recommended actions to be taken to address race matters in America and set a framework for building one America.

What is **racial profiling**?

Racial profiling refers to a discriminatory practice by law enforcement officials to use race, ethnicity, religion, or national origin to take action against individuals or groups. Those most frequently targeted have been African Americans, Hispanics, Native Americans, and sometimes gang members. After the bombing of the World Trade Center on September 11, 2001, Arabs, Muslims, and South Asians became popular victims as well. Those targeted may be stopped while driving in the "wrong" neighborhood, driving expensive cars, driving while no violation occurs, in airports, malls, and elsewhere. Racial profiling has included celebrities, college students, professional athletes, state legislators, military personnel, and others. On July 1, 2009, Harvard University Professor Henry Louis Gates Jr. was arrested for disorderly conduct in his Cambridge, Massachusetts, home when a witness reported to police that he was trying to break into a home, which was, in fact, Gates' residence. The case spurred President Barack Obama to raise the issue of racial prejudice and profiling. Recent accusations against law officials emerged in the state of Arizona, where Hispanics were the primary victims. Some black Americans react to racial profiling by wearing t-shirts or other paraphernalia with the lettering "driving while black" and similar messages.

Protesters march in San Francisco in July 2013 after George Zimmerman was found not guilty of murdering Trayvon Martin. Many felt Zimmerman, an armed neighborhood patrolman but not a police officer, confronted the young black Trayvon because of his race, initiating a confrontation that led to Trayvon's unnecessary death.

EDUCATION

EDUCATION DURING SLAVERY

What efforts were made to **educate Africans** in America in the **1700s**?

Since the first arrival of Africans in America, the African-American community has worked to sustain a system for educating its youth. White individuals and groups have worked to educate blacks as well. From the late 1600s to the mid-1700s, instruction of the newly arrived Africans was sporadic and haphazard. Pennsylvania Quakers, who opposed the institution of slavery, organized monthly educational meetings for blacks during the early 1700s. One such Quaker, Anthony Benezet, in 1750 established an evening school in his home, which remained successful until 1760. In 1774 Quakers in Philadelphia joined together to open a school for blacks. In 1751 the Society for the Propagation of the Gospel in Foreign Parts sent Joseph Ottolenghi to convert and educate blacks in Georgia. By the mid 1830s, however, states passed stringent laws to prohibit whites from teaching blacks; nevertheless, some efforts to educate blacks continued.

How did **Black Codes affect** the **education** of free and enslaved African Americans?

Black Codes grew out of Slave Codes, or laws that defined the civil status of African Americans prior to and after the Civil War. They also prevented African Americans from having equal access to education. South Carolina was the first state to establish Black Codes that specifically addressed education of free African Americans. All states added these codes to the state constitution. The codes resulted in varying educational outcomes from state to state. Depending on state regulations, blacks were relegated to segregated education by law, could attend mixed schools, were denied admission to schools, or could found privately funded schools for their own education. Blacks began to challenge Black Codes by filing suits against school systems; for example, in 1855 they succeeded in dismantling segregated school laws in Massachusetts. Throughout the nineteenth century, blacks protested in many states, such as Iowa, Indiana, and Illinois, and overturned de jure segregation in education. Although the *Brown v. Board of Education of Topeka, Kansas* decision of 1954 and cases in other states declared segregation in schools illegal, de facto segregation continues.

What support did the **anti-slavery movement** give toward **creating schools for blacks?**

The anti-slavery movement played an important part in the creation of schools for blacks. In 1787 the Manumission Society founded the New York African Free School; by 1820 more than five hundred black children were enrolled. Support increased as other African Free Schools were established in New York until 1834, when the New York Common Council took over control of the schools.

What are some of the efforts of the **Freedmen's Aid Society** to **educate blacks?**

At the close of the Civil War hundreds of thousands of free blacks were left without homes and adequate resources. As a means of providing temporary assistance to the newly freed slaves, numerous organizations were formed. The New England Freedmen's Aid Society, organized in Boston on February 7, 1862, was founded to promote education among free African Americans. Supporters included Samuel Cabot, William Lloyd Garrison, and William Cullen Bryant. In New York a similar organization was founded, the National Freedmen's Relief Association, on February 20, 1862. This was followed by the Port Royal Relief Committee, later known as the Pennsylvania Freedmen's Relief Association, founded in Philadelphia on March 3, 1862. In 1863 several of these organizations merged to form the United States Commission for the Relief of the National Freedmen, which in 1865 became the American Freedmen's Aid Union.

What did **Congress do** in the **1860s** to help **educate newly freed slaves?**

During the 1860s Congress passed several Freedmen's Bureau Acts, creating and financing an agency designed to provide temporary assistance to newly freed slaves. Under the acts, the bureau's chief functions were to provide food, clothing, and medical supplies. Working in conjunction with various benevolent organizations, Commissioner General Oliver Otis Howard established and maintained schools as well as provisions for teachers. By 1870 the bureau operated over 2,600 schools in the South, with 3,300 teachers educating 150,000 students; almost 4,000 schools were in operation prior to the abolition of slavery.

Who was the **first African American** to **graduate** from **Harvard University?**

Richard Theodore Greener (1844–1922), educator, lawyer, consular officer, and reformer, was the first black to graduate from Harvard University, in 1870. In October 1873 he became professor of metaphysics at the University of South Carolina. Greener assisted in the departments of Latin, Greek, mathematics, and constitutional history while also attending to his primary teaching duties. He was acting librarian, arranging the university's book collection of twenty-seven thousand volumes, and beginning preparations for a card catalog. During this same time, Greener studied law. In 1876 he graduated from the university's law school. He was admitted to the Supreme Court of South Carolina in 1877, and the next year practiced at the District of Columbia bar. He remained at South Carolina until March 1877, when the Wade Hampton legislature abruptly closed the door of the university to black students. He headed the law school at Howard University and developed a considerable reputation as a speaker and writer. Greener became active in the foreign service, serving in Bombay and Vladivostok. He retired in 1905.

Attorney and professor Richard Theodore Greener was the first black man to graduate from Harvard University, earning a B.A. He also earned a law degree from the University of South Carolina. In his later career he was a U.S. commercial agent in Russia and India.

Who was the **first African American** to **attend Yale University**?

Edward Alexander Bouchet (1852–1918), the first black to attend Yale, graduated in 1874. He was also the first to receive a doctorate from an American university when he was awarded the doctorate from Yale in 1876. The Institute for Colored Youth of Philadelphia, with which he was subsequently associated for twenty-six years as a teacher of chemistry and physics, supported his graduate work in physics. Bouchet was born in New Haven, Connecticut, and attended the oldest of four primary schools for blacks in that city. He was later able to attend the private Hopkins Grammar School, from which he graduated as valedictorian. He continued to be an outstanding student when he entered Yale College in 1870, which no doubt served to call him to the attention of the Institute for Colored Youth. While teaching there he became actively involved with the affairs of Philadelphia's black community. He also maintained a connection with Yale through his membership in the Yale Alumni Association. Bouchet, along with other faculty members at the Institute, was fired in 1902, on the grounds that the facility's academic department was being closed. The school did move and then reopened as what would eventually become known as Cheyney Training School for Teachers. In its new location, the curriculum followed the model of the Hampton and Tuskegee Institutes (as they were called then), with an industrial arts focus that Bouchet found unpalatable.

Between 1902 and 1905, Bouchet held various positions, including teacher at a public high school, business manager of Provident Hospital, and U.S. Inspector of Customs at the Louisiana Purchase Exposition. He spent the next three years as director of the academic department and teaching courses in several subjects at St. Paul's Normal and Industrial School in Lawrenceville, Virginia. He also served as principal at a high school in Gallipolis, Ohio, and faculty member at Bishop College in Marshall, Texas, before retiring for health reasons in 1916. Bouchet returned to New Haven and died less than two years later. In 1998 Yale unveiled a granite memorial at his previously unmarked gravesite in New Haven's Evergreen Cemetery.

Who was the **first African-American woman** to **graduate from a college** in the **South**?

Virginia E. Walker Broughton (c. 1856–1934) studied at Fisk University in Nashville for ten years before receiving her bachelor's degree in May 1875, and is said to be the first black woman in the South to graduate from college. She went on to teach in the public schools of Memphis and became active with Christian missionary activities. In both areas of endeavor, Broughton was often the victim of gender bias. As a teacher, a male teacher was given the promotion she should have received. As a woman missionary, male preachers often resented her efforts because she was more literate than they. Even her own husband initially questioned her dedication to missionary work. She is recognized as a religious feminist who was one of several Baptist women who used the Bible to defend women's rights during the latter decades of the nineteenth century and early in the twentieth century. She taught, lectured, and wrote throughout her life. Fisk University awarded her an honorary degree in 1878. She was a widow living in Memphis at the time of her death.

Who was the **first African American** to receive a **doctorate** from **Harvard University**?

In 1895 W(illiam) E(dward) B(urghardt) Du Bois (1868–1963), educator, writer, and Pan-Africanist, became the first black to receive a doctorate from Harvard University. He was also the first black to obtain a Ph.D. in history. While Du Bois is universally recognized as an important and influential leader, controversy surrounded

Educator, author, and Pan-Africanist W.E.B. Du Bois was the first black man to earn a doctorate from Harvard University.

his leadership and his progressive ideas on black-white relations often brought him into conflict with black leaders who espoused less radical approaches.

Du Bois was arguably the greatest African-American scholar-intellectual of the twentieth century. He employed his research and training to further the causes of social uplift and the educational and professional development of African Americans. One of his numerous writings, *The Souls of Black Folk,* is among the most influential texts of the twentieth century. His "Talented Tenth" theory, or the concept that the best-equipped tenth of the black race would lead the less advantaged 90 percent, countered Booker T. Washington's accommodationist platform. As a founder of both the Niagara Movement and the NAACP, Du Bois was a pioneer of the modern Civil Rights Movement. He dedicated his life to ending colonialism, exploitation, and racism worldwide. Born in Great Barrington, Massachusetts, Du Bois graduated from Fisk University, where he had great exposure to African-American culture and began to politicize his thinking. He entered Harvard University, but had to do so as a junior since the school failed to recognize his Fisk degree, regardless of the quality of his education.

Throughout the 1950s, Du Bois' criticism of American capitalism, imperialism, and racial inequality firmly tied him to leftist causes. He settled in Ghana in 1961, joined the Communist Party, and died there one day before the famous March on Washington.

Who were the **first African-American women** to earn **doctoral degrees**?

Eva Beatrice Dykes (1893–1986), Sadie Tanner Mossell Alexander (1898–1989), and Georgianna R. Simpson (1866–1944) were the first three black American women to earn doctorates. All three received their degrees in 1921.

Dykes was the first to complete requirements for a Ph.D. She was born in Washington, D.C., where her family had close ties to that city's Howard University. Four of her relatives, including her father, were Howard graduates. One of her sisters taught at Howard after graduating from the institution. Dykes herself graduated from Howard *summa cum laude* in 1914. She taught at the now-closed Walden University (Nashville, Tennessee) for a year, and then enrolled at Radcliffe College, where she was accepted as an unclassified student. She earned three degrees from Radcliffe: A.B. in English, *magna cum laude,* honors in English, and election to Phi Beta Kappa (1917); A.M. (1918); Ph.D. (1921). Before joining Howard's faculty in 1929, Dykes taught at what became Paul Laurence Dunbar High School in Washington; she retained her Howard position until 1944. She published several works while there. When she left Howard, she became the first woman to join the faculty at Oakwood College, a Seventh Day Adventist junior college (at that time) in Huntsville, Alabama. Dykes, who was known for her musical ability and her commitment to the Seventh Day Adventist Church in addition to her commitment to education, remained the only faculty woman for ten years. The rest of her career was spent at Oakwood. She first retired in 1968, returned in 1970 to teach a full load for three years, and taught a reduced load from 1973 until she retired permanently in 1975. During her stay at Oakwood, Dykes chaired the committee whose work led to Oakwood's accreditation in 1958 by the Southern Association of Colleges and Schools; in addition, she directed several Oakwood music groups. She was also instrumental in helping to establish a separate black conference of the Adventist Church.

Of the three black women who obtained doctorates in 1921, Dykes completed her requirements first. However, the commencement exercises of Sadie Alexander and Georgianna Simpson were both held before Dykes. Alexander received her degree in economics (the first black American to earn a degree in the field) from the University of Pennsylvania and Simpson earned her degree in German at the University of Chicago. Simpson attended commencement exercises on June 14, making her the first black American woman to earn a doctorate.

COLLEGE FOUNDINGS

What mainstream college was the first founded with a mission to educate African Americans?

The first college in the United States founded with a mission to educate blacks was Oberlin College in Ohio, established in 1833. One of the elements creating the institution was Lane Seminary in Cincinnati. When many of the students converted to abolitionism, it became expedient to move to northern Ohio and join the nucleus of students and instructors already established there. By the time of the Civil War, one-third of the student body was black.

HISTORICALLY BLACK COLLEGES AND UNIVERSITIES

What are the oldest historically black colleges in America?

Lincoln University (Pennsylvania) and Wilberforce University (Ohio), established in 1854, are the oldest historically black colleges established in America. Unlike Cheyney State, which had its origin in 1832, these institutions are still in their original locations and were the first to indicate their aim to award baccalaureate degrees and develop fully into degree-granting institutions. Lincoln University, the outgrowth of the Ashmun Institute, was incorporated January 1, 1854, and opened its doors to young black men on August 30, 1856. Wilberforce University was incorporated in 1856 and awarded its first baccalaureate degree in 1857. In 1862, Wilberforce came under black control, making it the oldest college controlled by blacks.

When were the majority of HBCUs founded?

Before the Civil War, three Historically Black Colleges and Universities (HBCUs) were founded—the Institute for Colored Youth (now Cheyney University of Pennsylvania) in 1837; Ashmun Institute, later known as Lincoln University in Pennsylvania (1854); and

Wilberforce University in Ohio in 1856. Most HBCUs, however, were founded in the years immediately following the Civil War. An impetus for their establishment was given by the Thirteenth and Fourteenth Amendments to the U.S. Constitution, for now slavery was abolished and blacks had full citizenship; this meant that they could pursue higher education. Independent philanthropists, religious denominations, and philanthropic organizations were crucial in establishing these institutions. Among these institutions, Morehouse College (est. 1867) in Atlanta retained its identity over the years as an all-male institution. Spelman College (est. 1881) in Atlanta survived as an institution established to educate African-American women. Bennett College (est. 1873) in Greensboro admitted male students at one time but is now a women's college and known as Bennett College for Women. There were 105 HBCUs in 1913, including two-year, four-year, and professional schools.

Why is **Cheyney State** sometimes considered the **oldest black college** in the United States?

Cheyney State College, sometimes referred to as the oldest black college in the United States, had its beginning in 1832. Richard Humphreys, a Philadelphia Quaker, willed $10,000 to a board of trustees to establish a school for blacks. A school for black boys was eventually established in 1839 and incorporated in 1842. The school became known as the Institute for Colored Youth in 1852. It reorganized in 1902 and moved to Cheyney, Pennsylvania, where it was renamed. It became a teacher training school in 1914 and a normal school in 1921, when it was purchased by the state. Since 1932 Cheyney State College (now Cheyney University of Pennsylvania) has been a degree-granting institution.

What **black college** was the **first established** by an **act of Congress**?

Howard University, located in northwest Washington, D.C., was the first HBCU established by an act of Congress; it was chartered on March 2 1867. Like several HBCUs founded during this period, the university has always been open to students regardless of race or gen-

The campus at Howard University in Washington, D.C. Howard was the first historically black college established by an act of Congress.

der. It would receive direct and continuing financial support from Congress, yet it remains privately controlled. Howard has become a comprehensive research university.

What **black college** was established by an **act of Congress** in the **twentieth century** and is sometimes called a **land-grant college**?

In 1966 Public Law 89-791, a public education act, was enacted. Following the passage of this act, two schools were established in Washington, D.C.: Federal City College and Washington Technical Institute. Both institutions were designed to serve the needs of the community and to direct resources and knowledge gained through education to help solve urban problems. The schools opened in 1968 and were given land-grant status in that year as well. On August 1, 1977, the District of Columbia Teachers College, Federal City College, and Washington Technical Institute merged to become the University of the District of Columbia. Lisle Carleton Carter Jr. (1925–2009) became the first president.

What historically black college was the **first to establish undergraduate, graduate, and professional schools**?

On January 8, 1867, Howard Theological Seminary changed its name to Howard University. On that date the university, located in Washington, D.C., became the first black school to establish undergraduate, graduate, and professional schools. The school was established under the auspices of the Freedmen's Bureau and named in honor of General Oliver O. Howard, who headed the Bureau from 1865 to 1874.

What **acts** were passed by **Congress** to **fund land-grant colleges**?

The Morrill Act of 1862 provided federal land-grant funds for higher education. In 1890 Congress passed the second Morrill Act, also known as the Land Grant Act of 1890. The second act stipulated that no federal aid could be provided for the creation or maintenance of any white agricultural and mechanical school unless that state also provided for a similar school for blacks. As a result, a system of separate black land-grant institutions developed, which became the basis of black higher education in the South. They were unequal to the traditional white institutions in the amount of funding they received. As well, they were excluded from the benefits of agricultural extension services and experiment stations. Although these schools now offer a variety of curricular programs, they often directly indicate their early and continuing emphasis on agricultural, industrial, mechanical, or technical interests by incorporating these subjects in their names: "A&T" for North Carolina Agricultural and Technical State University or "A&M" for Alabama A&M, Florida, Prairie View and Southern Agricultural and Mechanical Universities. The land-grant schools also developed a research mission with results that would aid government as well as industry. Their initial curricular offerings represented a radical departure from the classical liberal arts offerings seen in other Historically Black Colleges and Universities established before them, where history, law, and theology were emphasized.

What are the **1890 schools**?

Those Historically Black Colleges and Universities that received land-grant status under the second Morrill Act, or the Land Grant Act of 1890, are often referred to as the 1890 schools. They are Alabama A&M, Alcorn A&M, Delaware State, Florida A&M, Fort Valley State, Kentucky State, Langston, Lincoln (in Missouri), North Carolina A&T, Prairie View, South Carolina State, Southern, Tennessee State, University of Maryland Eastern Shore, Virginia State, and West Virginia State. Although Tuskegee University is not an official land-grant school, it is often included on the list.

What was the **first land-grant college** for **blacks**?

The first land-grant college for blacks was Alcorn Agricultural and Mechanical College in Lorman, Mississippi, which was established in 1871. This was made possible under the Morrill Act of 1862. Ironically, the college was named in honor of James I. Alcorn, a Reconstruction governor of the state who led the white branch of the Republican Party, and who opposed black legislators during his term of office. Hiram Rhoades (Rhodes) Revels (1827–1901), a former U.S. Senator, was the first president. For a considerable period of time, the college maintained a liberal arts curriculum, in spite of the disapproval of the legislature.

What **institution** of higher education did **Booker T. Washington establish**?

Booker T. Washington (1856–1915), with the assistance of his wife, Fanny Norton Smith Washington, founded Tuskegee Institute (now University) in Alabama on July 4, 1881. He was born a slave in Virginia, where he remained until he moved with his mother and siblings to join his stepfather in West Virginia after the end of the Civil War. He received his first formal schooling in Malden, West Virginia, but was unable to attend regularly. Despite this, at age sixteen he entered Hampton Institute in Virginia, which taught normal school classes and trades. It is said that the school's founder—who is alleged not to have believed in social equality for black people—became Washington's father figure. Washington did well at Hampton, and when he graduated he taught public school in Malden from 1855 to 1877. After studying briefly at Wayland Seminary in Washington, D.C., he returned to West Virginia. In 1879 he took a teaching job at Hampton, where he remained until he was asked in 1881 to open a new school in Alabama. He accepted,

Tuskegee University was founded in Alabama in 1881 by Booker T. Washington.

and in July of that year Tuskegee Normal and Industrial Institute was born. He was at first the only teacher, and Washington had to work to establish support of the white community. He followed the Hampton model, preparing students for crafts and encouraging them to be public school teachers. As the school prospered, so too did Washington's reputation as a leader. He became known increasingly for his conservative stance on racial issues, which was attributed to his belief that agitation by black people would not yield positive results. In time, other black figures, including W.E.B. Du Bois, emerged to question Washington's philosophy. A number of works list Washington as the author, although some are known to have been ghostwritten.

What were the **divergent views** between **Booker T. Washington** and **W.E.B. Du Bois** on educating blacks?

Booker T. Washington, renowned among many white philanthropists and political leaders, won the financial backing of rich and powerful whites who gave millions of dollars to Tuskegee Institute. He counseled Southern blacks to stay in the rural South. For their education and to prepare them for survival, his school offered agricultural, trade, and other industrial subjects. He wanted blacks to "pull themselves up by their bootstraps" to remove themselves from poverty, and develop a strong labor force for the nation. He never condemned lynching, segregation, disfranchisement, and other perils that the South practiced and that his students and graduates encountered in Southern society.

W.E.B. Du Bois, who became Washington's most noted opponent, challenged Washington's views on education, calling his educational program at Tuskegee "too narrow," and even questioning the type of industrial education that Tuskegee offered, saying that some trades, such as that of blacksmith, were becoming obsolete. To train blacks in industrial education would, in Du Bois' view, keep them in a subservient position and also set blacks back in their progress toward full civil rights. He also accused Washington of "deprecating institutions of higher learning." Without teachers who were trained at black colleges, common black schools as well as Tuskegee would close, he thought. Much time would pass before the two leaders respected each other's views.

What was the **first college** founded to **educate black women**?

Hartshorn Memorial College, the first black women's college in the country, opened on November 7, 1883. It began in Richmond, Virginia, in the basement of Ebenezer Baptist Church, with fifty-eight students. It was chartered on March 13 by the Virginia legislature as "an institution of learning of collegiate grades for the education of young women." The college awarded its first degrees in 1892, when three young women graduated: Mary Moore Booze, Harriet Amanda Miller, and Dixie Erma Williams. The college was never well funded and struggled to fulfill its mission as a college for black women. In 1918 Hartshorn students began enrolling in courses at nearby Virginia Union University; by 1922 Hartshorn had entered into an agreement for educating its students at Virginia Union. Rather than merge with Virginia Union, in June 1928 Hartshorn officials closed the college department and focused on its high school. In 1932 the college trustees conveyed the school's property to Virginia Union, merged with the school, and became Hartshorn Memorial College in the Virginia Union University.

What was the **first state-supported college** founded to **educate black teachers**?

Alabama State University was founded at Salem, as the State Normal School and University for Colored Students and Teachers in 1874. It was the first state-supported institution in the United States to train black teachers. In 1887 the institution moved to its present site in Montgomery.

What school was **founded** by **Mary McLeod Bethune**?

Mary McLeod Bethune (1875–1955) became founder and president of Daytona Normal and Industrial Institute in Daytona Beach, Florida, in 1904. In 1923 the school merged with Methodist-supported Cookman Institute in Jacksonville, which supported Bethune's desire to maintain a college. In 1929 the institution changed its name to become Bethune-Cookman College (now University) and retained Bethune as its president. Born in Sumter County, near Mayesville, South Carolina, she was the fifteenth of seventeen children. She attended a rural Presbyterian mission school in the area and came under the influence of Emma Jane Wilson, a pioneering black teacher. She later attended Scotia Seminary (now Barber-Scotia College), a Presbyterian school in North Carolina. After graduation she enrolled in the Bible Institute for Home and Foreign Missions (now

Mary McLeod Bethune was founder and president of Bethune-Cookman University. She was also a president of the Southeastern Association of Colored Women and of the National Association of Colored Women, and founded the National Council of Negro Women.

Moody Bible Institute) in Chicago where she prepared to enter foreign missions and become an African missionary. The Presbyterian Church, however, did not place black missionaries in Africa. Bethune went on to teach at the Presbyterian-supported Haines Institute in Augusta. There she came under the influence of Lucy Craft Laney, the school's founder and principal. In 1900 Bethune founded a Presbyterian school in Palatka, Florida, and then established an independent school. On October 3, 1904, in a sparsely furnished rented house, she founded Daytona Educational and Industrial Institute. Financial support from the Methodist church helped Bethune with some of the school's financial problems. In 1926 she accepted a full-time federal position in Washington, D.C., and the school suffered as she continued to divide her attention between the two positions. After a life-threatening illness, she resigned the presidency in 1942 but worked her way back into that office until 1947. Bethune was well known for her work in the black women's club movement. In 1920 she founded and became president of the Southeastern Association of Colored Women. From 1924 to 1928 she served as president of the National Association of Colored Women, an organization of some ten thousand women. On December 5, 1935, she founded the National Council of Negro Women and later pushed the organization into extensive lobbying in Washington. D.C. Under her leadership the organization sponsored the *SS Harriet Tubman* in 1944, the first liberty ship to honor a black woman, and fought for the acceptance of black women in the armed forces. Bethune wrote for several journals as well as a column for the *Pittsburgh Courier* and the *Chicago Defender.* One of her best-known works is her "Last Will and Testament," which serves as an inspiration for black people; it was subsequently published in a number of sources. Bethune was highly honored for her activities as an educator, clubwoman, and orator.

What **colleges** were founded by the **American Missionary Association**?

Since its founding in 1846, the American Missionary Association, with its social and religious interests, was concerned with enhancing the condition of black Americans. It was an anti-slavery crusader and relief agency during and immediately after the Civil War, and later founded and maintained a chain of schools throughout the South. In 1861 the American Missionary Association founded its first institution of higher learning specifically aimed at educating black people—Hampton Institute (now University) in Virginia. Those that followed were Atlanta University in Georgia (1865), Fisk University in Tennessee (1866), Talladega College in Alabama (1867), LeMoyne (now merged to become LeMoyne-Owen) College in Tennessee (1870), Straight (now merged with New Orleans University to become Dillard University) in Louisiana (1868), Tougaloo College in Mississippi (1869), and Tillotson (now Huston-Tillotson) in Texas (1877).

What **black leaders** were members of the **American Missionary Association's board**?

Four blacks were members of the first AMA board, including escaped slave and minister James William Charles Pennington, Charles Bennett Ray, Samuel Ringgold Ward, and Theodore S. Wright. In later years distinguished African Americans such as Henry Highland Garnet and Samuel E. Cornish were AMA board members. During the Reconstruction period, the AMA focused its resources and efforts on creating and supporting higher education institutions for African Americans. The list of Historically Black Colleges and Universities (HBCUs) that were founded by the AMA or received early support from the organization included Hampton Institute (later University), Fisk University, Howard University, Atlanta University (now Clark Atlanta), Straight University (now Dillard), Tougaloo College, Talladega College, LeMoyne College (now LeMoyne-Owen), Avery Institute, and Tillotson College (now Huston-Tillotson). African Americans were represented among the first AMA teachers in the South, including Mary Smith Peake, who is credited with being the first teacher at a school for freed slaves.

By the **end of the Civil War**, what **HBCUs** were founded and **supported by** the missionary spirit of **Northern white churches** and their denominational boards?

HBCUs in this group were aided by the Freedmen's Aid Society of the Methodist Church, which founded and/or supported Clark College in Atlanta, Georgia (1869); Claflin University in Orangeburg, South Carolina (1869); Shaw University (renamed Rust College) in Holly Springs, Mississippi (1866); Bennett College in Greensboro, North Carolina (1873); and Wiley College in Marshall, Texas (1873). Those founded and/or supported by the American Baptist Home Mission Society were Shaw University in Raleigh, North Carolina (1865); Benedict College in Columbia, South Carolina (1870); Morehouse College in Atlanta, Georgia (1867); Jackson College in Jackson, Mississippi (1877); and Virginia Union University in Richmond, Virginia (1865).

What **black churches** and **denominational boards** established and maintained **HBCUs**?

Several black church schools were founded before the Civil War but became colleges after the war ended. A number of black churches and denominational boards were involved in the development of such schools. The Cincinnati Conference of the Methodist Episcopal Church founded Wilberforce University, Tawawa Springs, Ohio, (1856); the

African Methodist Episcopal Church founded Allen University, Columbia, South Carolina (1870); Paul Quinn College, Waco, Texas (1872); Edward Waters College, Jacksonville, Florida (1883); and Morris Brown College in Atlanta, Georgia (1881). The African Methodist Episcopal Zion Church founded Livingstone College, Salisbury, North Carolina (1879). The Colored Methodist Episcopal Church founded or supported Lane College, Jackson, Tennessee (1882); Paine College, Augusta, Georgia (1882); Texas College, Tyler, Texas (1894); and Miles College, Birmingham, Alabama (1902). The Negro Baptist Convention founded or supported Arkansas Baptist College, Little Rock, Arkansas (1884); Shaw University, Raleigh, North Carolina (1865); Virginia College and Seminary, Lynchburg, Virginia (1888); and Morris College, Sumter, South Carolina (1905).

These schools prepared persons for the ministry and trained teachers to educate the struggling black community.

What role did **philanthropy play** in the development of **black colleges and schools**?

Northern philanthropic groups were among the organizations that aided the Historically Black Colleges and Universities early on. In 1867 George Peabody, a Massachusetts merchant, created the Peabody Education Fund to benefit elementary education. In 1882 Connecticut manufacturer John F. Slater established the Slater Fund to support four-year high schools as well as colleges. Established in 1888, the Daniel Hand fund began to provide for the needy and indigent blacks in the South. There were also the Anna T. Jeanes Fund for Rudimentary Schools for Southern Negroes, or the Jeanes Fund, founded in 1907, and the Julius Rosenwald Fund, which was created in 1917 and established rural schools and some high schools for blacks in the South. The Southern Education Foundation, established in 1937, the General Education Board, and the Carnegie Corporation were also sources of support for black colleges, library collections, library buildings on college campuses, as well as black branches of public libraries, teacher education, and other programs.

When was **medical training** provided in the **black colleges**?

Between 1868 and 1900, there were twelve institutions with a mission to provide medical education for African Americans. Some, but not all, were affiliated with colleges and universities. In 1870 Lincoln University in Missouri opened a medical school. Knoxville College in Knoxville, Tennessee, maintained a department of medicine from 1895 to 1900. The college also awarded a number of medical degrees during this period. Those admitted to the program were required to meet the standards for admission prescribed by the Association of American Medical Schools. The medical unit was gradually discontinued, and by 1931 the school was exclusively a liberal arts college. The Louisville National Medical College was established in 1888, and in 1889 Flint Medical College became a department of New Orleans University and was managed by the Freedmen's Aid Society of the Methodist Episcopal Church, North. In 1900 the University of West Tennessee College of Physicians and Surgeons was founded. Medical schools currently in existence are Howard University College of Medicine, Washington, D.C., (1867); Meharry

Medical College, Nashville, Tennessee (founded as a medical department and became a medical school in 1900); Charles Drew University of Medicine and Science, Los Angeles, California (1966); and Morehouse School of Medicine, Atlanta, Georgia (1975). Drew is the only dually designated historically black graduate institution and Hispanic-serving health professional institution in the United States.

What **historically black institution** offers the **only graduate program** in **veterinary medicine**?

Tuskegee University in Alabama established a School of Veterinary Medicine in 1945, when African Americans lacked the opportunity to study veterinary medicine in the South because of racial restrictions. It is the only such program located on the campus of a historically black college. Located within the College of Veterinary Medicine, Nursing and Allied Health, the school educates from fifty to sixty percent of African-American veterinarians in the country and, during its lifetime, has trained more than seventy percent of African Americans in that field in the U.S. During the past five to seven years, the school has also graduated ten percent of all Hispanic veterinarians. Among the schools of veterinary medicine in the country, Tuskegee is the most balanced racially, ethnically, and culturally. The school offers the doctor of veterinary medicine, master of science degrees in veterinary science and tropical animal health, a dual DVM/MS degree, and the Ph.D. degree in integrative biosciences. The program is accredited by the American Veterinary Medical Association.

What are some of the **independent schools** founded in the **South** beginning in the **late 1890s**?

Private institutions, also known as independent schools, were founded to provide education and equip African Americans for the work force and largely served this function until African-American land-grant institutions were established in 1890. Some, though not all, of these institutions became full-fledged colleges and universities. Among these schools are Tuskegee Normal and Industrial Institute (later Tuskegee University) in Alabama (1881), Haines Normal and Industrial Institute in Savannah (1883), National

Training School for Women and Girls in Washington, D.C. (1901), Palmer Memorial Institute in Sedalia, North Carolina (1901), and Daytona Normal and Industrial Institute for Girls (later Bethune-Cookman University) in Florida (1904).

What factors **led to rebellions** at **black colleges** during the **1920s**?

A growing racial consciousness, a demand for a change from an emphasis on vocational programs to higher-level curricula and a demand for more control of their colleges led students at several Historically Black Colleges and Universities to publicly protest. In 1922 students at Florida A&M protested the governor's requirement that the school shift its emphasis from teacher-training to training tradesmen. At Lincoln Institute (now University) in Missouri opposing groups protested against traditional academic programs and the need for vocational education. Students at Hampton demanded greater emphasis on academic subjects, resulting in the suspension of several hundred students.

Fisk University, like many other black colleges, was headed by a white president who was accused of instituting programs and regulations that preserved blacks' subordinate position and status in the community. In 1925 student unrest began a protest that lasted ten weeks and resulted in the president's removal and the hiring of a more liberal white president. It was not until 1946 that Fisk hired its first black president, Charles Spurgeon Johnson (1893–1956). A graduate of Virginia Union University, Johnson later earned a bachelor of philosophy degree from the University of Chicago. He had served as research director of the National Urban League, and in that position founded the journal *Opportunity*. He moved to Fisk in 1928, established the Department of Social Sciences and later the Race Relations Institute. Johnson wrote a number of books including studies of black college graduates and housing.

Although Fisk University was a black college, it was led by a white president until 1946, when Charles Spurgeon Johnson took over.

Disgruntled students, faculty, and alumni of Howard University demanded a curriculum with an emphasis on Africa and African Americans, and a black scholar to lead their institution. In 1926 Mordecai W. Johnson (1890–1976) became Howard's first African-American president. Johnson graduated from Atlanta Baptist College, Rochester Theological Seminary, and Harvard Divinity School. During his tenure at Howard, Johnson attracted some of the most talented persons of the era to his school, including Thurgood Marshall, Charles Hamilton Houston (who headed the law school), Harlem Renaissance architect Alain Locke, and scientist Charles Drew.

What is the purpose of the **"No Child Left Behind Act"**?

On January 8, 2002, the No Child Left Behind Act was signed into law by President George W. Bush. The Act was designed to close the achievement gap between whites and nonwhites. It also represented a reauthorization of the Elementary and Secondary Education Act of 1965, or ESEA. The assessment of the schools, known as the Nation's Report Card, suggested in 2005 that the achievement gap was lessening. Other educators disagreed with the improvement because of lack of funding, distribution of funds, and the lack of the federal government's commitment to imposing mandates in relationship to funding. Others charged that white schools are able to use political clout not available to minority schools to obtain waivers from compliance. The central issue continues to reflect the *Brown v. Board of Education of Topeka, Kansas* (1954) controversy of racial isolation. Critics claim that NCLB is funded at a level much lower than necessary to meet the mandate of the legislation. Although some improvement in the achievement of African-American students has been realized, the academic gap remains.

What is the only **black college consortium**?

The first and only black college consortium, the Atlanta University System, was founded in 1929. John Hope (1868–1936) became the first president of the system when Atlanta University (a co-educational institution), Spelman College (an undergraduate college for women), and Morehouse College (an undergraduate college for men), entered a consortia arrangement. Later Clark and Morris Brown Colleges (Morris Brown no longer exists) and the Interdenominational Theological Seminary (all co-educational) joined to form the largest educational center in the world for blacks. Atlanta and Clark merged in 1988, to become Clark Atlanta University, which remains a part of the consortium.

What was the **first college** established by the **Churches of Christ**?

The first institution of higher learning for blacks during the period of segregation, established in 1948 by the Churches of Christ, was Southwestern Christian College. Located in Terrell, Texas, it opened in the fall of that year with forty-five students. The

Xavier University of Louisiana in New Orleans is the first black Catholic university.

college began in Fort Worth under the name Southern Bible Institute. It moved into buildings that once housed Texas Military College and changed its name to Southwestern Christian College. Though founded to educate blacks, it has maintained an open-door policy to students regardless of race. The institution became a four-year college in the 1970s. The campus contains the first dwelling erected in Terrell—an octagonal-shaped house built by a man named Terrell. It exists as one of the twenty surviving Round Houses in the country.

What is the country's **only black Catholic college**?

Xavier University of Louisiana in New Orleans was founded by Katharine Drexel and the Sisters of the Blessed Sacrament. It opened on September 27, 1915, as a high school. The college department was added in 1925. Xavier was the first (and remains the only) black Catholic college.

COLLEGE INTEGRATION

Were **white colleges** in the **South open to blacks before** the **Brown v. Board of Education** decision of 1954?

The University of South Carolina was first opened to all races on March 3, 1868. B. A. Boseman and Francis L. Cardozo were elected to the board of trustees. There was a long series of disturbances which occurred between July 8 and October 26, 1876, and federal troops were sent in.

116

What **college south of the Ohio River** was the first founded to **educate blacks and whites together**?

Berea College in Kentucky, founded in 1858, was the first college south of the Ohio River established specifically to educate blacks and whites together. Activities of the college were temporarily suspended during the Civil War in 1865. The integrated school received numerous threats of violence, but also experienced periods without friction. The Kentucky legislature passed a law forbidding the racial mix, which ended the biracial experiment abruptly in 1904.

What **students gained national attention** for the efforts to **integrate colleges** in the **South**?

After three-and-a-half-years of legal efforts on the part of the NAACP, Autherine Juanita Lucy (Foster) (1929–) became the first black student admitted to the University of Alabama, on February 3, 1956. A riot followed, and she was suspended that evening. She was expelled on February 29, accused of making "false" and "outrageous" statements about the school.

Charlayne Hunter-Gault (1942–) and Hamilton Earl Holmes (1941–1995) were the first black students to enroll at the University of Georgia, on January 10, 1961. Students rioted in protest of their admission, and they were temporarily suspended in the interest of their safety. Nevertheless, both students graduated from the institution in 1963.

In 1962, the first black admitted to the University of Mississippi was U.S. Air Force veteran James Howard Meredith (1933–). Meredith was admitted after being denied admission three times. Although the U.S. Supreme Court ordered Meredith's admission, Governor Ross R. Barnett defied the decision. United States marshals were called to escort Meredith to classes on October 1, and federal troops were called out to quell disturbances. They remained on campus to protect Meredith until he graduated on August 18, 1963, with a bachelor's degree in political science.

Who was the **first black student** to **graduate** from the **University of Alabama**?

The first black student to graduate from the University of Alabama, on May 30, 1965, was Vivian Malone Jones (1942–1995). In 1956 Autherine Lucy (Foster) (1929–) was the first black student enrolled in the university. Malone along with another black student, James Hood (1943–2013), had to be escorted by the National Guard to register.

LAW SCHOOLS

What **historically black college** was the **first** to establish a **law school**?

In October 1868 John Mercer Langston (1829–1897) founded and organized the Law School at Howard University, the first in a black school. He headed the department when classes formally began on January 6, 1869, and was its dean for seven years. From 1873 to 1875 he was also vice president and acting president of the university.

Who was the first black student to become **editor** of the **Harvard Law Review**?

The first black student to become editor of the *Harvard Law Review* was Barack Obama (1961–), in 1990. A second-year law student and a native of Hawaii, Obama was employed in social work on Chicago's South Side before entering law school. In 2008 he was the first African American elected to the U.S. presidency; he was reelected in 2012.

OTHER SCHOOLS

What was the **first boarding school** for **black girls**?

Established in 1829, Saint Francis Academy of Rome in Baltimore, Maryland, was the first boarding school for black girls. The school was established by the Oblate Sisters of Providence, a group of black nuns who were French-educated. The school opened with twenty-four girls. The only secondary school for black women, Saint Francis became well known and attracted young women from all across the country as well as from Canada. The school had become co-educational by 1865 and was known then as the Saint Francis Academy.

Who was the **first black teacher** for **freed slaves**?

In 1861 Mary Smith Kelsick Peake (1823–1862), a free woman of color, was the first teacher for freed slaves. Supported by the American Missionary Association, she was appointed to teach children at Fort Monroe, Virginia, and on September 17, 1861, she opened a school in Hampton, Virginia, marking the beginning of the general education of blacks in the South. The school started as a day school, providing elementary education for children. A night school for adults was soon added. Hampton Institute (now University) had its roots in this school. Peake was born in Norfolk, Virginia, daughter of a prominent Englishman and a free mulatto woman. At age six, she was sent to live with relatives in Alexandria, Virginia, to attend a private school for free blacks. When Virginia passed laws closing all schools for blacks, she returned to Norfolk, where she became established as a seamstress. She moved to Hampton, Virginia, when her mother married in 1847. Concern for her people led her to begin teaching children in her home. The Hampton home she shared with her husband was burned shortly after the Civil War began, which led the Peakes and other blacks to seek harbor at Fortress Monroe. Unfortunately, Peake's health failed shortly after establishment of the school, and she died of tuberculosis on February 22, 1862.

When were **public schools** for blacks **established**?

America's first public school was established in 1635. The first schools in the United States were private and founded and/or supported by religious groups, such as Puritans and Roman Catholics. Their schools were also reflective of the particular belief system of the founding entity. By the mid-eighteenth century private schools catered to wealthy males. Many years would pass before the idea that a public school should provide an education for all children was generally accepted. Snowden School, Virginia, was the first state school for blacks. Founded in 1870, the school was short-lived. In 1872 the first recorded free public school established for blacks was founded in Salem, Massachusetts. Blacks continued to receive an unequal education and far less educational resources than whites.

The Preparatory High School for Colored Youth, the first public high school for blacks in the country, opened in the basement of the Fifteenth Street Presbyterian Church in Washington, D.C. It moved to its first permanent location in 1891, when it occupied a building on M Street, N.W. It then became known as the M Street High School, and twenty-five years later, was renamed to honor Paul Laurence Dunbar. The M Street/Dunbar High School was acknowledged as the best public high school for blacks in the country.

What **African-American woman** was the first to **head** a **major educational institution** for blacks?

In 1869 Fanny Jackson Coppin (1837–1913) became the first black woman to head a major educational institution for blacks, the Institute for Colored Youth of Philadelphia. The Society of Friends founded the school in 1837, and when Coppin graduated from Oberlin College in 1865, she became principal of the Institute's female department. The Institute was a prestigious school with a faculty consisting of some of the most highly educated blacks of the period.

Why was **Mary Church Terrell** important?

Mary Church Terrell (1863–1954) was the first black woman to serve on the Washington, D.C., Board of Education. She served from 1895 to 1901, and again from 1906 to 1911. In

1896 she was the cofounder and first president of the National Council of Colored Women. Terrell was born in Memphis, Tennessee, to parents who were former slaves. Her father was the son of his owner and opened a successful saloon after emancipation. Her mother ran an equally successful hair salon. Terrell was sent to Ohio for her early schooling, attending first the Antioch College Model School, then a public school in Yellow Springs, and finally the public high school in Oberlin. During this time, her mother moved to New York while Terrell was away in school. Terrell graduated from Oberlin College in 1884 and returned to Memphis, where her father, Robert Reed Church Sr. (1839–1912), had become wealthy. In 1885 she began her professional career at Wilberforce College, but left after a year to teach in the Latin department of

Cofounder of the National Council of Colored Women, Mary Church Terrell was the first black woman to serve on the U.S. Board of Education.

the colored high school in Washington, D.C. She completed work for her master's from Oberlin in 1888, while working in Washington.

What was the focus of the **National Training School for Women and Girls**?

In 1901 the National Training School for Women and Girls opened in Washington, D.C., to carry out the focus of its title—to educate women and girls. Its founding president was Nannie Helen Burroughs (1879–1961), a brilliant orator who was a lifelong booster of women's education and a tireless civic organizer. By the end of the school's first year, the enrollment had thirty students; twenty-five years later it boasted of a student population of more than one thousand women at the secondary and junior college levels. In 1934 the name was changed to the National Trades and Professional School for Women. The school was again renamed, becoming the Nannie Helen Burroughs School. Born in Orange, Virginia, Burroughs was the daughter of former slaves who advanced economically as soon as they were freed. She was educated at the M Street High School in Washington, D.C., which was one of the nation's outstanding secondary schools. She was well known for her unyielding advocacy of racial pride and worked tirelessly to advance women through education, the black women's club movement, and the National Baptist Convention.

What **school for young women** stressed **social graces** in its academic program?

On October 10, 1902, the Alice Freeman Palmer Institute opened in Sedalia, North Carolina, with Charlotte Hawkins Brown (1883–1961) as founder. The school was named in honor of Brown's friend and benefactor, with monies raised from Northern white philanthropists. Along with academic subjects, the Palmer Institute stressed industrial and vocational education, and cultural courses. It also focused on secondary and postsecondary components and attracted students from all across the nation. The school enjoyed the reputation of a finishing school for African Americans and was one of the nation's leading preparatory schools. Brown, who was born Lottie Hawkins, was a Henderson, North Carolina, native who moved with her family to Cambridge, Massachusetts, in search of better social and educational opportunities. She attended a two-year normal school in Salem, Massachusetts, and in 1901 was offered a teaching position at Bethany Institute which the American Missionary Association founded in Sedalia, near McLeansville, North Carolina. The school closed at the end of the year, when the AMA closed its one- and two-room schools. The Sedalia community urged Brown to remain, which was her impetus to interrupt her education and start a school of her own. Later on she studied at Harvard University and Wellesley and Simmons Colleges. In 1922 her school, Palmer Memorial Institute, graduated its first accredited high school class. Brown became a national leader on race issues and in the black women's club movement.

What was the **Jeanes teacher program**?

In 1907 Anna T. Jeanes, a philanthropist and teacher in Philadelphia, gave $1 million to

Booker T. Washington (founder and president of Tuskegee Institute in Alabama) and

Hollis B. Frissell (of Hampton Institute in Virginia) to strengthen rural schools for blacks in the South. Through the Fund for Rudimentary Schools for Southern Negroes, or the Jeanes Fund, the program supported industrial teachers who moved from school to school and taught industrial and utilitarian subjects. Later the program provided master teachers, or Jeanes teachers, who supervised other teachers in the schools. The program operated from 1908 until 1968, at which time counties assumed that responsibility and paid teachers' salaries.

Who was the **first Jeanes teacher**?

Virginia Estelle Randolph (1870–1958) became the first black Jeanes teacher in 1908. She was one of the most effective educators of her day. The Jeanes teacher program was fashioned after Randolph's notable practices in Henrico, Virginia. Through the Jeanes movement, Randolph was instrumental in bringing about improvements in the lives of thousands of teachers, children, and community residents. Born in Richmond, Virginia, to parents who were slaves, her early years were difficult. Her father died when she was young, and she took her first job when she was eight years old. After attending schools in Richmond, she obtained a job teaching in a county school at age sixteen, and moved to the Henrico school three years later. Her many achievements there extended beyond the regular school week; she organized a Sunday School, and taught in it herself for five years. Randolph left the Henrico School when she became a Jeanes teacher, and spent time working in a number of states, including Virginia, North Carolina, and Georgia. Her success led to expansion of the Jeanes movement, with Jeanes teachers supervising industrial education and building community support for black schools all over the South. The program was later broadened to include supervision of instruction in regular academic curricula. The Virginia Randolph Fund, established as a tribute to her in 1936, was merged with the Anna T. Jeanes Foundation, which had been renamed the Negro Rural School Fund. These funds were later merged with others to become the Southern Education Fund. It has been said that confusion over the role of the Jeanes teachers—whose successes were unquestioned—when desegregation was begun contributed to the death of the program. Many tributes to Randolph exist, including a Virginia museum named for her, which was designated a national historic landmark in 1976. She was living in Richmond at the time of her death.

What was the **Julius Rosenwald Rural Negro Schools** project?

In 1911 philanthropist and organization founder Julius Rosenwald (1862–1932) met Booker T. Washington of Tuskegee Institute in Alabama and the two developed a program that had a marked impact on the education of African Americans in the rural South. The relationship stimulated Rosenwald to build over five thousand schools, teachers' homes, shops, and other buildings in sixteen southern and border states, from 1909 to 1932. The buildings were funded on a matching basis, with states and local areas contributing some of the support. To enhance the educational program in these schools and uplift the education of black youth, many teachers who were a part of the Jeanes teacher program taught in the Rosenwald schools. Many of the school buildings are extant and now restored to serve as community centers.

What educator became nationally known as the **"Little Professor of Piney Woods"**?

Educator, school founder, and administrator Laurence Clifton Jones (1884–1975) uplifted the African-American community by establishing a school in the deep woods of Mississippi's Black Belt called Piney Woods Country Life School. He made it possible for thousands of black youth to receive elementary and high

Inspired by the work of Booker T. Washington, philanthropist Julius Rosenwald built thousands of schools and other educational-support buildings in sixteen states.

school educations. The school that he founded on faith in 1910 led Jones to be known affectionately as "The Little Professor of Piney Woods." Born in St. Joseph, Missouri, Jones worked his way through college and graduated from Iowa State University. He became fascinated with the philosophy and success of educator Booker T. Washington. Later he was offered a position at Tuskegee Institute (later University), which Washington founded, but instead decided to build a school in Piney Woods, where he thought his service was needed more. To help sustain the struggling school, Jones organized several small groups of singers known as the Cotton Blossom Singers, who went out on singing tours to raise money. They were called "the best-known ambassadors or musical messengers" for Piney Woods. In the later 1930s Jones also organized the International Sweethearts of Rhythm; they appeared at the Apollo Theater in New York City and at the 1939 New York World's Fair. Jones retired in the 1974–1975 school year and died in Jackson, Mississippi.

When did programs in **adult education begin**?

The Bureau of Refugees, Freedmen, and Abandoned Lands (or the Freedmen's Bureau) supported the first formally recognized adult education program in the United States in the post-Civil War period. Adult education for African Americans continued beyond this and concentrated in four areas: literacy, community education, continuing (or workplace) education, and academic or degree-granting programs. Perhaps the adult education program that is best known is that which was started in the early 1920s, and focused on helping adults lacking in basic skills.

SCHOOL DESEGREGATION

What **five different cases** dealing with **segregation in public schools** reached the U.S. Supreme Court in 1952?

In 1952 five different cases, all dealing with segregation in public schools, but with different facts and from different places, reached the U.S. Supreme Court. Four of the cases, *Brown v. Board of Education of Topeka* (out of Kansas), *Briggs v. Elliott* (out of South Carolina), *Davis v. Prince Edward County School Board* (out of Virginia), and *Gebhart v. Belton* (out of Delaware), were considered together; the fifth case, *Bolling v. Sharpe,* coming out of the District of Columbia, was considered separately since the district is not a state. The Court had difficulty reaching a decision after hearing the initial argument. Thurgood Marshall, legal counsel for the NAACP Legal Defense and Education Fund, presented arguments on behalf of the black students. The Court ruled in favor of the black students in each case, declaring that segregation in public education deprived minority children of equal protection under the Fourteenth Amendment. In the Bolling case, the Court determined that segregation violated provisions of the Fifth Amendment, since the Fourteenth Amendment is expressly directed to the states.

What was the **only public school desegregation case initiated** by **students**?

Formed in the Virginia Colony in 1754, Prince Edward County is widely known as the subject of *Davis v. County School Board of Prince Edward County*. Students in the system were the only ones who initiated such a case. While the case was eventually incorporated into the NAACP-led *Brown v. Board of Education of Topeka,* the Virginia General Assembly still passed a series of laws in 1956 to implement massive resistance. Efforts to fend off potential litigation by the NAACP resulted in the founding of the all-black Robert Russa Moton High School in 1939, which lacked a gymnasium, cafeteria, and teachers' restrooms. In 1951 the inadequate facilities, as well as repeated denials by the all-white school board to provide assistance, led Barbara Johns, niece of activist Reverend Vernon Johns, to lead a walkout in protest of the school's conditions. In response, school officials refused to appropriate any funds for the county's school board, effectively closing all of the county's public schools. For five years, the county's public schools remained closed until they were forced to reopen in 1963.

What is the origin and **purpose of freedom schools**?

The landmark case *Brown v. Board of Education of Topeka, Kansas* (1954) caused some public school systems to close their doors in reaction to the U.S. Supreme Court ruling to desegregate public schools. This occurred in Prince Edward County, Virginia, and elsewhere. This reaction, in turn, caused civil rights leaders to develop freedom schools to educate young African Americans and teach them leadership and political participation. The quintessential model freedom school was developed in 1964, during Freedom Summer in Mississippi—an effort that led to voter registration drives. The Mississippi Freedom

Schools offered academic courses as well and the subjects varied according to school location. They were established with the commitment of local communities and were offered in nontraditional locations, such as parks, kitchens, and private homes. Attendance fluctuated, ranging from fifteen in the first week to eight in the second. Later, as many as thirty-five students attended a particular school. Most freedom schools have since closed.

What was the work of the **"Little Rock Nine"**?

Daisy Bates (1920–1999), then president of the Arkansas state branch of the NAACP, led nine black students to integrate Central High School in Little Rock, Arkansas, on September 25, 1957. For their efforts, Bates and the "Little Rock Nine," as they came to be known, received the NAACP's Spingarn Medal on July 11, 1958. The medal was given "in grateful acknowledgement of their courageous self-restraint in the face of extreme provocation and peril." In 1998 the U.S. Senate voted to award Congressional gold medals to the nine at a White House ceremony and presented the awards in 1999. Bates was recognized again when the state of Arkansas declared the third Monday in February in her honor. Bates was born in Huttig, Arkansas, and was raised by adoptive parents. She grew up in a positive relationship with her surrogate parents and attended the poorly equipped segregated schools in her hometown. When she married in 1941, she moved with her husband to Little Rock, where she and her husband leased the *Arkansas State Press*. The paper's report of the beating death of a black army sergeant by a local white policeman led to loss of its advertising from white businessmen, but it survived and gained stature as an independent voice of the people, which worked to improve conditions for blacks throughout the state. When Arkansas moved slowly to follow the U.S. Supreme Court's 1954 desegregation order, the NAACP, under Bates' leadership, protested and developed several strategies to force quicker action. Daisy Bates and other NAACP officials surrendered to police on October 25, 1957, following an arrest order is-

Central High School in Little Rock, Arkansas, was the site where NAACP leader Daisy Bates led nine black students into the all-white school in 1957, bravely smashing the color barrier.

sued by the Little Rock City Council that charged the organization with violation of a new law requiring organizational information. Bates was convicted and fined, but the decision was later reversed. The *Arkansas State Press* ceased publication in 1959, but Bates continued to be active in voter registration drives and in work with the Democratic National Committee; the paper resumed publication in 1985.

What are **charter schools**?

A charter school is a publicly funded school that operates under contract with the local school system. Guidelines and regulations governing such schools differ from those of other public schools in that its accountability and expected productivity are governed by its charter. Its goal is to improve the public education system. Most are small schools: For example, in 1996–1997 the enrollment of an average charter school was about 150 students, as compared to 500 students in public schools in those states where the schools coexisted. Charter schools are popular in urban areas, with minority students in those areas constituting most of the enrollment.

Among the highly successful and nationally recognized urban charter schools serving black youth is the Harlem Children's Zone Promise Academies, founded by Geoffrey Canada; these schools use the community-based approach to stimulate learning. Another, Urban Prep Academy, was founded in the Englewood community, a troubled neighborhood on Chicago's South Side in 2006. It is the first all-boys public charter high school in the country. In 2010, all of the school's 107 graduates were accepted into different colleges and universities, including the University of Illinois, Northwestern, and historically black Fisk University, Morehouse College, and Howard University. Tim King, the academy's founder, said that the school was doing everything that it should to prepare the students for the academic rigors of college. The school "promotes a spirit of brotherhood from the students' earliest days in high school." It also promotes a spirit of family and community.

What is the **voucher system** in education?

The voucher system is a plan used to fund public and private education and at the same time improve the quality of education and the safety of schools. This system represents a strategy of sharing control at the local level. The vouchers follow the child to the school that the child or the parents choose. There are claims that vouchers especially improve the quality of education for African-American students, many of whom live in urban areas and receive a poor education. The voucher system has been proposed for private schools as well. One of the first voucher systems in the nation was implemented in Milwaukee, Wisconsin, in 1990, and produced great debate over its success. There is agreement, however, that the education of African-American students improved slightly as result of the voucher system.

What is **Head Start**?

A federally funded and comprehensive program in child development, Head Start serves young children and families in poverty. Since more than one in three children in the program are African American, Head Start is especially meaningful in the African-American community. Its assistance to the recipients is short-lived, lasting only a few years. When President Lyndon B. Johnson launched his "War on Poverty" and the 1964 Economic Opportunity Act was passed, Head Start emerged as well. It became a part of the Office of Child Development in the Department of Health, Education, and Welfare in 1969. The Civil Rights Movement and social and political activism strongly influenced the beginning of the Head Start program. Head Start has been studied through federally mandated evaluations and highly sophisticated investigations. Conclusions are that it is an insufficient remedy for the challenges that many African-American families and children face; however, it does have a broad and positive impact on the recipients.

What is **Ebonics**?

Ebonics was developed to improve the language skills of African-American students. It is Black English, renamed in 1996, and consists of a combination of the words "ebony" and "phonics." During the 1960s and 1970s, Black English was called Black Vernacular English (BVE) and in the 1980s and 1990s became known as African American Vernacular English (AAVE). Some scholars say that it is similar to other dialects, consisting of distinct grammar and syntax patterns. Ebonics reached national attention in 1996, when the Oakland, California, school board agreed to make it "a second language" and ordered all teachers to be trained in its grammar and to respect this speech used by so many African American students. This decision drew national criticism.

FUNDING
HIGHER EDUCATION

How does the **Higher Education Act of 1965** impact Historically Black Colleges and Universities?

President Lyndon B. Johnson's "War on Poverty" had as one of its components the Higher Education Act of 1965, which is an example of several laws that challenge the poverty, racism, and sexism that prevent equal access to education. Its goal was to advance the work of colleges and universities by supporting educational, economic, and social mobility among diverse groups, and to aid students from low-income families and those from underrepresented groups, making it possible for them to obtain postsecondary education. Johnson and Congress both recognized the importance of supporting Historically Black Colleges and Universities and their production of most African-American college graduates. Originally, the Higher Education Act of 1965 provided support specifically for HBCUs but was amended to include community colleges. Still, Title III of HEA—Minority-Serving Institutions—provides for graduate or professional training at HBCUs, tribal colleges, and other minority-serving institutions.

President Lyndon Johnson, shown here signing the 1964 Civil Rights Act, did much to help black Americans, including his 1965 Higher Education Act and his 1965 Voting Rights Act. He was committed to his "War on Poverty."

What is the **current impact** of **Historically Black Colleges and Universities** on the education of black students?

Historically Black Colleges and Universities, or HBCUs, are recognized as those institutions established prior to 1964 and whose mission, when founded, was to educate African-American students. A few of these institutions, such as Fisk and Talladega, that were founded by the American Missionary Association, were established to educate students regardless of race. Now the HBCUs as a whole portray themselves as institutions that serve a diverse student body Although they have a legacy of underfunding, HBCUs continue to ensure that African-American students have equal access to an education and work to ensure them academic success. Among the HBCUs founded before 1964 are three black medical schools, six law schools, one school of veterinary medicine, and one graduate library school. A number of the institutions offer master's and doctoral degrees. They offer nursing, pharmacy, engineering, and other programs that lead their graduates to successful careers and help the HBCUs remain attractive providers of higher education.

What is the *Adams v. Richardson* case?

The celebrated *Adams v. Richardson* case addressed the dismantling of dual systems of public higher education that existed well after the passage of the Civil Rights Act of   **127**

1964, which mandated, among other benefits to black Americans, the removal of racial discrimination in education. The Department of Health, Education, and Welfare and Welfare found that ten states still had segregated higher education systems during the period of January 1969 until February 1970. The mandate referred to those public colleges that received federal funds. HEW required each state to submit a desegregation plan. Five states then submitted plans that were unacceptable while the other five disregarded the mandate altogether. John Quincy Adams, a black Mississippian whose name appeared first in the list of plaintiffs, and others filed suit against HEW Secretary Elliot L. Richardson to force him to follow the congressional mandate and enforce Title VI in the states. The case was heard in the U .S. Court of Appeals for the District of Columbia, June 12, 1973. This case, and several others, was instrumental in breaking down barriers that prevented African Americans and other minorities from claiming their rights as U.S. citizens. The case also had a positive impact on public and private black colleges in several areas and underscored the need for their continued existence.

What is the **White House Initiative** on **Historically Black Colleges and Universities**?

In 1980 President Jimmy Carter signed Executive Order 12232 and established the White House Initiative on HBCUs. The purpose of the initiative was to provide a structure to help these institutions have access to, participate in, and benefit from federally funded programs. Those presidents who followed Carter, including President Barack Obama, have all signed executive orders reaffirming the mandate begun by Carter and, in doing so, strengthened the HBCU grants program while also giving it national attention. These presidents acknowledge the historic and ongoing contributions of HBCUs to the general welfare and prosperity of America. HBCUs were founded by visionary leaders and for over 150 years they have produced national leaders in business, government, academia, the military, and other arenas. They have also given generations of men and women hope and educational opportunity.

There are 106 HBCUs located in twenty states, the District of Columbia, and the U.S. Virgin Islands. They continue as important engines of economic growth and community service, and serve people of all ethnic, racial, and economic backgrounds,

President Jimmy Carter signed the executive order that helped HBCUs obtain benefits from federally funded education programs.

especially African Americans. Currently, the White House Initiative supports the HBCUs by providing funds from the U.S. Department of Education for the HBCU Capital Financing program. The initiative also provides support to strengthen the Historically Black Graduate Institutions program, for comprehensive science and technology workforce programs at the National Science Foundation, and Pell grants to help finance student tuition and fees at HBCUs.

What was an **important outgrowth** of the **White House Initiative** on **Historically Black Colleges and Universities**?

An outgrowth of the White House Initiative on Historically Black Colleges and Universities was the Secretary of the Interior's Historic Preservation, established to identify and restore those historic structures on the HBCU campuses considered to be the most historically significant and physically threatened. Without direct response to the needs of many of these colleges, which were presented with critical rehabilitation needs, their historic buildings may have been lost because the colleges lacked the resources to restore them.

What **White House Initiative complements** and **reinforces** the federal initiative on **HBCUs**?

President Barack Obama, on July 26, 2012, signed the first-ever Executive Order 13621, the White House Initiative on Educational Excellence for African Americans. The initiative, housed in the U.S. Department of Education, provides every child greater access to a complete and competitive education from birth until the child enters a career. This order is an extension of the White House effort to persuade colleges to cut costs so that every American can afford an education. The new initiative, along with the existing White House Initiative on Historically Black Colleges and Universities, supports educational outcomes for African Americans at every level. The new order also aims to result in a more effective educational continuum for all African-American students. Partnerships with public, private, and philanthropic organizations are encouraged. A President's Advisory Commission on Educational Excellence for African Americans, composed of twenty-five members appointed by the White House, is mandated by the order.

Are there **single-purpose schools** founded for African-American males?

Lincoln University in Pennsylvania (1854) and Morehouse College in Atlanta (1867)—both liberal arts institutions—were founded to educate black male students. Lincoln was strictly a privately supported institution until 1972, when it began a formal association with the Commonwealth of Pennsylvania and is now a state-related, coeducational institution. Since its charter had prevented female matriculation toward a degree, women were not graduated until 1953. In 1945 educator Horace Mann Bond (1904–1972) became the school's fifth president and its first African-American president; he served until 1957. From 1987 through 1998, Lincoln had its first woman president, Niara Sudarkasa (1938–).

Morehouse College has among its notable and long list of distinguished black graduates Martin Luther King Jr. The school began as Augusta Institute under the auspices of the Baptist Home Missionary Society. Its first African-American president was John Hope (1868-1936), who took office in 1913. In 1940 the school's renowned leader Benjamin Elijah Mays (1894–1984) became president and held that office until 1967. He is credited with promoting the college's philosophy termed "Morehouse Mystique," which is a spiritual and intellectual approach to leadership, brotherhood, and service reflecting much of Mays's own life and values.

COLLEGE CURRICULA

What are the **Afrocentric Movement** and **Afrocentricity**?

The Afrocentric Movement emerged in the early 1970s, at the hands of such scholars as Molefi Asante, a Temple University professor, and Maulana Karenga, a professor at the University of California, Los Angeles. Their vision was that Black Studies should be rooted in the African experience and should have a worldview which emanates from that experience. The view is that one should understand the whole of human history, and recognize that there are mutually beneficial exchanges that contribute to and enrich African humanity and human civilization. Although the movement faced strong dissent among some precincts of academia, it gained in popularity and was well received among primary and secondary teachers who wanted an alternative to Eurocentric education.

The Afrocentric Movement is an academic focus on African history, culture, and thought. It spanned the 1980s and 1990s and was manifest in academic areas as well as in dress, paraphernalia, literature, art, and modern cultural traditions. It embodies all things related to African-American culture. Both black and white colleges led the way in promoting and offering Afrocentric education in their institutions.

Afrocentricism is more than historical facts and figures centered on time and space. Afrocentricism is based on the principles of truth, justice, balance, and order. It presents to black students their own cultural life experiences. The classroom is transformed into a holistic learning envi-

Professors Molefi Asante (shown here) and Maulana Karenga spurred the Afrocentric Movement in the 1970s in which they emphasized that Black Studies should teach about the African experience.

ronment in which the student is the center. Although Afrocentricism benefits all students, the overall thrust of African-centered education is the re-centering of children of African descent.

What are **Black Studies programs**?

Black Studies is an activist-based discipline that embraces the study of the arts, humanities, and social behavioral sciences relating to African Americans. It is an interdisciplinary program and aims to help African Americans gain a full understanding of their experiences. Black Studies programs have been influenced by many events, actions, and people. Significant among the influences of society is the Civil Rights Movement, during which black academicians and leaders expressed dissatisfaction with the lack of courses and inaccurate content of those offered about the African-American experience, as well as agitation of the Black Student Movement. Black students themselves became proud of their heritage, culture, and lives, and concluded that they were underrepresented, misrepresented, and/or not represented in academic curricula. Black Studies programs were offered as early as 1966, beginning with black course offerings which, in later years, developed into undergraduate and graduate degree programs, including the doctoral degree. Nathan Hare (1933–) is often regarded as the founder of Black Studies programs; he was hired at San Francisco University to coordinate the first Black Studies program in the United States.

Who is one of the **forerunners of Black Studies**?

One of the forerunners in the field of black studies, theologian and educator Reverend Alexander Crummell (1819–1898), along with a group of black intellectuals, founded the American Negro Academy in Washington, D.C., in 1897. The purpose of the organization was to foster scholarship and promote literature, science, and art among African Americans. The organization's members hoped that through the academy an educated black elite would be born to shape and direct society. Crummell first conceived of the idea of an American Negro Academy while he was a student at Cambridge University in England. The organization's founding members included poet Paul Laurence Dunbar (1872–1906), William Sanders Scarborough (1852–1926), and educator and Pan Afri-

An Episcopalian priest and professor, Alexander Crummell cofounded the American Negro Academy in Washington, D.C.

canist W.E.B. Du Bois (1868–1963), among other noted educators. Following Crummell's death in 1898, Du Bois was elected president of the academy.

MAINSTREAM ACADEMIC INSTITUTIONS

What **actions** have **mainstream institutions** taken in an effort to give **blacks equal access to education**?

Equal access to primary and secondary education has long been a perplexing problem for the entire country. Even so, the problem in higher education has been deemed as great, if not greater, than in other areas of schooling, for many mainstream institutions were reluctant to open their doors to blacks. They denied that racial segregation was an issue. A black presence on white college campuses was well demonstrated in the acceptance of black athletes who were placed on varsity teams regardless of their overall graduation rate. As they sought to increase black enrollment, many of these colleges also did so through ordinary as well as innovative ways. They held special programs, established attractive scholarship programs, and some had set-asides for African-American students. Such practices continued until critics began to launch strenuous opposition to any program that practiced what they called race-based favoritism in higher education. Critics then began national protests to remove all vestiges of affirmative action in education as well as in employment.

Is affirmative action an issue practiced in admitting blacks to mainstream institutions?

Affirmative action has its roots in the Civil Rights Movement. On March 6, 1961, President John F. Kennedy signed Executive Order 10925, which established the President's Commission on Equal Employment Opportunity. It called for contractors doing business with the government to ensure that applicants are hired without regard to their race, creed, color, or national origin. President Lyndon B. Johnson developed the concept into public policies, declaring that affirmative steps must be taken to close the gap between blacks and whites and issued Executive Order 11246 to document such efforts. President Richard M. Nixon was the first to implement federal policies designed to guarantee minority hiring. By the late 1970s the U.S. Supreme Court continued to uphold affirmative action policies but placed certain restrictions on their implementation. In the *Regents of the University of California v. Bakke* case, the court held that it was unconstitutional for the medical school at the University of California at Davis to establish a rigid quota system setting aside sixteen of one hundred spaces for entering minorities. Other cases continued to challenge affirmative action into the last decade of the twentieth century.

In 1996 California governor Pete Wilson and Ward Connerly, a conservative African American and member of the University of California Board of Regents, pushed for and got passed Proposition 209, which ended all state-sponsored affirmative action programs. Two years later Connerly led Washington State's Initiative 200, which also sought to eradicate affirmative action. In 2003 the U.S. Supreme Court upheld the use of race as a factor in promoting educational diversity as long as the University of Michigan did not consider it in a "mechanical way." The Court rejected Michigan's undergraduate plan saying that it placed too much emphasis on race as a determining factor in its admission policies. On November 7, 2006, Michigan voters approved a referendum calling for an end to race-sensitive admissions at the University of Michigan and in the state's university system. Affirmative action has been a highly contentious and decisive issue since its inception. With state legislatures, the public, and the courts at variance, its continued status is uncertain.

Have **African-American educators headed mainstream** academic institutions?

In 1854 Patrick Francis Healy (1834–1910) became the first African-American president of Georgetown University in Washington, D.C. Healy, the first black Jesuit, was also the first of his race to earn a Ph.D. from Louvain University in Belgium. He was the son of an Irish plantation owner and a mulatto slave woman; his race was not widely known. The first black president of a major American university in the twentieth century was Clifton Reginald Wharton Jr. (1926–), who on January 2, 1970, became president of Michigan State University. He was born in Boston and graduated from Harvard University and Johns Hopkins University, and in 1958 was the first black to earn a doctorate in economics from the University of Chicago. In 1993 Wharton was named deputy U.S. secretary of state.

Mary Frances Berry (1938–) became chancellor of the University of Colorado in 1976 and left the next year to become assistant secretary of education in the U.S. Department of Health, Education, and Welfare. Several other educators, male and female, have headed mainstream institutions, notable among them Ruth Simmons (1945–), who was the first black president to lead one of the "Seven Sister" schools, Smith College in Northampton, Massachusetts. She moved to Brown University as its president on July 1, 2001, becoming the first woman to head two of the nation's premier institutions. Simmons was born in Grapevine, Texas, to parents who were sharecroppers, and graduated from historically black Dillard University in New Orleans. She earned her doctorate from Radcliffe College, now a part of Harvard University. In the Deep South, Rodney Bennett became the first black president of the University of Southern Mississippi. He took office in 2013.

LEADERSHIP TRAINING

What **leadership programs** for African Americans have been **offered**?

African Americans have begun to focus on leadership programs, whether gender-based or in other areas. Hampton University in Virginia aims to address the leadership training needs of newly appointed presidents, provosts, vice presidents, deans, and other executives in academia through its program "On the Road to the Presidency." Others have been held at Bennett College for Women, Fisk University, and Morehouse College. Still others have addressed the leadership training needs of other administrators; for example, in 2005 the HBCU Library Alliance held its first Leadership Institute called "Redefining Leadership for 21st Century Librarians," in Stone Mountain, Georgia.

JOURNALISM

AFRICAN–AMERICAN PRESS

What has been the **focus of the black press** in the United States?

The black press in America began in 1827; from then until the Civil War, it was one of many leaders against racial injustice. Black journalism has demonstrated from the outset a near total commitment to the cause of racial equality. Some claim that the early black press was not exclusively aimed at black audiences. If this is true, it follows that the older press was protest-oriented with a focus on slavery, lynching, and the overall brutal treatment of African-American men, women, and children. Much later the black press, particularly newspapers, focused on local news. Discrimination in housing and employment, and police brutality were among the common themes discussed. In time, however, the black press carried information of national interest. The national newspapers began to resemble large urban dailies more than the urban weeklies that they were. Like mainstream papers today, black newspapers and magazines have had a high mortality rate.

How was the **black press sustained** in **antebellum America**?

Self-expression in the black community, whether slave of free, always found a way to exist. During slavery, blacks were forbidden to read or write, yet many did so and gained access to the black-oriented publications that existed. An early black publication that was popular was David Walker's "Appeal, in Four Articles, Together with a Preamble to the Coloured Citizens of the World, but in Particular, and Very Expressly to Those of the United States of America," which was published in 1827. It was a pamphlet that was published in several editions, and which stirred the public in the South and the North. Blacks were imprisoned, in some instances, simply for possessing a copy. After the Civil War, many publications aimed at the black community were published in pamphlet form.

How have **black religious publications contributed** to the black press?

Black churches contributed to the black press by publishing newsletters and magazines; some of these publications, however, have had white ownership. Among the genuinely black religious publications are those from the National Baptist Convention of America, the National Baptist Convention, U.S.A., and the African Methodist Episcopal Church. Their publications have made an important contribution to black people, giving them a sense of hope, security, and identity.

NEWSPAPERS

What was the **first black biweekly newspaper**?

Published in 1862, *L'Union* was Louisiana's first black newspaper and the first black biweekly. The paper was published from September 27 until December 20, 1862, and became a triweekly beginning December 23, 1862. Publication was suspended on May 31, 1864, but the paper continued to struggle until it was disbanded on July 19, 1864. From early July 1863, the paper was published in both English and French. Its chief editor was Paul Trevigne, a black man who was born and reared in New Orleans. In 1864 Louis Charles Roudanez and his associates bought the defunct newspaper, revived it, changed the title to *La Tribune de la Nouvelle Orleans,* and published it irregularly until 1871.

What **journalist** was **fearless** in his writings on **abolition and slavery**?

David Ruggles (1810–1849), journalist and abolitionist, knew at an early age that he would fight against the injustices of slavery. When Ruggles was seventeen, he moved to New York and became secretary of the New York Committee of Vigilance. He was a steadfast advocate for escaped slaves and would assist them in their struggle for freedom. The most famous fugitive who found refuge with Ruggles was Frederick (Bailey) Douglass. While in hiding at Ruggles's home, Douglass married Anna Murray before continuing his escape. By this time, in 1838, Ruggles was already a notorious abolitionist. After an article he wrote in *Colored American* accused John Russell, a black lodge owner, of helping to kidnap blacks, the paper was sued for libel

An illustration of three men shows David Ruggles in the center. Ruggles, whose ill health led to blindness, was an abolitionist and journalist who published daring articles and pamphlets against slavery.

and Russell won. Samuel Cornish, the owner of the paper and a member of the Vigilance Committee, saw Ruggles's behavior as objectionable. This along with other radical acts resulted in Ruggles having to resign from the committee in 1839. As a journalist Ruggles produced numerous pamphlets and articles about the condition and situations of blacks at that time. He strongly disagreed with the American Colonization Society, which advocated black relocation, and in response published his own pamphlet, "Extinguished," in 1834. Ruggles continued to publish in abolitionist journals as his health deteriorated to the point that he was nearly blind. He was fearless in his confrontation with legal and political forces that supported slavery. Ruggles left New York for Massachusetts, in 1841, and later found some health improvement using water cures. By 1845 he had regained his health and continued to write about the abolitionist movement. He was considered a true warrior for the cause of abolition.

Who was called the **"dean of African-American journalism"**?

Journalist, civil rights activist, and printer T. Thomas Fortune (1856–1928), who was born in Marianna, Florida, had little formal education but was enthralled by the newspaper business and learned the trade. He became a printer, a publisher, and an outspoken and militant journalist. Fortune came to be known as the dean of African-American journalism: He worked for, owned, and published several newspapers. His ideas appeared in his journalistic writing and in his book, *Black and White: Land, Labor, and Politics in the South* (1884). While editor of the *New York Age,* he conceived of ideas which led to the formation of the Afro-American League, which became defunct in 1893; however, he was asked to aid in the development of the Afro-American Council (1898), which had almost the same concerns as the league. Many of these same issues are seen in the Niagara Movement and the National Association for the Advancement of Colored People. Fortune worked with civil rights organizations and leaders in addition to his editorial efforts for civil rights. He was well acquainted with Booker T. Washington and they shared many ideas. He became the editor of the *Negro World,* the organ of Marcus Garvey's Universal Negro Improvement Association, supported black women activists, and aided in the efforts of Ida B. Wells (Barnett) with information, employment, and help for her lecture engagements. The methodologies and proposals in Fortune's editorial writing foreshadow the direction of twentieth-century civil rights.

Who was the **only early black journalist** to serve a **major daily**?

In 1864 Thomas Morris Chester (1834–1892) became the first and only black correspondent for a major daily, the *Philadelphia Press,* during the Civil War. His dispatches covered the period from August 1864 through June 1865. He was previously editor of the *Star of Liberia.* For eight months he reported on black troop activity around Petersburg, Florida, and the Confederate capital, both before and after Richmond, Virginia, was taken. Chester was born in Harrisburg, Pennsylvania, to abolitionist parents. He studied first at Alexander High School in Monrovia, Liberia, and later at the Thetford Academy in Vermont. He read law under a Liberian lawyer, then spent three years at Middle

Temple in London, England. In April 1870 he became the first black American barrister admitted to practice before English courts.

What was Chicago's first black newspaper?

The Conservator was the first black newspaper published in Chicago, in 1878. Richard H. De Baptiste (1831–1901), who was pastor of Chicago's Olivet Baptist Church, assumed editorial control later that year. In the year that he headed the paper, he expanded circulation to reach the masses. He also became corresponding editor of the *Western Herald,* the short-lived *Saint Louis Monitor,* and the *Brooklyn Monitor.* De Baptiste was born into a prominent family in Fredericksburg, Virginia. Before joining the ministry, he was a bricklayer and plasterer. He moved to Detroit and later taught in Ohio. He was ordained in Mount Pleasant Baptist Church in Ohio in the late 1850s. From 1863 to 1882 he headed Olivet Baptist Church in Chicago. He later was elected president of the American Baptist Association, the first national black Baptist association in the country. He was elected president of the white Baptist Free Mission Society in 1870.

What are some black anti-slavery newspapers?

The first black anti-slavery newspaper was *Freedom's Journal,* published in New York in 1827. Among others were *Rights of All,* New York, 1829; *Colored American* (formerly *The Weekly Advocate*), New York, 1837; *The Elevator,* Albany, New York, 1842; *The Ram's Horn,* New York, 1847; *The North Star,* Rochester, New York, 1847; *The Christian Herald,* Philadelphia, 1848; *The Colored Man's Journal,* New York, 1851; *The Alienated American,* Cleveland, 1852; *The Mirror of the Times,* San Francisco, 1855; and *The Anglo African*, New York, 1859.

What was the importance of *Freedom's Journal*?

Freedom's Journal advocated the abolition of slavery and attacked anti-black sentiment. The newspaper was founded at 5 Varick Street in New York City. The first issue appeared on March 30, 1827. It was the first black-owned newspaper that opposed slavery and advocated for autonomy for slaves. It also sought to put the black cause before the American public, celebrated black achievement, and promoted racial pride. The editors wrote, "We wish to plead our own cause. Too long others have spoken for us." This statement has been quoted frequently in the history of the black newspaper. Later the newspaper changed names to become *Rights of All.* It was owned and edited by Presbyterian minister Samuel Eli Cornish (1795–1858) and abolitionist and colonizationist John Brown Russwurm (1799–1851).

When did black illustrated newspapers begin publication?

Edward Elder Cooper (1859-1908), journalist and editor, established *The Freeman,* in Indianapolis, Indiana, in 1888. This was the first black illustrated newspaper and the first to make a feature of portraits and cartoons. First published July 14, 1888, the news-

> ## What is the oldest, non-church, continually published black newspaper?
>
> The *Philadelphia Tribune,* first published in 1885, is the oldest continually published non-church newspaper.

paper reached national prominence and made a fortune for its owner. It also was a part of an exchange list with white newspapers and periodicals, something that no other black newspaper enjoyed at the time. Cooper was born in Smyrna, Tennessee, but moved to Philadelphia and then to Indianapolis. He enrolled in school in Indianapolis, graduating first in his class of sixty-five. He was the only black in the class. By 1882 he was working with the U.S. railway mail service. In 1883 Cooper joined Edwin F. Horn and others in publishing *The Colored World* in Indianapolis. Although the paper was an immediate success, sometime later Cooper severed his connection with it. In 1886 he returned to the paper, now known as the *Indianapolis World.* He sold out his interest a year later and began publishing *The Freeman.* The quality of the paper, coupled with his business skills, led I. Garland Penn in *The Afro-American Press* to call Cooper the greatest black journalist. Cooper's friend and neighbor W. Allison Sweeney noted in his sketch of Cooper in the *New York Age,* "I am glad that Edward Elder Cooper belongs to the negro [sic] race."

What **black woman journalist** was **society editor** for the *Boston Guardian* in the early 1900s?

Geraldine "Deenie" Pindell Trotter (1872–1918) was an editor, activist, entrepreneur, and civic worker. She came from a family of Boston militants and moved in Boston's elite black militant society as a staunch supporter of activism. In the 1850s, her uncle had led a movement to integrate public schools in Boston. Both Geraldine and her partner and husband William Monroe Trotter were dedicated to the cause of equal rights. She became society editor for the *Boston Guardian,* a journal that promoted equal rights for African Americans. It was founded by Monroe Trotter, W.E.B. Du Bois, and other black militants and anti-Booker T. Washington supporters. When the National Association for the Advancement of Colored People was founded in 1909, Geraldine Trotter became a member. She had joined the failing Niagara Movement but resigned because of internal conflict; it soon lost out to a new organization, the NAACP. Monroe Trotter's illness, around 1916, and subsequent imprisonment catapulted Geraldine Trotter to a higher leadership role at the paper. Then she saw first-hand the realities of racial agitation. Beyond the *Guardian,* Geraldine Trotter had a number of civic interests, including supporting the Saint Monica's Home for elderly black women. Later on, she formed a woman's antilynching committee and also joined the National Equal Rights League, which Monroe Trotter had helped to establish. During World War I she spoke before black soldiers at Camp Devens and she continued other efforts on behalf of the men. Her friend W.E.B. Du Bois said at her death that she "died as one whom death cannot conquer."

What newspaper was known as "The World's Greatest Weekly"?

Robert Sengstacke Abbott (1870–1940) first published the *Chicago Defender* in 1905. On May 6, 1905, he established what he called "The World's Greatest Weekly." The *Defender* reached national prominence

The building that once housed the offices of the *Chicago Defender.*

during the great black migration from the South during World War I, and by Abbott's death, he had turned it into the most widely circulated black weekly. Abbott was born in St. Simon's Island, Georgia; his father was of fully African heritage, while his mother was born in Savannah, Georgia. Abbott's father died in 1869, and when his mother remarried, he added his stepfather's name and became known as Robert Sengstacke Abbott. He studied at Claflin University in Orangeburg, South Carolina, Hampton Institute (later University), and Kent College of Law in Chicago. At Hampton, he focused on learning the printing trade, having worked earlier as an apprentice at the *Savannah Echo*. When he graduated from law school, as Robert Sengstacke Abbott. Abbott, he was the only African American in his class. At both Claflin and Hampton, Abbott, who was dark-skinned, was looked down upon by his lighter-skinned schoolmates; he was told by a prominent African-American lawyer that his complexion would be a disadvantage to him in the practice of law. These experiences influenced his decision to turn to printing. After he launched the *Defender,* the paper grew slowly, and Abbott had difficult financial years before the paper became a success. It became a full-sized newspaper in 1915, the first black newspaper to achieve this feat. In the beginning, Abbott's paper was focused on the black masses. As time passed, he came to favor gradualism as the approach to racial progress and became more entrenched in the Chicago establishment. In 1929 he was the first to attempt publication of a well-financed black magazine, *Abbott's Monthly*; the magazine survived until 1933. Abbott's news and columns as published in the *Defender* established him as a major spokesman for blacks during his lifetime.

What journalist was the **only black official war correspondent** during **World War I**?

In 1818 Ralph Waldo Tyler (1859–1921), reporter and government official, became the first, and only, black official war correspondent during World War I. Tyler worked in a variety of jobs on the way to becoming a well-known journalist. His job as a stenographer at the *Columbus Dispatch* in Columbus, Ohio, gave him his start in 1888. While working there Tyler gained journalistic skills and also developed and strengthened his interest in politics. He stayed with the *Dispatch* for seventeen years, serving for a while as society editor. After working for the *Ohio State Journal* from 1901 to 1904, Tyler's political activities and a friendship with Booker T. Washington led to his being appointed by President Theodore Roosevelt as an auditor in the Navy Department, where he served for nine years. Tyler lost this position in 1913 when the Woodrow Wilson administration removed black officeholders from their positions. While working as an organizer for the National Negro Business League, Tyler wrote columns that discussed the position of blacks in the South. In 1914 his columns were syndicated by the American Press Association.

Ralph Waldo Tyler was the only black journalist to cover World War I.

By 1917 Tyler was back in Washington as secretary of the National Colored Soldiers Comfort Committee. When both a representative of the government and black newspaper editors agreed that a first-class journalist was needed to document the experiences of black soldiers in France during wartime, Tyler was a logical choice. He continued to write on this subject for the remainder of his life, even after the war ended.

WOMEN AND THE EARLY PRESS

What **African-American woman** became an **early black newspaper editor**?

Mary Ann Shadd (Cary) (1823–1893) became the first black woman editor of a newspaper in North America, in 1853. She was editor and financier of the *Provincial Freeman,* published in Windsor, Ontario, Canada, one of several black anti-slavery newspapers. The paper condemned slavery, attacked the all-black settlements in Canada, and solicited funds to help fugitive slaves. Shadd was a dedicated abolitionist who used her many talents in journalism as a teacher and lawyer to fight vigorously for the cause. She grew up free and well-to-do in her parents' Delaware home, which often served as a shelter for runaway slaves. She attended a Quaker school in Pennsylvania for six years, after which she founded a Wilmington, Delaware, private school for black children where she taught from 1839 to 1850. Largely as a consequence of the Fugitive Slave Act of 1850, Shadd and one of her brothers moved to Windsor in 1851, and she became an advocate for black emigration to Canada. Shadd and her brother both began to teach in a segregated school, and in 1853 she published the first copy of the *Provincial Freeman*. The paper competed with Henry Bibb's publication, *Voice of the Fugitive,* which former slave Bibb also targeted toward blacks. Bibb and Shadd differed greatly in philosophy. Bibb saw Canada as a temporary home for American blacks and supported segregation; Shadd's views were just the opposite. She lectured frequently on racial themes and is recognized by both Canadian and American historians as the first educated black woman lecturer. After the Civil War, Shadd, who had married Canadian Thomas Cary in 1856, moved to Washington, D.C., where she was principal of three large school districts for seventeen years. She became the first woman to enroll in fledging Howard University's law department. In 1883 she received her law degree. Shadd later turned her attention to women's suffrage and became a staunch advocate, arguing the case before the House of Representatives Judicial Committee. Shadd's paper had a limited audience, and her writings often offended some, but she is recognized as one of the best editors in Canada at the time.

What was the **first black woman's weekly column** published in the *New York Freeman*?

Editor, journalist, and feminist Gertrude Bustill Mossell (1855–1948) began the first black woman's weekly column in the *New York Freeman,* in 1885. The column was known as "Our Women's Department"; it appeared in the first issue of the *Freeman,* in December. Mossell introduced her first column, on the subject "Woman's Suffrage," by saying that it was to be "devoted to the interest of women," and that she would continue to "promote true womanhood especially that of the African race." An educator and feminist, Mossell was born in Philadelphia into an elite free black family. She campaigned for equal rights and women's rights. For seven years she taught at various places in New Jersey and in Delaware, but left teaching after she married, as married women were forbidden to teach. After that she developed her career in journalism and became active in women's rights and in social reform movements.

What **newspaper** was the first **written** for and by **black women**?

The first newspaper written for and by black women was the *Woman's Era*. It began in 1894 and published news and activities of women's clubs throughout the country. The official organ of the National Association of Colored Women, *Woman's Era* had Josephine St. Pierre Ruffin (1842–1924) and her daughter, Florida Ruffin Ridley (1861–1943), as editors until 1900. Josephine Ruffin, a clubwoman, civic leader, and reformer, was born in Boston. She became a founding member of the Woman's Era Club (which she, Florida Ridley, and Maria Baldwin organized), the National Federation of Afro-American Women, the National Association of Colored Women, and the Northeastern Federation of Women's Clubs. Florida Ridley was a writer, educator, and social worker, as well as a clubwoman. She was born in Boston and educated at Boston Teachers College and Boston University. Ruffin became a teacher in Boston's public schools. In 1890 she founded the Society for the Collection of Negro Folklore, one of the earliest groups of black folklorists. She also aided her daughter in promoting a national organization of black clubwomen.

What **black woman** is thought to be the **first** to **own and publish a newspaper** in this country?

Charlotta Bass (1874–1969) is thought to be the first woman to own and publish a newspaper in this country. She bought the *California Owl* in 1912 and ran it for some forty years. Bass was the Progressive Party's vice-presidential candidate in 1952, another first for a black woman. Through her journalistic and political interests, she worked tirelessly on behalf of the elimination of racism and sexism. Bass was born in Sumter, South Carolina, and moved to Providence, Rhode Island, at age twenty, to work for a local newspaper. Ten years later,

Charlotta Bass (seen here with civil rights leader Paul Robeson) was owner and publisher of the *California Eagle*.

health reasons prompted her to move from Providence to Los Angeles, where she took a part-time job with the *Eagle*. The paper was suffering from both poor management and its editor's ill health. When Bass assumed control of the paper, in 1912, she renamed it the *California Eagle*. She was married to John Bass in the same year, and they combined their efforts toward combating racial discrimination.

The film *Birth of a Nation,* injustice in the military during World War I, the 1919 Pan-African Conference, the 1931 alleged rape case in Scottsboro, Alabama, and discrimination in employment were among the concerns that came under the *Eagle*'s scrutiny. In her lifetime, Bass ran for three political offices, but was not successful in any of these races. She was, however, the first black grand jury member for the Los Angeles County Court. Her memoirs, published in 1960 as *Forty Years: Memoirs from the Pages of a Newspaper,* reveal the important part that black people played in the development of Los Angeles.

What was the **first black daily newspaper** published in **twentieth-century** America?

On March 13, 1932, the *Atlanta Daily World* became the first black daily paper published in twentieth-century America. Although its founder, William A. Scott III, established the paper in 1928, it was at first a weekly and later expanded to become a daily paper. Scott envisioned the paper as an anchor for a chain of operations that he would establish, and he formed the Scott Newspaper Syndicate which, by 1934, printed over forty black newspapers. Scott's son, C. A. Scott, became editor in 1934 and ran operations until 1997, when he retired. The daily continues to serve metropolitan Atlanta; it is a weekly in print format and a daily online. M. Alexis Scott, granddaughter of the founder, is publisher.

PRESS CORRESPONDENTS
AND JOURNALISTS

Who was the first **black correspondent** to be admitted to a **White House press conference**?

Harry S. McAlpin (1906–1985) became the first black correspondent to be admitted to a White House press conference, in 1944. A correspondent for the National Negro Press Association and the Atlanta *Daily World,* he first attended a White House press conference on February 8, 1944. In 1947 the Negro Newspaper Publishers Association and individual newspaper correspondents were accredited to the Congressional Press Galleries and to the State Department. The journalists accredited at this time were James L. Hicks, accredited to the State Department; and Percival L. Prattis and Louis Lautier accredited to the House and Senate press galleries.

Who was the first **black woman** accredited to the **White House and the Congressional press galleries**?

In 1944 Alice Dunnigan (1906–1983) of the Associated Negro Press became the first black woman accredited to the White House and the State Department, and the first to gain access to the House of Representatives and Senate press galleries. At the State Department, she joined James L. Hicks, assistant chief of the Negro Newspapers Publishers Association, who had been the first black accredited to the department shortly before. Dunnigan was also the first black elected to the Women's National Press Club. In 1948 she became the first black news correspondent to cover a presidential campaign, when she covered Harry S. Truman's whistle-stop trip. She was chief of the Washington bureau of the Associated Negro Press for fourteen years. Dunnigan was born on April 27, 1906, near Russellville, Kentucky. She attended Kentucky State College (now University), earning a teaching certificate in elementary education, and later graduated from West Virginia Industrial College (now West Virginia State University); she often taught and attended school at the same time. Poor salaries for teachers and the need to do menial jobs when the schools were not closed led her to seek a government job. In 1942 Dunnigan obtained a job with the War Department in Washington, D.C., and by the end of the war she had risen to the level of economist in the Office of Price Administration. Her interest in writing had begun in her childhood; she wrote a local news column for the *Owenborough Enterprise,* a black-run publication, and continued to write in a variety of formats during her years in Kentucky. It was this background that led to her appointment as chief of the Associated Negro Press in Washington. Dunnigan served in a variety of government positions until 1970, when her Democratic Party allegiance proved to be a disadvantage. She continued to write after leaving government service, publishing her autobiography in 1974 and a second book in 1979. Dunnigan received numerous awards during her career, including induction into the Journalism Hall of Fame at the University of Kentucky in 1982.

What journalist was the first **full-time black reporter** for the *Washington Post*?

Journalist Simeon S. Booker (1918–) was the first full-time black reporter for the *Washington Post,* from 1952 to 1954. In 1982 he was the first black to be awarded the Fourth Estate Award by the National Press Club in Washington, D.C. Booker began his career as a reporter for the *Baltimore Afro-American*. During the 1950s he was a reporter for the *Cleveland Call and Post*. He left the *Post* in 1955 to work for the Johnson Publishing Company; he later became its Washington bureau chief. His reports of civil rights activities were highlighted in 1955, when he covered the trials of the men who lynched Emmett Till in Mississippi. He rode with the Freedom Riders in May 1961—the only journalist to do so—to protest segregated facilities on interstate bus travel. Although he was not harmed when the riders were attacked in Anniston, Alabama, he witnessed the beatings first-hand, reported the attacks to Attorney General Robert Kennedy, and later wrote about the experiences in *Ebony* magazine. He continued to write about the civil rights struggles of the 1960s and early 1970s. Booker interviewed U.S. presidents, a number of senators, and other Washington leaders and wrote about the interviews in his column "Ticker Tape U.S.A." Born in Baltimore, he and his family moved to Youngstown, Ohio, when he was five years old. He graduated from Virginia Union University in Richmond and did graduate study at Cleveland College. In 1992 Booker became the second black journalist to receive the Nieman Foundation Fellowship for study at Harvard University. The next year the Washington Association of Black Journalists presented him the Career Achievement Award for groundbreaking service in the field of journalism. The National Black Media Coalition, in 1998, awarded him the Master Communicator's Award.

What journalist used the *Pittsburgh Courier* as an advocate for **social change** for African Americans?

Activist Robert Lee Vann (1887–1940) used the newspaper that he edited, the *Pittsburgh Courier,* as an advocate for social change for African Americans. Born in North Carolina, he studied for a while at Virginia Union University in Richmond and became disturbed over deteriorating racial conditions in the South. He was affected by Booker T. Washington's autobiography, *Up from Slavery,* which helped to shape his ideas on racial pride and economic self-help for his race. Vann relocated to Pittsburgh where he continued his studies. After completing his law degree, he became one of only five black attorneys in Pittsburgh. By 1910 he was editor of the *Pittsburgh Courier*. He used

An illustration honoring Robert Lee Vann, who championed social change for African Americans as the editor of the *Pittsburgh Courier.*

the paper to crusade for improvement in areas of housing, health, education, employment, crime, and other issues that affected African Americans. Vann urged blacks to form their own financial institutions. He wanted more blacks to become medical doctors and pleaded for a hospital to serve the needs of the black community. The crafty journalist also worked to dispel negative images of blacks that the white press had promoted. He provided blacks with positive news on the local community—facts that the mainstream presses disregarded. The new black immigrants from the South were able to use the *Courier* to read news about their home states. His work with the *Courier* demonstrated his continuing interest in promoting racial pride.

Who was **Hazel B. Garland**?

Hazel B. Garland (1913–1988), who was named editor-in-chief of the *Pittsburgh Courier* in 1974, was the first woman head of a nationally circulated black newspaper in the United States. For more than fifty years her columns were published in various editions of the *Courier*. Some sources say that her greatest contributions were made behind the scenes, as she determined newspaper policy, made staff assignments to reflect social needs, and prepared those who would carry on her work. Hazel Barbara Maxine Hill Garland was born outside Terre Haute, Indiana, and died in McKeesport, Pennsylvania, where she had lived for over fifty years. She worked as a maid and at night spent her time dancing, singing, and playing the drums. Her plan was to become an entertainer. Her contact with the *Pittsburgh Courier* in 1943, when she was a reporter for the local YWCA in Pittsburgh, led to her appointment in 1946 as a full-time staff member. She wrote the column "Things to Talk About." In 1966 John Sengstacke purchased the paper and renamed it the *New Pittsburgh Courier,* and Garland became women's and entertainment editor. She was named editor-in-chief in 1972. The National Newspaper Publisher's Association named her "Editor of the Year" in 1974, the year in which Garland stepped down from her post.

Why was **Robert C. Maynard** known as an important journalist?

Robert C. Maynard (1937–1993) was the first black to direct the editorial operations of a major American daily, the *Oakland Tribune* in California, in 1979. In 1983 he became owner and publisher of the *Oakland Tribune* and the first black to become a majority shareholder in a major metropolitan daily newspaper. Maynard spent ten years at the *Washington Post* as its first black national correspondent, and later as ombudsman and editorial writer. On October 15, 1992, the name and certain assets of the *Oakland Tribune,* then the nation's only black-owned major daily newspaper, were sold to the Alameda Newspaper Group. Maynard was a high school dropout whose interest in writing surfaced when he was eight years old. While in high school in Brooklyn, he chose to spend his time at the offices of the *New York Age,* a black weekly newspaper of the time, instead of attending class. His involvement with the newspaper, which published some of his articles, led to his dropping out of school. Maynard's first big journalistic break came when he was hired as a police and urban affairs reporter for the York, Pennsylvania, *Gazette and Daily* in 1961; he later covered the Civil Rights Movement as well. Maynard added to his formal journal-

> ## Who was the first African-American journalist to win a Pulitzer Prize?
>
> In 1989 Clarence Page (1947–) became the first black columnist to be awarded a Pulitzer Prize. He joined the *Chicago Tribune* staff in 1969 and later became a syndicated columnist and editorial writer for the paper. His interest in journalism began in high school, and while there he won an award from the Southeast Ohio High School Newspaper Association for best feature article. He received a bachelor's degree in journalism from Ohio University in Athens in 1969 and went to work for the *Tribune* soon after. Following a brief tour of duty in the military, which interrupted his employment, he returned to the *Tribune* and made rapid progress. Page's column is nationally syndicated, and his freelance writings have appeared in a variety of sources. Among his other accomplishments, he is an author of longer works, having written his first book in 1996; a regular analyst for *ABC News*; and an occasional participant on several television news shows and PBS documentaries.

istic training when he was awarded a one-year Nieman Fellowship for journalists at Harvard University. His work at the *Post* led to national visibility: he was one of the only three journalists chosen as questioners for the final debate between presidential candidates Gerald Ford and Jimmy Carter. He was hired by the Gannett newspaper chain while on leave from the *Post* to pursue his strong interest in provision of training programs for aspiring minority journalists. When Gannett made him editor of the *Oakland Tribune,* Maynard made many improvements, but the paper ran into financial difficulties. After putting together sufficient funding, he purchased the *Tribune* when Gannett put it up for sale in 1983. The paper was financially unsuccessful, but it became a symbol of racial pride, and it won a Pulitzer Prize for its photographic coverage of the 1989 Bay Area earthquake. The *Tribune* was sold in 1992 after Maynard became terminally ill.

What African American was the first to **head** the *Los Angeles Times*?

The first black journalist to lead a top newspaper in United States was Dean P. Baquet (1956–). Baquet, who had already made a name for himself with the *Chicago Tribune* and the *New York Times,* took the number two spot at the *Los Angeles Times*—that of managing editor. In 2005 he was appointed editor of the paper and became the first black to head a major mainstream newspaper. He left that post in November 2006 and returned to the *New York Times* as chief of the Washington bureau and assistant editor. A native of New Orleans, Baquet studied at Columbia and Tulane Universities but gave up formal training without completing a degree. For seven years he did investigative reporting with the *States-Item* (later subsumed under the *Times-Picayune*) but left the New Orleans press in 1984 to join the *Chicago Tribune.* Later he became associate metropolitan editor for investigations. In 1988 Baquet shared a Pulitzer Prize for investigative reporting with fellow journalist Ann Marie Lipinski. He helped the paper receive thirteen Pulitzer prizes. He left the *Tribune* in 1990 and began investigative reporting for the *New York Times,* becoming deputy metro editor later on, and in 1995 national editor.

PERIODICALS

Who publishes *The Crisis* magazine?

The first issue of *The Crisis* magazine, the official organ of the National Association for the Advancement of Colored People (NAACP) and the vehicle for the dissemination of educational and social programs for blacks, was published in April 1910. Edited by W.E.B. Du Bois, *The Crisis* was first printed in one thousand copies, but by 1920 circulation had increased one-hundred-fold.

What **journal** was the official organ of the **National Council of Negro Women**?

In 1940 Sue Bailey Thurman (1903–1996) was the founder-editor of *Aframerican Women's Journal,* the first published organ of the National Council of Negro Women. (The title of the journal was changed to *Women United* in 1949.) Its purpose was to inform black women about major women's issues, legislation that affected them and blacks in general, to highlight women's accomplishments, and to report the projected work of the NCNW. Thurman also founded and was first chairperson of the council's library, archives, and museum department. The pioneering activist and wife of theologian Howard Thurman died in her sleep at a hospice in San Francisco, at age ninety-three.

Who was *Newsweek* magazine's **first black editor**?

In 1998 Mark Whitaker (1957–) became the first black editor of a major news weekly in the United States when he became editor of *Newsweek*. Whitaker, a Norton, Massachusetts, native, graduated from Harvard University in 1979. During the early 1980s he attended Balliol College at Oxford University as a Marshall Scholar. As early as 1977 he became associated with *Newsweek,* working as a reporting intern in the San Francisco office. In 1981 Whitaker became a stringer for the bureaus in Boston, Washington, and Paris. He became a full-time staff member in 1981, and worked with the New York City office. Whitaker became business editor for *Newsweek* in 1987, just in time to report on the stock market crash of that year. Then he reported on such scandals as insider trading and the savings-and-loan crisis. Whitaker was promoted again in 1991 when he was named assistant managing editor; he oversaw the publication of special issues, such as those devoted to the Olympics and the first inauguration of Bill Clinton as President of the United States. Whitaker was named editor of the magazine on November 10, 1998, and was the first black to hold such an influential position with a national weekly news magazine. Although he is interested in racial matters in this country, he has downplayed the issue of race in his selections and his work. He left that post in 2006 and became vice president and editor-in-chief of New Ventures at the

Washingtonpost.Newsweek Interactive. In 2007 he was named senior vice president of *NBC News* and Washington bureau Chief for *NBC News,* succeeding Tim Russert when Russert died. Whitaker became one of NBC's two highest-ranking black executives. In February 2011, he became executive vice president and managing editor for *CNN Worldwide*.

PHOTOJOURNALISM

What contributions did **Gordon Parks** make to **photojournalism**?

Gordon A. Parks Sr. (1912–2006) became the first black photojournalist on the staff of *Life* magazine, in 1949. Born Gordon Roger Alexander Buchanan Parks in Fort Scott, Kansas, he was the youngest of fifteen children. After his mother died when he was sixteen, Parks moved to St. Paul, Minnesota, to live with his sister and her family. He moved back and forth from St. Paul to Minneapolis and Chicago. While working as a waiter on the North Coast Limited, he was inspired to become a photographer. He began his career in 1937 with a camera purchased in a pawnshop; it became what he called his "weapon against poverty and racism." He returned to Chicago where he captured much of the South Side slums on his camera. Parks was the first black to receive a Rosenwald Fellowship for

photography; in 1942 he was the first black to work for the United States Farm Security Administration as a photographer; and, in 1943, the first to work for the United States Office of War Information as a photojournalist and war correspondent. Parks was named the Magazine Photographer of the Year in 1961. A gifted film director, he was the first black to direct movies for a major studio, including the feature film *Shaft*. He also gained fame for his autobiographical books, *A Choice of Weapons* and *The Learning Tree*.

What **photojournalist** became well-known for his **civil rights images,** but monitored activities of activists?

Trained as a photographer in World War II, Ernest C. Withers (1922–2007) documented over sixty years of African-American history. His visual images were devoted to the Civil Rights Movement, Negro Leagues Baseball, and the blues and R&B perfor-

In a twist on artist Grant Wood's well-known painting "American Gothic," photographer Gordon A. Parks Sr. titled this photo of cleaning woman Ella Watson as a comment on racism and poverty in America.

mances that he witnessed on Beale Street in his Memphis hometown. While serving in the war, the Army Corps of Engineers trained him as a photographer. When the war ended he returned to Memphis and established a commercial studio. Withers served the black newspaper industry, working as a freelance journalist for such newspapers as the *Tri-State Defender* and the old *Memphis World*.

In 1955 two white men had been accused of killing a black teenager from Chicago, Emmett Till, for supposedly whistling at the wife of one of the defendants. The men were acquitted but much later admitted that they committed the crime. Withers covered the trial in Sumner, Mississippi, and published the photographs that he took in booklet form. The booklet led to other assignments for Withers. The black press, including the *Chicago Defender, Jet,* and the *Baltimore African American,* gave him assignments, as did mainstream outlets including the *New York Times, Life, Time,* and the *Washington Post.*

As the Civil Rights Movement progressed, Withers captured key moments and events in the South. Among his subjects were Martin Luther King Jr. and Ralph Abernathy riding a bus in Montgomery, Alabama; the photograph was taken on December 1956, the first day that desegregation of the buses occurred. In 1957 Withers chronicled the integration of Little Rock High School in Arkansas and James Meredith's entrance into the University of Mississippi in 1962. He documented the funerals of Medgar Evers in 1963 and King in 1968. After his death, the real purpose of Withers's work became known. Recruited in 1958, he was a "racial" informant for the FBI. He helped the FBI infiltrate black power groups and monitored the work of activists during the Civil Rights Movement. He especially followed celebrities who visited his hometown of Memphis.

What photojournalist won a **Pulitzer Prize** for a **feature photograph**?

Moneta J. Sleet Jr. (1926–1996) won a Pulitzer Prize in 1969 for his photograph of Coretta Scott King and her daughter at the funeral of Martin Luther King Jr. Sleet covered many historical moments of the Civil Rights Movement, including the Montgomery Movement and the Selma to Montgomery March. He was with King in Norway when King accepted the Nobel Peace Prize. Sleet was born in Owensboro, Kentucky. A box camera that his parents gave him when he was a child marked the beginning of his enchantment with photography. He continued his training and graduated from Kentucky State College (later University), and then obtained his master's degree in journalism from New York University. He was staff photographer for Johnson Publishing Company for over four decades.

TELEVISION NEWSCASTERS

Who was **Louis Lomax**?

The first black newscaster, for WNTA-TV in New York City, was Louis Emanuel Lomax (1922–1970), in 1958. Lomax, an author, educator, and civil rights activist, was born in Valdosta, Georgia, and graduated from Paine College in Augusta, Georgia. He later received a master's degree from American University and a doctorate from Yale University. From 1947 to 1958 he was a journalist for both the *Baltimore Afro-American* and the *Chicago American*; he covered lynchings, riots, and leadership problems in the black community. Lomax was a freelance writer from 1958 to 1970. For two years he was also a news commentator on WNTA-TV in New York City, and from 1964 to 1968 for Metromedia Broadcasting. Around this time as well, Lomax was news analyst for KTTV in Los Angeles, news director for WNEW-TV in New York City, and news writer for the *Mike Wallace Show.* He was also a syndicated columnist for the North American Newspaper Alliance. For a while Lomax hosted his own television program in Los Angeles, called *Louis Lomax.* In addition to teaching at Georgia State University and Hofstra University, he wrote a number of books and contributed articles to *Life, Look,* and the *Saturday Evening Post.*

What was newscaster **Mal Goode**'s importance?

Mal (Malvin) Russell Goode (1908–1995) became the first black network news correspondent for any major television network when he was hired by ABC in 1962. Following that, CBS hired George Foster and Lee Thornton as White House correspondents. Born in White Plains, Virginia, Goode became the first black member of the National Association of Radio and Television News Directors, in 1971. He was well-known for his coverage of civil rights and human rights activities during the 1960s. From his parents, Goode received the dual message of the importance of both work and education. During his youth, and after his family moved to Homestead, Pennsylvania, he worked in the local steel mills to earn enough money to attend the University of Pennsylvania. After graduating from college, Goode had a number of jobs, including serving as manager of a Pittsburgh housing development, which was at the time one of the country's few racially integrated housing units. He began his career in radio journalism as a commentator for station KQV in Pittsburgh in 1949, moving soon after to station WHOD in Homestead to join his sister, who was a disc jockey there. During this same year, he began work in print journalism by working in the circulation department of the *Pittsburgh Courier*. His duties and responsibilities expanded at both WHOD and the *Courier,* and in 1952 he became the station's news director. When the station closed in 1956, he went to work at a McKeesport, Pennsylvania, station and also sought work at major stations in Pittsburgh, but was unsuccessful. Ten years later he was hired by ABC, based on a recommendation from baseball legend Jackie Robinson and his years of experience. He became nationally known for his coverage of the Cuban missile crisis, when he had major responsibility for reporting United Nations activities. He was one of three journalists chosen by ABC to conduct seminars for African students in 1963. He retired from ABC after twenty years, but remained an ABC consultant. He was a mentor to George Strait and to Bernard Shaw, who followed him as black television journalists.

What was *Black Journal*?

Tony Brown (1933–) became host of the first and longest-running minority affairs show on television, *Black Journal,* beginning in 1970. He also became a leading voice on black issues. He was founding dean of the School of Communications at Howard University in Washington, D.C., designed to provide blacks with a better chance of success in the field of communications. Brown was born in Charleston, West Virginia, and raised by a family friend. He graduated from Wayne State University in Detroit in 1959 and received his master's degree in social work from that school in 1961. He left the social work field to become drama critic for the *Detroit Courier*. After working his way up to city editor, Brown moved to WTVS, Detroit's public television station, where he worked in public affairs programming. He went on to produce *C.P.T. (Colored People's Time)*, which was the station's first program aimed toward a black audience. He later produced and hosted another community-oriented program, *Free Play*.

In 1968 the Corporation for Public Broadcasting (CPB) funded a new program, *Black Journal,* which was produced in New York at WNET-TV and broadcast nationally on public television. Brown was hired as executive producer and host of the show in 1970. His concern, however, was that its content failed to represent the national black community. First an hour show which aired once a month, he changed it to become a thirty-minute weekly. He hired a predominantly black staff to run the show. CPB cut off funding from 1973 to 1974. In 1977 Brown received funding from Pepsi Cola Company, changed its name to become *Tony Brown's Journal,* and moved to commercial stations. Another program of equal success, *Tony Brown at Daybreak,* later aired on WRC-TV in Washington, D.C. In 1982 he returned *Journal* to public television. Continuing his efforts to enhance black people, in 1980 he initiated Black College Day, designed to help save and support black colleges. Brown has been widely honored for his achievements. Among his awards were the National Urban League's Public Service Award in 1977, and an NAACP Image Award in 1991. In 1995 he received the Ambassador of Free Enterprise award; he was the first black so honored.

What **woman anchored** the newscast *The MacNeil/Lehrer Report*?

Charlayne Hunter-Gault (1942–) was the first black woman to anchor a national newscast, *The MacNeil/Lehrer Report,* in 1978. She left that post in 1997 when she moved to South Africa. In 1999 she joined CNN in Johannesburg, South Africa, as bureau chief. She was born in Due West, South Carolina, and moved to Atlanta with her parents and siblings in 1954. In January 1961 she and Hamilton Holmes were the first two black students to attend the University of Georgia, where they were confronted with a student riot protesting their admission. She started college at Detroit's Wayne State University while waiting for a federal court order that would allow her to attend the University of Georgia. She graduated with a bachelor's degree in journalism in 1963. Hunter-Gault's first job after graduation was as a secretary for *The New Yorker* magazine. While there she contributed articles to a feature section and wrote short stories.

A Russell Sage Fellowship allowed her to study social science at Washington University in St. Louis, Missouri, in 1967. She edited articles for *Trans-Action* while there and covered the Poor People's Campaign in Washington, D.C. This coverage led to her first television job as investigative reporter and anchorwoman of the evening local news at WRC-TV in Washington. A ten-year position at the *New York Times* followed, after which she went on to *MacNeil/Lehrer*. Hunter-Gault says her interest in journalism began at age twelve, with the comic strip reporter Brenda Starr as her idol. She gives the University of Georgia credit for her style of reporting. The university awarded her the prestigious George Foster Peabody Award in 1986. She also won two Emmys for her work with PBS.

Who was the **first** black person to **anchor** at **Cable News Network** (CNN)?

Bernard Shaw (1940–) was appointed chief Washington correspondent and became the first black anchor at Cable News Network (CNN), in 1980. In 1987 Shaw joined the major television networks in a nationally televised interview with President Ronald Reagan. The next year he moderated the second presidential debate in Los Angeles. Born in Chicago, Shaw attended the University of Illinois-Chicago. He received an early push toward a career in news when his father routinely brought four Chicago daily newspapers with him every day when he returned home from work. Edward R. Murrow, whose reporting was prominent on CBS, became his role model, and Shaw decided to become a broadcaster. He bought the *New York Times* regularly, visited Chicago commentator Clifton Utley, and frequented newsrooms as he sought to become familiar with the profession. Shaw was in the U.S. Marine Corps and stationed in Hawaii in 1961 when, after repeated attempts, he was able to get an appointment with Walter Cronkite to talk about a news career. The persistence shown by Shaw in his preparations came to be noted as one of the characteristics of his approach to reporting. While attending college after leaving the service, he worked without pay in the wire room of a Chicago radio station and became a paid reporter for the station when its format was changed to all-news. Before joining CNN, Shaw worked at other stations, both radio and television, until he decided to leave college when he was offered a job as White House correspondent for WIND in Washington, D.C., a position he held from 1968 to 1971. He worked for CBS for the next three years, and in Miami for ABC, from 1974 until 1979, as chief of the Latin American bureau. His move to CNN the next year resulted in the position he held until his retirement on February 28, 2001. During his tenure at CNN, Shaw was able to break a number of important news stories, including almost a full day's continuous coverage on the Persian Gulf War. Shaw's work has resulted in numerous awards, including an Emmy in 1989 in the News and Documentaries category, the Award for Cable Excellence as best news anchor in 1990, and the Cable Ace Award from the National Academy of Cable Programming for best newscaster of the year in 1991.

What **black television journalist** became well-known for his work on *60 Minutes?*

Ed (Edward R.) Bradley (1941–2006) became the first black co-editor of *60 Minutes,* a CBS television network weekly news program, in 1981. He replaced Dan Rather in 1980, but his first story aired in 1981. His previous assignments included serving as principal correspondent for *CBS Reports,* CBS News White House correspondent, anchor of the *CBS Sunday Night News,* and writing reports shown on *CBS Evening News with Wal-*

ter Cronkite. The Pennsylvania native graduated from Cheyney State College (now University). Bradley's first job after his 1964 college graduation was teaching sixth grade in Philadelphia. He had become a friend of a Philadelphia radio disc jockey while in college and continued to visit him at the station and to work as a volunteer jazz disc jockey and sometimes newscaster. After he personally covered the breaking story of a riot in Philadelphia, he accepted a paying job with the station in 1965. Bradley taught school by day and did his station work, which included music, news, and sports reporting, by night. His first CBS job came when he was hired at New York's WCBS Radio, an all-news station, in 1967. The stress of this job led him to move to Paris to live a less constrained and more artistic life, but his money soon ran out. CBS was able to lure him back in 1971 as a stringer for the Paris bureau. This was part-time work with payment by the story, and Bradley went back to work full-time as a CBS war correspondent. He was wounded while covering Vietnam and Cambodia and returned to the United States after the fall of Saigon, where his first assignment was coverage of Jimmy Carter's presidential campaign; he was assigned to cover the White House after the election. He remained a fixture at CBS. He had additional CBS assignments other than *60 Minutes* while on that program, but it is *60 Minutes* that made him a familiar and respected face on the television screen. Bradley earned an Emmy in 1981 for his interview of actress Lena Horne. Altogether, he earned eleven Emmys and numerous other awards.

Who was the *Chicago Tribune*'s first black **syndicated columnist**?

Vernon D. Jarrett (1921–2004), journalist and radio and television moderator, was a radical and fiery career journalist and an aggressive agitator. He used journalism to ensure that the achievements of blacks would be recognized. He also used the media to promote race matters, politics, urban affairs, and the history of his race. He was articulate and persuasive in his presentations in print and non-print media. Born in the small town of Saulsbury, Tennessee, near the Mississippi border, he was the son of Annie Sybil Jarrett and William Robert Jarrett, the children of former slaves. He graduated from historically black Knoxville College in Tennessee (1941) and continued his studies in 1946 at Northwestern University, where he studied journalism. From there he moved to the University of Kansas in Missouri in 1956, studying television writing and producing. Still later, in 1959, he studied urban sociology at the University of Chicago. By now he was well prepared for the positions that he would hold.

Although Jarrett taught at Northwestern University and at City Colleges of Chicago, as time passed his primary interest was journalism. In 1946 he joined the *Chicago Defender* as general assignment reporter. He joined the *Chicago Tribune* in 1970, becoming its first black syndicated columnist. He was also a columnist and a member of the editorial board for the *Chicago Sun Times,* posts that he held from 1983 to 1996. Then Jarrett became a talk-show host, producer, and commentator for WLS-TV, ABC's station in Chicago. Now he was in position to broadcast his views, which he did on the show *Black on Black,* serving as first moderator. Renamed *For Blacks Only,* and then *Face to Face with Vernon Jarrett,* the hour-long program gained popularity. Chicago's only black-owned radio station, WVON-AM—of which he was part-owner—aired his *Jarrett's Journal* beginning in 1996. The elder statesman was a part of numerous national and international media productions, and in 1992 the *MacNeil/Lehrer Report* selected Jarrett to analyze the final debate between President George H. W. Bush and presidential candidates Bill Clinton and Ross Perot. Jarrett was also a featured commentator for four of the five shows in the British Broadcasting Corporation's *The Promised Land*—a television series on black migration to the North after World War II. Jarrett was instrumental in promoting black journalists and their work, as seen in the Chicago Association of Black Journalists, the National Association of Black Journalists, and the Monroe Trotter Group at Harvard University, which he founded. He was a constant presence at the NABJ conventions and charged those presidents who succeeded him to keep advocacy for black journalists at the head of the association's goals. In founding the Trotter Group, he commemorated the work of William Monroe Trotter, a journalist and elite militant integrationist, who in the early twentieth century was an important black spokesperson. Jarrett further demonstrated his interest in race matters from 1977 until his death, serving as a member of the Advisory Board for the Race Relations Institute at Fisk University.

One of his prized activities was ACT-SO (Afro-Academic, Cultural, Technological and Scientific Olympics), which he founded and chaired. The program recognizes the academic and artistic talents of young blacks in grades nine through twelve in a manner similar to that given to star athletes. In 1977 the NAACP adopted ACT-SO as one of its major programs. With NAACP support and Jarrett's devotion to activities for young people, the program is active in over one thousand cities across the country.

Who was the first **black co-host** of *The Today Show*?

The first black co-host of *The Today Show* was Bryant Charles Gumbel (1948–), beginning in 1982. He had been co-host of NBC's Rose Bowl Parade since 1975, worked as chief anchor of NBC's televised football games, and in 1977 was co-host for Super Bowl XI. In 1988 he was NBC's host for the Olympics in Seoul, South Korea. When he replaced Tom Brokaw as co-host of *Today,* after sitting in for him for a few months before being officially named co-host, most of his previous broadcast experience had been in sports, which he acknowledges as his true love. Gumbel was born in New Orleans, Louisiana, but the family moved to Chicago

Sportscaster Bryant Gumbel became co-host of *The Today Show* in 1982 and later appeared on programs such as *The Early Show.*

when Bryant and his older brother Greg were infants. He is a 1970 graduate of Bates College, where he played both baseball and football. He wrote an article about Harvard's first black athletic director for *Black Sports,* which led to a contract with the magazine and to his becoming its editor nine months later. He became a weekly sportscaster for Los Angeles' KNBC-TV in 1972, moved to sportscaster on the evening news, and to sports director in a span of just eight months. For a time he worked for both KNBC and as co-host of the NFL pre-game show, commuting back and forth from Los Angeles to New York. He began to do more shows for NBC, and in 1980 was assigned to do three sports features a week for *Today.* When he took over the plum job of co-host of the show, it was in second place in the ratings. By spring 1985, it was in first place, where it remained for most of the Gumbel years. His stay on *Today* was not without controversy. Gumbel is regarded as a hard taskmaster and was given to expressing his opinions about aspects of the show and its cast members in sometimes unflattering terms. This and other instances of creative differences between Gumbel and the producers played a part in his decision to leave the show in 1997. He soon accepted a CBS offer to host *Public Eye,* a prime-time, magazine-format, weekly interview show. This show lacked *Today*'s longevity, and in 1999 Gumbel returned to the morning show beat as co-host of CBS's *The Early Show;* he left the show in 2002. He maintained multiple projects and still appears on his HBO sports show, *Real Sports.* Over the years he earned three Emmys and numerous other awards and honors, including two Image Awards from the National Association for the Advancement of Colored People, and was named Journalist of the Year by the Association of Black Journalists in 1993. He has also become known for his philanthropies, particularly his work on behalf of the United Negro College Fund.

Who is **Gwen Ifill**?

Gwen Ifill (1955–) was hired as moderator of Public Broadcasting System's *Washington Week in Review* in 1999, becoming the first black woman to host a prominent political talk show on national television. The veteran news reporter began her work in journalism in 1977, when she was a reporter for the *Boston Herald-American.* She left that post in 1989, and from 1981 to 1984 she was a reporter for the *Baltimore Evening Sun.* She joined the *Washington Post* in 1984 as a political reporter. From 1991 to 1994 Ifill was first congressional correspondent for the *New York Times'* Washington, D.C., bureau, then became White House correspondent. Her first assignment as congressional correspondent

A former journalist for the *Washington Post* and *New York Times,* Gwen Ifill was a panelist for *Washington Week in Review* in the 1990s and is a senior political correspondent for *PBS Newshour.*

was to join other reporters on a bus that trailed presidential candidate Bill Clinton. She served as panelist and occasional moderator from 1992 to 1999, before becoming moderator and managing editor of *Washington Week in Review*. When she made her debut on the show in the fall of 1999, producers began an advertising campaign for it, called "TV's Voice of Reason Has a New Face." Ifill is also senior political correspondent for *PBS Newshour* (previously *The News Hour with Jim Lehrer*). She received widespread public attention when she moderated the vice-presidential debate between Alaska Governor Sarah Palin and Senator Joe Biden on October 2, 2008. Born in New York City, Ifill was educated at Simmons College. In 2009 her book, *The Breakthrough: Politics and Race in the Age of Obama,* was published.

LITERATURE

EARLY AFRICAN–AMERICAN POETS

Who was the **first black American poet**?

In 1746 Lucy Terry Prince (c. 1730–1821), a slave and orator, was the first black American poet. "Bars Fight," written this year (her only known poem), was inspired by an Indian ambush of haymakers in the Bars, a small plateau near Deerfield, Massachusetts. It was not published until 1855, in Josiah Gilbert Holland's *History of Western Massachusetts*. Terry was kidnapped as an infant in Africa and brought to Rhode Island. In 1756 Terry married Abijah Prince and obtained her freedom. She is also noted for her determined, if unsuccessful, attempt to persuade Williams College (Massachusetts) to accept her son as a student—she is reported to have argued before the board of trustees for three hours.

Why was **Phillis Wheatley** important?

In 1773 Phillis Wheatley (c. 1753–1784), born on the west coast of Africa, published the first book of poetry by a black person in America (and the second published by a woman). *Poems on Various Subjects, Religious and Moral* was published in London, England. A Boston merchant, John Wheatley, had bought Phillis as a child of about seven or eight, and had allowed her to learn to read and write. Wheatley's first

A slave to merchant John Wheatley of Boston, Phillis Wheatley was the first black person to publish a book of poetry in America.

published poem, "On the Death of the Reverend George Whitefield," appeared in 1770 in a Boston broadside. In 1773 she traveled abroad with the Wheatley's son, partly in the hope of restoring her health with exposure to sea air, and she attracted considerable attention in England as a poet. It was at about this time that she was freed. Deaths had ended the connection with the Wheatley family by 1788, when she married a freeman, John Peters. Her first two children died, and at the end of her life she worked as a maid in a boarding house to support herself. She died in December, followed the same day by her third child, an infant.

Who was the **first poet** and tract writer to **publish a poem** as a **separate work**, in America?

In 1760 Jupiter Hammon (1711–c. 1806), poet and tract writer, was the first black to publish a poem as a separate work, in America. This poem was the eighty-eight lines of "An Evening Thought. Salvation by Christ, with Penitential Cries: Composed by Jupiter Hammon, a Negro belonging to Mr. (Henry) Lloyd of Queen's Village on Long Island, the 25th of December, 1760." Born a slave on Long Island, Hammon revealed an intensely religious conviction of the Methodist variety in this and his other publications. He became noteworthy as well for providing the first and most comprehensive writing on black theology and was the first to write anti-slavery protest literature in America.

Who was the **first Southern black** to publish a **collection of poetry**?

George Moses Horton (1797–c. 1883) was the first Southern black to publish a collection of poetry. *The Hope of Liberty,* containing twenty-one poems, was published in Raleigh, North Carolina, in 1829. He anticipated that proceeds from this volume would pay his way to Liberia. As with all his attempts at gaining freedom before Emancipation, this was unsuccessful. Somehow Horton managed to educate himself and establish a connection with the University of North Carolina in Chapel Hill. He purchased his own time from his owners at twenty-five cents a day, later fifty cents. A tolerated character at the university, he seems to have earned part of his money by writing poems for undergraduates. In 1866 he had moved to Philadelphia and toward the end of his life wrote and published prose to earn a living. He also adapted Bible stories by changing names and events to fit the times. His works were found in different publications, since he sold them where he could. He may have returned South before he died around 1883.

Who was the **first black poet** to gain **national fame**?

Paul Laurence Dunbar (1872–1906) was the first black poet to gain national fame, in 1893. Born in Dayton, Ohio, Dunbar was accepted wholeheartedly as a writer and widely recognized in the late nineteenth century. His literary promise was recognized first when he graduated from high school in 1891. At that time he delivered the class poem that he had written. Financially unable to support himself while he studied law, Dunbar developed his literary talent and became a man of letters. He first worked as an elevator operator while he read widely and honed his writing skills, which led him to become founder and editor of the Dayton *Tattler* (1889–1890). After that he worked briefly as a clerk at Chicago's World's Columbian Exposition (1893), as court messenger (1896), and assistant clerk at the Library of Congress (1897–1898). His writings began to appear in print and reflected his use of dialect and standard English in his work. Dunbar's poems were published in the *Dayton Herald* as early as 1888. His first book, *Oak and Ivy,* appeared in 1893, and two years later his second book, *Majors and Minors,* attracted the attention of the celebrated critic William Dean Howells. His third book, *Lyrics of Lowly Life* (1896), gained him his national reputation. He published a number of other works, including collections of short stories, collections of poems, and works of fiction.

Best known as a poet, Paul Laurence Dunbar was a writer who gained national renown with collections published in the late-nineteenth century.

EARLY BLACK AMERICAN PROSE

Who was the **first African American** to have works of **prose published**?

Briton Hammon was the first black American writer of prose, in 1760. His fourteen-page work, *A Narrative of the Uncommon Sufferings and Surprising Deliverance of Briton Hammon, A Negro Man-Servant to General Winslow, of Marshfield in New England; Who Returned to Boston, after Having Been Absent almost Thirteen Years,* was published in Boston. This fourteen-page account tells of his providential escape from captivity by Indians, and then from his Spanish rescuers. Although it is known that Hammon was an autobiographer, little else is known about him.

What black American was the **first** to publish a **short story**?

In 1859 Frances Ellen Watkins Harper (1825–1911) wrote "The Two Offers," the first short story published by a black woman in the United States. It appeared in the *Anglo-African* magazine in 1859. Harper was born in Baltimore, Maryland, of free parents. By age fourteen she had a fairly good education for the time and was already established as a writer and scholar. She became a noted speaker in the abolition movement, including that as permanent lecturer for the Maine Anti-Slavery Society. After the Civil War her lectures addressed such issues as the suffrage and temperance movements as well as women's rights. Often she interspersed poetry throughout her lectures. Although her poems addressed a variety of issues, Harper is often referred to as an abolitionist poet; she was also the most popular black poet of her time. Her first volume appeared in 1845, when she was twenty-one years old. She was an extremely successful poet—*Poems on Miscellaneous Subjects* launched her career and is reported to have sold fifty thousand copies by 1878, and her novel *Iola Leroy* (1892) had three editions printed.

SLAVE NARRATIVES

What is a **slave narrative**?

A slave narrative is an intimate view of the life of one who was a slave in America during its early times. It is an autobiography and a memoir. Since few slaves learned to read or write, their stories were often told to another: a scribe, or a sympathetic white person of good social standing and importance. Whether or not the scribe took editorial liberties with the story is unknown, and in some cases this is exactly what makes some scholars skeptical about the truth of the slave narrative.

In 1789 *The Interesting Narrative of the Life of Olaudah Equiano, or Gustavus Vassa, the African, Written by Himself* was published; it has been called the first critically important slave narrative. As the title indicates, it was, indeed, written by Equiano, or Gustavus Vassa. Unlike American slaves, he was educated and financially able; he gave testimony to his work for abolition in Great Britain and the United States.

The best known slave narrative is *Narrative of the Life of Frederick Douglass, an American Slave, Written by Himself* and published by Boston's Anti-Slavery Office in 1845. Written in the slave narrative genre as well were Douglass's *My Bondage and My Freedom* (1855) and *The Life and Times of Frederick Douglass* (1881). Other popular slave narratives were *Slave Insurrection*, by Nat Turner (1831), who gave accounts of his plan to lead a great destruction to bring about freedom for slaves; *Narrative of William W. Brown, a Fugitive Slave, Written by Himself* (1845); *Narrative of Sojourner Truth, a Northern Slave, Emancipated from Bodily Servitude by the State of New York, in 1818* (1850);

Frederick Douglass's slave narrative was so enormously popular it launched his successful speaking career.

Running a Thousand Miles for Freedom; or the Escape of William and Ellen Craft from Slavery (1960); and Harriet Ann Jacobs's *Incidents in the Life of a Slave Girl, Written by Herself* (1861).

So popular was Douglass's work that it spurred a speaking career for him; others had invitations as well to tell their stories and to work on behalf of the abolition movement. Some slave narratives remain unpublished and thus were lost to literary history for many years. Supplementing this source of information on slaves are the oral history interviews on former slaves collected by the Federal Works Progress Administration in the 1930s, and others that sociologist Charles Spurgeon Johnson collected while leading studies at Fisk University, which were published as *God Struck Me Dead* (Pilgrim Press, 1969). The slave narrative is often included in literature courses on college and university campuses and discussed as well in works on African-American literature.

Who wrote the **first pamphlets** calling for **slave revolts** in America?

In 1829 David Walker (c. 1796–1830) published the first pamphlet by an American black calling for a slave revolt, *David Walker's Appeal*. Born in Wilmington, North Carolina, he was the son of a free mother and a slave father. Since his mother was free, by law he took her status and was also free. He wandered across the South before settling in Boston in 1825, where he was the proprietor of a shop buying and selling secondhand clothing. Walker worked quickly to make his mark on Boston's black community, becoming active in the Massachusetts General Colored Association. He assured his fame by publishing *Appeal, in Four Articles, Together with a Preamble, to the Colored Citizens of the World, But in Particular, and Very Expressly to Those of the United States of America*. Despite efforts to suppress it, the *Appeal* became one of the most widely circulated pamphlets of the time. The circulation of the work became a crime in the South, and a bounty was placed on Walker's life. In 1848 *The Appeal* was published with Henry Highland Garnet's *Address* (1843), another call to revolt, in a volume financially supported by abolitionist John Brown.

What was the **earliest unpublished novel** written by a black **woman slave**?

The earliest known manuscript of an unpublished novel by a black woman slave, *The Bondswoman's Narrative,* by Hannah Crafts, was written around 1857. (Analysis of the document places its authorship between 1853 and 1860.) The manuscript, which went unnoticed for over 140 years, is probably the earliest known novel by a black woman anywhere, slave or free. It may be one of only a few novels by black slaves in America as well. Years later a book dealer in New Jersey acquired the work. In 1948 Dorothy Porter Wesley (1905–1995), then head of the Moorland-Spingarn Research Center at Howard University, acquired the manuscript in the belief that the author was a black American slave woman. She helped to authenticate her belief by noting that the author introduced and treated black characters as people without regard to race, while white writers introduced them with assured reference to their race. The manuscript surfaced again in 2001 at auction at the Swann Galleries in New York. Henry Louis Gates (1950–), chair of Harvard University's Black Studies Department, was the single bidder for the manuscript and acquired it for less than $10,000. He sold the rights to Warner Books for an undisclosed advance against royalties. The novelist, Hannah Crafts, was a slave on the John Hill Wheeler plantation in North Carolina. In spring 1857 she escaped to New Jersey and wrote the novel, combining accounts of her life as a house slave, stories from works she had seen earlier, and her experiences later on as a teacher in the North. Gates edited the work and it was published by Warner Books in April 2002.

What was the **first dissertation** written by an **African slave**?

The first dissertation written by an African slave was *The Agony of Asar: A Thesis on Slavery by the Former Slave, Jacobus Elisa Johannes Capitein, 1717–1747*, published in 1742. It is also the first scholarly work by an African slave. Capitein's master took him from Guinea to Holland in 1828 and freed him. After that, grants from the wealthy enabled him to receive an education at the University of Leiden. Capitein returned to Guinea as a missionary. His work refutes the authors of antiquity and shows that slavery violated the principles of natural freedom and equality. He also rebuts Aristotle's doctrine of natural slavery.

When did the **first known slave narrative** written by a black American appear?

A Narrative of the Life and Adventures of Venture, a Native of Africa: But Resident Above Sixty Years in the United States of America Related by Himself, published in 1798, was the first slave narrative written by a black American. The work is also important because it illustrates the life of slave and free blacks in Connecticut during the eighteenth century. Venture (Broteer Smith; 1729–1805) recalls his royal descent in Africa, his slavery in Connecticut and Long Island, New York, and his prosperity after he was able to purchase his freedom by the age of forty-six. There are precursors to Venture's narrative, but they were written down by whites, like *Some Memoirs of the Life of Job* (1734), by Thomas Bluett; difficult to credit fully, like *A Narrative of the Lord's Dealings with John Marrant* (1789); or complete fictions. The author of the very important *The Interesting Narrative of the Life of Olaudah Equiano* (1789) spent only a few days in the American Colonies.

Who was the first black **woman** to publish a **slave narrative**?

The first slave narrative published by a black woman in the Americas was *The History of Mary Prince, West Indian Slave*. The narrative was published in 1831.

Who was the **first black woman** to publish a **novel**?

Harriet E. Adams Wilson (c. 1827–1870) was the first black woman to publish a novel. *Our Nig; or, Sketches from the Life of a Free Black, In A Two Story White House North, Showing That Slavery's Shadows Fall Even There* was published on August 18, 1859, in Boston, where she was living alone after her husband had abandoned her and her son. She hoped to realize money from the book to reunite herself with her son, but he died before this was accomplished. The book was also the first novel published in the United States by a black man or woman; William Wells Brown's *Clotel* and Frank J. Webb's *The Garies and Their Friends* were both published in England. *Our Nig* presents social, racial, and economic brutality suffered by a free mulatto woman in the antebellum North. Although several copies of the work are extant, including one at Fisk University, in the early 1980s scholar Henry Louis Gates rediscovered the book and removed it from obscurity.

What was the **first autobiography** published by an **American black woman**?

The first autobiography by an American black woman was *The Life and Religious Experiences of Jarena Lee, a Coloured Lady* by religious leader Jarena Lee (1783–?), published in 1836. Lee was a nineteenth-century evangelist and itinerant preacher who called herself "the first female preacher of the First African Methodist Episcopal Church." In her lifetime she published two autobiographies; the second, *Religious Experiences and Journal of Jarena Lee,* was published in 1849. Little is known about her life after that time.

What was the **first black history** founded on **written documentation**?

The first black history founded on written documentation is *The Colored Patriots of the American Revolution* by William Cooper Nell (1816–1874). Although deficient as history by modern standards, it nonetheless contains materials of lasting value. Nell's work began as a twenty-three-page pamphlet in 1851 and was published in 1855. A native of Boston, Nell came from a relatively privileged family. He joined the First African Baptist Church, that Thomas Paul founded, and was educated in the black school that operated in the church's basement. In 1826 he was a founding member of the Massachusetts General Colored Association and became an associate of David Walker, who wrote *Walker's Appeal*. Nell was a major leader in the ultimately successful fight to desegregate the Massachusetts public schools, as well as an associate of William Lloyd Garrison and Frederick Douglass in the abolition movement.

William Cooper Nell penned *The Colored Patriots of the American Revolution,* the first black history based on documentation.

Who was **William Wells Brown** and why was he important?

In 1853 William Wells Brown (1814–1884) became the first black novelist. His novel, *Clotel; or, The President's Daughter: A*

Narrative of Slave Life in the United States, was published in England. The son of a slave mother and plantation owner, Brown was born near Lexington, Kentucky. In 1816 his master, John Young, moved his family and his slaves to a farm in the Missouri Territory and later to St. Louis. While in Missouri, Brown worked as Young's office boy and learned to prepare medicine and administer to slaves who were ill. After being sold several times and several escape attempts, Brown escaped successfully on January 1, 1834. He became active in the abolitionist movement, and in 1843 he became an agent of abolitionist societies. Brown spent five years in Europe championing emancipation and wrote the first book of travel, *Three Years in Europe,* in 1852, and the first dramatic work by an American black, *Experience; or How to Give a Northern Man a Backbone,* in 1856. His second play, *Escape; or, A Leap for Freedom,* also written in 1856, was the first play published by an American black. Brown wrote more than a dozen books and pamphlets. He was also a physician and maintained a practice until his death; his interest also turned to writing the history of black achievement.

The first black American novelist was William Wells Brown, who published *Clotel; or, The President's Daughter: A Narrative of Slave Life in the United States* in 1853.

What was the **mood of black writers** in **post-Reconstruction** America?

Perhaps the greatest satisfaction for black writers early on was to have the freedom to write; in fact, knowing how to read and write was a tremendous accomplishment for many post-Reconstruction African Americans.

For Frederick Douglass to write stirring diatribes against slavery powerful enough to shake the consciousness of a nation was more a political than an artistic accomplishment. Likewise, when Jupiter Hammon, George Moses Horton, and Frances E. W. Harper prosaically wrote about the evils of slavery and racism, their verse seemed somewhat stilted; they followed the molds of Methodism, neoclassicism, and the Bible, traditions ill-suited to their subject matter. However admirable their writing was, they never quite found a vehicle that fit their revolutionary thoughts.

As the bonds of slavery were loosened, black writers clamored to be heard, but the range of their work was limited. Since slavery and plantations were practically the only subjects in their repertoire, early African-American works were often locked into these themes. In addition, being a black writer before 1920 was a unique profession, almost an oddity. Many writers were essentially unknown during their lives. Still others, like

Phillis Wheatley and George Moses Horton, gained a certain amount of acclaim. In fact, a number of blacks, including Paul Laurence Dunbar and Charles W. Chesnutt, became appreciated as writers.

White society controlled much of the early publishing in America, and African-American works were often filtered and distorted through this lens. As a result, much of the post-Reconstruction era work by African Americans was an attempt to prove that blacks could fit into middle-class American society. Much of the literature was an attempt by blacks to appear happy with their assigned lot. Yet some writers—Paul Laurence Dunbar and Charles Waddell Chesnutt, for example—tried to break the chains of this imposed expression by presenting a view of black life as it really was, not as society wanted it to be.

What is the importance of **George Washington Williams**?

George Washington Williams (1849–1891) was the author of the first major history of blacks in America. His *History of the Negro Race in America from 1619 to 1880,* published in 1882 in two volumes, was a major event and earned him respect for meeting the standards of professional historians. Williams was born in Bedford Springs, Pennsylvania, and spent time in a home for refugees. A wayward teenager, he changed his name and, in the summer of 1864, joined the Union Army. After his discharge in 1868, Williams received a license to preach in a church in Hannibal, Missouri, and attended Wayland Seminary in Washington, D.C. On June 10, 1874, he completed the theological program at Newton Theological Institution near Boston. While he was pastor of Twelfth Baptist Church in Boston, he wrote his first historical work, *History of the Twelfth Baptist Church*. In 1875 he was ordained as a Baptist minister but later turned to law and politics, serving a term in the Ohio legislature. Williams passed the Ohio Bar in 1881 and returned to

Boston in 1883, where he became a member of the Massachusetts Bar. His active life did not preclude the collection of materials for his histories. His other writings include the valuable *History of the Negro Troops in the War of the Rebellion* in 1877. His last efforts were attacks on the inhumane government of the Congo Free State, following an 1890 visit there.

Who was the **first** known black writer to depict a **black detective** in a **novel**?

Between 1907 and 1909, John Edward (Bruce Grit) Bruce (1856–1924) serialized "The Black Sleuth" in *McGirt's Magazine* and became the first known writer to depict a black detective in a novel. His work was a forerunner of detective novels by such au-

George Washington Williams's *History of the Negro Race in America from 1619 to 1880* is the first major history of blacks in America to be published.

thors as Rudolph Fisher and Chester Himes. Born a slave in Piscataway, Maryland, he studied at Howard University for a while and then became a journalist, editor, historian, and a popular public speaker. A militant writer for the black press, during his career he wrote for over twenty newspapers, some of which appeared in the white press. His famous column that appeared in the *Cleveland Gazette* and the *New York Age* was called "Bruce Grit," the name by which he was also known. In 1911 he was a cofounder, with Arthur A. Schomburg and others, of the Negro Society for Historical Research. John Cullen Gruesser of Kean University edited Bruce's work and published it in book form in June 2002.

LITERATURE OF THE HARLEM RENAISSANCE ERA

When did the Harlem Renaissance occur?

The Harlem Renaissance, sometimes called the New Negro Movement and the Negro Renaissance, has been variously dated. Dates for its beginning have been cited as around 1910, the mid-1910s, and 1920. Some claim that it formally began in 1925, when scholar, Howard University professor, and architect of the Harlem Renaissance Alain Leroy Locke published the anthology, *The New Negro*, bringing out works by rising African-American writers. Some sources believe that it ended in 1929, with the stock market crash, which sent the writers and artists out of Harlem to look for new opportunities. Most sources agree that it ended around the mid-1930s. The end has also been marked as 1940, when Richard Wright published his famous *Native Son,* which led to a new direction of black writing. Still others say that it closed when Langston Hughes, the last major writer of that period, died in 1967.

What led to the literary developments during the period known as the Harlem Renaissance?

The Harlem Renaissance is generally regarded as the first literary movement in African-American literature. Although its title suggests that the movement occurred in the Harlem section of New York City, it existed as well in other large urban areas of the United States where many African Americans from the South had relocated. Alain Leroy Locke led and shaped the movement during which Upper Manhattan became a hotbed of creativity in post–World War I America. It also marked the beginning of when white Americans (principally intellectuals and artists) gave serious attention to the culture of African Americans. This literary and cultural movement resulted from black America's need to celebrate its culture and racial identity. No longer were they preoccupied with the ills that slavery caused, and they sought new ways to define themselves, their ancestors, their talents, and their culture.

Literature only partially characterized the full developments of the renaissance period. Jazz and blues music also flourished during the prosperous times of the postwar era. During the 1920s and 1930s Louis Armstrong, "Jelly Roll" Morton, Duke Ellington, Bessie Smith, and Josephine Baker rose to prominence as well. Their contributions to music performance are still felt by artists and audiences today.

Who supported the literary developments of the Harlem Renaissance?

During this cultural movement, the benevolence of a handful of individuals ensured the success of the writers, poets, and artists who emerged and achieved lasting literary success. One of them, Charlotte Osgood Mason (or Charlotte Vandervere Quick), an enormously wealthy and influential white woman, became known as "Godmother" of the Harlem Renaissance. Among her "subjects," or those she supported, were Langston Hughes, Claude McKay, Zora Neale Hurston, and Alain Leroy Locke. At one time Hughes, who according to esteemed historian David Levering Lewis was her "most precious child," received the equivalent of a "blank check" from Mason to sustain himself while writing and studying at Lincoln University.

Further, Lewis identified what he called "The Six," (six artists who led the Renaissance) including three that Langston Hughes named and three more that Lewis added. Hughes saw Jessie Redmon Fauset at *The Crisis,* Charles S. Johnson at *Opportunity,* and Alain Locke, a Howard University professor who helped to shape the movement. Charles S. Johnson, editor of *Opportunity,* the official organ of the National Urban League, also gave the new writers a chance to showcase their poems, short stories, and novels in that journal. He and the journal also sponsored annual literary contests and offered awards to those whose works were considered especially noteworthy during a particular year. Lewis named Walter White, an NAACP officer and writer, who was also influential among powerful people in America; Caspar Holstein, wealthy numbers king; and James Weldon Johnson, sometimes called "Godfather of the Harlem Renaissance." Despite the work of influential W.E B. Du Bois, Lewis (who won two Pulitzer Prizes for biographies on Du Bois) declared that Du Bois "would never join The Six." As literary editor of the NAACP's *The Crisis* magazine, however, Du Bois published works by the emerging writers and artists. Without these influential contributors, there would have been a much shorter list of what Lewis identified as "twenty-six novels, ten volumes of poetry, five Broadway plays, innumerable essays and short stories, two or three performed ballets and concerti, and the large output on canvas and sculpture." In 1926, the magazine *Survey Graphic* showcased the work of these artists in its special issue on Harlem. The influential white patron and lesser benefactor was Carl Van Vechten, who helped to underwrite the literary prizes given to black cultural artists in 1926. Publisher Boni and Liveright announced a $1,000 prize that year for the best novel on black life written by a black author. Prizes were also funded by donations from black banks, black insurance companies, Amy Spingarn, and elsewhere.

Who were the literary artists of the Harlem Renaissance?

Important writers of this era include Countee Cullen, Jessie Redmon Fauset, Langston Hughes, Zora Neale Hurston, Nella Larsen, and Claude McKay. They were the younger

literary artists of the time, and older writers, established writers, critics, and editors encouraged them to produce.

Poet Countee Cullen (1903–1946) was born in Baltimore and adopted by the Reverend Frederick Cullen, who was pastor of New York's Salem Methodist Church. While a student at New York University in 1925 he completed a volume of poetry called *Color* and two years later received the Harmon Foundation's first gold medal for literature. He received his master's degree from Harvard in 1926 and the next year completed *The Ballad of the Brown Girl* and *Copper Sun*. In 1929 his work *The Black Christ* was published. Cullen spent two years in France on a Guggenheim Fellowship, returned to New York and taught in the public schools while continuing to write. He wrote *One Way to Heaven* (1932), *The Medea and Other Poems* (1925), *The Lost Zoo* (1940), and *My Lives and How I Lost Them* (1942).

Poet Countee Cullen relaxing in New York's Central Park. Cullen was known for such works as *The Black Christ* and *The Medea and Other Poems*.

Author, educator, and editor Jessie Redmon Fauset (1882–1961), came from a family with a strong commitment to racial uplift. She graduated from Cornell University in 1905, held membership in the prestigious honor society Phi Beta Kappa, and was the first black woman to graduate from that university. After receiving her master's degree from the University of Pennsylvania in 1919, she spent several years as a teacher. Fauset was a key figure during the Harlem Renaissance and is often referred to as "the Mother of the Harlem Renaissance." While editor of *The Crisis* magazine from 1919 to 1927, she supported the careers of many young artists, including Zora Neale Hurston and Langston Hughes. Fauset wrote her first novel, *There is Confusion,* in 1924. She left *The Crisis* in 1927 and established a literary career by publishing novels *Plum Bun* (1929), *The Chinaberry Tree* (1931), and *Comedy American Style* (1933). Her works focused on the racism and sexism that black women confronted, while educating her audience about the abilities of blacks and the opportunities that African Americans should have received. She returned to teaching in her later years.

Langston Hughes (1902–1967), poet, novelist and playwright, was born in Joplin, Missouri, and moved to Cleveland when he was fourteen. He spent a year in Mexico and then studied at Columbia University. He roamed the world as a seaman, wrote poetry during his travels, and returned to the United States. While attending Lincoln University in Pennsylvania, Hughes won the Bynner Prize for undergraduate poetry. He received the Harmon Award in 1930 and a Guggenheim Fellowship in 1935, which enabled him to travel to Russia and Spain. Hughes's prose works include *Not Without Laughter* (1930), a novel *The Big Sea* (1940), and his autobiography *I Wonder as I Wander* (1956). His collections of poetry include *The Weary Blues* (1926), *The Dream Keeper* (1932), *Shakespeare in Harlem* (1942), *Fields of Wonder* (1947), and *Selected Poems* (1959). Hughes was an accomplished song lyricist, librettist, and columnist for the *Chicago Defender*. Through his columns, he created Jesse B. Simple, a Harlem character who saw life on the musical stage in *Simply Heavenly*. Hughes edited several anthologies published in the 1960s, and his play *Mulatto* was produced on Broadway in the 1930s.

A gifted novelist, playwright, poet, and columnist, Langston Hughes was a leader in the Harlem Renaissance frequently noted for his innovative jazz poetry.

Novelist Nella Larsen (1891–1964), was born in Chicago and attended the high school program at Fisk University. In 1915 she received a nursing degree from the Lincoln School of Nurses in New York City. Although she worked in nursing, her interest in writing never waned. In the 1920s she became immersed in the literary and political activities of the times. She is best known for two novels, *Quicksand* (1928), which won her a bronze medal from the Harmon Foundation, and *Passing* (1929), for which she received a Guggenheim Fellowship in creative writing in 1930. Larsen's work focused on black women's sexuality and the social expectations of women of color, particularly those who were of mixed race as she was.

Poet and novelist Claude McKay (1889–1948) was born in Jamaica (then British West Indies). He began writing at an early age. Two books of his poems, *Songs of Jamaica* and *Constab Ballads,* were published just after he turned twenty; they include extensive use of Jamaican dialect. McKay moved to America in 1913 to study at Tuskegee Institute (now University) and at Kansas State University. His interest in poetry prompted him to relocate to New York City, where he published his work in small literary magazines. He visited England and, while there, completed a collection of lyrics, *Spring in New Hampshire*. In 1922 he completed *Harlem Shadows,* a landmark work of the Harlem Renaissance. McKay turned to the writing of novels, and produced *Home to Harlem* (1928), *Banjo* (1929), and four other books, including an autobiography and a study of Harlem. He wrote his famous poem, "If We Must Die," to assail lynchings and mob violence in the South. His *Selected Poems* (1948) was published posthumously in 1953.

Why has **Zora Neale Hurston** become a cultural **icon of the Renaissance?**

Novelist and folklorist Zora Neale Hurston (1891–1960) was born in Eatonville, Florida, an all-black town. Eatonville, sometimes called the first incorporated black town in America, is now an all-black town of current celebration. Hurston left home at age fourteen to work with a traveling Gilbert and Sullivan theatrical troupe. She left the troupe when it arrived in Baltimore, Maryland, and entered high school, graduating in 1918. She entered Howard University in 1924, taking courses intermittently. While there she was influenced by Alain Leroy Locke. In 1921 Hurston published her story, "John Redding Goes to Sea," in the school's literary magazine. Hurston moved to New York in 1925 and became absorbed in the Harlem Renaissance; she befriended and worked alongside such writers as Claude McKay, Eric Waldron, Jean Toomer, Langston

Best remembered for her acclaimed 1937 novel *Their Eyes Were Watching God*, Zora Neale Hurston was also a short story writer, folklorist, and anthropologist.

Hughes, and Wallace Thurman. She also served on the editorial board and collaborated with Hughes, Thurman, and others in publishing the short-lived literary magazine *Fire!* In 1928 Hurston graduated from Barnard College and continued graduate study at Columbia University under renowned anthropologist Franz Boas. She returned to Eatonville and collected black folklore. Her book *Mules and Men,* published in 1935, includes the folklore that she collected in Florida, Alabama, and Louisiana from 1929 to 1931, as well as her hoodoo essay written in 1931 for the *Journal of American Folklore.* Issued by Lippincott, *Mules and Men* became the first such collection of folklore compiled and published by a black American woman. It was also the first by a woman indigenous to the culture from which the stories emerged. Hurston's other works include *Jonah's Gourd Vine,* a novel (1934); *Their Eyes Were Watching God,* considered her best novel (1937); *Tell My Horse,* her second collection of folklore (1938); *Moses, Man of the Mountain,* her third novel (1939); *Dust Tracks on a Road,* her autobiography (1942); and *Seraph on the Sewanee,* her fourth and last novel (1948).

Hurston's career began to slide in the 1950s, forcing her to take a series of menial jobs in Florida's small towns. After suffering a stroke in 1959, she was confined to Saint Lucie County Welfare Home in Fort Pierce, Florida, and she died in poverty on January 28, 1960. Writer Alice Walker rediscovered Hurston's work in 1973, placed a headstone at the approximate site of her unmarked grave, and arranged Hurston festivals to be held regularly in Eatonville to celebrate her life and work. The Zora Neale Hurston Festival, held in Eatonville each year, now honors the author's life and work. Hurston's play *Polk County* resurfaced in 1997 at the Library of Congress and was produced at the Arena Stage in Washington, D.C. Between 1925 and 1944, Hurston had deposited typescripts of ten of her unpublished and unproduced plays at the Library of Congress for copyright protection. Once rediscovered in 1997, these works were placed in the library's Manuscripts, Music, and Rare Books and Special Collections division. Hurston is celebrated for her writings, which include her perspectives as a black woman, feminist, anthropologist, and a keeper of the culture.

What black writer was the **first** to publish a **detective novel** in book form?

In 1932 Rudolph Fisher (1897–1934) became the first black writer to publish a detective novel in book form, *The Conjure Man Dies,* which revealed Fisher's medical and scientific knowledge within the storyline. The Federal Theater Project at the Lafayette Theater in Harlem produced his work as a play posthumously in 1936. In 2001 it was brought back to life and ran through February 11 at the Henry Street Settlement on the Lower East Side of New York City. Fisher was born in Washington, D.C., and earned both his bachelor's and master's degrees at Brown University. He received his medical degree from Howard University Medical School in 1924. The next year Fisher continued his medical education at Columbia University's College of Physicians and Surgeons. After that he trained for years in bacteriology, pathology, and roentgenology, becoming a radiologist. Fisher was said to have been conflicted over his involvement in two disparate professions—medicine and creative writing—but managed to do well in both. He wrote a number of very good short stories and two novels (including *The Walls of Jericho,* 1928), in addition to his detective novel. He was considered one of the wittiest of the Harlem Renaissance group. Fisher died of cancer in 1934, while he worked on a dramatization of *The Conjure Man Dies*. He was only thirty-seven years old.

What were the **lasting effects** of **Harlem Renaissance literature** on American and African-American culture?

There were numerous programs and developments in African-American culture that were influenced by the Harlem Renaissance and its giants. These include the emergence of Black Studies programs in black and mainstream institutions and a study of the works of Harlem Renaissance scholars, sometimes with separate courses concentrating on the works of particular literary artists, such as Zora Neale Hurston and Langston Hughes. There are courses on black writers with strong focus on those of the Harlem Renaissance, which continues to stimulate a greater demand for their works and a need to republish works long since out of print. Their works are examined and reexamined, and rarely lose their importance in the study of African-American literature. Early issues of journals such as *The Crisis* and *Opportunity* are useful sources for a study of developments in Harlem as written during the period of the renaissance. Courses on race relations in America also look at the treatment of blacks in the literature of the Harlem Renaissance.

POETS AND POETRY

Who was the **first** African American poet to serve as **consultant in poetry** to the **Library of Congress**?

Poet, essayist, and educator Robert Hayden (1913–1980) was consultant in poetry to the Library of Congress from 1976 to 1978. In 1985 the position was renamed Poet Laureate Consultant in Poetry to the Library of Congress. Born Asa Bundy Sheffey in Detroit, Hayden's parents separated before his birth, and then next-door neighbors Sue Ellen Westerfield and William Hayden became his foster family. The severe visual problems that he had as a child continued throughout his life. Young Hayden turned to reading. He attended Detroit City College (later Wayne State University) and left in 1936 to work for the Federal Writers' Project until 1938. In 1942 he received his master's degree from the University of Michigan. Hayden had been influenced by such black writers and poets as Countee Cullen, Langston Hughes, and Arna Bontemps, as well as several white writers. In 1940 he published his first volume, *Heart-Shape in the Dust*. Other works include *Selected Poems by Robert Hayden* (1966), *Words in the Mourning Time: Poems by Robert Hayden* (1970), *Angle of Ascent: New and Selected Poems by Robert Hayden* (1975), and *Collected Poems: Robert Hayden* (1985).

Who was the **first black** poet to win a **Pulitzer Prize for poetry**?

Gwendolyn Brooks (1917–2000), poet and novelist, was the first black to win a Pulitzer Prize for poetry, with *Annie Allen,* on May 1, 1950. She became established as a major American poet and, in 1976, she was the first black woman inducted into the National Institute of Arts and Letters. A sensitive interpreter of Northern ghetto life, Brooks began to write poetry at age seven; her first poems were published in the *Chicago Defender*.

Gwendolyn Brooks won the 1950 Pulitzer Prize for Poetry for her collection *Annie Allen*.

From 1969 on she promoted the idea that blacks must develop their own culture. She changed her writing style in an effort to become accessible to the ordinary black reader. Brooks was poet laureate of Illinois for sixteen years, and was named poetry consultant to the Library of Congress in 1985. Brooks was born in Topeka, Kansas, and began to write poetry when she was seven years old. While in high school, she met Langston Hughes who, on her request, read her poems and gave her enthusiastic inspiration. After graduation she attended Woodrow Wilson Junior College. In the 1940s and 1950s, Brooks concentrated on learning poetry and on writing it as well. In 1945 she published *A Street in Bronzeville,* the book that launched her career. Her autobiographical novel, *Maude Martha,* was published in 1953, followed by the first of four books of poetry for children in 1956, then *The Bean Eaters* (1960), *In the Mecca* (1968), *The Riot* (1969), and other works.

SCIENCE FICTION

Who was the **first black** writer to earn acclaim as a **science-fiction writer**?

The first black American to earn acclaim as a science-fiction writer was Samuel R. Delany (1942–), in 1962. Delany was born in Harlem and had a privileged childhood. He was a versatile and talented person who began to write at an early age. He was also a talented musician and composer by age fourteen, and studied physics and mathematics in high school. It was then that he was diagnosed with dyslexia. Delany won a number of awards for his writing, including a fellowship to the Bread Loaf Writers' Conference in Vermont. There he met poet Robert Frost. Delany studied at City College of New York for a while, but failed to complete his degree. His first science-fiction novel, *The Jewels of Aptor,* was published in 1962, when he was twenty years old. In 1973 he published a graphic novel, *The Tides of Lust*. That helped to set the course for his novels that followed. Around the mid-1970s he came to grips with his identity as a gay man. Delaney continued to write, producing in 1977 the first of his well-received works of criticism, *Jewel-Hinged Jaw,* followed by *The American Shore* in 1978. He has been highly recognized for his writings, receiving the Pilgrim Award in 1984 from the Science Fiction Research Association and the William Whitehead Memorial Award for Lifetime Contribution to Lesbian and Gay Writing in 1993.

Who was the **first black American woman** to **publish science fiction**?

In 1976 Octavia Butler (1947–2006) became the first black woman science-fiction writer to be published. Butler was born in Pasadena, California, and grew up in a racially integrated community. She suffered from unrecognized dyslexia, the consequence of which at first led to poor performance in school. However, her problem never interfered with the fantasy stories and romances that she wrote when she was ten and eleven years old. After graduating from high school, Butler worked during the day and enrolled in fiction writing courses at Pasadena City College at night. After completing the two-year program, she studied for a while at California State College. By now seriously interested in writing, she enrolled in writing courses at the University of California at Los Angeles, attended writing workshops that the Writers Guild of America West sponsored, and participated in the Clarion Writers Workshop in Clarion, Pennsylvania. Butler has published a number of short stories, several of which were award winning. She also wrote a number of science-fiction novels, most falling within a series. Her most successful stand-alone novel is *Kindred* (1988), which she called "grim fantasy" and not science fiction, for there is no science in it.

LITERATURE OF THE
CIVIL RIGHTS MOVEMENT

What was the **focus of black writers** during the **Civil Rights Movement**?

African-American literature is traditionally polemical and thus indicative of the political and social concerns of black people. This is evident in African-American literature at the height of the Civil Rights Movement in the 1950s and 1960s, which was characterized as consciousness-raising and self-affirming. Beginning in the 1950s, writings by African Americans increasingly shifted from integrationist literature directed toward a primarily white audience to a literature that was reflective of intra-communal issues and validation of black experiences. Gwendolyn Brooks' *Annie Allen,* James Baldwin's *Go Tell It on the Mountain,* Ralph Ellison's *Invisible Man,* and Lorraine Hansberry's *A Raisin in the Sun* are among the most prominent works of the decade. The works are reflective of the concerns of the Civil Rights Movement. Unlike the naturalistic and social-realist writings of the 1940s, this literature celebrated life in the black community, at times in relation to the white community, but more often not. These works revealed the humanity of black people and thus suggested that the political and social rights of African Americans are an obvious extension of that humanity.

The 1960s marked a decidedly more pronounced shift in the literature. Like literature of the 1950s that focused on interpersonal and intra-communal issues of black people, the 1960s literature emphasized political and social awareness and black pride. The Society of Umbra meetings in 1962–1963 served as precursor to the Black Arts Movement. Black writers Tom Dent, Askia Toure, David Henderson, and Calvin Hernton were among the writers who developed and attended Umbra meetings. At these meetings writers discussed their work, as well as social and political issues. Despite the efforts of the Umbra writers, the assassination of Malcolm X and Amiri Baraka's establishment of the Black Arts Repertory Theatre/School (BARTS) in 1965 are generally considered the beginning of the Blacks Arts Movement. Under the leadership of Amiri Baraka and Larry Neal, black writers sought to promote an

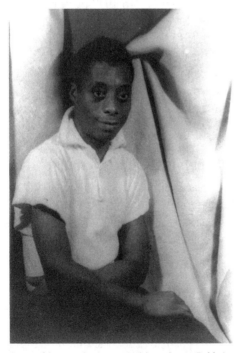

Among his many important writings, James Baldwin is best remembered for the semi-autobiographical 1953 novel *Go Tell It on the Mountain,* which examines racism, community, and the role of the Christian Church in the lives of African Americans.

aesthetic that was truly reflective of African artistic values and celebrated the lives of black people. Amiri Baraka's essay "Black Art" and his poem by the same title both provide insight into the radical black aesthetic espoused by the most prominent writers of this period. Larry Neal's essay, "The Black Arts Movement," further provides insight into the agenda of writers of this era. The movement largely produced poetry and drama.

Some of the other dominant writers of the period included Sonia Sanchez, Etheridge Knight, Haki Mutabuti (Don Lee), Nikki Giovanni, Ishmael Reed, Alice Childress, Adrienne Kennedy, Ed Bullins, and Douglas Turner Ward. Despite the empowering nature of the black aesthetic promoted by the writers of the Black Arts Movement, the efforts of the writers were marred by concerns of artistry being overshadowed by the didactic nature of the writing and problems of misogyny, vulgarity, violence, and a glamorization of impoverished mind-set and lifestyle. With the assassination of Martin Luther King Jr. and the decline of the Civil Rights Movement, the Black Arts Movement ended in the early 1970s.

THE BLACK AESTHETIC

What is the **Black Aesthetic in literature**?

The 1960s ushered in a period that some called the Black Aesthetic, which is used to define African-American literary history. It embraces recurring elements in African-American culture, whether in literature, art, poetry, drama, or music. It may range from violent rhetoric to black self-discovery. Some black aestheticians followed W.E.B. Du Bois' "double consciousness," or always seeing oneself as an American and as a black person. The Black Aesthetic covers the works of writers from the nineteenth and twentieth centuries. Writers such as Paul Laurence Dunbar, Charles Waddell Chesnutt, Pauline Hopkins, and James Weldon Johnson—some of them precursors of the Harlem Renaissance—are among the leading early writers. Those of the twentieth century, particularly during the Harlem Renaissance period, include Langston Hughes, Alain Leroy Locke, Zora Neale Hurston, and Richard Wright. Later writers of the 1950s and 1960s are represented by such luminaries as Amiri Baraka (LeRoi Jones), Lorraine Hansberry, Ishmael Reed, and Haki Madhubuti. The poets of this time included Sonia Sanchez, Mari Evans, and June Jordan. Some writers of this era also produced literature during other eras, including the Civil Rights Movement and the Black Arts Movement.

THE BLACK ARTS MOVEMENT

What was the **Black Arts Movement**?

The Black Arts Movement had as its goal "to transform the manner in which African Americans were portrayed in literature." The literature of mainstream American had portrayed them as "criminal, servile, misfit, or dependent." Some sources call the Black

Arts Movement the Black Aesthetic Movement, while others separate the terms. The Black Arts Movement began in the early 1960s, and began to subside in the mid-1970s. It was the first major African-American artistic movement since the Harlem Renaissance. Unlike the Harlem Renaissance in which white Americans played some part in its development, this movement was brought on by the anger of notable African-American writers, including Ralph Ellison and Richard Wright.

This artistic movement was closely paralleled by the civil rights marches and the call for independence being experienced in the African-American community. As phrases like "Black is beautiful" were popularized, African-American writers of this movement consciously set out to define what it meant to be a black writer in white culture. While writers of the Harlem Renaissance seemed to stumble upon their identity within, writers of this movement were serious about defining themselves and their era before being defined by others. Writers of this movement tended to be revolutionaries rather than diplomats—Malcolm X was more of an idol than Martin Luther King Jr. In addition, they believed that artists had more of a responsibility than just art: artists also had to be political activists in order to achieve nationalistic goals.

Writers of this movement include some seen in the Black Aesthetic Movement, such as Ellison and Wright. It also includes Haki R. Madhubuti (Don L. Lee), a poet and essayist who was overwhelmingly popular, selling over 100,000 copies of his books without a national distributor. Ishmael Reed, A. B. Spellman, Nikki Giovanni, and Jayne Cortez are among the poets of the movement—the largest group of artists in the Black Arts Movement.

The period saw the emergence of black publishing houses, such as Third World Press in Detroit and Broadside Press in Chicago. Broadside Press published more than one hundred books and recordings, including the works of over four hundred poets. Black journals emerged as well and included such titles as *Black Dialogue, Journal of Black Poetry,* and *Negro Digest* (renamed *Black World*).

The academic world was impacted by the Black Arts Movement as well, as seen in the Black Studies programs that were developed during this period. The movement saw a change in terminology—the use of "black" rather than "Negro," and certainly the death of the word "colored" that had been used for many years.

VARIETY IN AFRICAN-AMERICAN WRITING

What is the **nature** of African-American literature **following** the **Black Arts Movement**?

Since the Black Aesthetic Movement and the Black Arts Movement, African-American writing has become more legitimized in America. Variety was the key to African-American writing after 1950 and barriers went down in various genres. The period from 1975 to the twenty-first century brought more black writers into the mainstream and greater attention to African-American literature and Black Studies programs. Women poets such as Gwendolyn Brooks and Nikki Giovanni, writers such as Margaret Walker, Paule Marshall, and Nobel-Prize-winner Toni Morrison were key in literary studies. Writers offered a broad view of the black experience, while bringing new perspectives inclusive of post-modern aesthetics and mixing of genres. Accomplished writers emerged, such as August Wilson, Ntozake Shange, and George Wolf in theater; Rita Dove and Yusef Komunyakaa in poetry; and Alice Walker, Charles Johnson, and John Edgar Wideman in fiction. Other writers who exerted their influence in other genres were Walter Mosley with detective novels and Octavia Butler in science fiction, as well as BeBe Moore Campbell, Charles Fuller, Charles Johnson, Gayle Jones, Terry McMillan, and Gloria Naylor, who used mixed genres of history revision, magical realism, and popular culture storylines.

AWARD-WINNING WRITERS

Who was the **first** African-American writer to **win** the **National Book Award**?

Ralph Waldo Ellison (1914–1994) was the first black to win the National Book Award for his novel, *Invisible Man,* in 1953. Written in 1952, the book deals with a black man's "place" in a white man's world. Born in Oklahoma City, Oklahoma, Ellison studied at Tuskegee Institute (now University) before going to New York in 1936, intent on studying sculpture. He quickly met Langston Hughes, who introduced him to Richard Wright. Ellison became interested in writing and joined the Federal Writers' Project in 1942, hoping to develop his skills. In 1944 he began to write what would become his celebrated

novel, *Invisible Man,* which also won the Russwurm Award. Between 1943 and 1950 he worked on as many as four novels. His most distinguished short story, "Flying Home," was a long excerpt from one of his unfinished novels. He also published a collection of essays, *Shadow and Act* (1964). After *Invisible Man* was published, Ellison made a living primarily from teaching, lecturing, and royalties from his book. In 1999 Ellison's literary agents published *Juneteenth,* a novel completed before his death.

Who was the **first African-American woman** to win a **Pulitzer Prize** for fiction?

Alice Walker (1944–) was the first black woman writer to win a Pulitzer Prize for a

Best known for his National Book Award-winning 1953 novel, *Invisible Man,* Ralph Ellison was one of the leaders in the Black Aesthetic Movement.

179

work of fiction, on April 18, 1983. The novel, *The Color Purple,* was popular but controversial. It also won the American Book Award and established Walker as a major American writer. Her third novel, *The Color Purple* was made into an Oscar-nominated movie, which intensified discussion among black men and women over her presentation of black men. Walker is also a poet, essayist, and short-fiction writer. The Georgia-born writer was labeled a rebel and forced to leave Spelman College; she graduated from the more liberal Sarah Lawrence College in 1965, and worked in the Civil Rights Movement in Mississippi after graduation. An ardent feminist, Walker uses the term "womanist" to describe her work. Her works include *The Third Life of Grange Copeland* (1970), *In Search of Our Mother's Garden: Womanist Prose* (1983), *Temple of My Familiar* (1989), *Meridian* (1999), *The Way Forward Is with a Broken Heart* (2002), *We Are the Ones We Have Been Waiting For* (2006), *Hard Times Require Furious Dancing* (2011), *The Chicken Chronicle* (2012), and *The Cushion in the Road* (2013).

Who was the **first** black person to win a **Nobel Prize for literature**?

In 1986 Wole Soyinka (1934–), Nigerian playwright, poet, and novelist, became the first African and the first black writer of any nation to win a Nobel Prize for literature. His works have been acclaimed for his portrayals of the human condition in emergent Africa. Soyinka was born in Abeokuta, a village on the banks of the River Ogun in western Nigeria. He was educated at Government College and University in Ibadan. He also received a degree in English from the University of Leeds in 1960, and worked as a teacher and scriptwriter in London at the Royal Court Theater. He returned to Nigeria in 1960 and soon established himself as a dramatist, actor, and director. In 1994 he went into exile in the United States and Europe. While in the United States, he was distinguished visiting professor at Emory University in Atlanta. In 1997 his home country Nigeria charged him with treason, asserting that he was involved with bombings against military installations, which he denied. Soyinka has written many works in various genres and received a number of awards and honors. Since 2007 he has been professor in residence at Loyola Marymount University in Los Angeles.

Who was the **first African-Caribbean** to win a **Nobel Prize** in **literature**?

Derek Walcott (1930–), poet, educator, playwright, journalist, and painter, was the first African-Caribbean to be honored with the Nobel Prize in literature, in 1992. The prize was given for his "melodious and sensitive" style and "historic vision." His writings reflect the cultural diversity of his native Caribbean homeland, St. Lucia. A teacher at Boston University, Walcott also won a $250,000 John D. and Catherine T. MacArthur Foundation grant eleven years earlier. He is regarded as one of the finest living poets in England. Born of mixed racial and heritage background in Castries, St. Lucia, Walcott was educated as a British subject. He was founding director of Trinidad Theatre Workshop in 1959.

AFRICAN–AMERICAN LITERATURE
IN AMERICAN CULTURE

How has **African-American literature been accepted** or acknowledged in modern times?

African-American writers and their works have increased in acceptance and, according to Gates and McKay in *The Norton Anthology of African American Literature,* have been "enjoying renaissance in quality and quantity for the past few decades." A host of women writers, such as Maya Angelou, Rita Dove, Gloria Naylor, and Terry McMillan, have helped to lead the national interest in African-American literature. They have won Pulitzer prizes, international and American Book awards, and other recognitions. Several black writers have appeared together on the *New York Times* best-seller list. "This magnificent flowering of black literature crosses all racial boundaries," according to Gates and McKay, and black literature is now prominent in the marketplace as well as in school curricula. "Black literature courses have become a central part of the offerings in English departments and in departments of American studies, African American studies, and women's studies," they claim.

Recognition of the writers and poets in black culture has been seen in a variety of other ways. For example, poet Maya Angelou wrote and delivered a poem for the inauguration of President Bill Clinton in 1993, and Rita Dove was Poet Laureate of the United States for an unprecedented two terms. By the twenty-first century, African-American literature still continued to flourish, along with the academic study of the field. Bearing out the findings of Gates and McKay, libraries continue to collect "critical studies, anthologies, encyclopedias, companions, chronological histories, reprints, and reference works" that enable researchers and students of the literature to capture the new and/or continuing literary tradition of African-American writers.

Who was the **first black American** and the **second American woman** to win the **Nobel Prize in literature**?

Toni Morrison (1931–), novelist, educator, and editor, was the first black American and the second American woman to win the Nobel Prize in literature, which was awarded on October 7, 1993. The Swedish Academy called her "a literary artist of first rank," one who "gives life to an essential aspect of American reality," and one who wrote prose "with the luster of poetry." Informed of the honor, Morrison said that her work was inspired by "huge silences in literature, things that had never been articulated, printed or imagined and they were the silences about black girls, black women." Her novel *Song of Solomon,* published in 1977, won the National Book Critics Award for fiction that year, and in 1988 she won the Pulitzer Prize for Fiction for her work *Beloved.* Her other novels include *The Bluest Eye* (1970), *Sula* (1974), *Tar Baby* (1981), *Jazz* (1992), *Paradise* (1999), *Love* (2003), *A Mercy* (2009), *Desdemona* (2012), and *Home* (2013). Morrison was born in Lorain, Ohio,

Author and educator Toni Morrison received a Presidential Medal of Freedom from President Barack Obama in 2012.

and graduated from Howard University in Washington, D.C., in 1953. She received a master's degree in English from Cornell University in 1955. In 1965 Morrison became a textbook editor for a subsidiary of Random House Publishing in Syracuse, New York, and three years later she moved to New York City as a senior editor in the trade department at Random House. She mixed her editorial work with a teaching career and taught at a number of colleges. She left the publishing field in 1984 and in 1989 became the Robert F. Goheen Professor of the Council of the Humanities at Princeton University. She resigned from Princeton in 2006. In 1996 the National Endowment for the Humanities named her Jefferson Lecturer in the Humanities.

What African American won **two Pulitzer Prizes**?

In 1993 historian and educator David Levering Lewis (1936–) won a Pulitzer Prize for his biography, *W.E.B. Du Bois: Biography of a Race: 1868–1919*. In 2001 he published the second volume of the Du Bois biography, *W.E.B. Du Bois: The Fight for Equality and the American Century, 1919–1963,* and again won a Pulitzer Prize, becoming the first biographer to win twice for back-to-back books on the same subject. Lewis was born in Little Rock, Arkansas, and relocated with his parents to Wilberforce, Ohio. He entered Fisk University in Nashville, Tennessee, in the fall of 1952, as a member of the university's Early Entrants Program for bright students who had not finished high school; he graduated in 1956 with Phi Beta Kappa honors and a bachelor's degree in history. He received his master's degree in history from Columbia University in 1958 and enrolled in England's London School of Economics. There Lewis focused on Modern European and French history and received his doctorate in 1962. All the while he maintained an interest in U.S. history and continued to develop intellectually in that area. Lewis held a number of teaching posts at such institutions as the University of Ghana in Africa, Howard University, the University of Notre Dame, Morgan State University, the University of the District of Columbia, and finally Rutgers University, where he holds the Martin Luther King Jr. Chair. His biography of Martin Luther King Jr. titled *King: A Biography,* published in 1978, was well received by the academic community. His book *When Harlem Was In Vogue,* published in 1981, was likewise well received and helped to enhance the resources on that cultural period in history. Lewis' crowning achievement came with the publication of his monumental biographies of W.E.B. Du Bois that chronicle the life of one of the twentieth century's most brilliant and fertile minds.

MILITARY

FROM THE AMERICAN REVOLUTION TO THE SPANISH–AMERICAN WAR

Why is **Crispus Attucks** important?

In 1770 Crispus Attucks (c. 1723–1770) became the first black casualty in the American Revolution. He was not enlisted in the army but instead was a part of a Boston group protesting the Townshend Acts. Tensions in Boston were already high when Attucks and his companions, who are said to have come from the Boston docks, approached the British garrison. While protesting at the garrison housing the British soldiers who were to enforce the acts, Attucks and several others were shot. The event came to be known as the Boston Massacre and is considered to have triggered the American Revolution. The details of Attucks' early years are not well known. It is believed that he was of African and Native-American ancestry, that his father was a slave, and that the family lived in Framingham, Massachusetts. He is also identified as a merchant seaman. Further speculation, based on a 1750 advertisement in the *Boston Gazette,* identifies Attucks as a runaway

Killed at the Boston Massacre, Crispus Attucks was the first black man to die in the American Revolution.

slave. The Crispus Attucks Monument, in honor of the victims, was dedicated in the Boston Commons in 1888.

Who was **Salem Poor**?

Salem Poor (1747–?) was the first black soldier to win a battle commendation. The recommendation for his acknowledgement was made on December 5, 1775, to the General Court of Massachusetts Bay. It commended Poor for his bravery at the Battle of Charlestown, describing him as "a Brave & gallant Soldier." The recommendation was signed by fourteen colonial army officers and was entered into court records twice. There is no record as to when or if he received notice of the commendation. The earliest record of Poor appears when he was baptized in Andover, Massachusetts, in 1747. He was an indentured servant until he purchased his freedom in 1769. Poor enlisted in a Massachusetts militia company in April 1775, and on June 17, 1775, fought valiantly at the battle of Bunker Hill, where he wounded a British officer. Other blacks at the battle were Barzillai Lew, Cuff Whittemore, Titus Coburn, Charlestown Eads, Peter Salem, Sampson Taylor, and Caesar Brown. Poor's military record extends from 1775 to 1780, with only brief absences of no more than a few months at a time. He was with George Washington at Valley Forge, but he is not listed among the five thousand blacks who lost their lives during the Revolutionary War and for whom there is a memorial in Pennsylvania's Valley Forge National Historical Park. He fought in a number of other crucial battles, and was finally given recognition for his contributions to the colonial army on March 25, 1975, when the U.S. Postal Service issued a series of stamps during its Revolutionary War Centennial. The stamp series was entitled "Contributors to the Cause." A ten-cent stamp recognized "Salem Poor—Gallant Soldier." The date of Poor's death is not recorded.

When did the **exclusion of blacks** in the **military** become law?

Congress restricted military service to "free able-bodied white males" in 1772; thus the exclusion of blacks from the military became law in that year. Six years later, the Secretary of War reiterated this law and issued an order to the Commandant of the Marine Corps that "no Negro, mulatto or Indian is to be enlisted."

When was the **Continental Army racially integrated**?

America's founding fathers grudgingly accepted free black men for service in the Continental Army. On January 16, 1776, Congress proclaimed that "free Negroes who have served faithfully in the Army at Cambridge may be reenlisted therein." Thus, by 1778, the Continental Army was racially integrated.

Did black troops in combat contribute to the American victory at the **Battle of New Orleans**?

The War of 1812, in New Orleans, was mainly fought by naval forces, and black sailors made up approximately twenty percent of naval crews. While the army and Marine Corps continued to exclude blacks, the Louisiana legislature authorized enlistments of free black landowners in the militia. The black troops' bravery in combat was a key factor in the American victory at the Battle of New Orleans, although it was fought after the war had officially ended.

What **African Seminole led raids** during the first and second Seminole Wars?

John Caesar (c. 1750–1837) led raids in the First Seminole War in 1817 and convinced runaway slaves and free blacks to join his efforts. He was successful again in 1835 during the Second Seminole War. The men burned homes, wrecked mills, and confiscated livestock and corn. In 1836 Caesar led successful raids of sugar plantations outside St. Augustine, Florida, and as a result freed slaves who were on the plantations. Native Seminoles, escaped slaves, and African Seminoles aided in the raids again. His leadership in recruiting slaves from plantations compelled the U.S. military to enter into negotiations with African Seminoles and remove them from enslavement on the plantations. While attempting to steal horses from a plantation, on January 17, 1837, Caesar and his men were discovered and attacked. Three warriors and Caesar were killed. Caesar became well known in Florida as an outstanding and brave military leader.

Did **black soldiers** participate in the **Civil War**?

As soon as the Civil War began, blacks outside the rebel territory volunteered for the army. Some army leaders sought to recruit blacks as soldiers, but President Abraham Lincoln's administration countermanded such actions. The Confederacy, however, relied on slave labor to construct fortifications and assist in related combat service support tasks. By 1862, after significant military setbacks, Congress lifted the ban on blacks in the military and approved their use as Union Army laborers.

What was the importance of the **54th and 55th Massachusetts Infantry** during the **Civil War**?

After the Emancipation Proclamation was issued in September 1862, Massachusetts was permitted to organize two black regiments: the 54th and 55th Massachusetts

During the American Civil War, blacks fought on the Union side after Congress lifted a ban preventing them from serving, while the Confederacy used them for slave labor.

A painting commissioned by the U.S. National Guard depicts the 54th Massachusetts Volunteer Infantry Regiment attacking Confederate soldiers at Fort Wagner, South Carolina, on July 18, 1863.

Infantry. The 54th Massachusetts Regiment was the first regiment raised in the North during the Civil War. Black leaders helped to recruit blacks from free states, slave states, and Canada. The regiment fought valiantly at Fort Wagner in July; the regiment commander, Colonel Robert Gould Shaw, was killed and buried with his black soldiers. The attack at Fort Wagner was the first major engagement seen by black troops. The regiment objected to the pay differential between black and white enlisted men and served a year without pay rather than accept discriminatory wages.

Why was **Sergeant William H. Carney** important?

William Harvey Carney (1840–1908), sergeant of Company C, 54th Massachusetts Colored Infantry, was the first black in the Civil War to earn the Medal of Honor, on July 18, 1863. Born in Norfolk, Virginia, he was educated privately and later settled in New Bedford, Massachusetts, where he became a seaman. Carney enlisted on February 17, 1863, and earned his Medal of Honor five months later at Fort Wagner, South Carolina. When the color bearer was wounded in the battle, Carney, also hurt, sprang forward and seized the flag before it slipped from the bearer's grasp. By doing so, he prevented the flag from touching the ground. Carney was discharged from the infantry with disabilities caused by the wounds he had received. His Medal of Honor was not issued until May 23, 1900. Upon Carney's death, the flag on the Massachusetts state house was flown at half mast—an honor formerly restricted to presidents, senators, and governors.

What movie was based on the 54th Massachusetts Infantry?

The exploits of the 54th Massachusetts Infantry formed the basis of the motion picture *Glory* (1989). Starring Denzel Washington, the film portrays black soldiers who were trained to fight in the Civil War. Under the supervision of Colonel Robert Gould Shaw, a white colonel from Boston, the men displayed courage and strength which enabled them to engage in a heroic battle that ended on July 18, 1863. The men attacked Battery Wagner, a key fortification in Charleston, South Carolina. Washington played the part of a former slave named Trip, whose slave experiences had embittered him and left him angry and tough. For his role in the film, Washington won his first Oscar and his second Academy Award nomination for Best Supporting Actor.

Who were the **United States Colored Troops**?

In May 1863 the severe manpower shortage forced the War Department to approve the organization of additional black regiments led by white officers. The units were designated as the United States Colored Troops (USCT). The USCT constituted 13 percent of the Union Army. The 54th and 55th Massachusetts regiments were excluded from this designation. Over thirty such regiments were in place by the mid-1860s. After the USCT regiments were established, black Americans fought and died in all major actions during the Civil War. Usually their pay was much less than that of white soldiers. Blacks in some units, however, refused to accept the lesser pay. When black Union soldiers fell into Confederate hands, they were enslaved, re-enslaved, or executed, thus breaching the land warfare standards in place. One of the most brutal acts against black soldiers was the Fort Pillow Massacre, which occurred at Fort Pillow, Tennessee, on April 24, 1864. Even though the Union forces had surrendered, Confederate troops massacred the Union troops, killing more than three hundred African Americans, including fleeing civilians. Confederate leader General Nathan Bedford Forrest was identified as the responsible person in the act; he became a principal founder of the Ku Klux Klan after the war ended.

Why was **Robert Smalls** important?

Robert Smalls (1839–1915) was the first and only black to attain the rank of captain in the U.S. Navy during the Civil War. He was a skilled pilot who took control of the armed Confederate dispatch boat, *The Planter,* in Charleston, South Carolina, on May 12, 1862. With the help of eight black crewmen, Smalls put his family and other fugitives on board and sailed it out of the harbor to turn it over as a prize of war to the Union Navy on May 13, 1862. The boat was eventually refitted as a gunboat, and Smalls was made a captain in the Union Navy. At the time of his heroic deed, Smalls was a slave. He was born in slave quarters in Beaufort, South Carolina, and his father is believed to have been a Eu-

ROBERT SMALLS, CAPTAIN OF THE GUN-BOAT "PLANTER."

Captain Robert Smalls was the only African American to achieve that rank during the American Civil War.

ropean. He was sold in 1851 to a slave owner who lived in Charleston, South Carolina. The owner allowed Smalls to work for pay outside of the plantation, and it was on his job as a ship rigger that he learned about sailing and became a superior sailor. He was employed on *The Planter* in 1861 and began hatching his plan to escape. He was initially commissioned as a second lieutenant in Company B, 33rd Regiment, U.S. Colored Troops; he was denied enlistment in the Federal Navy because he was not a graduate of the naval academy. His promotion to captain came as a result of his actions at the battle at Folly Creek, South Carolina. He was serving on *The Planter* when Confederate troops opened fire on it. Smalls took over after the white commander panicked, and he was able to bring the ship safely back to port. He left the navy at the end of the Civil War, but went on to a career as a politician. As a Republican congressman from South Carolina, he served longer than any other black during Reconstruction, although not in consecutive terms. When he left the House of Representatives in 1887, he became a customs collector, with his last post in his hometown of Beaufort. He held that position until his death.

Who were the **Buffalo Soldiers**?

Congress approved the first all-black units in the regular army in 1867. These soldiers, known as "buffalo soldiers" or the U.S. Colored Troops, served in the West and made up the 9th and 10th Cavalry Regiments as well as the 24th and 25th Infantry Regiments. Their nickname came from Native Americans, who believed their short curly hair was similar to that on the buffalo's neck and that their brave and fierce fighting matched that of the buffalo. Eleven black soldiers earned the Congressional Medal of Honor in combat against Utes, Apaches, and Comanches. Soldiers served in black regiments until the integration of U.S. forces in 1952. A monument honoring the buffalo soldiers was unveiled at Fort Leavenworth in 1992.

Why was **Second Lieutenant Henry Ossian Flipper** important?

In 1877 Henry Ossian Flipper (1856–1940) became the first black to graduate from the U.S. Military Academy at West Point, New York. (Another student, James W. Smith, was the first black to enter the academy in 1870.) A native of Georgia and a student at Atlanta University at the time of his appointment, Flipper graduated fiftieth out of a class

Ninth Cavalry non-commissioned officers of the U.S. Army had their picture taken at Fort Robinson, Nebraska, in 1889. Along with the 10th Cavalry and the 24th and 25th Infantry Regiments, they were nicknamed "buffalo soldiers" by Native Americans because their hair reminded them of the curly hair of bison.

of seventy-six after suffering four years of exclusion and ostracism by white cadets. He joined the 10th Calvary in 1878, one of the all-black cavalry regiments making up what became known as the "buffalo soldiers." He served in Oklahoma and Texas. The only black officer in the U.S. Army, Flipper was cleared of an embezzlement charge in 1882, but was convicted of conduct unbecoming an officer and dishonorably discharged. He remained in the West and, for the next fifty years, engaged in engineering, mining, and survey work. He also lived in Atlanta for a number of years with his equally renowned brother, Josephus Flipper, a bishop in the African Methodist Episcopal Church. In 1976 the U.S. Army exonerated Flipper posthumously and granted him a retroactive discharge. On May 3, 1977—the centennial of his graduation—a bust by black sculptor Helene Hemmans was unveiled in Flipper's honor at West Point. Buried at first in a family plot in Atlanta, his remains were moved to his hometown, Thomasville, where he was reburied with full military honors. His *Colored Cadet at West Point* (1878) gives a penetrating insight into his early life. In 1999, 117 years after his wrongful discharge, President Bill Clinton granted him a posthumous pardon at a ceremony held in the White House.

Who was the **first black** American to hold the **rank of lieutenant colonel**?

In 1906 Allen Allensworth (1842–1914) became the first black American to hold the rank of lieutenant colonel. Born a slave, he taught under the auspices of the Freedmen's Bureau, operated a number of businesses, and served as a chaplain in the army. He founded an all-black town named Allensworth in Tulare County, California.

Who was **Charles Young**?

Charles Young (1864–1922) was the first black military attaché in the history of the United States; he was accredited to Haiti. In 1889 Young was the third man of color to graduate from the U.S. Military Academy, entering the academy after his graduation from historically black Wilberforce University in Ohio. He was a five-year graduate, having dropped out for a year because of deficiencies in mathematics; he also had to cope with racial affronts during his experience at West Point. When he graduated he was commissioned as a second lieutenant in the U.S. Cavalry. During the Spanish-American War, Young served as a major in charge of the 9th Ohio Regiment, an all-black volunteer unit. He served in Haiti, the Philippines, and Mexico, and by 1916 he had attained the rank of lieutenant colonel. Young was the second person and the first military person to be honored with the NAACP's Spingarn Medal in 1916. In 1917 at the advent of World War I, Young was forced to retire for reasons of "physical unfitness for duty." (He was suffering from extremely high blood pressure and Bright's disease.) He held the rank of full colonel at the time. In response, Young mounted his favorite horse at Wilberforce, Ohio, and rode five hundred miles to Washington, D.C., to prove that he was indeed fit for service. The army reinstated him in 1918, and he was assigned to train black troops at Fort Grant, Illinois. In 1919 Colonel Young was sent as military attaché to Liberia on a second tour of duty. He died in Lagos, Nigeria, during an inspection tour. He was given a funeral there with full military honors, but was later exhumed at the request of his widow and buried in Arlington Cemetery. Black schools in the nation's capital were closed to honor him on the day of his burial. Born the son of slaves in Mayslick, Kentucky, Young grew up in Ripley, Ohio. During the early part of his army career, he taught military science and other subjects at Wilberforce. As a diplomat in foreign countries he used his cartography skills to draw new maps and revise existing ones. In May 1974 his home in Xenia, Ohio, was declared a National Historic Landmark by the Department of the Interior.

How was the military involved in the **Civilian Pilot Training Program**?

Educator and college founder Mary McLeod Bethune was instrumental in garnering support from Historically Black Colleges and Universities in participating in the Civilian Pilot Training Program. One of these colleges, Tuskegee Institute (now University), became the federal government's most important center for civilian pilot training when World War II began. The first black pilots trained there began their course on July 19, 1941, and completed rigorous programs in navigation and meteorology before their flight training at the Tuskegee Army Base. The first five who earned their "silver wings" graduated as fighter pilots on March 7, 1942. Some 962 black pilots were trained at Tuskegee during the war years; 450 of them flew in combat.

What was the **"Tuskegee Experiment"** and who were the **Tuskegee Airmen**?

The 100th Squadron of four fighter squadrons comprising solely of black men was activated on October 13, 1942, at the Tuskegee Army Air Field in Alabama; it was the first black American military aviation group. Later three other black fighter squadrons were combined and became known as the Tuskegee Airmen. By the end of the year, the 99th Pursuit Squadron, the first black air unit in the history of the United States, was ready for action. The 99th was sent to North Africa and on June 2, 1943, they flew their first combat mission against the island of Pantelleria. About six hundred black pilots received their wings during World War II. The Tuskegee Experiment proved that black men could fly state-of-the-art aircraft and could conduct highly successful combat operations.

Increasingly, the Tuskegee Airmen have received public acclaim. In April 2007 President George W. Bush awarded the legendary airmen the Congressional Gold Medal, the

The Tuskegee Airmen fought bravely during World War II in the European theater. In 2007, the 99th Pursuit Squadron received the Congressional Gold Medal from President George W. Bush.

highest honor Congress can award to civilians. President Bush told the men, "You helped win a war, and you helped change our nation for the better." He continued, "And the medal that we confer today means that we are doing a small part to ensure that your story is told and honored for generations to come." Public Law 105-355, which President Bill Clinton approved on November 6, 1998, established the Tuskegee Airmen National Historic Site at Moton Field in Tuskegee, Alabama. In 1996 an HBO movie titled *Tuskegee Airmen,* starring Laurence Fishburne, was released, followed by a movie *Red Tails,* in 2012, which also told the story of the legendary airmen. The airmen's brand is seen on hats, shirts, jackets, and other paraphernalia that honor the iconic black units.

Who was **Benjamin O. Davis Sr.**?

Benjamin Oliver Davis Sr. (1877–1970) was the first black American general in the U.S. Army and the highest-ranking black in the armed forces when he was promoted to brigadier general on October 25, 1940. Born and educated in Washington, D.C., he graduated from Howard University in 1898. He entered the army after graduation. Davis served as a temporary lieutenant in the 8th U.S. Volunteers Infantry (an all-black unit) from 1898 to 1899, fighting in the Spanish-American War. In 1899 he enlisted as a private in the Ninth Cavalry, a unit of the regular army, and soon rose to the highest rank held by any black soldier at the time: sergeant-major. Determined to become an officer, he passed the examinations in 1901 and was promoted to second lieutenant, assigned to the 10th Cavalry. Davis was sent to Wilberforce University in Ohio in 1905 to teach military science, where he remained for four years, after which he served as a military attaché in Liberia. He returned to active duty in the Philippines in 1917 after an assignment in Mexico and a repeat tour of duty at Wilberforce. He was by this time a captain. After a teaching assignment at the Tuskegee Institute (now University), during which he was promoted to lieutenant colonel, he became an instructor to the Ohio National Guard in 1924. Davis was given his own regiment to command, the 369th Cavalry New York National Guard, in 1937; he held the rank of colonel at the time. Throughout his army career, Davis was confronted by and fought against segregation and discrimination in the armed forces. His value to the country as a symbol of the army's somewhat belated good intentions is perhaps indicated by the fact that he was past the official age for military promotions when he was elevated to brigadier general. He retired from the army in 1948, having served in the U.S. armed forces for half a century; his career dated from the Spanish-American War to World War II. Davis was a highly decorated soldier, including the French *Croix de Guerre* and the Bronze Star among his awards. He also served as a mentor to the troops during World War II, and was noted as a diplomatic negotiator on racial problems and an advisor to then-General Dwight Eisenhower (who did not fully accept Davis' advice) on integration in the army. Davis continued to be active in public life until poor eyesight and other health problems forced him to cease much of his activity in 1960. He was in a hospital in North Chicago, Illinois, when he died of leukemia. His son, Benjamin O. Davis Jr., followed in his father's footsteps and grew up to become the first black general in the U.S. Air Force.

It is of note that Davis Sr. was denied admission to the U.S. Military Academy when he applied after graduating from high school.

Who was **Benjamin O. Davis Jr.**?

Benjamin Oliver Davis Jr. (1912–2002) became the first black U.S. Air Force general on October 27, 1954. He also became the first black air force officer to complete a solo flight in 1941 and the first black man to command an airbase. During World War II Davis received two promotions in one day in 1943 when he was promoted first to major and then to lieutenant colonel. President Bill Clinton elevated Davis to the rank of four-star general, and in 1994, President Clinton named him to the Board of Visitors of the U.S. Military Academy. Davis' career paralleled that of his father, U.S. Army Brigadier General Benjamin O. Davis Sr., in rising to the rank of general, albeit in another branch of the armed forces. Davis was born in Washington, D.C., and began his college education in 1929 at Western Reserve University (now known as Case Western Reserve University) in Ohio. He attended the University of Chicago from 1930 to 1932, after which he was able to enter the U.S. Military Academy when he passed the qualifying examinations on his second try. Davis faced racial bias just as his father had during his army experience. It has been reported that none of Davis's West Point classmates spoke to him during his years at the academy, except when absolutely necessary. With a class rank of 35 out of 278, he graduated from West Point in 1936 as the first black with this achievement in the twentieth century. He was commissioned a second lieutenant and elected to serve in the U.S.

Brigadier General Benjamin O. Davis Sr. (left) served in the U.S. Army from the Spanish-American War through World War II. His son, Air Force General Benjamin O. Davis Jr., served in Korea and Vietnam. Father and son were both highly decorated soldiers.

Air Force. He was informed that blacks were ineligible for that branch and was assigned to Fort Benning, Georgia, where he was excluded from membership in the officers' club. In 1941, after a tour of duty at Fort Riley, Kansas, Davis was chosen to command the 99th Pursuit Squadron, an all-black flying unit authorized by President Franklin Roosevelt. The squadron trained at Tuskegee Army Air Base in Alabama and went on to fame as the "Tuskegee Airmen," despite the fact that they were subjected to tremendous racial bias. Davis commanded the 332nd Fighter Group, comprising four black squadrons. This group saw action in Europe and achieved an enviable escort duty and combat record. When it flew escort duty, the group never lost a bomber to the enemy. The exploits of the 332nd are considered to have been instrumental in the 1948 decision of the U.S. armed forces to become integrated. In 1951 Davis became the commander of the integrated 51st Fighter Interceptor Wing in Korea and the Thirteenth Air Force in Vietnam. He became a lieutenant general in 1965. Davis retired from the air force in 1970 and took a position as director of public safety in Cleveland, Ohio. From 1971 to 1975 he served as the director of civil aviation security, assistant secretary of environment, safety, and consumer affairs for the U.S. Department of Transportation. Davis was inducted into the Aviation Hall of Fame in 1944. He received numerous military awards, including the Distinguished Flying Cross. When the White House ceremony at which he was promoted to four-star general was held, twenty of the original Tuskegee Airmen were in attendance to give praise to his courageous leadership of the 332nd unit. President Clinton was given an honorary signature Tuskegee Airman jacket at the time. Davis published his book, *Autobiography: Benjamin O. Davis Jr.: American,* in 1991.

Who were the **Harlem Hellfighters**?

The Harlem Hellfighters, or the 369th Infantry Regiment, was the first all-black U.S. combat unit shipped overseas during World War I. This outstanding unit became the best-known all-black unit in the war; it was in continuous combat longer than any other American unit in World War I. The unit began in 1916 as the 15th New York National Guard Infantry Regiment. It was manned by black and white enlisted soldiers. In 1917 the regiment was federalized and prepared to serve in Europe, arriving in Brest, France, in December. They had become a part of the 93rd Division (Provisional). Meanwhile, France requested military help, and General John J. Pershing responded by assigning the 369th and other regiments in the 93rd Division to the French army, where they were under French command. The regiment received federal designation in March, was reorganized according to the French model, and that summer integrated into the French 161st Division. Now they called themselves "Men of Bronze" and went into combat for over six months—possibly serving the longest period of continuous combat of any American unit. They were said to be the first unit to cross the Rhine and acquitted themselves well at Chateau-Thierry and Belleau Wood. Their enemies gave them the moniker "Hell Fighters." Almost one-third of the unit died in combat, yet the French government awarded the full regiment the Croix de Guerre. The men were well-received when they returned home and were honored with a parade in February 1919. They were then reabsorbed into the National Guard.

Who were **Henry Johnson** and **Needham Roberts**?

Henry Johnson (1897–1929) and Needham Roberts (1901–1949) were the first black soldiers to be awarded the French *Croix de Guerre* as individuals, in 1918. As privates with the 369th Infantry, they were injured on May 14, 1918, in an assault by German soldiers, but continued to fight and succeeded in routing their attackers. Johnson went to Roberts' rescue when he was being taken away by the enemy, and rescued him. During World War I, Johnson, of Albany, New York, joined the Army National Guard's "Harlem Hellfighters" unit. Roberts was only fifteen or sixteen years old when he joined the regiment. The segregated unit fought under the French in Europe. After France awarded each man in the unit its highest honor for bravery, President Theodore Roosevelt also cited Johnson as one of the five bravest Americans during the war. The U.S. military, however, failed to decorate him. When Johnson died, he was buried at Arlington National Cemetery with full military honors. In 1996, efforts were made to award him the Medal of Honor. Errors in military records prevented him from receiving the medal posthumously; eventually, the errors were corrected, and efforts to award him the medal continued. In 1996 Roberts was awarded the Purple Heart. Johnson also received the Purple Heart that year, and in April 2000 the Distinguished Service Cross, both posthumously.

What African American became a **hero** during the Japanese attack on **Pearl Harbor**?

Doris (Dorie) Miller (1919–1943) was the first national black hero during World War II. He was honored with the Navy Cross in 1942, after pressure from newspapers and civil rights groups. Miller was a U.S. Navy messman first class on the battleship *Arizona* at Pearl Harbor when the Japanese attacked on December 7, 1941. He manned a machine gun and shot down at least four Japanese planes despite the fact that, as a messman, he had not been trained in the use of a weapon. He moved his wounded commander to a safe place before going into action and stopped firing only when he ran out of ammunition and was ordered to abandon ship. His career in the U.S. Navy was cut short by wartime tragedy. He was among the crew of the carrier USS *Liscome Bay* when it sank at sea after being struck by a torpedo on November 24, 1943. Thirty years later, in June 1973, the U.S. Navy commissioned the USS *Miller* (a destroyer escort) in his honor. Born in Waco, Texas, to parents who were sharecroppers, Miller joined the U.S. Navy when he was nineteen, thinking that he would be eligible for

An illustration by Charles Henry Alston for the Office of War Information commemorates the selfless act of bravery committed by Dorie Miller in defending Pearl Harbor from the Japanese attack.

fighting service. He, like all other black sailors, was assigned to a menial job in the only rank that was then open to blacks in the navy. Miller was denied promotion after his heroic deeds, and returned to his old navy duties after receiving the Navy Cross medal for gallantry, becoming the first black so honored.

What role did **Samuel L. Gravely Jr.** play in the U.S. Navy?

In 1944 Samuel Lee Gravely Jr. (1922–2004) became the first black ensign commissioned during World War II. He was released from active service after the war, but was recalled in 1949. In January 1962 Gravely was given command of the destroyer USS *Falgout*. This was the first time a black officer had been given command of a ship in the modern U.S. Navy. In 1963 Gravely and George I. Thompson were the first two blacks chosen to attend the Naval War College. Three years later, he entered the history books again as the first black commander to lead a ship, the USS *Taussig,* into offensive action. Gravely became the first black admiral in the U.S. Navy in 1971; he had earlier been the first black to achieve the rank of captain. His contributions to the navy continued when he became commander of the 3rd fleet in 1976. He was transferred from Hawaii to Virginia in 1978, when he became director of the Defense Communications Agency. Gravely retired from the navy in 1980 as a three-star admiral. He was born in Richmond, Virginia, into a family committed to government service. Gravely interrupted his college studies at Virginia Union University to enlist in the U.S. Naval Reserve in 1942. By the time he was assigned to his first ship in 1945, he had risen to the rank of captain; he was the first black officer on the ship. During his brief hiatus from the navy, Gravely completed his college work, graduating in 1948. He returned to active duty in the navy in 1952. After his retirement from the navy, he remained active as a consultant and a speaker. During the mid-1980s, he served as executive director of education and training for the Educational Foundation of the Armed Forces Communications and Electronics Association. His thirty-four years in the navy included service in three wars: World War II, the Korean War, and the Vietnam War. Gravely held numerous medals commemorating his service, including the Defense Distinguished Service Medal and the Bronze Star. On November 20, 2010, Gravely was honored posthumously when a guided-missile destroyer, the USS *Gravely,* was commissioned in Wilmington, North Carolina. The vessel was hailed as "one of the most advanced ships ever developed." It is over 508 feet long and draws 31 feet of water. Over 380 officers and enlisted personnel serve aboard.

The "Golden Thirteen" were twelve black ensigns and one warrant who were commissioned in the U.S. Navy in 1944, breaking a long-standing barrier in that branch of the military.

Who were the **"Golden Thirteen"**?

African Americans were enrolled in the U.S. Navy in 1932, but in a separate branch. When World War II came, the navy broke its racial barrier and accepted fourteen thousand black enlistees in its various ratings and branches. In March 1944 twelve black ensigns and one warrant officer were commissioned in the U.S. Navy. They had broken the color barrier in the navy and, without public knowledge, were given intensive training. The men later dubbed themselves the "Golden Thirteen." The navy subsequently accepted their designation in recognition of their pioneering efforts to integrate that branch of the military. During World War II, the U.S. Navy commissioned about sixty black Americans.

Why were the **Triple Nickels** important?

On December 19, 1943, the Army Ground Forces Headquarters called for the activation of the 555th Parachute Infantry Battalion, an all-black volunteer unit with officers and enlisted men. The unit was officially activated on December 30 at Fort Benning, Georgia. The first black enlisted paratrooper was Walter Morris. The unit trained for several weeks and then on November 25, 1944, moved to Camp Mackall, North Carolina, when it was reorganized as Company A, 555th Parachute Infantry Battalion, formally becoming the world's first black paratroopers. The unit became popularly known as the Triple Nickels. The battalion was never sent overseas during the war; it was instead sent to the west coast of the United States to remain alert for possible Japanese attacks. Its mission there was also to fight forest fires, and the battalion responded by assisting with a number of dangerous fire-fighting missions. The men made over one thousand jumps as they fought fires in Oregon and California, which earned them a second nickname, "Smoke Jumpers." **197**

After a distinguished military career in the field, General Colin Powell was chairman of the Joint Chiefs of Staff under President George H. W. Bush and secretary of state under President George W. Bush.

After the war the group organized as the 555th Parachute Infantry Association, using the motto "Before them there weren't many, after them there weren't any." Three buffalo nickels stacked in pyramid form became their logo.

Why is **General Colin Powell** important in military history?

Colin L. Powell (1937–) became the first black National Security Advisor in 1987. Born in Harlem in New York City to Jamaican immigrants, Powell received his bachelor's degree from City College of New York in 1958 and his master's in business administration from George Washington University in 1971. He graduated from the National War College in 1976. Powell joined the Reserve Officers Training Corps while at City College and was commissioned as a second lieutenant when he graduated. He made his best grades in the ROTC courses and graduated as a Distinguished Military Student. His first assignment after basic training was in Germany, where he was made a first lieutenant. An assignment to Boston completed his ROTC-required three years of military service in 1961, but he chose to remain active in the military. Powell was trained as a military advisor in 1962 and saw his first tour of war duty in Vietnam. An injury there resulted in his being given first the Purple Heart and later the Bronze Star. He was assigned to the Pentagon in 1971, after another tour of duty in Vietnam. Powell was sent to South Korea in 1973. By 1976 he was a full colonel. In 1979 Powell was promoted to brigadier general and worked for a brief time as an assistant to the Department of Energy. For the 1980 presidential election, he switched his political allegiance from the Democratic to the Republican Party. He was offered an administrative position with the army after the election, but chose to return to more traditional army duty, as he had done many times previously when similar opportunities were presented to him. Between 1983 and 1986 Powell rose from major general to three-star general. As such, he commanded the Fifth Corps in Frankfort, Germany. He was back in the United States serving as assistant national security advisor when President Ronald Reagan named him national security advisor. Just short of a year later, he became the first national security advisor to be given the Secretary's Award, for distinguished contributions.

Who was **Daniel "Chappie" James Jr.**?

In 1975 Daniel H. "Chappie" James Jr. (1920–1978) became the first black four-star general in the U.S. Air Force and was named commander-in-chief of the North American Air

Defense Command (NORAD). He was not only the first black air force four-star general, but also the first to be promoted to that rank in any of the U.S. armed forces. James was born in Pensacola, Florida. He was educated at Tuskegee University but was expelled for fighting in his senior year; he was not actually awarded his degree until twenty-seven years later. He enrolled in the Army Air Corps program, part of the government's Civilian Pilot Training Program, while a student at Tuskegee and was commissioned as a second lieutenant in 1943. James earned renown as a military pilot as one of the original members of the famed "Tuskegee Airmen," the all-black flying unit that faced tremendous racial bias during its training days and its initial flying engagements. Although his military career began in 1944, he was still flying combat missions during the Korean and Vietnam wars. In 1970 James was promoted to the rank of brigadier general, to major general in 1972, and to lieutenant general in 1974. His career spanned thirty-four years, ending with his retirement in 1978. He died of a heart attack less than a month after retirement. James' many civilian and military awards included the Distinguished Flying Cross, a Distinguished Service Medal for Valor, and the George Washington Freedom Foundation Honor Medal, given to him in 1967 for his essay "Freedom—My Heritage, My Responsibility," which he had written for a contest in the *Stars and Stripes*. James, who was the first black to command an integrated combat unit in the U.S. Army, endured much and achieved much. His career almost ended in 1950 when he was in a serious crash while flying in a two-seater plane. He is remembered as a patriotic American, a courageous and dedicated airman, and an advocate of racial equality in the armed forces.

Who was **the first African-American general counsel** for the **U.S. Navy**?

Business executive and attorney Togo Dennis West Jr. (1942–) was the first black U.S. Navy general counsel. He had served also as associate deputy general for the Department of Justice, and special assistant to the secretary, deputy secretary, and general counsel for the Department of Defense. From 1993 to 1998, West was secretary of the U.S. Army. He then became acting secretary for Veterans Affairs. Born in Winston-Salem, North Carolina, he received his bachelor's and law degrees from Howard University in Washington, D.C.

THE MILITARY AND JIM CROW

When was **racial segregation** in the **U.S. military outlawed**?

President Harry S. Truman issued Executive Order 9981 on July 26, 1948, signaling an end to legal segregation in the U.S. military. The order read, "It is hereby declared to be the policy of the President that there shall be equality of treatment and opportunity for all persons in the armed services without regard to race, color, religion or national origin. This policy shall be put into effect as rapidly as possible, having due regard to the time required to effectuate any necessary changes without impairing efficiency or morale." Increasingly the demand for desegregation of the military became a key political issue in black America. Although blacks had served in the military, they did so in racially segregated units. When the Korean War (1950–1953) was fought, it was a "battlefield test of integration in the making." The integration of blacks in military units in Korea rose from 9 percent to 30 percent between May and August 1951. By then there was also an overall gain of blacks in the army. For the first time in America's history, the military officially accepted blacks as an integral part of its service units.

Were **African-American doctors allowed** to serve in the **Navy?**

In 1942 Bernard Whitfield Robinson (c. 1918–1972) became the first black commissioned officer in the U.S. Naval Reserve on June 18. The navy sought to increase the number of doctors in service and then offered commissions to medical students who, upon graduation, began tours of duty. After graduating from Harvard University, Robinson became the first black commissioned through the program, eventually serving as a doctor in the U.S. Naval Reserve. The Bureau of Naval Personnel, however, claimed that his commission had been a "slip." Robinson reported for duty after the "Golden Thirteen" were commissioned in March 1944.

AFRICAN-AMERICAN WOMEN IN THE MILITARY

In what **capacities** have African-American **women served in the military?**

During World War II, African-American women served in a number of capacities. Lieutenant Harriet Ida Pickens (d. 1969) and Ensign Frances Eliza Willis were the first to be commissioned in the Women Accepted for Volunteer Emergency Service (WAVES). Over four thousand African-American women joined the Women's Army Corps (WAC). The Army Nurse Corps discouraged black women nurses in many sites, such as field hospitals, hospital ships and trains, and medical transport planes. Black women felt the sting of racial segregation practices in some military units. It was not until 1945 that the Army Nurse Corps, and soon the navy, ceased racial exclusionary practices, but not before the Draft Nurse Bill (H.R. 1284) was introduced in Congress. By the end of the war, some seventy-six thousand black nurses served in hospitals in the United States, Africa, Asia, and Europe.

What role did the **Women's Auxiliary Army Corps** play in **bringing black women** into the **military?**

President Franklin D. Roosevelt signed the act that created the Women's Auxiliary Army Corps (WAAC) on May 14, 1942, which made it possible for more African-American women to serve in the military than previously. The volunteer unit consisted of both black and white recruits. Charity Adams Earley (1918–2002) completed basic training in the WAAC that year, and two weeks later became the first black woman commissioned in that organization. When she retired from the Corps, after the end of World War II, she was the highest-ranking black officer in the service. Earley grew up in Columbia, South Carolina, the daughter of a Methodist minister and a former schoolteacher. The influence of segregation was apparent in Columbia, and Earley went on to become a vigorous opponent of racial segregation. She worked her way through Wilberforce University and graduated in 1938. She taught mathematics in Columbia, until she was influenced by the recruitment efforts of Mary McLeod Bethune to enlist in the WAAC. Bethune, a noted educator and influential leader, served as an assistant to the secretary of war and was the black representative on the Advisory Council to the Women's Interests Section, a group organized by the War Department in 1941 to attract women to the armed services. Commissioned as a lieutenant, Earley was named company commander of the women's Basic Training Company on her post. She faced several problems as she sought to expand opportunities for blacks in the WAAC. The organization became known as the Women's Army Corps (WAC) when "Auxiliary" was dropped from the unit's name. The name change, made under the guidance of WAAC director Oveta Culp Hobby, was designed to make the unit a direct branch of the military and attract more women with better educational backgrounds. By 1943 Earley was a major, and she was proposed to head a special Negro training regiment. She refused this position and the segregated unit was never formed. In 1944 she became the first black WAC given overseas duty and commanded a unit in Birmingham, England. She was made a lieutenant colonel in December 1945. When Earley left the army, she resumed graduate studies in psychology at The Ohio State University. She was recognized as a highly effective administrator during her period of military service. She died in her hometown on January 13, 2002.

Who was **Harriet M. Waddy (West)**?

On August 21, 1943, Harriet M. Waddy West (1904–1999) became the first black woman major in the Women's Army Auxiliary Corps (WAAC), which later became the Women's Army Corps (WAC). She was at the time chief of planning in the Bureau of Control Division at WAAC Headquarters in Washington, D.C. Waddy was born in Jefferson City, Missouri, and was a graduate of Kansas State College of Agriculture and Applied Science. During the Great Depression, she worked as an aide to noted educator and civic leader Mary McLeod Bethune, who no doubt influenced Waddy's decision to join the WAAC. She entered officer candidate school in 1942. During World War II, Waddy was one of the two highest-ranking black officers in the WAAC and served as its wartime advisor on racial issues. She was promoted to lieutenant colonel in 1948 and served on active duty until she retired in 1952; she remained in the Reserves until 1969. During her time after retirement from active military duty, she worked for the Federal Aviation Administration and also served as a counselor for girls at a Job Corps Center in Oregon. Waddy was an active recruiter of black women for the WAAC and served for a time as an aide to its director, Oveta Culp Hobby. She also campaigned against the existing racial discrimination in the military. She moved to Las Vegas in 1998 and was in residence there at the time of her death.

Who is **Marcelite J. Harris**?

Marcelite Jordan Harris (1943–) became the first black woman brigadier general in the U.S. Air Force, in 1990. She became the first black woman major general in 1995. Born in Houston, Texas, Harris's ancestry can be traced back to slavery and reveals the achievements of her forebears. Her maternal great-great-grandfather was the mayor of Donaldsonville, Texas, and served in both houses of the state legislature. Her maternal great-grandfather founded the first school for blacks in Fort Worth, Texas. Harris was educated at Spelman College, Central Michigan University, Chapman College, the University of Maryland, and Harvard University. She entered the air force in 1965 through Officer Training School, and in 1971 she became the first black woman aircraft maintenance officer. (She had to apply three times before her application for training in aircraft maintenance was accepted.) In 1978, as commander of a cadet squadron at the U.S. Air Force Academy, Harris became one of the first two female air officer commanders. She retired from the air force in 1997. While in the service, she was the highest-ranking woman on active duty in the air force and the highest-ranking black woman in the Department of Defense. She also served for a time as social aide to President Jimmy Carter. Her many military honors include the Bronze Star, the Presidential Unit Citation, and the Vietnam Service Medal. President Barack Obama appointed her to the Board of Visitors to the United States Air Force Academy.

Brigadier General Marcelite Harris was the first black woman to achieve that high rank in the air force.

Who was the **first black woman general** in the U.S. **Army**?

Hazel Winifred Johnson (1927–2011) climbed the ranks in the military and became the first black woman general in the U.S. Army, in 1979. She was born in Malvern, Pennsylvania, one of seven children raised on the family farm in West Chester. She knew early that she wanted to be a nurse, and took her first step in this direction when she entered Harlem University School of Nursing in 1950. After receiving her bachelor's degree, she took a job at a veterans hospital in Philadelphia. She was working there when she joined the army in 1955. In 1960 Johnson achieved the rank of second lieutenant. She found no problems because of her race, and was able to continue her education while in the army, going on to earn degrees from Villanova University (bachelor's in nursing), Columbia University (master's in nursing education) and Catholic University (doctorate in educational administration). Johnson progressed steadily in the army, and by the 1970s her rank of colonel made her the highest-ranking black woman in the armed forces. On her way to becoming a general, Johnson held many responsible positions, including serving as assistant dean of the School of Nursing at the University of Maryland and as chief nurse of the U.S. Army Military Command in Korea. She remained chief of the Army Nurse Corps until 1983, when she retired from military service. Johnson turned her attention to teaching after retirement, holding faculty posts first at George Washington University (while also working with the American Nursing Association), and then at George Mason University. Johnson was named Army Nurse of the Year in 1972, and held several honorary doctorate degrees and military awards.

NURSES IN THE MILITARY

Who was the **first black army nurse**?

In 1948 Nancy Leftenant-Colon (c. 1920–) became the first black member of the Regular Army Nurse Corps in March of that year. She was a graduate of Lincoln Hospital School for Nurses, in the Bronx, New York, which enrolled primarily minority students. She joined the army reserve nurse corps in February 1945. At the time of her enlistment, black nurses were not highly regarded and were not given the status of regular nurse, but in eleven months she was promoted from second to first lieutenant. Her performance as a nurse was no doubt a factor in the acceptance of her 1948 application for admission into the Regular Army Nurse Corps. During her service career she was an air force flight nurse. Leftenant-Colon retired from the army, with the rank of major, in 1965. She worked from 1971 to 1984 as a nurse at Amityville High School in New York, having moved to Long Island when she left the army. She achieved another "first" as the only woman to be president of the Tuskegee Airmen. She was president of the group from 1989 to 1991.

When did the **Coast Guard's Women's Reserve admit** black women?

The Coast Guard's Women's Reserve was created on November 23, 1942, when President Franklin D. Roosevelt signed Public Law 772. The Women's Reserve became known by an acronym based on the Coast Guard's motto: "Semper Paratus—Always Ready," or SPAR. Black women were initially denied admission into the organization. In October 1944, the first black SPAR was Yeoman Second Class Olivia Hooker (c. 1922–). A twenty-two-year-old high school graduate, Hooker had worked in a clerical or sales position before joining the SPARs. Most SPARs enlisted for six years; thus, by December 1944 SPAR recruiting virtually ended. Altogether, only five black women were recruited for SPARs, representing tokenism; they were trained at Manhattan Beach Training Station in New York and were assigned to district offices of the Coast Guard without regard to race.

Who was the first African-American **woman** to become **brigadier general** in the army?

In 1985 Sherian Grace Cadoria (1943–) became the first black woman to be given the rank of brigadier general in the regular U.S. Army and the first black woman to command a male battalion. That same year she became the first black woman director of manpower and personnel for the Joint Chiefs of Staff. Cadoria served as one of four women army generals. Her tours of duty included service in Vietnam. She held key posts with the Law Enforcement Division and the Criminal Investigation Command. She retired from the army in 1990. Cadoria's route to advancement in the army was unlike that of many of her women colleagues, who were able to advance through the nursing corps; she advanced through her involvement with the military police. She was born in Marksville, Louisiana, where in the 1940s she had to walk five miles to school rather than run the risk of riding the bus. She graduated from Southern University in Louisiana in 1961 and enlisted in the Women's Army Corps (WAC). This led to another "first" for her: she was the first black woman to attend the army's Com-

U.S. Army Brigadier General Sherian Grace Cadoria became the first black woman to command a male battalion in 1985.

mand and General Staff College, from which she received a diploma in 1971. She earned a master's degree from the University of Oklahoma and a diploma from the U.S. War College (where she was, again, the first black woman to attend); she also studied at the National Defense University Institute of Higher Defense Studies. Cadoria's rise through the ranks was accompanied by the frustrations encountered because of her race and her gender—white racism in the South and the army's stereotypical belief that there were army jobs women could not do. Her last army assignment, which began in 1987, was as Deputy Commanding General and Director for the U.S. Total Army Personnel Command in Alexandria, Virginia. During her almost thirty-year army career, Cadoria received many medals and commendations, including three Bronze Stars. She returned to Louisiana when she retired, where she organized the Cadoria Speaker Service.

MEDICAL OFFICERS IN THE MILITARY

Who was the **first black commissioned medical officer** in the **army**?

In 1863 Alexander T. Augusta (1825–1890) became the first black commissioned, and the highest ranking black officer, in the segregated army. Augusta headed the old Freedmen's Hospital located at Camp Barker in Washington, D.C., becoming the country's first black to direct a hospital. There he oversaw the treatment of escaped slaves who were sick and came to Camp Barker for treatment. In 1865 it came under the auspices of the newly created Freedmen's Bureau. Born free in Norfolk, Virginia, Augusta studied medicine under private tutors in Baltimore. After he was refused admission to the University of Pennsylvania's medical school, a professor at that school, William Gibson, taught him privately. He moved to Canada and in 1856 received his medical degree from the University of Toronto's medical college. By April 1863, Augusta had received a medical commission and was appointed surgeon of the U.S. Colored Troops. With the rank of major, he became the first of eight black physicians commissioned in the army. In 1868 he taught at Howard University's newly organized Medical Department. The school awarded him an honorary M.A. degree in 1872.

Why was physician and abolitionist **Martin R. Delany** important during the **Civil War**?

Upon the order of President Abraham Lincoln, Martin Robison Delany (1812–1885) was the first black commissioned as a field officer with the rank of major in the regular infantry, in 1865. Assigned to Charleston, South Carolina, he recruited two regiments of blacks. Delany was born in what is now Charles Town, West Virginia, the son of a slave father and a free mother. He is reputed to have believed that he was descended from African royalty, and this may have influenced his later activities as a founder of Black Nationalism and advocate of emigration to Africa. The family relocated to Chambersburg, Pennsylvania, after facing racial problems in Charles Town, and Delany was educated in Chambersburg until 1827, when he had to go to work. Four years later he left for Pittsburgh, which was his home for the next twenty-five years. In Pittsburgh he established his leadership as an advocate for blacks and continued his education. In or around 1843, Delany began publishing *The Mystery,* said to be the first black newspaper west of the Alleghenies. In 1850 he entered Harvard Medical School, but left after one semester because of the protests of white students; he gave himself the title of "doctor" and did indeed practice medicine in Pittsburgh. Delany moved to Wilberforce, Ohio, in 1864. It was at this time that he advanced a plan to recruit black troops commanded by black officers to fight on the side of the Union in the Civil War. It was after an interview with President Abraham Lincoln with regard to the plan that Delany became an army officer. The war ended before his plan could be put into effect. He was assigned to the Freedmen's Bureau in Beaufort, South Carolina. He remained there until he ended his army career in 1868. He transferred his attention to politics and served as a judge briefly, but was removed after being charged with fraud. Some considered Delany a radical, but he was, for a time, a recognized leader among blacks. He returned to Wilberforce shortly before his death.

Who was the first African-American **woman medical officer** in the U.S. **Army**?

Clotilde Dent Bowen (1923–2011), who was commissioned in the U.S. Army in 1955 with the rank of captain, became the first black woman medical officer in the army. When she was promoted to colonel, she was the first black woman to receive this rank. Bowen began accumulating "firsts" before she entered the army. When she graduated from The Ohio State University Medical School in 1947, she was the first black woman to receive a medical degree from the institution. Bowen's medical specialty was neuropsychiatry. During the Vietnam War she served in that country, and was awarded the Bronze Star and the Legion of Merit in 1971, in recognition of her service; the Meritorious Service Medal was given to her in 1974. Several awards from Ohio State, including The Ohio State University Professional Achievement Award in 1998, also recognized her achievements. Bowen was born in Chicago, Illinois, and did both her undergraduate and professional studies at Ohio State. Before she entered the army, she practiced in New York City and was associated for a time with Harlem Hospital. Before going to Vietnam, Bowen was assigned to Veterans Administration hospitals. Her last post before entering private practice was a position as staff psychiatrist at the Veterans Affairs Medical Center in Denver, Colorado, from 1990 to 1996. Bowen's professional skills resulted in a certificate in psychiatry from the American Board of Psychiatry and Neurology in 1966, and designation as a Fellow of the American Psychiatric Association. She served in the army for thirty years.

THE MILITARY ON BLACK COLLEGE CAMPUSES

What was the **impact** of **ROTC programs** on black college campuses?

Many black students have found it necessary to rely on federal aid to support their college education. Before federal grants were available, the Reserve Officers Training Corps (ROTC) established campus-based detachments on Historically Black Colleges and Universities (HBCU) campuses. This provided the major federal subsidy program for higher education for black men. The men entered campus-commissioning programs that had financial benefits for them once they graduated and entered military service as officers. In the late 1990s there were twenty-one HBCUs that produced approximately one-half of all black ROTC commissions in the army. After the Vietnam War ended, many traditionally white colleges abolished their ROTC programs and the Pentagon responded by adding more such programs to HBCUs. There are claims that ROTC training in these institutions is significant in producing black leaders for American society, and that their importance should not be overlooked.

Where are the **largest ROTC programs** in the HBCUs?

In 1995 the largest ROTC programs on HBCU campuses were at Alabama A&M University and Tuskegee University in Alabama, Florida A&M University, Jackson State University in Mississippi, Howard University in Washington, D.C., North Carolina A&T State University in Greensboro, South Carolina State University in Orangeburg, Prairie View A&M University in Texas, and Hampton and Norfolk State Universities in Virginia. Among these, only Hampton and Tuskegee are privately supported institutions. Some of the small, private institutions, such as Fisk University in Nashville, have provided ROTC and NROTC training for its students at nearby institutions, such as Vanderbilt

University. The U.S. Navy's presence on the HBCU campuses has been small. The HBCU programs also have on campus professors of military science who are revered names among black officers. Earlier, some of these professors were former Tuskegee Airmen. Among those on campus in fairly recent times were Colonel James Robinson at South Carolina State and Lieutenant Colonel Hiram Chase of Howard and Prairie View.

DISSIDENTS AND THE WAR EFFORT

What were the **war protest efforts** of black students during the **Black Power Movement**?

Activist black students joined those of other races on college campuses during the late 1960s and sometimes burned draft cards, protested against the ROTC and the Vietnam War, and promoted such slogans as "Make Love, Not War," and "Hell No, We Won't Go!" Violence at predominantly white Kent State University resulted in tragedy in early May 1970, when antiwar demonstrators were shot; four demonstrators were killed, and nine wounded. Violence at all-black South Carolina State University in Orangeburg on February 6, 1968, which drew national attention, appeared to be less focused on anti-war efforts than on racial protests.

What action did world heavyweight boxing champion **Muhammad Ali** take against the **Vietnam War draft**?

Muhammad Ali, born Cassius Clay, became defiant around the time of the Vietnam War, changed his name to Ali, and used his membership in the Nation of Islam to protest his draft into the United States Army. He argued that "military service was incompatible with his membership in the Nation of Islam." In 1967 he was convicted of violating the Selective Service Act. As further punishment, he was barred from fighting and stripped of his title, but remained free on bond. After appealing his case in 1971, the United States Supreme Court reversed the conviction. Ali regained his title on October 30, 1974.

KOREA AND VIETNAM

What were **race relations** like during the **Korean War**?

Black solders found a much segregated army at the outbreak of the Korean War. When the all-black 24th Infantry Regiment was called to duty, false reports circulated that the black soldiers were unreliable; however, combat troops were much needed, which led to at least ad hoc integration by the end of the war. Large numbers of blacks enlisted; by mid-1951, blacks accounted for one out of every four new army recruits. Before long, all of the army's basic training centers were integrated and blacks joined all-white combat units. By the end of the Korean War, over 90 percent of the blacks in the army were in integrated units. Both the U.S. Air Force and the Marine Corps also eliminated their racially segregated units.

What **risks** did blacks in the military face during the **Vietnam War**?

During the Vietnam conflict, reports indicated that blacks in the military were more likely to be drafted, sent to Vietnam to serve in high-risk areas, and to be killed or wounded in combat. The loss of blacks during the war amounted to one-fourth of the army casualties for enlisted personnel. This took black leaders' concerns back to the Selective Service System: some claimed that the system favored drafting blacks and the poor, and that many local draft boards had few black representations or none at all. Protests citing racial overtones spread to the Air Force, the Marine Corps, and naval stations.

MUSIC

MUSIC AND SLAVERY

What was the nature of **black music during slavery**?

Slaves, who lived a life of suffering, hardship, and pain, used a variety of styles and forms of expression in the music of the time. From Africa they had used music as a part of daily life—in work, communication, celebration, unity, and rites of passage. Because theirs was an oral tradition, the slaves had no need for sheet music to bring their songs and dances with them—they carried it all in their heads. Their musical styles consisted of moans, cries, hollers, shouts, work songs, and dances. As early as 1620, moans, cries and hollers were described by slave traders and others who kept journal records. Whether on slave ships, auction blocks, in the fields, or slave coffles, moans were heard and focused on repetitive words. As a form of exchange between slaves, field cries were used. Hollers were used to share a sentiment or to alert fellow slaves about a particular issue, while moans were used as "brief sighs or expressions." Work songs gave slaves an outlet to express emotion and were used by slaveholders as a form of motivation or to account for their presence or work. Styles varied, however, according to the type of work, such as gang labor or domestic activities. Musical styles and forms of entertainment of the enslaved began to take various forms as early as 1620, as they produced songs for children's play, dances, storytelling, and other forms of cultural expression. The role of the African griot (a West African oral historian, storyteller, praise singer, poet, and/or musician) was copied as well, as elder slaves passed on the essential music and cultural traditions in the slave community by singing songs and telling stories.

As slaves assimilated the culture of their owners, they learned the European's language, religion, and music. Between 1770 and 1865, they sang English psalms and hymns in church as they converted to Christianity and, along with whites, attended church services on Sundays and holidays. Their worship was in a segregated area of the

Black slaves, such as these sweet potato workers in a circa 1862 Southern plantation, would use songs to communicate to one another or express emotions. Styles varied depending on the type of labor and purpose of the song.

church. Camp meetings and outdoor revivals were popular in the South at that time as well. It was at such meetings that slaves gave full expression to their lifestyle and feelings by singing, dancing, shouting, and praying. The ring shout has been called the "first form of religious expression adapted from an African religious dance." It was performed in a call-and-response form, as some sang while others danced in a circle.

Some slaves in the South studied with itinerant music teachers. The most talented musicians gained professional-level skills that were quickly put to use by the whites. Bonded servants and slave musicians, playing instruments such as the violin, flute, and piano, provided much of the recreational music for their masters, playing at dance balls and dancing schools. On self-sufficient plantations, the most musical of the domestic slaves provided evening "entertainments." Once public concerts became possible and popular in the New World, a few talented slaves gave public concerts.

What are **Negro Spirituals**?

Negro Spirituals are religious songs that black Americans sang from the earliest days of their enslavement in America; they have been called "the foremost prominent style of Southern slave music." The exact development of the spiritual is difficult to trace, since the music was not recorded but passed on orally. However, the spiritual is said to have emerged in the late 1770s and became prominent during the antebellum period and the Civil War, between 1830 and the 1860s. Spirituals were taught by rote and not notated music. The spirituals have been called "strongly African" as well as "strongly American," as slaves brought with them from Africa a rich musical heritage. Slaves sang their songs while at work on plantations, when at play, at rest, and during their ritual worship ser-

What blind musician received national fame as a pianist?

In 1858 the first black pianist to win national fame was Thomas Greene Bethune, or "Blind Tom" (1849–1909). He was also the first black artist known to have performed at the White House. Then about ten years old, he played the piano for President James Buchanan. Born a blind slave near Columbus, Georgia, Bethune's talent as a composer and a pianist was soon recognized by Colonel Bethune, who had purchased him in 1850. The child prodigy made his debut in Savannah, Georgia, and for more than forty years amazed his audiences "with his artistry and his gift for total recall" of the more than seven hundred pieces that he played. Blind Tom had sporadic formal training and is said to have composed more than a hundred works. He began playing public concerts while still a slave and continued to perform after emancipation. The most celebrated of the early black pianists, he began a tour of Europe in 1866 that netted $100,000.

vices. They were powerful shields against the inhumanity of slavery and provided a healthy escape from sorrow and violence. Slave songs often spoke of God, heaven, and freedom; such as, chariots coming to carry them out of slavery. Some spirituals refer to the Jordan River, which slaves considered the "river of escape." They referenced the river as a route to freedom, or a return route to Africa. Thus, spirituals also held hidden messages to facilitate escape from slavery.

Who introduced spirituals to the world?

In February of 1882 the Fisk Jubilee Singers, who introduced the spiritual to the world as an American art form, became the first black choir to perform at the White House. Their rendition of "Safe in the Arms of Jesus" moved President Chester Arthur to tears. The night before their performance, the singers were denied lodging in every hotel in the district. On October 6, 1871, the nine men and women singers—all former slaves or freedmen—set out on their first tour to raise money to save fledgling Fisk University, located in Nashville, Tennessee. Under the direction of George Leonard White, their first tour took them to Ohio. While there, they assumed the name Jubilee Singers, after the Year of the Jubilee in the Old Testament. Although they were hungry and cold, they donated their first purse of less than fifty dollars to the Chicago Relief Fund to aid victims of the great Chicago fire. After that, they traveled widely, singing in the Boston Coliseum and in churches, and electrified audiences wherever they performed. They sang the songs of their ancestors—slave songs and spirituals. Following a successful performance in New England, President Ulysses Grant invited them to sing at the White House. The singers made their first tour of England in 1873–1874, where they sang before royalty and in cathedrals and palaces. Queen Victoria was so impressed with them that she commissioned her court painter, George Edmund Havel, to paint a portrait of the group that now totaled eleven members. His life-sized rendition now hangs in Fisk's Jubilee Hall, the residence hall that the school erected in 1875 from funds that the singers earned while on tour. The singers toured Europe in 1875 and continued to sing throughout the United States, electrifying audiences with their moving rendition of slave songs and spirituals. In November 2000 the then-current singers were inducted into the Gospel Music Hall of Fame in Nashville, Tennessee. President George W. Bush awarded the singers the National Medal of the Arts in 2008.

Hampton Institute, as the school was called earlier, had singers as well; they, too, sang spirituals as they traveled throughout the United States and Europe, covering England, Holland, France, Germany, Austria, and elsewhere, but this group lacked the international reputation of the Fisk singers.

RAGTIME MUSIC

What **composer** of instrumental rags was called the **"King of Ragtime"**?

In 1911 Scott Joplin's opera *Treemonisha,* the first black folk opera written by a black composer, was first performed in private. A talented musical composer, Joplin (c. 1868–1917) was born in northeastern Texas. Around 1875 the family relocated to Texarkana, Texas. By the late 1880s Joplin had settled in St. Louis and later in Sedalia,

Scott Joplin, the "King of Ragtime," also wrote the first black folk opera, *Treemonisha.*

Missouri. He studied at George R. Smith College in Sedalia. Joplin established himself as a composer of instrumental rags. His first major success was "Maple Leaf Rag," which earned him the title "King of Ragtime." He worked with several publishers but changed frequently in search of better terms. In 1913 he established his own publishing company. After his first major success, Joplin continued to compose. His works included the full-length ragtime opera, *A Guest of Honor* (1903), and *Treemonisha* (written in 1910 and published a year later), and *Magnetic Rag* (1914). He moved from St. Louis, where he had settled again, to New York City in July 1907, and earned his living as a composer and teacher. After he died, he was remembered for little more than "Maple Leaf Rag" until the 1960s, when he was rediscovered, and his work became the score for the movie *The Sting*. On January 28, 1972, *Treemonisha* premiered in Atlanta and was well-received. For his contribution to American music, in 1976 Joplin received a special Bicentennial Pulitzer Prize.

BLACKS IN COUNTRY MUSIC

What was **DeFord Bailey Sr.'s contribution** to **country music**?

DeFord Bailey Sr. (1899–1982), a harmonica player, became the first black musician to perform on the Grand Ole Opry in Nashville, Tennessee, on December 26, 1924. Originally called "The Barn Dance," the show's name was changed to "The Grand Ole Opry" in the autumn of 1927. Bailey was perhaps the first black heard on nationwide radio. The next year, he was the first black to have a recording session in Nashville, Tennessee. Bailey recorded eight sides for RCA. Known for his train sounds, he was one of the most influential harmonica players in blues and country music and one of the most popular performers in the first fifteen years of the Opry, the longest-running radio show in the country. Bailey was fired in 1941 as a result of the dispute between ASCAP and the newly formed BMI over payment for music played on the radio. In 1991, a memorial marker was erected near his birth site in Wilson County, Tennessee.

Who was the **first black singer** with the **Grand Ole Opry**?

In 1967 Charley Pride (1939–), singer and guitarist, became the first black singer with the Grand Ole Opry. His interest at first was in baseball, and at age sixteen he left his home state of Mississippi to seek employment with the now-defunct Negro American Baseball League. He was a pitcher-outfielder with the Memphis Red Sox, later played with the Birmingham Black Barons, and in 1961 played in the majors with the Los Angeles Angels. Opry star Red Foley heard Pride sing country music in 1963 and encouraged him to go to Nashville, where he charmed RCA Records and entered the country music field. The white audience at his first major concert in 1967 did not know his race until he appeared on stage. His recording "Just Between Me and You" launched him into super-stardom and made him a number-one country music attraction. In 1971 Pride was the first black named Entertainer of the Year and Male Vocalist of the Year in the field of country music.

Charley Pride was the first black country singer to be inducted into the Grand Ole Opry.

213

Pride became the first black American voted into the Country Music Hall of Fame, located in Nashville, Tennessee, in 2000. He and singer Faron Young were the seventy-third and seventy-fourth members to be inducted into the Hall of Fame at the Thirty-fourth Annual Country Music Association Awards. Their selection was the result of the votes of about 350 CMA members. During Pride's extraordinary career, he had twenty-nine country hits, representing the first major success by a black American in commercial country music. During the awards program Pride performed "Kiss An Angel Good Morning," "Crystal Chandelier," "Is Anybody Goin' to San Antone," and "Kaw-Liga." Pride was honored again, on May 14, 2001, when the Country Music Hall of Fame held its first official event at its new facility in Nashville; he received a medallion commemorating his induction into the hall in the previous year.

What **two successful pop singers-songwriters** crossed over into country music?

Former front man with the rock band Hootie & the Blowfish, Darius Rucker (1966–), a successful pop singer-songwriter, made his debut in country music in 2008, producing his debut disc, *Learn to Live,* with three hit singles. The disc went No. 1 on the country charts. With that success, Rucker became the first black singer to win the Best New Artist Award at the Country Music Association Awards in November 2008. Rucker calls himself a country singer. "I've always liked country music but never really told anybody," he said. Some sources say that Rucker is "sitting on top of the country music world." His single "Come Back Song" was on *Billboard*'s Top 10 country singles. *Charleston, SC 1966,* his 2010 CD, was number one on *Billboard*'s top country CDs, and after two months was still in the Top 20. Rucker is the first black to crack country music's top 20 singles since 1988 and the first black to reach number one since 1983, when Charley Pride achieved that honor. He is also the first black with a number-one country CD or album since 1985, when Ray Charles achieved that success. A singer and songwriter, Rucker was born on May 13, 1966, in Charleston, South Carolina. He graduated from the University of South Carolina, and in 1986 cofounded the band Hootie & the Blowfish, named after two of his college classmates. They played the college circuit for several years and toured full-time, breaking into the mainstream in 1994. Rucker continues his relationship with the band. His new album was released in 2013.

Lionel Brockman Richie Jr. (1949–), singer, songwriter, and pianist, crossed over into country music in 2012. He is known also as a singer of soul, R&B, and pop rock. The Tuskegee, Alabama, native grew up on the campus of Tuskegee Institute (later University). While a freshman at the school, Richie formed the Mighty Mystics who, along with members of the Jays, became the Commodores. The group combined gospel, classical, and country-western music and emerged as a formidable live act throughout the 1960s and 1970s. They signed with Motown and had their first hit in 1974 with the song "Machine Gun." In 1981 Richie recorded the hit theme song for Franco Zeffirelli's film *Endless Love.* In 1982 he released his first album, *Lionel Richie,* which featured the hits "Truly," "You Are," and "My Love." His follow-up album in 1983, *Can't Slow Down,* produced more hits, including "All Night Long" and "Stuck On You." He collaborated with Michael Jackson in 1985 and co-wrote "We Are the World." In 1985 he received an Oscar nomination for his composition "Say You, Say Me." Richie was inducted into the Songwriters Hall of Fame in 1994. His music has reached across generations and allowed new listeners to enjoy the smooth sound of this five-time Grammy winner, Oscar winner for best song, Golden Globe winner, and winner of numerous American Music Awards. His album *Tuskegee,* released in March 2012, contains thirteen of his hit singles and features such country singers as Shania Twain, Rascal Flatts, Blake Shelton, Willie Nelson, Darius Rucker, and others. It also represents his cross-over into the country music genre and has become another of his number-one albums.

RECORD COMPANIES

What was the **first record company owned** and operated by **blacks**?

In 1921 the Pace Phonograph Company, which used the Black Swan label, was the first record company owned and operated by a black. It was established in January 1921 by Henry Pace (1897–1943), who had been owner of a music publishing company with W. C. Handy. Two former workers for the Pace-Handy Company joined him: Fletcher Henderson (1897–1952) as a recording manager and William Grant Still (1895–1978) as

an arranger. In spring 1921 Ethel Waters (1896–1977) recorded the company's first hit, "Down Home Blues/Oh, Daddy." During its first six months the company reportedly sold more than half a million records. The company went broke in 1923, and was sold to Paramount Records the following year.

Who was the **first** African American to **record** with the **Victor Talking Machine Company**?

Bert (Egbert Austin) Williams (1873–1922) was the first black to record with the Victor Talking Machine Company, in 1901. Between 1901 and 1903 he recorded fifteen titles, primarily show tunes or comedy routines that he had done on stage. In 1910 he was the first black to receive feature billing in the Ziegfeld Follies and remained with them until 1919. Williams

A vaudeville comedian, Bert Williams was one of the most popular black entertainers of the early twentieth century and a best-selling recording artist.

was born in Antigua, British West Indies, and moved with his family to New York and California. He studied civil engineering for a period, before entering show business. He and George Nash Walker formed a successful vaudeville team that reached New York City in 1896. Their show, *In Dahomey,* opened in a Times Square theater in 1902 and had a command performance during a tour abroad in 1903. The team became known for characterizations—Walker as a citified dandy, and Williams as a blackface comic, wearing an outlandish costume and using black dialect. In 1914 Williams became the first black to star in a movie, *Darktown Jubilee.* The film is said to have caused a race riot when it was shown in Brooklyn. *Darktown Jubilee* was his only movie. Williams's trademark was the song "Nobody," which he wrote and sang. He is regarded by many as the greatest black vaudeville performer in American history.

BIG BANDS AND BANDMASTERS

What is the **importance of big bands** in African-American culture?

Big bands, playing jazz music, dominated African-American musical culture from 1920 until the 1950s. The bands were most prolific in the 1930s and 1940s, or the Swing Era. Bands during this era usually had twelve to fifteen members, and the bands were divided into four sections: saxophone, trumpet, trombone, and rhythm. By the time the bebop style emerged in the 1940s, the Swing Era had ceased. Jazz clubs, such as the Cotton Club and the Savoy in New York City and Chicago's Sunset/Grand Terrace Café were the common sites for the big bands. Radio broadcasts and recordings gave national spread to the music of the big bands.

What **big band leaders defined jazz** and American music in the early decades of the twentieth century?

Those black musicians whose names are commonly associated with the big band era are Fletcher Henderson, Louis Armstrong, Don Redman, Duke Ellington, Count Basie, and Cab Calloway. Much credit is given to Fletcher Henderson (1877–1952), who in 1921 became musical director for the Black Swan label, a black-owned company. His career began to soar when he became bandleader for Harlem's Club Alabam, and his orchestra became one of the dominant bands in New York. By the next decade his was one of America's most important black musical groups. A number of black musicians who would form their own bands later own had their start with Henderson. Don Redman (1900–1964) came from musically talented parents in Maryland. While playing with Fletcher Henderson, he developed a new jazz sound, playing the clarinet and saxophone. He became known, however, as an arranger, combining European classical, African-American brass band, and church music. His big band aesthetic influenced many big band leaders who followed him. He left Henderson's band in 1927 and later formed the

Don Redman Orchestra, whose residence was at legendary Connie's Inn in New York City. The work of Henderson and Redman helped to usher in the Swing Era.

In Chicago, Earl "Fatha" Hines (1903–1983) became notable as the Swing Era was born. He first played the trumpet and then the piano, and formed his own band in 1928. For many years his style of piano playing influenced pianists. Legendary personalities who emerged from his band included Dizzy Gillespie, Charlie Parker, Billy Eckstine, and Ella Fitzgerald. The most prolific bandleader of the Swing Era was Edward Kennedy "Duke" Ellington (1899–1974). He dropped out of high school in his native Washington, D.C., and made a living by playing the piano around town. He and his band moved to New York City in the early 1920s. The band spent four years at the Hollywood Club, later known as the Kentucky Club, and also recorded their music for sale. The group became the Cotton Club's house band in 1927, and then left in 1931. Billy Strayhorn joined the orchestra in 1938 and helped it along its most fertile period. Strayhorn composed or collaborated with Ellington on over two hundred works, the most notable being "Take the A Train."

Count (William) Basie (1904–1984) began playing the piano as a teenager and studied with Fats Waller. Basie's own band, formed in 1935 in Kansas City, Missouri, took the flowering of that city's style to Chicago and New York City. He is said to have helped to invent big-band swing. The band established itself as one of the leaders in jazz. Basie performed extensively until the 1970s, using slide piano. His was an almost exotic sound heard during the Big Band Era. In 1959, Basie was the first black man to win a Grammy Award. He was also the first black from the United States to have a band give a command performance before Queen Elizabeth.

Who popularized scat singing?

Cab (Cabell) Calloway III (1907–1994) was a renowned bandleader, singer, and entertainer. Born in Rochester, New York, Calloway and his family later moved to Chicago, where he studied at Crane College. He was an important big band leader of the 1930s and 1940s and used as his theme song "St. James Infirmary." He played at the Cotton Club, calling his band the Cab Calloway Cotton Club Orchestra, and later the Cab Calloway Band. He remained popular after the Big Band Era, appearing in several movies, including the role of Sportin' Life in *Porgy and Bess* (1953), *Stormy Weather* (1943), *Hello Dolly* (1967), and *The Blues Brothers* (1980). He was a flamboyant dresser who often performed in a zoot suit—his most famous was yellow, with a matching hat—and pleased his audiences with his famous scat singing style, "Hi-de-ho-de-ho-de-hee," which he championed. His most popular song was "Minnie the Moocher." He remains a legendary jazz figure in African and African-American culture.

Who was "**Lady Day**"?

When jazz great Billie "Lady Day" Holiday (1915–1959) teamed up with the Artie Shaw Band and toured the country, it was the first time a black woman and a white band shared the same stage. She was born Elenora Fagan in Baltimore, Maryland. She later moved to New York and, at age fifteen, sought work in various nightspots. Although she had no formal training as a singer or dancer, customers liked her, and she was hired. She became a regular in Harlem clubs and was in demand as a singer. In 1937 she toured with Count Basie's orchestra and became soloist with Artie Shaw's white band. Jazz saxophonist Lester Young nicknamed her "Lady Day"

Billie "Lady Day" Holiday was an early giant of American pop and jazz singing.

when she was with Count Basie's band. She assumed the name "Billie" from movie star Billie Dove. Holiday was known for wearing gardenias in her hair and performing with her eyes nearly closed. Her protest song "Strange Fruit" was a ballad about lynching; the fruit represented black men hanging from trees. At the peak of her career in the late 1930s and early 1940s, she began to struggle with drug and alcohol addiction. After being jailed on a drug charge, she tried to recapture her life, but her addiction led to poor health and death.

When were **black bandmasters** first appointed to **black infantry regiments**?

In 1908 the first black bandmasters were appointed to the U.S. Army Ninth and Tenth Cavalry regiments and the Twenty-fourth and Twenty-fifth Infantry regiments. President Theodore Roosevelt signed a special order in November ordering black bandmasters assigned to the four regular military regiments; white bandmasters were to be transferred out of these units as soon as possible. Four bandmasters were then promoted to the rank of chief musicians: Wade Hammond, Alfred Jack Thomas, William Polk, and Egbert Thompson.

CLASSICAL MUSIC

What **concert singer** became the **first black** to give a command performance **before royalty**?

Elizabeth Taylor Greenfield (c. 1819–1876), the nation's first black concert singer, became the first black singer to give a command performance before royalty when she appeared before Queen Victoria on May 10, 1853. Born in Natchez, Mississippi, she was called "The Black Swan" because of her sweet tones and wide vocal compass. Greenfield toured the United States and Canada extensively during her career and became the best-known black concert artist of her time. In the 1860s, she organized and directed the Black Swan Opera Troupe.

Who was **Roland Hayes**?

In 1917 Roland Hayes (1887–1976) became the first black to sing in Symphony Hall in Boston. Born in Curryville, Georgia, the son of former slaves, Hayes studied at Fisk University, where he was a member of the Fisk Jubilee Singers. He left Fisk to study voice in Boston, then traveled and studied in Europe. The 1917 concert attracted little public attention but another in the same venue on December 2, 1923, was a triumph. It was the beginning of a major career for Hayes. In 1923 he sang

A former member of the Fisk Jubilee Singers, Roland Hayes sang for the Boston Symphony and became the first black singer to perform at Symphony Hall.

with the Boston Symphony, and may have been the first black to sing with a major orchestra. Hayes became the first black to give a recital at Carnegie Hall in 1924. He was known in the United States for his interpretation of classical lieder and Negro spirituals and was the leading black singer of his time.

GOSPEL MUSIC

Who was known as the **"Father of Gospel Music"**?

Thomas Dorsey (1899–1993), the "Father of Gospel," founded the first black gospel choir in the world with Theodore Frye at Chicago's Ebenezer Baptist Church in 1931. He established the first music publishing firm, Dorsey Music, dedicated to only gospel music, in 1932. In 1930 the National Baptist Convention, U.S.A., was the first major religious group to publicly endorse gospel music. From this endorsement followed the first choruses, the first publishing houses, the first professional organizations, and the first paid gospel concerts. The action of the Baptist convention, which had been carried away by Dorsey's "If You See My Savior," called public attention to a major change that had been taking place in the music of black churches, and is often considered the starting point for the history of gospel music. Dorsey wrote more than two thousand blues and gospel songs during his lifetime. "Precious Lord, Take My Hand" has been declared one of the most profound expressions of Christian faith ever published. Dorsey was born in Villa Rica, Georgia, to an itinerant preacher who moved about until he settled in Atlanta. Dorsey left school after grade four, when he was around the age of thirteen. By age fourteen he was playing for dances at rent parties and in brothels. By 1919 he had settled in Chicago, where he enrolled in the Chicago School of Composition to develop his skills. He became music director at New Hope Baptist Church and began to write songs; his first religious piece was "If I Don't Get There." He was soon earning his living by arranging music. He wrote the famous "Precious Lord, Take My Hand" after mourning the loss of his newborn son.

Who was **Lucie (Lucy) Campbell Williams**?

In 1919 Lucie (Lucy) Campbell Williams (1885–1963) published "Something Within" and became the first black woman composer to have a gospel song published. In her lifetime she wrote more than eighty songs—a number of them became classics in the field of gospel. These included "Jesus Gave Me Water," "There Is a Fountain," and "In the Upper Room with Jesus"; her songs for liturgical use included "This Is the Day the Lord Has Made." Campbell, along with Charles A. Tindley (1851–1933) and Thomas Andrew Dorsey (1899–1993), is considered a gospel music pioneer. Campbell, who had a great influence on Tindley, selected songs for his hymnal, *Gospel Pearls*. Born in Duck Hill, Mississippi, Campbell graduated from Rust College in Holly Springs, Mississippi, in 1927, and received a master of science degree from Tennessee State University in 1951. A self-taught musician, she played the piano and organ at the Metropolitan Baptist Church in Memphis. In 1909 she began to organize young people's choirs, and by 1916 she was musical director of the Sunday School and Baptist Young People's Union. Her songs are still heard at Baptist conventions and at the Grand Ole Opry in Nashville. In addition to her musical talent, Campbell was a dynamic speaker.

Who was the **first** black to **take gospel** music into a **secular setting**?

"Sister" Rosetta Tharpe (Rosetta Nubin; 1915–1973) was the first black to take gospel music into a secular setting, when she sang on a Cab Calloway show from the Cotton Club in 1938. When she signed with Decca, she became the first gospel singer to record for a major company. Born in Cotton Plant, Arkansas, and raised in the Church of God in Christ—a Pentecostal denomination—Tharpe began touring as a professional when she was six. She took the lead in bringing gospel music to the mainstream. Tharpe was the first major gospel singer to tour extensively in Europe, and in 1943 she was the first to sing gospel at the Apollo Theater in New York City.

Who was known as **"Queen of the Gospel Song"**?

Through her recordings she became the first to bring gospel singing to the general public, Mahalia Jackson (1912–1972) was the first gospel singer to appear on the *Ed Sullivan Show* and became the first gospel artist to sing at the Newport Jazz Festival in 1958.

She was known as the "Queen of the Gospel Song." Born in New Orleans and nicknamed "Halie," she moved to Chicago at age sixteen, and met gospel musician and songwriter Thomas A. Dorsey, who invited her to sing at the Pilgrim Baptist Church. Dorsey became her musical advisor and accompanist. In 1937 Jackson recorded four sides for the Decca label, including the song "God's Gonna Separate the Wheat from the Tares." Her big break came in 1947 when she released gospel music's first million-selling record "Move On Up a Little Higher." In 1949 her song "Let the Holy Ghost Fall on Me" won the French Academy's Grand Prix du Disque. Soon afterward she toured Europe and recorded the gospel hit "In the Upper Room." During the 1960s Jackson became a musical ambassador. She performed at the White House as well as at London's Albert Hall. Her voice was heard during the Civil Rights Movement, when she sang at

The "Queen of the Gospel Song," Mahalia Jackson was hailed as a national institution.

the 1963 March on Washington and at Martin Luther King's funeral ceremony in 1968. Jackson died in Chicago, and some forty-five thousand mourners gathered to pay their respects to her at the Great Salem Baptist Church where her funeral was held. She was hailed as the world's greatest gospel singer, and her rich contralto voice became a national institution. Through live performances, recordings, and television appearances, Jackson elevated gospel music to a level of popularity unprecedented in the history of African-American religious music.

CHOIRS AND OTHER ORCHESTRAS

Who held a **historic first**—a **concert** of black music **for a largely white audience**?

James Reese Europe (1880–1919) and his Clef Club Orchestra—the leading black orchestra in the country—held a concert on May 2, 1912, for a largely white audience at Carnegie Hall in New York City for a historic first "Concert of Black Music" by black singers and instrumentalists. The program was more comprehensive than others that Europe had directed and reflected a full range of African-American musical expression, including secular, religious, traditional, modern, vocal, and instrumental selections.

221

Europe was born in Mobile, Alabama, and moved to Washington, D.C. He took violin lessons from Joseph Douglass, who was Frederick Douglass' grandson, and later switched to the mandolin and piano. To hone his skills in music, Europe was active in musical and dramatic activities at his church. He became active in the musical theater and directed the orchestra for such productions as *A Trip to Africa* (1904) and *Shoo-Fly Regiment* (1905). Europe became a successful bandleader and officer in the U.S. Army. On December 29, 1913, Europe, with his Society Orchestra, began a historic series of recordings of dance music for Victor Records. Europe received one of the first contracts that a major record company had given to a black musician, and the musical group received the first ever given to a black orchestra. On January 12 of the next year, Europe led the first black orchestra to perform at a leading white vaudeville theater— the Palace Theater in New York City. During this performance the group complied with the union's ban on black musicians by appearing on stage and not in the orchestra pit. While touring in 1914, Europe, who often experimented with new musical ideas, was the first bandleader to play W. C. Handy's "Memphis Blues."

Who was **Eva Jessye**?

Eva Jessye (1895–1992), composer, musician, choral director, educator, writer, and actress, became the first black woman to achieve acclaim as director of a professional choral group, in 1926. The Eva Jessye Choir performed regularly at New York City's Capitol Theatre from 1926 until 1929. Jessye directed the choir in Hollywood's first black musical, *Hallelujah,* in 1929. She was born in Coffeyville, Kansas, graduated from Western University (Quindaro, Kansas), and later attended Langston University in Oklahoma. In 1935 Jessye became choral director for the premiere of George Gershwin's *Porgy and Bess.*

COMPOSERS

Who was the **first black composer** to have an **opera performed** by a **major orchestra**?

William Grant Still (1895–1978) was the first black to have a symphony performed by a major orchestra, when on October 29,1931, the Rochester Philharmonic Orchestra presented his first work—*The Afro-American Symphony*. Born in Woodville, Mississippi, Still studied at Wilberforce University, Oberlin Conservatory of Music, and the New England Conservatory of Music. He worked in a great variety of musical settings, from playing in dance and theater orchestras to supplying arrangements of popular music for black show people. He was also a prolific composer in the art music tradition, writing more than 150 compositions. In 1936 Still was the first black to conduct a major symphony orchestra, the Los Angeles Philharmonic, and became the first black American to have an opera performed by a major opera company, in 1949, when the New York City Opera put on *Troubled Island.*

Who composed "Carry Me Back to Old Virginny"?

In 1878 James Bland (1854–1911), composer and minstrel entertainer, was the first black to compose a song that became an official state song. "Carry Me Back to Old Virginny," was adopted by the state in April 1940, although few knew that it was by a black composer. Bland wrote approximately seven hundred songs in his career, including "Oh, Dem Golden Slippers" and "In the Evening by the Moonlight." Born in Flushing, New York, he attended Howard University Law School but gave up his law studies to join the entertainment world.

What **symphony** was the first by a **black woman composer** performed by a **major orchestra**?

Florence Beatrice Smith Price (1888–1953) was the first black woman to have a symphony performed by a major orchestra. The Chicago Symphony, under Frederick Stock, first played her *Symphony No. 1 in E Minor* at the Chicago World's Fair in 1933. Born in Camden, New Jersey, Price was the first black woman to achieve distinction as a composer. She was a graduate of the New England Conservatory of Music in 1906 and furthered her music education at Chicago Music College, the American Conservatory, the University of Chicago, Chicago Teachers College, and elsewhere. She taught music at Shorter College in Arkansas and later gave private lessons in violin, piano, and organ. One of her mentees, Margaret Bonds, later became known in the music world. Price won her first Harmon prize for composition in 1925. She wrote a number of works, many of which were published. She also made recordings, but no extensive list of these works in known to exist.

Who was **Margaret Allison Bonds**?

Margaret Allison Bonds (1913–1972) became the first black American guest soloist with the Chicago Symphony Orchestra, performing Price's *Piano Concerto in F Minor"* at the 1933 World's Fair. Although Bonds was a skilled composer, her output is largely in the area of vocal music. Her arrangements of spirituals for solo voice and chorus are well known. Her arrangement of "He's Got the Whole World in His Hands," commissioned and recorded in the 1960s by Leontyne Price, is among Bonds's best-known pieces. Bonds was born in Chicago into a musical family. In high school she studied piano and composition with Florence Price and later William Daw-

Margaret Allison Bonds is most often remembered for her vocal music, including the famous "He's Got the Whole World in His Hands."

son. She received her bachelor of music degree in 1933 and her master of music degree in 1934, both from Northwestern University. She remained active as a concert musician throughout her life.

What black **composer** was the first of his race to **conduct the New York Philharmonic**?

In 1941 Dean Charles Dixon (1915–1976) was the first black to conduct the New York Philharmonic and was possibly the first black American recognized as a symphonic conductor of international stature. He was the first to hold permanent positions for long periods with symphony orchestras and toured worldwide as a guest conductor. Born in New York City, Dixon was educated at Julliard School of Music and Columbia University Teachers College. In 1949 he settled in Europe, where he remained until 1970.

RACIAL SEGREGATION AND BLACK SINGERS

What **black singer** was **denied** an opportunity to perform before the **Daughters of the American Revolution** (DAR), resulting in embarrassment for the nation?

Marian Anderson (1897–1993), one of the twentieth century's most celebrated singers, was the first black to sing a principal role with the Metropolitan Opera. She made her debut as Ulrica in Verdi's *Un Ballo in Maschera* on January 7, 1955, and remained with the opera for seven performances. In October 1930 Anderson received critical acclaim for her concert at the Bach Saal in Berlin and from there embarked on an extensive tour of Europe. She made national news in 1939 when the Daughters of the American Revolution (DAR) refused to allow her to appear at their Constitution Hall. On Easter Sunday of that year, she gave what is perhaps her most remarkable concert—singing on the steps of the Lincoln Memorial after having been barred from appearing at Constitution Hall because of her race. Anderson continued to tour until her farewell trip in the 1964–1965 season. She established scholarships to support and encourage other singers who had to endure and eventually break the racist barrier that permeated America. Anderson was a Philadelphia native, who demonstrated her vocal talents as a young choir girl and who at the age of nineteen began studying with Giuseppe Boghetti.

URBAN BLUES

Who **combined blues** and **guitar** to create **urban blues**?

In 1943 Muddy Waters (McKinley Morganfield; 1915–1983) was the first person to combine blues and amplified guitar to create urban blues. A guitarist and singer, he was born in Rolling Fork, Mississippi, and grew up in Clarksdale, Mississippi. It is said that he was nicknamed "Muddy" because as a child he liked to play in the mud; the name Waters was added later. He left the Mississippi Delta and toured with the Silas Green tent show. In 1943 he settled in Chicago, where he adopted the electric guitar. Waters was discovered by folklorist Alan Lomax. In 1948 Waters signed a recording contract and became known as the "King of the Delta (or Country) Blues."

POP MUSIC

When did **pop music emerge**?

Pop music, the shortened form of popular music, embraces blues, jazz, hip hop, rock, funk, rhythm and blues, rap, and other genres. It has been recognized since the first

Combining traditional blues with electric guitar, Muddy Waters originated the urban blues.

quarter of the nineteenth century, when black and other ethnic performers began to change the musical landscape of America. Nonblack audiences have consumed much of the music that developed out of black musical traditions. This trend followed even when public audiences were largely racially segregated. Beginning in the 1960s, when Motown Records was founded, talented black singers appealed to larger, mixed audiences and also propelled pop music to international acclaim. Michael Jackson's album *Thriller* (1982) was a megahit and also played a major role in exposing pop music to an international scene. Beginning in the 1980s, the fusion of styles and genres and the use of modern technology produced music that reflected and appealed to the culture of the younger generation.

Who was called the **"King of Pop"**?

Singer, songwriter, dancer, and choreographer Michael Jackson (1958–2009) had a vocal style that attracted fans from every racial and age group. His album *Thriller* (1982) was the first to produce five top singles: "The Girl is Mine," "Billie Jean," "Beat It," "Wanna Be Startin' Somethin'," and "Human Nature." In 1981 the *Guinness Book of Records* certified *Thriller,* for which Jackson won eight Grammy Awards, as the best-selling album to date. *Guinness* also cited Jackson for winning the most awards (seven) at the American Music Awards in 1984. Jackson was born in Gary, Indiana, into a musical family. The Jackson brothers—Jackie, Tito, Jermaine, Marlon, and Michael—became known as The Jackson Five and received their first big break at Harlem's Apollo Theater in 1968. They caught the attention of Motown and its president Berry Gordy, and, in 1969, released their

The self-proclaimed "King of Pop," Michael Jackson earned fame as a boy with his family group The Jackson Five and went on to have a hugely successful solo career.

Starting off her career with the girl group Girls' Tyme, Beyoncé now has a successful solo career that includes seventeen Grammys and many other awards.

debut album, *Diana Ross Presents the Jackson Five*. While the group was with Motown (from 1969 to 1975), the Jackson Five scored thirteen consecutive top-twenty singles such as "ABC," "The Love You Save," and "I'll Be There." Michael Jackson began his solo career by acting in the 1977 movie *The Wiz*. His enormous record sales and success in concerts earned him the title "King of Pop." Since his death in 2009, sales of his works have soared.

Who is **Beyoncé**?

A singer and actress, Beyoncé Gisele Knowles (1981–), a Houston native, is popularly known simply as Beyoncé. She began her singing career in 1990 with a group called Girls' Tyme. The group added Kelly Rowland as a member in 1992, and LeToya Luckett in 1993. After several name changes the group chose Destiny's Child as their name. Although the group signed with Elektra Records in 1995, it dropped that company and signed with Columbia Records the next year. Their debut album *Destiny's Child* (1998), which went platinum, was followed by *The Writing's on the Wall* (1999), which earned them two Grammys. The group made changes in the members but continued to release records well into 2004, with phenomenal success.

Beyoncé released her first solo album, *Dangerously in Love,* in 2003. The album was so successful that it went multiplatinum, and it was selected by the Rock and Roll Hall of Fame as one of the two hundred definitive albums in music history. Beyoncé's musical talents have also earned her four MTV awards, seventeen Grammy awards, and nine Billboard Music awards. She is the first African-American woman to win the American Society of Composers,

Authors and Publishers Songwriter of the Year Award (2001), and she is only the second woman to receive the award. The iconic singer and actress has performed with numerous artists and contributed to film soundtracks, such as *Men in Black* (1997) and *Dreamgirls* (2006). In January 2013 she sang at Barack Obama's second-term inauguration as President of the United States, and at half-time during Super Bowl XLVII held in New Orleans. She continues to explore different entertainment opportunities and interests, including collaborating with her mother on a clothing line, while also being actively involved in philanthropic endeavors.

What **prominent black artist** successfully **integrated pop** with other genres, especially in the 1980s?

In the 1980s, pop, rock, and R&B artist Prince (1958–) rose to prominence with a style that is difficult to categorize because of his eclectic mixtures of musical form, as well as his heavy use of synthesizers and drum machines. His most influential album is *1999* (1982), which was followed by his most commercially successful album, *Purple Rain* (1984). Tracks from these albums crossed over into white rock audiences. His *Purple Rain* made him one the biggest pop stars of the 1980s.

Born Prince Rogers Nelson in Minneapolis to parents who were both musical, he withdrew from family problems and settled into music. Prince signed a lucrative recording contract with Warner Brothers in 1977, while he was still a teenager, and had almost total control of the studio. He soon produced three albums that all went gold: *Prince* (1979), *Dirty Mind* (1980), and *Controversy* (1981). For a while he experienced some commercial flops and an ebb in popularity, yet by 2004 sales of his album *Musicology* brought critical acclaim. His innovative ways of promoting his concerts, such as including a CD with the purchase of a concert ticket, enabled him to gross millions. Prince changed his name several times—from Prince to The Artist Formerly Known as Prince (or simply The Artist), and then back to Prince.

SOUL MUSIC

What is **soul music**?

As early as the 1950s, the term "soul" was used to refer to music. Gospel quartets of that era used the term as a label for the spiritual nature of their music. Jazz musicians used it as early as the 1960s in their reference to hard bop (a style of jazz with bebop influences). Soul music often refers to all black popular music. *Billboard* magazine has been credited with using the term in 1969, after changing its reference to black popular music to race music, and then to rhythm and blues. Clearly soul music is not a homogeneous form of music but a reflection of identity. It is a reflection of black consciousness and has some connection with Black Power and politics. The political message comes through clearly in singer James Brown's song, "I'm Black and I'm Proud," and in Aretha Franklin's call for respect in her rendition of Otis Redding's song by that name. Since the 1960s the term "soul" has also been used to describe food and as a term of endearment.

Who is known as the **"Queen of Soul"**?

Aretha Franklin (1942–), singer, pianist, and songwriter, earned the title "Queen of Soul" early in her career, and has a musical career that spans over fifty years. Her music incorporates gospel, jazz, blues, pop, and funk. She began singing blues in the 1960s, and in 1967 two of her albums sold more than a million copies each. At age fourteen, Franklin left school and went on the road with her father, a seemingly endless tour in which the family traveled thousands of miles by car. After four years on the road, Franklin traveled to New York to establish her own career as a pop artist. In 1960 she signed with Columbia Records and in 1966 moved to Atlantic Records. Two of her well-known hits were released the next year: "I Never Loved a Man (The Way That I Love You)," and her signature piece, "Respect." Other well-known pieces that she has recorded are "You Make Me Feel Like a Natural Woman" and "Chain of Fools." In 1986 Franklin became the first black woman selected for induction into the Rock and Roll Hall of Fame Museum. In 2005 she was awarded the Presidential Medal of Honor. She has won twenty Grammy awards. Franklin sang at the inauguration of President Barack Obama in January 2009, and when Oprah Winfrey ended her television show *Oprah* in May 2011, she sang at the television mogul's twenty-five-year celebration. Franklin was inducted into the Grammy Music Association Hall of Fame in 2012. Born in Memphis, Franklin is the daughter of the famous Reverend Charles L. Franklin. She grew up on the east side of Detroit and sang at her father's New Bethel Baptist Church. She refused to learn what she considered juvenile and simple tunes and learned piano by ear, occasionally receiving instruction from individuals like the Reverend James Cleveland. Her singing skills were modeled after gospel singers and family friends, including Clara Ward, and R&B artists like Ruth Brown and Sam Cooke.

The Queen of Soul, Aretha Franklin is a megastar with numerous smash hits, including "Respect" and "You Make Me Feel Like a Natural Woman."

MUSIC OF THE CIVIL RIGHTS ERA

What purpose did black music serve during the modern Civil Rights Movement?

From the spirituals and work songs to the later forms of blues, jazz, R&B, and gospel, African-American music from the time of slavery to the climax of the Civil Rights Movement in the 1950s and 1960s has inspired protest and progress. During this period, a number of songs served to empower civil rights demonstrators. Some of these songs were performed by the Freedom Singers of Albany, Georgia, to raise money for protesters and the Student Nonviolent Coordinating Committee. The same songs performed, and later recorded, by the Freedom Singers were sung at marches and rallies to inspire protesters, giving them a common orientation and sense of purpose and direction. Prominent among the singers were Cordell Reagon and Bernice Johnson Reagon. "We Shall Overcome" was the theme song of the movement in its early days. Martin Luther King Jr. and other leaders of the movement commonly referred to that freedom song as a spiritual, probably because it resembled the nineteenth-century slave song "No More Auction Block for Me." Among other prominent songs of protest were "I Shall Not Be Moved," "Oh, Freedom," "Keep Your Eyes on the Prize," "This Little Light of Mine," and "Ain't Gonna Let Nobody Turn Me Around." Some of these songs, including the spiritual "We Shall Overcome," were actually anti-slavery songs later adopted for the Civil Rights Movement. Singer, songwriter, and pianist Nina Simone, who was passionately committed to the Civil Rights Movement and the Black Power Movement, is said to have given musical expression to both. She contributed her talent to the movements by singing at benefit marches. Her song "Mississippi Goddam" became a classic during the Civil Rights Movement. Sam Cooke's "A Change Gonna Come" and James Brown's song "I'm Black and I'm Proud" were two of the most well-known, popular songs to inspire and serve the Civil Rights Movement.

JAZZ MUSIC AND MUSICIANS

Who invented jazz?

Ferdinand "Jelly Roll" Morton (1885–1941), a New Orleans pianist, claimed credit for having invented jazz. And to some degree, it was fair of him to think so—after all, his recordings with the group the Red Hot Peppers (1926–1930) are among the earliest examples of disciplined jazz ensemble work. But in truth, the evolution of jazz from ragtime and blues was something embraced by many musicians in several cities. Most regard Morton as one of the founders of jazz; the other founders include Bennie Moten (1884–1935), Eubie Blake (1887–1983), Duke Ellington (1899–1974), and Thomas "Fats" Waller (1904–1943).

Some would go back even farther to trace the roots of jazz. From 1899 to 1914 Scott Joplin (1868–1917) popularized ragtime, which was based on African folk music. Even astute music critics may be unable to draw a clear-cut distinction between ragtime and early jazz. Both musical forms rely on syncopation (the stressing of the weak beats), **229**

The late pianist, composer, and orchestra leader Duke Ellington is credited with being one of the originators of jazz music, along with "Fats" Waller, Eubie Blake, Bennie Moten, and "Jelly Roll" Morton.

and either style can be applied to an existing melody to transform it. The definitions and boundaries of the two terms have always been subject to debate, which is further complicated by the fact that some musicians of the time considered ragtime to be more or less a synonym for early jazz. But there are important, albeit not strict, differences between the two genres as well: Rag was composed and written down in the European style of notation, while early jazz was learned by ear (players would simply show one another how a song went by playing it); jazz encourages and expects improvisation, whereas ragtime, for the most part, does not; and the basic rhythms are also markedly different, with jazz having a swing or "hot" rhythm that ragtime does not.

Whatever its origin, jazz became part of the musical mainstream by the 1930s and influenced other musical genres as well—including classical music. Perhaps more than any other composer and musician, Miles Davis (1926–1991) expanded the genre: through decades of prolific work, Davis constantly pushed the boundaries of what defines jazz and in so doing set standards for other musicians.

Who was **King Oliver**?

Joe "King" Oliver (1885–1938) was born in Abend, Louisiana, and started his career playing the trombone, but switched to the cornet. He began playing with the Melrose Brass Band in 1907 and played with several other brass bands as he perfected his skills. Oliver first earned the sobriquet "King" in 1917, after establishing himself as the best cornetist against the likes of Freddie Keppard, Manuel Perez, and a host of other early New Orleans jazz musicians. Oliver soon teamed up with Kid Ory and organized what would become the leading jazz band in New Orleans. During the Storyville era of the early twentieth century, Oliver met and befriended Louis Armstrong. Lacking a son of his own, Oliver became Armstrong's "unofficial father," sharing with him the musical knowledge that he had acquired over the years. In return, Armstrong treated him with great respect, referring to him as "Papa Joe." In 1922 Oliver summoned Armstrong to Chicago to play in his Creole Jazz Band as second cornetist; a year later the band made the first important recording by a black jazz group. The work of Oliver and Armstrong put Chicago on the jazz map of the United States. However, changing tastes caused Oliver's music to decline in popularity, and by the time he moved to New York, in 1928, his best years were behind him.

Who formed the **first black jazz band**?

In 1891 Charles "Buddy" Bolden (1877–1931) was the first black to form what may have been a real jazz band, in New Orleans. His band incorporated blues and ragtime. He has been called the patriarch of jazz, and because of his fierce, driving tone, he was known as "King Bolden." A plasterer by trade, Bolden developed a cornet style that influenced musicians such as King Oliver and Dizzy Gillespie. Bolden was born in New Orleans and took his first formal music lesson from a neighbor around 1895. Soon he adapted his own style of playing from the music that he heard around town, in barbershops, and at parades. He also played in small string bands, often for parties and dances. A friendly and gregarious person, Bolden was a ladies' man. As a performer, he was more comfortable in uptown New Orleans than downtown and never played at the Creole society halls. His greatest rival was John Robichaux, a Creole whose band played for wealthy plantation owners, brokers, and other white professionals. Bolden's popularity peaked in 1905. In an effort to remain ahead of his competitors, he took on more and more jobs but soon realized that his style was no longer new. Frustrated, he began to drink heavily, had spells of depression, and sometimes was jailed for his behavior. He was diagnosed as paranoid in 1907, and on June 5 of that year he was committed to East Louisiana State Hospital in Jackson, Louisiana, where he spent the last twenty-four years of his life. While there, however, he played a horn on some occasions, but was not a member of the patients' band. He died in Parker Hospital, on the grounds of the institution where he had been institutionalized, on November 4, 1931, at age fifty-four.

Who was **one** of the **most influential jazz artists**?

Jazz trumpeter (Daniel) Louis "Satchmo" Armstrong (1900–1971), was born in New Orleans and claimed to have been born on the Fourth of July, rather than on August 4 (which was his actual birthday). He learned to play the coronet and read music while in the Negro Waifs Home for Boys and later became leader of its band. Between 1917 and 1922, he played with various Dixieland jazz bands in New Orleans, including that of Kid Ory. Armstrong moved to Chicago in 1922, where he became second cornetist with King Oliver's Creole Jazz Band. He was also Oliver's protégé. He married Lil Harding in 1924; although they later divorced, she remained a strong influence in his life. Harding persuaded him to become independent of Oliver. He left Oliver's band and later moved to New York where he provided a spark in Fletcher Henderson's band and made the jazz band a viable entity. In 1927 Armstrong formed a band called Louis Armstrong and His

One of the most influential jazz artists of all time was trumpet player and band leader Louis Armstrong.

Stompers. During the early years of the Great Depression he was unemployed for a while, but from 1932 to 1935 he toured Europe, playing before King George V of England.

He appeared in several noteworthy films, including *Pennies from Heaven* and *Cabin in the Sky*. At the height of his popularity in the 1950s and 1960s, Armstrong had become well known as an entertainer. His recording of "Hello Dolly," which he made in the 1960s, brought him to the top of the charts. His hits "Mack the Knife" and "Blueberry Hill" added to his popularity. Although he took a stance against racial segregation by refusing to play in New Orleans for many years, blacks often misunderstood Armstrong and accused him of pandering to whites. They also criticized his wide grin and use of a large white handkerchief—his trademark—to wipe perspiration from his face. In time, however, he became recognized as one of the most influential jazz artists of all time. A superb showman, he was known for his gravelly, growling vocal style. In 1932 an editor of the *Melody Maker* gave him the nickname "Satchmo."

BLUES

Is **blues** music **older** than **jazz**?

Only slightly—and only if the definition of jazz excludes ragtime. In reality, the two musical traditions developed side by side, with blues emerging about the first decade of the

1900s and hitting the height of its early popularity in 1920s Harlem, where the songs were seen as an expression of African-American life. Great blues singers like Ma Rainey (1886–1939) and Bessie Smith (1894-1937) sang of the black reality—determined but weary. During the Harlem Renaissance the music was a symbol for African-American people who were struggling to be accepted for who they were. Poet Langston Hughes (1902–1967) saw the blues as a distinctly black musical genre and as helping to free blacks from American standardization.

Who is called the **"Father of the Blues"**?

In 1909 "Memphis Blues," by W(illiam) C(hristopher) Handy (1873–1958), composer, cornetist, band leader, and publisher, was the first written blues composition. It was also the first popular song to use a jazz break. Written in 1909 as a campaign song for legendary "Boss" Edward H. Crump when he ran for mayor of Memphis, it was published in 1912. The song was the third blues song published; black songwriter Artie Matthews published the first, "Baby Seals Blues," in August 1912. A white composer published the second in September 1912, and Handy's song came three weeks later. He was the first person to codify and publish blues songs. Handy led the way in the adaptation of Southern black folk blues into popular music. His "St. Louis Blues," published two years later, carried the blues all over the world and has become one of the most frequently recorded songs in popular music. Other well-known works are "Beale Street Blues," and "Careless Love." Handy was born in a log cabin in Florence, Alabama, and began playing in a minstrel band at a young age. He was bandmaster and director of a dance orchestra in the Mississippi Delta, and then returned to Memphis where he continued band activities. In 1918 he established himself in New York City, where he made his first recordings and co-founded a music company. Handy lost his sight after World War I, partially regained it, but became totally blind in 1943. Over the years he continued to write music, arrange spirituals and blues, and compose marches and hymns. One of the most celebrated musicians of his time, Handy is known as the "Father of the Blues."

Who was **Ma Rainey** and why was she called the **"Mother of the Blues"**?

Ma Rainey (Gertrude Pridgett; 1886–1939), of the Rabbit Foot Minstrels, was the first black to sing the blues in a professional show, in 1902. She learned a blues song from a local woman in Missouri, and audience response was such that she began to specialize in blues and became known as the "Mother of the Blues." Born in Columbus, Georgia, she began public appearances at age fourteen, performing in a local talent revue. She went on to perform in tent shows and sing the blues. After marrying Will Rainey, the husband-and-wife team traveled with the Rabbit Foot Minstrels and performed as "Ma" and "Pa" Rainey. They toured the South with several companies. Ma Rainey became especially popular, receiving separate billing. She sang in a raw and gritty style and became a flashy dresser who loved jewelry and glitter. Rainey met Bessie Smith sometime between 1912 and 1916 and greatly influenced Smith's musical career. Rainey increased her audience through the recordings that she made with Paramount Record Company, beginning December 1923, and through performances on the Theatre Owners Booking Association (T.O.B.A.) circuit. After the T.O.B.A. collapsed around 1931, at the time of the Great Depression, Rainey's career suffered as well. In 1935 she returned to her native home in Columbus and operated two theaters that she owned.

Who was **Bessie Smith**?

Singer Bessie Smith (1894–1937) became one of the most important women in the history of American music, both as a stage performer and recording star. Between 1923 and 1933, she gave the public such works as "Backwater Blues" and "Do Your Duty," which became twentieth-century landmarks. In 1923 "Downhearted Blues/Gulf Coast Blues" was the first record by a black to sell more than a million copies. Born in Chattanooga, Tennessee, Smith first performed on the city streets. She eventually performed with Ma (Gertrude) Rainey (1886–1939), the first professional to sing the blues, in the Rabbit Foot Minstrels. Smith's only movie appearance was in the first film short featuring black musicians, *Saint Louis Blues* (later retitled *Best of the Blues*), in 1929.

Who are **B. B. King** and **"Lucille"**?

B. B. (Riley B.) King (1925–) has reached legendary status as a singer, guitarist, and bandleader and has become one of the most successful artists in the history of the blues. King, who never finished high school, was born in Indianola, Mississippi. He began his musical career singing with a gospel group in 1940, but soon learned he could earn more money by playing and singing the blues on the street. In 1946 he moved to Memphis, Tennessee, where he had his own radio show on station WDIA, and later became a disc jockey. The station named him "The Boy from Beale Street," and thereafter he was known as "B.B." By the 1960s he was a successful performer. In 1979 he was the first black blues artist to perform in what was the Soviet Union. The recordings of such musicians as Blind Lemon Jefferson

Blues artist B. B. King performed for many decades with his guitar "Lucille."

(1897–1929) influenced his early style. King participated in the Vatican's 1997 Christmas concert, after which he and a group of international artists held a special audience with Pope John Paul II. At the end of the concert, King donated "Lucille," his famous fifty-year-old guitar, to the pontiff. His love for music and women and his struggles to succeed in the music business are among the details of his life included in his mid-1990s autobiography, *Blues All around Me: The Autobiography of B. B. King.* He is noted for his philanthropy, including a huge gift of vintage, collector's-item records. He received an honorary doctorate from Tougaloo College in Mississippi in 1973, becoming the first black musician to receive an honorary degree for work in the blues. King also holds an honorary degree, conferred in 1977, from Yale University. He won a Grammy for his blues album *Blues 'n' Jazz* in 1984, a Grammy for lifetime achievement in 1988, was inducted into the Rock and Roll Hall of Fame in 1987, was awarded the Presidential Medal of Arts in 1990, and honored at the Kennedy Center in 1995.

HIP HOP

What is **hip hop**?

Music historians claim that hip hop music can be traced to speech and songs heard in America during the nineteenth and early twentieth centuries, or even earlier. It derives from "stylized talk between verses" that are "characteristic of blues and rhythm and blues," and comes from black game chants and songs, sounds heard in fraternity and sorority step shows, pool halls, barber and beauty shop talk, and elsewhere. It is associated with the American dream—the dream of moving beyond one's circumstances and becoming self-empowered. The art form is often used interchangeably with "rap." As a cultural expression, hip hop became known in the 1970s, in the South Bronx, New York. Elements of hip hop include rapping, deejaying, and break dancing, all characterized by heavy back beats and repetitive rhythms.

Who are some influential **hip hop artists**?

Kool DF Herc, Jamaican-born, who was a deejay in the South Bronx, has been called the pioneer of hip hop. A generation of singers who came of age in the 1980s, such as Mary J. Blige, Erykah Badu, and Lauryn Hill, are examples of earlier artists. Others include Public Enemy and Queen Latifah.

Who is called the **"Queen of Hip Hop Soul"**?

Singer, songwriter, and actress Mary Jane Blige (1971–), known as the "Queen of Hip Hop Soul," had a difficult childhood in the Bronx, New York, where she grew up living with a drug-using mother. She quit school early and went to work, becoming a singer in 1989 when a tape that she made was passed from her mother to a friend and

Mary Jane Blige has been called the "Queen of Hip Hop Soul."

then to R&B record executives Jeff Redd and Andre Harrell of Uptown Records. As a result, Blige began singing backup for artists at Uptown Records. In 1991, with the help of Sean "Puffy" Combs, Blige cut her first solo album, *What's the 411*, which went multiplatinum; it was followed in 1995 with *My Life*. Blige moved to MCA Records after 1997 and continued to write many of her songs, which are based on her life experiences. Blige produced albums including *Mary* (1997), *No More Drama* (2001), *Reflections* (2006), and *Growing Pains* (2008). She has also made appearances on television specials (such as a Christmas performance with blind opera singer Andrea Bocelli), television series, and in movies. In respect for the difficult journey that resulted in her sobriety, she started the first phase of her foundation to help other women by opening the Mary J. Blige Center for Women in 2003. Blige's awards include six Grammys and seven multiplatinum records. She continues to write and produce her award-winning music, which is a combination of soul and hip hop.

REGGAE

What is **reggae**?

A popular and expanding music genre, reggae music originated in Jamaica. The popular artist Bob Marley claims that reggae came from the Spanish term *regis,* meaning "the king's music." It emphasizes off-beat music, often by a "rhythm guitar, piano, or synthesizer." At first only one or two chords made up an entire song; it is often played in 4/4 time. The lyrics of reggae originally included only messages of "peace, love, positive social and family values, and culture and history." It traditionally embraces aspects of the Rastafarian lifestyle, but some contemporary reggae artists use lyrics that debase women and "encourage crime and violence." Those who popularized reggae worldwide included Bob Marley, Prince Buster, Desmond Dekker, Kackie Mittoo, and Bunny Wailer. Marley, however, has been called the music's greatest pioneer.

RHYTHM AND BLUES

What is **R&B**?

New forms of black dance music emerged after World War II ended, sending forth a blend of boogie-woogie and sounds from blues, jazz, Latin, and gospel music. This music began and continues to be sentimental, with both slow and fast numbers. By the early 1950s, America began to draw from the work of popular singers Big Joe Turner, Louis Jordan, T-Bone Walker, and Dinah Washington to form a music heard in dance halls and on variety shows. They called this sound rhythm and blues (R&B). Detroit's Motown popularized R&B artists and their sounds, and promoted the work of Smokey Robinson, the Miracles, the Temptations, Diana Ross (then The Supremes, with Diana Ross), Marvin Gaye, Stevie Wonder, the Jackson Five (with Michael Jackson), Gladys Knight, and a host of other artists.

ORGANIZATIONS

ORGANIZATIONS AND SOCIETAL FORCES

Why did African Americans **develop** their own **organizations**?

As African Americans recognized a need to find ways to address the economic, social, cultural, and educational necessities of their communities, they developed various types of organizations to serve as a vehicle for meeting their goals. Much of their work was stimulated by the church. This led to the development of literary societies for young people, and welfare leagues in major cities that had seen a wide influx of migrants from the South. Historically, African-American organizations have been the voices of the particular groups that they serve and function as influential forces in American society. While such organizations have existed for many years, the founding date of the first African-American organization cannot be determined. It is possible, however, to group such organizations by type, such as abolitionist, business, civil and human rights, educational, financial, journalism, medical, political, social and social service, religious, and women. There are also organizations concerned with urban problems, African and Caribbean issues, and so on.

BUSINESS AND UNIONS

What was the purpose of the **Colored Merchants Association**?

Among the various cooperative movements that took place in the African-American community was the Colored Merchants Association, or CMA. The association aided in the development of black-owned grocery stores. In addition to grocery stores, the early cooperatives involved department stores, shoe stores, and other enterprises, and their work brought about meaningful results. The CMA's purpose was to stimulate black business, effect cost-savings for customers, and provide jobs for blacks. Founded on August 10, 1928, in Montgomery, Alabama, by local grocer A. C. Brown, the organization soon spread to other states and then adopted the slogan "Quality, Service, and Price." The voluntary chain would operate under the banner "C.M.A. Stores" and display the proprietor's name below the CMA designation. The association promoted cooperative buying and intensive selling—a pronounced difference between the CMA and other cooperatives. CMA taught its members to move their merchandize quickly, in an effort to increase profit. Each week the member stores advertised cooperatively and promoted their businesses in weekly newspapers, taking care to promote special bargains. The advertisements were reprinted and distributed to black homes in communities where the stores were located. The members also worked to enhance business practices; thus, a uniform accounting system was installed in each store.

How was the **National Negro Business League** involved in the development of **CMA stores**?

After the success of the initial stores, Albon L. Holsey (1883–1950), national secretary of the National Negro Business League (NNBL), became involved, visited some of the stores, and became so impressed with the "Montgomery Plan," as he called it, that he recommended that the NNBL support the project. The league complied and Holsey became national organizer. He advanced the CMA's objectives of promoting modern methods of selling, promoting the psychology of the black consumer, and uniting local jobbers and wholesalers. The plan spread to Winston-Salem, North Carolina, in May 1929, making it the second city to open a CMA store. Holsey helped the plan to move elsewhere, and soon stores were seen in most major American cities, including Dallas, Tulsa, Atlanta, Nashville, Louisville, and Richmond in the South; and Omaha, Detroit, Philadelphia, New York, and Brooklyn outside the South. Most transactions were for cash, with greater sales coming on Fridays and Saturdays. As Holsey moved the plan to Harlem, he emphasized the necessity of training in modern merchandising methods, under the tutelage of experts. Membership grew rapidly, reaching a total of twenty-three stores in two years. Even the stock market crash of 1929 did not substantially affect the CMAs. By 1936, however, many CMA stores withdrew membership, some claiming that the chain was white-owned, others claiming that members intentionally oversold each other on the "specials" that were offered, and still others preferring to sell different brands. Despite their eventual failure, the CMAs had benefited from "oneness of action," witnessed the purchasing power of blacks, provided jobs for blacks, and promoted black pride in business ownership.

What was the purpose of the **National Negro Business League**?

Controversy surrounds the history of the National Negro Business League (NNBL). W.E.B. Du Bois is said to have called for such an organization "in every town and hamlet" where blacks lived in 1899, but was unable to follow through with his plan. Credit has been given to Tuskegee Institute (now University) president Booker T. Washington

(1856–1915) for actually bringing the organization to life. He visited African-American businesses all over the country, observed their struggles, noted that banks denied them loans, and concluded that a league was needed to enable the business owners to work together on their own behalf. He wanted the group to be political and thought that many wealthy black leaders could work collectively to benefit many areas of American life. He also called for representation from every business in which black men and women were involved. The first meeting of the league was held in Boston in 1900, with three hundred delegates present. The delegates elected Washington president, an office he held until he died. He saw the organization as an instrument for a new emancipation that could come about through black economic independence. After Washington died, leaders from Tuskegee continued to head the organization until 1945. Until 1953 the NNBL was actually based at Tuskegee. The organization is still in existence. Its mission is to encourage African-American business leaders and youth to become entrepreneurs. Since its founding the NNBL has closely adhered to this mission. Among its various initiatives, the league helps blacks establish new ventures, promotes youth business developments, and encourages African Americans to buy from members of their race.

Tuskegee University president Booker T. Washington is considered largely responsible for creating the National Negro Business League, although the idea originally came from W.E.B. Du Bois.

CIVIL AND POLITICAL RIGHTS

What was America's **first-known African-American organization**?

Established as a mutual aid society on April 12, 1787, in Philadelphia, the Free African Society is generally regarded as the first African-American organization of note in this country because it quickly became the nucleus for two black churches. (The African Union Society of Newport, Rhode Island, was formed in 1780. In Philadelphia, the Female Benevolent Society of Saint Thomas's Episcopal Church was formed in 1793, and the male African Friendly Society of Saint Thomas in 1795.) The Free African Society was founded by religious leaders Richard Allen (1760–1831) and Absalom Jones (1746–1818). It became an important organization that addressed political consciousness and welfare for blacks nationwide. The society combined economic and medical aid for poor blacks and supported abolition of the enslaved blacks in the South. On October 12, 1794, the original Free African Society building in Philadelphia was dedicated as Saint Thomas' African Episcopal Church, the first black Protestant Episcopal church, with Jones as its unofficial leader.

What was the **National Equal Rights League**?

Historically, organized efforts to promote civil rights of African Americans have been numerous. The National Equal Rights League (NERL) was one such effort. It was founded in 1864, with John Mercer Langston (1829–1897) as its first president. A second league was formed in early 1908, with William Monroe Trotter (1872–1934) as founder. The NERL was a forerunner of the Niagara Movement that W.E.B. Du Bois helped to organize to protest Booker T. Washington's conservative views. It was also a forerunner of the NAACP, formally founded in 1910. For a number of years Trotter worked through the organization to agitate for the rights of black people. Those who were unable to accept the principles of the NAACP had as an alternative the NERL. Trotter and his followers, known as Trotterites, did not fully embrace the NAACP. The two organizations also competed with each other for members. The NAACP, with its moderate approach to matters of race, grew in importance and membership numbers. Trotter, however, employed discordant tactics, which made his organization less successful. He openly criticized Republican William Howard Taft's election to the presidency, attacked President Woodrow Wilson's racial policies, and met with Presidents Warren G. Harding and Calvin Coolidge to attack the federal government's racial practices. The league folded in the 1920s after Trotter was unsuccessful in his aim to form a relationship among the NERL, Marcus Garvey's Universal Negro Improvement Association movement, and the African Blood Brotherhood.

How was the **Afro-American League** involved in **civil rights**?

The Afro-American League was launched under the leadership of Timothy Thomas Fortune (1856–1928), the editor of the newspaper *The New Age*. Delegates representing twenty-three states met in Chicago in October 1890 and officially formed the league, which grew from the ideas of Fortune. The league's aim was to fight for the civil and political rights of Negroes and to seek full citizenship for all Americans. It espoused racial solidarity, self-help, and confrontation in the face of racial oppression and revolution. These goals were in response to rising discrimination, including: the overturning by the Supreme Court of the 1875 Civil Rights Act by declaring it was unconstitutional; the weakening of the Fourteenth and Fifteenth Amendments; lynchings; and other practices of disenfranchisement. Branches were located in forty cities. J. C. Price (1854–1893), the president of Lincoln University in Missouri, was elected the league's president. As a vehicle for the fight for civil rights, the league was active for four years. However, it re-emerged in 1898 as the Afro-American Council established by Timothy Thomas Fortune and Alexander Walters, an African-American Episcopal Bishop. The council advocated and supported aggressive action and direct challenge; it ceased to exist in 1908. Other organizations, such as the Afro-American Council, Niagara Movement (1905), and NAACP (1909) filled the vacuum left behind.

What was the **Niagara Movement**?

As the first American civil rights organization of the twentieth century, the Niagara Movement arguably influenced all modern civil rights initiatives that followed. Founded in 1905 by W.E.B. Du Bois (1868–1963) and William Monroe Trotter (1872–1934) and comprising the leading African-American intellectuals of the time, the organization was established as a challenge to Booker T. Washington's accommodationist stance. While the movement disbanded soon after its founding, its commitment to affecting legal change and its efforts to address issues of crime, economics, religion, health, and education were reborn in the NAACP, which many of its members helped to establish.

How was the **Niagara Movement founded** and **named**?

After a closed-door meeting was held at New York's Carnegie Hall in 1904 and the Committee of Twelve for the Advancement of the Interest of the Negro Race was created, infighting led the group to disband. The following year, Du Bois and Trotter extended invitations to fifty-nine leading African Americans who opposed Booker T. Washington to attend a meeting in western New York that summer. In addition to being the nation's eighth largest city, Buffalo had historically been associated with the struggle for freedom from slavery, and western New York was considered an important crossing point on the Underground Railroad for runaway slaves headed to safety in Canada. However, a Buffalo hotel refused to accommodate the attendees, forcing them to move their organizational efforts to the Canadian side of Niagara Falls. Twenty-nine African-American businessmen, writers, teachers, and clergy met from July 11 to 14, 1905, to form the Niagara Movement. Its name honored the place of its founding and acted as a constant reminder of the "mighty current" of protest its founders wished to unleash on American society. Du Bois was named general secretary of the organization. Booker T. Washington's determined opposition to the movement barred virtually all white assistance to it and limited its effectiveness. It was not until a violent race riot in Springfield, Illinois, in 1908 that the Niagara Movement effectively paved the way for the creation of the more powerful interracial NAACP in 1909.

What is the **NAACP**?

Founded in 1909, the National Association for the Advancement of Colored People (NAACP) has been at the helm of the American freedom struggle since the turn of the twentieth century. As the nation's first racially integrated institution of its kind, the NAACP had a militant platform that demanded civil rights as well as educational and political equality for all Americans. Following the Springfield, Illinois, race riot of August 1908, an eminent interracial group of white progressives and black militants, including Niagara Movement founder W.E.B. Du Bois and member and social worker Mary White Ovington, sent out "The Call" for a national conference on black rights. The meeting was planned for the centennial of Abraham Lincoln's birthday, February 12, 1909. In May of the same year more than forty people attended the organization's conference in New York and formed the National Negro Committee. During the group's second conference, in May 1910, the organization was formally renamed the NAACP and incorporated the following year. Its mission was to promote equality, eradicate class and racial prejudice, and to advance the interest of colored citizens by securing truly universal suffrage, justice under the law, and education for all children.

Benjamin Todd Jealous was elected president of the NAACP in 2008, one hundred years after the organization was founded.

Who are some **prominent leaders** of the **NAACP**?

From its beginning in 1909, the NAACP has been under the leadership of a number of influential people, among them Walter White, 1931 to 1955; Roy Wilkins, 1955 to 1976; and Benjamin L. Hooks, 1976 to 1993. The current president and chief executive officer, Benjamin Jealous (1973–), took office in 2008. He faced the challenges of increasing the organization's visibility, expanding the membership, and strengthening the organization's financial base. Immediately Jealous reached out to other civil rights advocates, religious leaders, and consultants to help him develop a plan to strengthen the organization. Jealous concentrated also on legislative issues that would affect racial disparities in education, health care, criminal justice, the home-mortgage crisis, and other issues. The California native has long been active in political and community organizations, first in a voter-registration drive for Jesse Jackson's presidential bid, later in Harlem for the Legal Defense Educational Fund, and still later as field organizer and campaigner in Mississippi to prevent the closing of two public historically black colleges.

What is the **NAACP Legal Defense and Educational Fund**?

The NAACP Legal Defense and Educational Fund (LDEF) is the legal arm of the NAACP and, since the mid-1950s, functions independently of its parent organization. Its primary interest is in African Americans, other racial minorities, and women. The LDEF works to help these groups exercise their legal and constitutional rights, defending them against discrimination in areas such as employment, education, and housing. Civil rights groups and others who have bona fide civil rights claims are represented as well. Financial support given to the organization is used to support campaigns for prison reform, land use, and health care delivery. Those who have been influential in the organization include Thurgood Marshall, Constance Baker Motley, Julius L. Chambers, and Oliver W. Hill. The LDEF won a number of notable legal cases. For example, with the

Supreme Court's *Brown v. Board of Education of Topeka, Kansas* decision in 1954, the LDEF succeeded in overturning *Plessy v. Ferguson*'s doctrine of "separate but equal," which had consequences far beyond educational arenas. Through its education arm, scholarships are given to African-American students who attend state colleges and universities. It also awards scholarships to African-American law students through its Earl Warren Legal Training Program.

Who **founded** and **edited** the **NAACP's official publication**?

W.E.B. Du Bois served as the founder and editor of the NAACP's official publication, *The Crisis* magazine, a current affairs journal showcasing black literature, history, and culture. The organization's most salient victories include the now legendary *Brown v. Board of Education of Topeka, Kansas* (1954) ruling, which arguably signaled the beginning of the modern Civil Rights Movement. The organization has also enjoyed successes second to none among American civil rights organizations. It continues to fight for social justice to ensure that the voices of African Americans are heard.

What was the purpose of the **Universal Negro Improvement Association**?

Marcus (Mozian Manaseth) Garvey (1887–1940), black nationalist and orator, founded the Universal Negro Improvement Association (UNIA) in 1914. It was the first black mass-movement organization. Garvey initially organized the UNIA in Kingston, Jamaica. However, when he came to the United States in 1916, the organization developed a more extensive following. The UNIA had members from around the world. There were 996 branches of the organization in 43 countries. During the early 1920s the association had grown larger than any other black organization in U.S. history. The UNIA served as the basis for Garvey's Black Nationalist and consciousness-raising movement. The motto of the organization was "One God! One Aim! One Destiny!" Later its divisions and subsidiaries included the African Legion and the Black Cross Nurses. The organization's agenda included racial pride, self-help, and racial segregation. The establishment of a black homeland in Africa and black economic independence were considered national extensions of that agenda.

Garvey was a controversial figure who was attacked by other black leaders be-

Black nationalist and orator Marcus Garvey founded the Universal Negro Improvement Association.

243

cause of his views on civil rights for African Americans in the United States. Garvey and his UNIA questioned whether black people could achieve equality in a white majority country. The UNIA, therefore, promoted migration of people of African descent back to Africa. As a part of the organization's emphasis on self-help and black economic enterprise, the UNIA established the Negro Factories Corporation. Black-owned grocery stores, restaurants, and other service-oriented businesses were a part of the corporation. By mid-1919 Garvey established the Black Star Shipping Line to help create economic opportunities for blacks, who bought stock in the line. Garvey and his stockholders later expanded the business to form a cross-continent steamship trade.

What African-American woman was the **only woman president** of the **UNIA**?

The only woman to serve as president general of the Universal Negro Improvement Association (UNIA) was Henrietta Vinton Davis (1860–1941). She became president in 1934. Born in Baltimore, Maryland, Vinton became an elocutionist, actress, and political organizer. She taught school in Maryland and Louisiana and then became a copyist in the Office of the Recorder of Deeds in Washington, D.C. During her stay in that office, she came under the supervision of Frederick Douglass, who encouraged her to study drama. She followed his suggestion and studied drama in Washington and at the Boston School of Oratory. She toured principal cities and gave a range of selections, from Negro dialect to Shakespeare's works. Davis also became an organizer for Marcus Garvey's UNIA in 1919, and continued in that role until her death in 1941. She was a strong advocate of racial pride. She embraced the Populist Party and later the Socialist Party. She was among the UNIA's top leadership in the 1920s and 1930s.

Why was the **Southern Christian Leadership Conference** established?

The first organization to coordinate the work of nonviolent groups devoted to racial integration and improved life for black Americans was the Southern Christian Leadership Conference (SCLC), established on February 14, 1957. Known in the Civil Rights Movement for its nonviolent and direct action, the SCLC grew out of the 1955–1956 Montgomery Bus Boycott. As the bus boycott sparked a chain of protests across the South, it became apparent to Martin Luther King Jr., Ralph David Abernathy, Fred Shuttlesworth, Bayard Rustin, and others that there was a need for a central coordinating body for these boycotts. Thus, from January 10 through 11, 1957, sixty disparate regional groups from ten states met in Atlanta and formed the Southern Leadership Conference on Transportation and Non-Violent Integration. Its initial objectives were to use nonviolent tactics and appeal to the moral conscience of America. Participants asserted at their meeting that civil rights are a basic part of democracy, that segregation should end, and that it was incumbent upon all black people to oppose segregation. The media's coverage of the SCLC's campaigns and its voter registration endeavors served to move the nation toward the passage of the Civil Rights Act of 1964 and the Voting Rights Act of 1965. It was involved in organizing the March on Washington for Jobs and Freedom in 1963, when Martin Luther King Jr. delivered his "I Have a Dream" speech.

Why was the **Student Nonviolent Coordinating Committee** founded?

The Student Nonviolent Coordinating Committee (SNCC), a youth political organization, was organized under the leadership of Ella Josephine Baker (1903–1986), a founder and executive director of the Southern Christian Leadership Conference (SCLC). Baker saw a need for students to become involved in the fight for equal rights, anticipating that they would need to organize and coordinate their efforts. She invited students to a meeting held from April 15 to 17, 1960, at Shaw University in Raleigh, North Carolina. Over two hundred college and high school students came from thirteen states, though most were from Nashville, Tennessee. This meeting followed a smaller meeting held at Highlander Folk School in Monteagle, Tennessee, where a number of the issues considered at Shaw were discussed. It was at Shaw that the fight for civil rights gained a new organization, the SNCC. It was independent of other civil rights groups even though these groups wanted them to affiliate. At the urging of Baker, they determined to have a decentralized leadership, maintain strong local leaderships, and keep the lines of communication open among college campuses and students. The group asserted its commitment to "the philosophical or religious ideal of nonviolence." SNCC concentrated on direct action and voter registration, with an emphasis on the power of the ballot. It saw itself as a movement against injustice and not racially exclusive in membership or focus.

What was the **New Negro Alliance** and why was it formed?

The New Negro Alliance (NNA), established in Washington, D.C., in 1913, was formed to improve accommodations, fair treatment, and employment of African Americans in Washington, D.C., during the period preceding World War II. Activists and founders of the alliance included John Aubrey Davis, Belford Lawson, and M. Franklin Thorne, who worked with Ralph Bunche, Thurgood Marshall, William Hastie, James Nabrit, and others. The alliance participated in a boycott of the Hamburger Grill in Washington after it fired black employees in August 1933. They used the then-popular campaign called

Among those prominently associated with the Student Nonviolent Coordinating Committee are activist (and one of SNCC's founders) Ella Josephine Baker, along with Marion Barry, James Forman, Fannie Lou Hamer, John Lewis, and Ruby Doris Smith-Robinson. As the group changed leadership later on during the Civil Rights Movement, and moved away from its nonviolent philosophy, its leaders were such figures as Stokely Carmichael (later known as Kwame Turé), and H. Rap Brown.

"Don't Buy Where You Can't Work" and mobilized support from black Washingtonians in the academic, legal, and religious communities; the boycott was a success. The NNA was formally organized in 1935 for direct action to secure economic rights, but the organization is not to be confused with Alain Locke and the "New Negro" cultural movement of the 1920s. The NNA achieved its greatest success in *New Negro Alliance v. Sanitary Grocery Company* (1938). Lawson, Marshall, Hastie, and Nabrit were members of the NNA's legal team that argued the case before the U.S. Supreme Court on March 5, 1938; it was decided in their favor by a vote of the justices on March 28. This legal victory led to President Franklin Delano Roosevelt's Executive Order 8802, mandating fair treatment of employees in agencies of the federal government and establishing the Fair Employment Practices Committee (FEPC). Davis began work with the FEPC, and the NNA ceased to exist soon after he left in the 1950s.

What is the purpose of the **National Urban League**?

One of the earliest organizations of its kind, the National Urban League (NUM) has been a grass-roots leader in the twentieth-century struggle to secure African-American civil rights and economic opportunities. Founded as the Committee on Urban Conditions Among Negroes on September 29, 1910, by Ruth Standish Baldwin, the widow of railroad magnate and philanthropist William H. Baldwin Jr., and by Fisk University and Columbia University graduate George Edmund Haynes, the league was fostered through the consolidation of the Committee for Improving the Industrial Conditions of Negroes in New York and the National League for the Protection of Colored Women, both founded in 1906. Renamed the National Urban League in 1911, the interracial organization was committed to securing economic and social parity for blacks as well as advocating racial integration. Its goals were particularly geared toward Northern populations of blacks who had migrated during the great black migration in search of economic opportunity, only to find that racism also pervaded the North and often reduced them to manual laborers. The league quickly emerged as a leader in the fight for blacks in urban settings. Through its artful mastery of negotiation and persuasion, for a century the league has successfully pushed for better educational and employment opportunities for African Americans.

How was the **National Urban League** involved in **civil rights activities**?

In the educational sector, the National Urban League pressured schools to expand vocational opportunities, all the while pursuing its strategy of "education and persuasion." Throughout the 1960s, the league kept pace with the efforts of other groups that demanded African-American civil rights during the modern Civil Rights Movement. With the election of Whitney M. Young Jr. (1921–1971) as the organization's president in 1961, the league was able to expand its fundraising ability and become more involved with its cohorts, who focused primarily on direct action as a means of achieving racial equality. In 1963 the league participated in the planning of the A. Philip Randolph- and Martin Luther King Jr.-led March on Washington. While his ten-year tenure was tragically cut short by death in 1971, Young's vision for the closure of economic racial disparities and his commitment to health, job training, and educational services to communities was extended by subsequent directors. Among these are Vernon E. Jordan Jr. and, more recently, through the leadership of president and chief executive officer Marc H. Morial, a former mayor of New Orleans.

What is the **National Urban League Guild**?

Mollie Moon (1912–1990) was the organizer and founding president of the National Urban League Guild, a fundraising organization for the league, established in 1942. She headed the organization until her death. Moon was born in Hattiesburg, Mississippi, and graduated from Meharry Medical College in Nashville, Tennessee, with a degree in pharmacy. She worked as a pharmacist in New Orleans; Gary, Indiana; and New York City. She became interested in social work, however, and left pharmacy to work with the Department of Social Services in New York City. She had wide contacts in New York's social circles and used her connections to help support the National Urban League. Moon and a group of friends held a benefit for the league in early 1942; the Victory Cocktail Party was highly successful and became a New York tradition. The black-tie ball continued to be held each February and was renamed the Beaux Arts Ball. Moon became the founding president of the Council of Urban League Guilds that

Randall Robinson is an activist and attorney who founded TransAfrica, which works to lobby Washington, D.C., about foreign policy in Africa and the Caribbean.

247

functioned to raise money for the league. At the time of her death in 1990, she had been its only president.

What is **TransAfrica**?

Randall S. Robinson (1941–), founded TransAfrica in 1977 and continues to serve as its director. The organization is concerned with the human rights of people of African descent throughout the world. Robinson led the group in lobbying Congress and the White House on foreign policy matters that involved Africa and the Caribbean. When Robinson and TransAfrica demonstrated before the South African embassy in Washington, D.C., in 1984 and 1985, they were arrested. TransAfrica supports the United Nations and its work in Africa, and through its research and education arm, TransAfrica Forum, provides reviews and perspectives on political, economic, and cultural issues that affect African-American communities worldwide.

EDUCATIONAL ORGANIZATIONS

What was the **American Negro Academy**?

Founded in Washington, D.C., on March 5, 1897, the American Negro Academy (ANA) was the first major African-American learned society. Its constitution defined the ANA as "an organization of authors, scholars, artists, and those distinguished in other walks of life, men of African descent, for the promotion of Letters, Science, and Art." Members of the organization hoped that through the academy educated black elites would be molded to shape and direct society. Papers of the academy appeared in print until 1924. A leading figure in the founding of the academy was Alexander Crummell (1819–1898), a minister. He conceived of the idea of an American Negro Academy while he was a student at Cambridge University in England. The academy's membership of forty included such scholars as Pan Africanist and educator W.E.B. Du Bois (1868–1963), educator Kelly Miller (1863–1939), poet Paul Laurence Dunbar (1872–1906), and educator William Sanders Scarborough (1852–1926). Noted contributors to its publications were Du Bois and Theophilis G. Steward. After Crummell died in 1898, Du Bois was elected president of the academy. Until its demise in 1928, the ANA claimed some of the black community's most important leaders. Only a handful of educated blacks ever belonged to the organization. During its existence, only ninety-nine were members at various times.

Who founded the **Negro Society for Historical Research** and what was its purpose?

Founders of the Negro Society for Historical Research were sociologist E. Franklin Frazier (1894–1963), historian George Washington Williams (1849–1991), journalist John Edward Bruce (1856–1924), and library curator and bibliophile Arthur Alphonso Schomburg (1874–1938). The organization was founded in Yonkers, New York, on April 8, 1911,

What is the purpose of the Association for the Study of African American Life and History?

In 1915 the Association for the Study of Negro Life and History, since 1972 known as the Association for the Study of African American Life and History, was organized by Carter G. Woodson (1875–1950) as the first learned society specifically devoted to the professional study of black history. The association's first meeting was on September 9, 1915, in the office of the Wabash Avenue YMCA in Chicago. Woodson was born in New Canton, Virginia, and educated at Berea College in Kentucky (B.Litt., 1907), the University of Chicago (B.A., 1907; M.A., 1908) and Harvard (Ph.D., 1912). The first issue of the *Journal of Negro History* appeared in 1916. This organization first sponsored Negro History Week in 1926. Since 1976, the celebration has been known as Black History Month. In 1926 Woodson, who became known as the "Father of Black History," received the NAACP's Spingarn Medal for his contributions to the advancement of black people.

at the same time that other black organizations began to preempt some of the American Negro Academy's goals. According to its constitution, the NSHR's purpose was "to instruct the race and to inspire love and veneration for its men and women of mark." Members committed themselves to collect data, pamphlets, and books that related to the history and achievements of the race, to build a circulating library for its members, and to publish works by black people and their friends that supported the upward struggle of the race. While there were never formal ties between the NSHR and the American Negro Academy, some members belonged to both organizations and "stimulated feelings of connectedness and mutual interest."

Who founded the **College Language Association**?

Hugh Morris Gloster (1911–2002) was the founder and first president of the College Language Association in 1937. A native of Brownsville, Tennessee, Gloster graduated from Morehouse College in Atlanta in 1931 and received a master's degree from Atlanta University in 1933. After teaching at LeMoyne-Owen College in Memphis, he returned to Morehouse where he taught until 1943. In that year he also received a doctorate from New York University. Gloster worked for the United Service Organizations in Arizona and Atlanta. Later he moved to Hampton Institute (now University) in Virginia and rose in rank to become dean of the faculty. He was a Fulbright professor of English at Japan's Hiroshima University and became a part of the international educational exchange program at the University of Warsaw in Poland. Gloster's distinguished career in education was capped with his presidency of Morehouse College from 1967 to 1987. While there he strengthened the college's endowment, doubled the size of the campus as well as the faculty, doubled faculty salaries, increased to 65 percent the total number of faculty with

Ph.D. degrees, and quadrupled the enrollment. He was the school's seventh president and its first alumnus to lead the institution. Among Gloster's publications were *Negro Voices in American Fiction* (1948) and *My Life—My Country—My World* (1952). He died in Decatur, Georgia, on February 16, 2002, at age ninety.

What organization has as its slogan "A mind is a terrible thing to waste"?

The United Negro College Fund (UNCF) began on April 24, 1944 in response to the need to address economic conditions on private black college campuses. It aimed to coordinate the fund-raising efforts of forty-one private, accredited, four-year schools.

Frederick Patterson—seen here with President Lyndon Johnson in the Oval Office—founded the United Negro College Fund, as well as the only black veterinary school, which is at Tuskegee University.

After black colleges were founded in the 1800s, they received some support from religious and charitable groups. By the end of the century, however, funding from such groups had dwindled; fortunately, new groups or philanthropists emerged and lent support to these colleges. Northern industrialists like George Foster Peabody, Andrew Carnegie, and Julius Rosenwald were among the leading supporters. Later John D. Rockefeller Jr. and Massachusetts senator John F. Kennedy became key supporters. As funds from philanthropists dwindled, Tuskegee Institute president Frederick D. Patterson called on presidents of the private black colleges to pool their resources and raise money together. At that time Patterson, Mary McLeod Bethune, and presidents of other historically black colleges coordinated their fund-raising efforts. A year earlier, Patterson came up with the idea for the fund and urged other members of the incorporating group to raise money through a collective "appeal to the national conscience." This fund-raising agency now consists of thirty-nine members from private and fully accredited black colleges. UNCF began an annual televised fund-raising event called *Lou Rawls Parade of Stars,* later called "An Evening of Stars," and showcased member colleges as well as students who benefitted from UNCF funding. The organization provides information on educational programs, administers scholarships, and offers programs supported by corporate bodies and foundations. Native American, Latino, and Asian students currently receive scholarship support. UNCF also established the Institute for Capacity Building, a grants-awarding initiative that helps small colleges and universities expand their network of donor support. Located in Fairfax, Virginia, the organization continues to contribute significantly to the survival of black higher education. In 1972 Forest Long coined the phrase "A mind is a terrible thing to waste," and since then UNCF has used the phrase as its slogan.

UNCF founder Frederick D. Patterson (1901–1988), a veterinarian, also founded the nation's first and only black veterinary school at Tuskegee Institute (now University). Until his retirement in 1953, he served as president of Tuskegee for twenty-five years. Patterson was born in Washington, D.C., and graduated from Iowa State University in 1923 with a degree in veterinary medicine. After teaching at Virginia State College (now University), he returned to Iowa and obtained his master's degree in veterinary medicine. He joined Tuskegee's faculty in 1932 and established a friendship with researcher George Washington Carver that lasted until Carver died. Patterson continued his education at Cornell University and returned to Tuskegee with his doctorate in bacteriology; he was the first Tuskegee faculty member to earn the terminal degree. While president of Tuskegee, he established the Commercial Aviation program and trained Tuskegee students as pilots. The program became well-known for training the group of black military pilots known as the Tuskegee Airmen. After he left Tuskegee, Patterson became president of the Phelps Stokes Fund in New York City and remained there until 1970. He was awarded the Presidential Medal of Freedom on June 23, 1987.

Where are chapters of **Phi Beta Kappa** on **black college campuses**?

Phi Beta Kappa was organized at William and Mary College in Williamsburg, Virginia, on December 5, 1776. Initially it was a secret social club, but abandoned its secrecy in 1826 when it became an honor organization based on scholarship. In 1877 Phi Beta Kappa accepted its first African-American member—George Washington Henderson—who was a student at the University of Vermont. Chapters of this most prestigious honorary society for undergraduate achievement in the humanities have been established on several black college campuses. The first chapter of the society at a black university was established at Fisk University in Nashville on April 4, 1953. The chapter at Howard University in Washington, D.C., was formed four days later. Since then, the only other black colleges with a Phi Beta Kappa chapter are Morehouse and Spelman Colleges in Atlanta. Phi Beta Kappa elected its first black national president in 1973, when historian and scholar John Hope Franklin (1915–2009) became its leader. He held office until 1976 and presided over the society's two-hundredth anniversary celebrations.

FRATERNAL, SOCIAL SERVICE, AND RELIGIOUS ORGANIZATIONS

What was the origin of the **Masonic lodge**?

In 1775 Prince Hall (1735–1807) and fourteen others joined a Masonic lodge sponsored by British Army officers at Castle William near Boston on March 6. These are the first American black Masons and the origin of the Masonic movement among blacks. On September 29, 1784, the British Grand Lodge approved the formation of African Lodge No. 459, but the notification did not arrive until 1787. The African Grand Lodge was established on June 24,

> ## What was the first national Catholic black fraternal order?
>
> The Knights of Peter Claver, founded in Mobile, Alabama, in 1909, was the first national Catholic black fraternal order. It embraces some 100,000 Catholic families in the United States. Its girls' auxiliary was established in 1909, junior auxiliary for boys in 1917, and ladies' auxiliary in 1922.

1791; Prince Hall was the grand master. A second black lodge was formed in Philadelphia in 1797. In 1808 the existing black lodges formed the Prince Hall Masons, an organization that declared itself independent from all other Masonic lodges. During the American Revolution, Prince Hall became the most famous black in the Boston area. His work, and that of the early lodges, set the stage for the Masonic lodges that followed.

Why was **Sigma Pi Phi** (the Boulé) founded?

The first black Greek letter organization, Sigma Pi Phi, known as the Boulé, was formed at a meeting in the Philadelphia home of physician Henry McKee Minton (1870–1946) on May 4, 1904. Six men were present for the initial meeting. The Boulé was founded for men "who had made places for themselves in their communities through useful service"; it was designed to meet the social needs of black professional and business leaders, and to address social issues. It focused on post-college years of the black elite who provided meaningful service in the community. It was expected that the members would have similar attributes in education, skills, and level of accomplishment. Minton became the first grand sire archon.

What is the purpose of **black Greek letter organizations**?

Near the beginning of the twentieth century, Greek letter organizations emerged on college campuses. For the African-American community they have been vital contributors to life and culture, by offering communal identity and spearheading initiatives in education, health, careers, teenage pregnancy, family issues, juvenile delinquency, and in community life. Greek letter organizations, whether on college campuses or graduate chapters in the community, provide scholarships for the education of black students, mentoring programs, leadership programs, and other initiatives. Rather than serve as social organizations, they are clearly service organizations that contribute to the uplift of the black community.

The oldest Greek letter organization for blacks on a college campus is Alpha Phi Alpha, founded at Cornell University in 1906. Notable among the early members were U.S. Supreme Court Justice Thurgood Marshall, activist and scholar W. E. B. Du Bois, and, later, civil rights leader Martin Luther King Jr. Following the Alphas, the Omega Psi Phi fraternity was established at Howard University in 1911. Among its prominent members are activist and minister Jesse Jackson Sr. and civil rights leader and minister Benjamin Hooks. Phi Beta Sigma was founded in 1914; among its ranks were scientist George Washington Carver and, much later, actor Blair Underwood.

What was the **first black women's sorority** founded?

African-American women joined sororities as early as 1908, when Alpha Kappa Alpha sorority was founded at Howard University. It aims to provide "services to all mankind." Civil rights activist Coretta Scott King was among its well-known members. Also founded at Howard University was Delta Sigma Theta sorority, in 1913. The organization is concerned with public and mental health, economic health, and other issues. Famed members now deceased or living include actresses Lena Horne and Ruby Dee, and singer Roberta Flack.

What was the **first black ecumenical organization**?

Reverdy C. Ransom (1861–1959), bishop in the African Methodist Episcopal Church, organized the Fraternal Council of Negro Churches in 1934; it was the first black ecumenical organization. It had an explicit agenda that included social change and racial uplift within a religious context. Concerned that the predominantly white Federal Council of Churches had failed to address black concerns in a substantive way, Ransom and other black church leaders saw the new council as the "authoritative voice" coming from a "united Negro church." Sixteen predominantly black communions and six predominantly white churches formed the council. Two of the thirty-nine members of the executive committee were women: Belle Hendon of Chicago, who represented the National Baptist Convention of America; and Ida Mae Myller of Gary, Indiana, representing the Community Center Church. Ransom was born in Flushing, Ohio, and then moved to a small farm near Old Washington, Ohio. The family later moved to Cambridge, Ohio. Ransom attended a local summer normal school and later enrolled at Wilberforce University, where he came to the attention of Bishop Daniel A. Payne and Benjamin W. Arnett. He attended Oberlin College the next year, but returned to Wilberforce later and graduated in 1886 with a bachelor's degree in divinity. Ransom edited the *AME Church Review* from 1912 to 1924. He was elected bishop in the African Methodist Episcopal Church in 1920.

Who was the **first African-American president** of the **World Council of Churches**?

Vinton Randolph Anderson (1927–) became the first black president of the World Council of Churches, in 1991. He retired from the post in 1998. Anderson was born in Somerset, Bermuda, and received his bachelor's degree from Wilberforce University in Ohio, his master's degree in divinity from Payne Theological Seminary, and a master of arts degree from Kansas University. He did further study at Yale Divinity School. Anderson had a stellar career in the ministry, including serving as pastor for a number of African Methodist Episcopal churches in Wichita, Kansas, and in St. Louis, Missouri. He was presiding bishop and chief pastor of the Ninth Episcopal District in Alabama from 1972 to 1976, and served the Third Episcopal District of Ohio, West Virginia, and West Pennsylvania from 1976 to 1984. From 1984 to 1988 he was with the Office of Ecumenical Relations and Development, and in 1988 he was assigned to the Fifth Episcopal District serving fourteen states and 255 churches west of the Mississippi River. Among his numerous accomplishments, Anderson developed the bicentennial edition of a church hymnal.

MEDICAL AND DENTAL ASSOCIATIONS

What was the **first black medical association**?

Founded in 1884, the Medico-Chirurgical Society of the District of Columbia was the first established black medical society. Its formation on April 24 was the result of refusal of the white medical society to admit blacks. It would not be until the early 1950s that black physicians could join the local American Medical Association branch. A national organization for blacks would be formed in 1895, when the Medico-Chirurgical Society was reactivated and incorporated. Although three of the eight incorporators were white, by 1920 the membership was entirely black.

When was the **National Medical Association** formed?

The National Medical Association was organized in October 1895 in Atlanta, Georgia, during the Cotton States and International Exposition. The association was formed in reaction to the racial practices of predominantly white associations. The American Medical Association refused to urge all its local members to remove restrictive provisions until 1950. Founded as the National Association of Colored Physicians, Dentists, and Pharmacists on September 18, 1895, the NMA had a small membership of fewer than fifty in 1904, which grew to over five hundred by 1912; the association name change was effected in 1903. The first president of the black association was R. F. Boyd of Nashville, Tennessee. The *Journal of the National Medical Association* became the chief means of spotlighting the work of its members. The journal remained the primary source of information on black doctors and dentists until the mainstream press covered their contributions to health care. The NMA continues to serve the black medical community.

Who was the **first black president** of the **American Medical Association**?

In 1995 Lonnie R. Bristow (1930–) became the first black president of the American Medical Association. A New York City native, Bristow was the son of a Baptist minister and a nurse. He grew up in Harlem and spent many hours at the Sydenham Hospital where his mother worked and where he went to escort her home at night. His experiences there stimulated him to become a doctor and to provide quality health care to patients regardless of race. Bristow graduated from City College of New York (B.S., 1953) and New York University College of Medicine (M.D., 1957). He completed several residencies, the last at the University of California's School of Medicine in San Francisco. He established a private practice in San Pablo, California, in 1964, and became highly active in medical societies. He became the first black president of the American Society

What organization was founded to address the needs of black nurses?

The founding meeting of the National Association of Colored Graduate Nurses (NACGN) was held at St. Mark's Methodist Church in New York City in 1908. The organization, the first national organization for black nurses, aimed to meet the increasing concern of black nurses to enhance themselves professionally. Few mainstream nursing schools of the North—and none in the South—admitted blacks for training. Fifty people attended the first meeting. Martha Minerva Franklin (1870–1968), who was the force behind the gathering of black nurses, became the founding president. The NACGN soon attacked the practice of setting up separate black and white state boards of nursing; it also promoted legislation to benefit its members and the black community as a whole. The association established a national headquarters in 1934, with nurse Mabel Keaton Staupers (1890–1989) as executive secretary. After obtaining full participation in the American Nurses Association, the NACGN board voted the black organization out of existence on January 25, 1951.

of Internal Medicine in 1982. Bristow served the American Medical Association in a variety of posts, such as alternate delegate to AMA's House of Delegates in 1978, chair of the Council of Medical Service in 1979, and chair of the board of trustees in 1993. In 1985 he was the first black elected to AMA's board.

What is the **professional organization** for **black dentists**?

Origins of the National Dental Association are traced back to the Washington Society for Colored Dentists, which in 1900 began meeting in the District of Columbia. In May of 1901 D. A. Ferguson of Virginia led the formation of the National Association of Colored Dentists at Howard University's College of Dentistry. For a brief period in 1907 the organization was known as the Robert T. Freeman Dental Society, named in honor of the first black man to graduate from a dental college. Freeman had graduated from Harvard in 1867. The organization focused on education, seminars, lectures, papers, debates, and social activities. When membership had declined five years later, Ferguson led the group that reestablished the organization in 1913 as the Tri-State Dental Association. Membership included dentists from Virginia, Maryland, and Washington, D.C. The group flourished, and by 1918 membership embraced fourteen states. As it gained momentum, counting members from twenty-one states, the association was renamed the Interstate Dental Association; in 1923 members began a movement for a national organization. In 1932 the IDA merged with the Commonwealth Dental Society of New Jersey, organized in 1927, to form a national organization known as the National Dental Association. Its mission is to represent people of color and various ethnic groups in the profession, to address the dental needs of the poor and underprivileged, and to improve the educational and financial goals of the membership. There are chapters in forty-eight states and the Caribbean, and the organization has a student organization as well. The *NDA Today* is the organization's professional journal.

Who were some of the **early leading black nurses**?

Among the notable black nurses were Martha Minerva Franklin and Mabel Keaton Staupers. Franklin (1870–1968) was the force behind the founding meeting of the National Association of Colored Graduate Nurses (NACGN) in 1908, and was its founding president. A civil rights activist, she was one of the first black nurses to campaign publicly and nationally for parity for black nurses. Franklin's goals became the NACGN's goals: "to eradicate discrimination in the nursing profession, develop leadership among black nurses, and promote higher standards in administration and education." Staupers (1890–1989), who became president of the NACGN in 1949, was the association's executive secretary from 1934 to 1949. She led a decades-long protest by black nurses who sought full integration into the mainstream nursing profession. Staupers became best known for the leadership role that she took in desegregating the Armed Forces Nurse Corps in World War II.

WOMEN'S ORGANIZATIONS

What was the purpose of the **National Conference of Colored Women**?

The National Conference of Colored Women met in Boston, Massachusetts, in August 1895. The leading spirit in organizing the conference was Josephine St. Pierre Ruffin (1842–1924), the founder of the Women's New Era Club. One hundred women from twenty clubs in ten states came together for the session. The meeting led to the formation of the National Federation of Afro-American Women, which was merged into the National Association of Colored Women the following year, on July 21, 1896. The new organization was founded as a national coalition of black women's clubs and was the first and foremost national organization of black women at the time. Mary Church Terrell (1863–1954) became the first president of the National Association of Colored Women.

What was the **White Rose Mission**?

Victoria Earl Matthews (1861–1907) and Maritcha Lyons (1848–1929) founded the White Rose Mission on February 11, 1897. Matthews was the organization's first superintendent. Its mission was a home for black girls and women, the purpose of which was to train them for "practical self-help and right living." The home operated from the San Juan Hill district in the Manhattan section of New York City and provided food and living quarters for Southern and West Indian migrants. Matthews was born in Fort Valley, Georgia, one of nine children of a slave mother. Her mother relocated to New York after emancipation, taking with her the only two of her children that she could find. Although she had little formal education, Matthews was an avid reader and took advantage of every opportunity to grow intellectually and culturally. She used the pen name "Victoria Earle" and wrote a number of works. She became founder and first president of the Woman's Loyal Union of New York City. Lyons, an educator, writer, and lecturer, was born a free black in New York City. After graduating from high school, she became a teacher, since a high school education, at that time, qualified one to teach. She taught in the Brooklyn schools for forty-eight years and later became an assistant principal and teacher trainer. She was also active in the women's club movement.

What is the purpose of the **National Council of Negro Women**?

Mary McLeod Bethune (1875–1955) was instrumental in founding the National Council of Negro Women on December 5, 1935— the first national coalition of black women's organizations established in the twentieth century. It aims to advance issues that are important to black women and their families. The organization was founded in New York City when fourteen black women's organizations came together at the 137th St. YWCA. Bethune was its first president, a post she held until 1949. The organization had a cen-

Dorothy Height is shown here presenting former First Lady Eleanor Roosevelt with the Mary McLeod Bethune Human Rights Award in 1960. Height was president of the National Council of Negro Women from 1957 to 1998. **257**

tralized direction and purpose that Bethune found lacking in the National Association of Colored Women. The NCNW was originally located at 1318 Vermont Avenue, NW, Washington, D.C., which in 1995 was designated an historical landmark. The Bethune Museum and the National Archives for Black Women's History, which document Bethune's life as well as the history of NCNW, are located at this site.

What was the importance of **Dorothy Height** to the **National Council of Negro Women**?

The fourth president of the National Council of Negro Women, Dorothy Irene Height (1912–2010) held this position from 1957 to 1998, when she retired and was named chair and president emeritus. She continued to make appearances on behalf of the organization and kept NCNW at the forefront of black and women's organizations. Height spent most of her life working as a leader in the struggle for equality and human rights for all people. In her early years, the Richmond, Virginia, native worked in government and social service associations. She rose through the ranks of the YWCA in Harlem and in Washington, D.C, and became a staff member of the National Board of the YWCA USA. There she developed leadership training programs for volunteers and staff. She became known for her internationalism and humanitarianism. Her leadership skills made her a natural choice as leader of NCNW when Mary McLeod Bethune retired. Through the organization, Height worked tirelessly to strengthen the black family and to develop model national programs. She led the organization in issue-oriented politics, promoted voter registration drives in the North and South, and strengthened communication between women of all races. Height was also a leader in the Civil Rights Movement and worked with Martin Luther King Jr., Roy Wilkins, Whitney Young, A. Philip Randolph, and others. She was active in practically all of the major civil and human rights activities of that time. She conceived and organized the Black Family Reunion Celebration, first held in 1986, to strengthen the traditional values of black families. For several years these successful celebrations were held in separate locations throughout the country. When Height died on April 20, 2010, President Barack Obama called her "the godmother of the civil rights movement."

Who are **The Links Incorporated**?

The Links, Incorporated, was established on November 9, 1946, as an international, not-for-profit corporation. Two Philadelphia matrons, Margaret Hawkins (1908–1963) and Sarah Strickland Scott (1901–1988), were its founders. Currently twelve thousand professional women of color compose the membership in 276 chapters located in 41 states, the District of Columbia, and the Commonwealth of the Bahamas. Its members are individual achievers, civic leaders, business leaders, mentors, activists, educators, and other volunteers who contribute annually over 500,000 documented hours of community service. The Links is now the largest black volunteer service organization. Its programs are organized into five facets: National Trends, The Arts, Services to Youth,

International Trends and Services, and Health and Human Services. The home office is located in Washington, D.C.

Why was the **National Coalition of 100 Black Women** established?

The National Coalition of 100 Black Women was founded on October 24, 1981, in response to the New York Coalition's nationwide call to develop a leadership forum for professional black women representing the public and private sectors. Following this call, a network was established to meet the professional needs of the contemporary black woman, her community needs, and her access to mainstream America. The organization is involved in economic development, health, employment, education, housing, voting, the arts, and other issues. It encourages leadership development for black women, role-model programs, guidance for teenage mothers, and networking opportunities between the organization and the political and corporate world. Currently there are over six thousand members in sixty chapters representing twenty-five states and the District of Columbia.

What **organizations** are among those that serve the **needs and interests of black women**?

Among the numerous organizations (and their headquarters) established to address the interests of black women are Black Women in Church and Society (Atlanta), Black Women in Publishing (New York City), Black Women Organized for Educational Development (Oakland), Black Women's Roundtable on Voter Participation (Washington, D.C.), Jack and Jill of America (Orlando), National Association of Black Women Attorneys (Washington, D.C.), and National Association of Negro Business and Professional Women's Clubs (Washington, D.C.).

POLITICS AND GOVERNMENT

EARLY POLITICAL ACTIVITIES

What **African Americans** were involved in **political gatherings** of the **Liberty Party**?

In 1843 Henry Highland Garnet, Charles B. Ray, and Samuel Ringgold Ward were the first blacks to participate in a national political gathering, the convention of the Liberty Party. Garnet (1815–1882) was pastor of a New York Presbyterian church and preached a social gospel. In that year he attended the Convention of Free Men held in Buffalo, New York, and outlined a brilliant plan for a general slave strike. Ray (1807–1886), one of the convention's secretaries, was a minister best known for his work as publisher of *The Colored American* and as president of the New York Society for the Promotion of Education among Colored Children. Ward (1817–1866), who led a prayer at the convention, was the leading black abolitionist before Frederick Douglass.

Along with Charles B. Ray and Samuel Ringgold Ward, Presbyterian pastor Henry Highland Garnet was one of the first black men to attend a national political gathering.

What leading African American was the **first black delegate** to a **national political convention**?

In 1866 Frederick Douglass (1817–1895) was the first black delegate to a national political convention, that of the National Loyalists' Union Party. In 1872 he was the first black to be nominated as a vice-presidential candidate at the Republican Convention, by the National Woman Suffrage Association. He received one vote. During Reconstruction, he demanded the vote for the freedman. He moved to the nation's capital and became the first black recorder of deeds in 1881 and U.S. minister to Haiti in 1889.

POLITICS DURING
THE RECONSTRUCTION

How was black America represented in **political office** during the **Reconstruction**?

Black Americans during the Reconstruction were represented at every level of government—local, state, and federal. They held numerous federal patronage appointments, such as postmaster, deputy U.S. marshal, treasury agent, and federal office clerk. They were also represented in virtually every county with a sizeable black population. Blacks were seen on county governing boards, police juries, boards of supervisors, and boards of police. Many free-born blacks were of mixed racial ancestry and so identified. Of those who were former slaves, ten black office holders escaped slavery before the Civil War. Most of these were born in Virginia, which made their flight north easier than from the Deep South. Some became militant leaders.

What African Americans held **gubernatorial positions** during the **Reconstruction**?

African Americans were able to work around the obstacles to their advancement in politics that remained even after the passage of the Civil Rights Acts of 1866 and 1870, and passage of the Fourteenth Amendment, which aimed to ensure their full citizenship. While African-American males were granted the right to vote by 1870, some states still denied them this privilege. Yet, between 1879 and 1901, over one thousand African Americans were elected to local and state office. There were six lieutenant governors and one governor. In Louisiana, P.B.S. Pinchback (1837–1921), disliked by many whites because he was a staunch advocate for equal rights for members of his race, became the first African-American governor. He had served as lieutenant governor in 1871 and then governor when Henry C. Warmouth was impeached. He held this post from December 8, 1972, to January 13, 1873, when he was defeated in elections. A Republican, Pinchback was later elected to the U.S. Senate and House of Representatives but denied his seat because of allegations of impropriety. Around 1883 he was surveyor of customs in

New Orleans and in the 1890s moved permanently to Washington, D.C. He was born of a white father and a freed slave mother in Mississippi. Pinchback held a law degree and was a New York U.S. Marshal. He also served as an Internal Revenue Agent.

What African Americans served in **Congress** during the **Reconstruction period**?

In 1868, John Willis Menard (1839–1893), a public official, was the first black elected to Congress. He was awarded his full salary but never seated. The committee on elections ruled that it was too early to admit a black to Congress. Menard was appointed inspector of customs of the Port of New Orleans. Born of French Creole parents living in Illinois, Menard moved to Louisiana after the Civil War to work for the Republican Party. When he was allowed to plead his own case on February 17, 1869, he became the first black to speak on the floor of the House.

Twenty African Americans were U.S. representatives and two were U.S. senators during the period of the Reconstruction. As early as 1869, Ebenezer Don Carlos Bassett (1833–1908) was named consul general to Haiti, becoming the nation's first African-American diplomat. In 1857, prior to this appointment, he was principal of Philadelphia's Institute for Colored Youth. After completing his Haitian assignment in1877, he served for ten years as a general consul from Haiti to the United States. Hiram Rhodes Revels (1822–1901) was the first black U.S. senator. He was elected to fill the seat of Confederate President Jefferson Davis on January 20, 1870. He was born of free parents in North Carolina, and educated by Quakers in North Carolina and at Knox College in Illinois. He became a minister in the African Methodist Episcopal Church, a teacher, and a Freedmen's Bureau worker in Mississippi. Revels was elected to the state senate in 1869 and elected U.S. Senator by the legislature. He served from February 21, 1870, to March 3, 1871. After serving in the Senate, he became the first president of the newly founded Alcorn College for Negroes in Mississippi.

Blanche Kelso Bruce (1841–1898) was Mississippi's second black in the U.S. Senate. He took his seat in 1875 and was the only black senator elected to serve a full term, until the mid-twentieth century. In 1878 he became the first black to preside over the Senate. President Ulysses S. Grant appointed him register of the treasury in 1881. Born a slave in Virginia, Bruce was educated at Oberlin College. He became a wealthy Mississippi farmer and a successful banker.

What were the **political achievements** of blacks at the **state and local levels** in the **1800s**?

The contributions of blacks in the political arena were far more impressive at state and local levels than at the national level in the 1800s. For example, there were thirty-one black delegates at Georgia's constitutional convention of 1868. In 1871 Atlanta elected blacks to city council for a one-year term. In this group was William Finch, who, while in office, worked to start a public school system for black children. After leaving office, he successfully pressured Atlanta to establish black schools.

South Carolina elected Francis L. Cardozo (1837–1903) secretary of state in 1868. He served for four years in the position and became secretary of the treasury; he was elected to two terms in 1872 and 1874, and claimed the election in 1876, but did not try to maintain his position after the downfall of the Republican regime in 1877. During the last fourteen months of his tenure as secretary of state, Cardozo employed a deputy in South Carolina while he served as professor of Latin at Howard University. A free-born native of Charleston, he pursued an education in Scotland. From 1884 to 1896 he was principal of the Colored Preparatory High School, Washington, D.C., and its successor, the M Street High School.

Another Southern state, Tennessee, elected a black to the state house. When the Tennessee legislature convened on January 6, 1873, Sampson W. Keeble (c. 1833–c. 1880) became the first black member of the state house of representatives. Born a slave in Rutherford County, Tennessee, prior to the Civil War he had worked as a roller boy and pressman for newspapers in Murfreesboro, Tennessee. Toward the end of the war he moved to Nashville, and around 1866 he established the Rock City Barber Shop. He was a member of the Freedman's Savings and Trust Company board and treasurer of the Colored Agricultural and Mechanical Association's board. The Davidson County Republican Party was the party of choice for blacks during Reconstruction. Keeble became involved and in 1872 was nominated for a seat in the state house. He won in the November 1872 election by a slim margin and took office on January 6, 1873. While in the legislature, Keeble introduced several bills that related to black businesses, the protection of black laborers, and the support of the Tennessee Manual Labor University, but the bills were defeated. Among these bills, the third was vastly important in Keeble's political career. Black leaders who were artisans, craftsmen, and small entrepreneurs organized the Colored Agricultural and Mechanical Association. In December 1866 the association's leaders organized the Tennessee Manual Labor University. The association was a strong political base for Keeble and others; it held an annual fair in the fall and attracted national black Republican leaders, such as John Mercer Langston and Frederick Douglass. Keeble held a second political office: he was elected magistrate of Davidson County and served from 1877 to 1882. He lost his bid for a return to the general assembly in 1878.

POLITICAL PARTIES AND POLITICS

What was the **impact of migration** on **national party politics**?

By the end of 1878 thousands of blacks had migrated to Kansas and other states in the Midwest. The Great Migration occurred from about 1910 to 1970, with a break between 1930 and 1940. African Americans migrated from the rural South to urban centers in the North, to Kansas, and to other states in the Midwest. They settled also in major

What caused African Americans to lose their fidelity to "the Party of Lincoln"?

When the Great Depression began in the 1930s, many blamed President Herbert Hoover for causing it. Although two-thirds of black voters still favored Hoover at the ballot box, Franklin D. Roosevelt won the election. Roosevelt's implementation of New Deal programs provided some relief for blacks as well as whites; however, blacks were disproportionally represented on relief rolls and in poverty. Federal initiatives led to jobs for blacks, offered training and educational programs, and gave blacks a voice in policy-making. Roosevelt's second run for office in 1936 won the support of African Americans, who switched parties in his favor.

cities, like New York, Cleveland, Detroit, Chicago, and Los Angeles, and dramatically altered the political landscape of urban areas. Economic desperation, racism, and difficult living conditions caused this migration. The migration then spurred a political resurgence in black patronage of Republican presidents and a call for a greater African-American voice in politics. Now they could embrace politics at the local, state, and national levels. When Republican Herbert Hoover won the presidential election with Southern white votes, blacks were alienated and believed that Hoover catered to whites and not blacks. Yet they rejoiced with blacks who won political office; for example, in 1928 Oscar DePriest of Chicago was elected to the U.S. House of Representatives. This paved the way for other blacks to be elected to office.

What African American first chaired the Republican National Convention?

John Roy Lynch (1847–1939) was elected chair of the Republican National Convention on September 19, 1884, the first black to be elected to that post. An eloquent speaker, he was also the first black to deliver the keynote address to the convention. In 1869, when Lynch was only twenty-two years old, he was elected as a member of the Mississippi State House of Representatives, and in 1871 he was elected Speaker of the House.

How have African Americans been involved in national committees of Democrats and Republicans?

Ron (Ronald) Harmon Brown (1941–1996) was named chair of the National Democratic Party in 1989, the first black to hold this office. In 1980 he was the first black American chief counsel of the Senate Judiciary Committee. He was spokesperson and deputy director of the Urban League's Washington operations and worked in the offices of Senator Edward Kennedy.

In 2009 the Republican Party named Michael S. Steele (1958–) as head of the Republican National Committee, the first black to hold this post. A controversial figure,

The first African American to be named chair of the National Democratic Party was Ron Harmon Brown in 1989.

Steele was frequently at odds with members of his party. In January 2011 he announced that he would not seek reelection and left office. Steele was also the first African American to serve in a Maryland statewide office and the state's first Republican lieutenant governor—a post created in 1970.

When did **black political candidates** become **successful** at **state and local** levels during the **twentieth century**?

Beginning in 1930 and through the 1940s, African Americans in large urban areas, such as Ohio, Illinois, Pennsylvania, and New York, began to agitate more for involvement in labor matters, foreign policy, race, and other issues of concern. Republicans as well as Democrats were aware of this new posture, and saw sizeable numbers of African-American voters in both parties. The strength of the black vote was demonstrated as an increasing number of African Americans gained seats in state legislatures, became municipal judges, were elected to city councils, and held other political positions. About thirty blacks were elected to legislatures in ten states in 1946.

What was the **"Black Cabinet"**?

This network of African-American advisers to President Franklin Delano Roosevelt represented black interests and concerns during the Great Depression and the New Deal economic recovery programs of the 1930s. The NAACP, the Julius Rosenwald Fund, and other organizations lobbied the Roosevelt administration to appoint blacks as advisers to federal agencies and New Deal programs. The administration, however, was hesitant to act because of the potential backlash from powerful Southern Democrats in Congress. After considerable political maneuvering, the appointments began to occur.

During the Roosevelt administration, African Americans gained considerable political clout and became specialists and advisors in a number of governmental departments. Advice of African Americans was seen early on; for example, with Booker T. Washington, educator, school founder, and founder, in 1910, of the National Negro Business League. He advised U.S. Presidents Theodore Roosevelt and William Howard Taft. By Franklin Delano Roosevelt's time, however, the administration had selected a fairly large group of black advisors, rather than focusing on a small group or select individuals, as other Presidents had done. Whether or not the earlier advisers actually had access to the President is questionable. FDR's advisers, however, were put in positions of importance with enough clout to be deemed significant. Under his New Deal administration, which included many programs to aid in recovery from the Great Depression, these advisors (who were not politicians) performed specific functions that required use of their intelligence and education. Some also referred to them as the "black brain trust," primarily because they were college presidents, lawyers, and/or held doctoral degrees.

The Black Cabinet was not a formal body. Included in the Black Cabinet were newspaper editor Robert L. Vann, Howard University Law School dean William H. Hastie, National Urban League executive Eugene Kinckle Jones, college founder and president Mary McLeod Bethune, and Ralph Bunche, later known for his work as undersecretary of the United Nations. By the late 1930s the cabinet members called themselves the Federal Council on Negro Affairs. The Black Cabinet also provided a model of successful coalition-building for leaders and organizations during the Civil Rights Movement of the 1950s and 1960s.

LAW AND THE SUPREME COURT

Who was the **first black woman lawyer** in the United States admitted to **practice law** before the **Supreme Court**?

The first black woman lawyer in the United States, and the third woman admitted to law practice in this country, was Charlotte E. Ray (1850–1911). As a graduate of Howard Law School (Washington, D.C.), she was automatically admitted to practice in the lower courts of the district, and on April 23, 1872, she became the first black woman admitted to practice before the Supreme Court. Ray was born in New York City. Hampered by her gender, she eventually became a teacher in the Brooklyn schools. She attended the National Woman Suffrage Association held in New York City in 1876, and she was active in the National Association of Colored Women. Ray's father, Charles Bennett Ray (1807–1886), was a noted abolitionist, minister, and editor. Charlotte Ray's sister, Florence T. Ray (1849–1916), was an accomplished poet.

LAW ENFORCEMENT

What black American gained fame as an **early law enforcement officer**?

When Bass Reeves (?–1910) was sworn in as a federal deputy marshal in Fort Smith, Arkansas, in 1875, he became the first black federal law enforcement officer on the early Western frontier. For thirty-two years he was a deputy U.S. marshal in Indian Territory and served also with the Muskogee, Oklahoma, police department. Reeves worked as deputy marshal with Judge Isaac C. Parker, who was known as the "hanging judge." For twenty-one years Reeves and Parker worked in the federal territory that later became Oklahoma. Born into slavery on a Texas cotton plantation, Reeves fled his master, who had allowed him to demonstrate his skill as a marksman but had refused to teach him to read. Reeves was a fugitive in the Oklahoma territory until the Civil War ended. As a free black, he became a farmer until Parker was named federal judge for the Western District of Arkansas (the early name for the Oklahoma territory). When Parker dedicated himself to rounding up the fearless bands of desperados, murderers, and outlaws in his district, he sought equally fearless men to enforce the law. Reeves, a crack shot and one who knew the territory, befriended the local Native Americans and was said to fear "nothing that moves or breathes." He trailed and ended the life of notorious Bob Dozier and later captured his own son, a fugitive charged with killing his wife. Rather than retire in 1907 when other law enforcement agencies took over the marshal's duties, Reeves worked for two years with the Muskogee police force. In 1994 the Bass Reeves Foundation was formed in Muskogee, Oklahoma, to perpetuate the legacy of the legendary lawman. A memorial was placed in city hall at Muskogee, Oklahoma, in his honor.

THE U.S. CONGRESS IN MODERN TIMES

Why was the **Congressional Black Caucus** organized?

The Congressional Black Caucus of the House of Representatives was the first concerted effort on the part of black representatives to influence congressional party politics. An affiliation of black members of Congress, originally, the caucus was an all-Democratic group representing mainly Northern big-city districts; it has included some Republican members over the years. It was formally organized in 1971 and is permanently headquartered on Capitol Hill with a director and staff. It maintains political liaison with other black groups and promotes a black agenda to influence and promote economic, social, and political goals favored by African Americans. Michigan congressman Charles C. Diggs Jr. was the founder and first head of the organization.

What **Southern black woman** was the first of her race **elected to the House**?

Barbara Charline Jordan (1936–1996) was the first Southern black woman elected to

Representative Barbara Jordan of Texas served in the U.S. Congress from 1973 to 1979.

the House, in 1972. Houston-born Jordan gained recognition from a nationwide television audience as the House Judiciary committee considered articles of impeachment against President Richard Nixon. She received her education at Texas Southern University and Boston University Law School. She was elected to the Texas legislature in 1965. Her reputation as one of the twentieth century's great orators was sustained by her keynote address before the 1976 Democratic Convention. Jordan decided in 1978 to retire from Congress. She became the Lyndon B. Johnson Centennial Chair in National Policy Professor at the University of Texas at Austin.

STATE OFFICE HOLDERS

Who was the nation's **first black elected governor**?

In 1986 L. (Lawrence) Douglas Wilder (1931–) was the first black lieutenant governor of Virginia. In 1990 Wilder became the nation's first black elected governor. In a hard-fought race, he defeated his Republican opponent and was elected to office on November 7, 1998. (In 1872 Pinckney Benton Stewart Pinchback [1837–1921] became the country's first black governor, but he was appointed to the short-term post.) Wilder was born in segregated Richmond, a mere two miles from the Governor's Mansion where he would live later on. He earned his bachelor's degree at Virginia Union University in 1951 and his law degree at the Howard University School of Law in 1959. Wilder served in the U.S. Army and was sent to Korea. He became a sergeant and was awarded the Bronze Star. After his discharge, he entered Howard University's law school and graduated in May 1959. Wilder joined his father's law firm in Richmond and became known as a very effective trial lawyer. He made a successful bid for the Virginia State Senate in 1969, becoming the first black to hold that position. In his first address before the senate, he criticized the state song, "Carry Me Back to Old Virginny," stating that some of the lyrics glorified slavery and were offensive to blacks. Nonetheless, Virginia retained its song until 1997, when it was retired because some of the lyrics being deemed offensive. Wilder continued to enjoy political success, as was seen in 1989 when he ran for governor. On September 13, 1991, he announced that he would seek the 1992 Democratic nomination for president but

A politician from Virginia, L. Douglas Wilder became that state's lieutenant governor in 1986 and governor in 1990, the first black man to win those seats in the United States.

later withdrew his name and devoted his efforts to solving the state's financial problems. In 1997 Virginia Union University named its new library and learning center in his honor. From 2005 to 2009, Wilder was mayor of Richmond and the first black to hold that post.

How did African Americans fare in the **2006 statewide** and **local elections**?

African Americans took top posts in several 2006 statewide and local elections. For example, in Massachusetts, Deval Patrick was elected governor, the second black since Reconstruction to hold a state's top post. Anthony Brown was elected lieutenant governor in Maryland and David Paterson was elected lieutenant governor in New York. (Paterson became New York's governor from 2008 to 2010.)

A political newcomer in the race for mayor was Cory Booker, who made his first bid for mayor of Newark, New Jersey, in 2002 but was unsuccessful. He ran again in 2006 and was elected to office; he was reelected to a second term in 2010. His close connection to New Jersey governor Christopher "Chris" Christie and his bold and successful steps to improve the lives of the citizens of Newark by reducing crime, improving housing, combating drug abuse, and improving education brought him attention in the national media. In Washington, D.C., Mayor Adrian Fenty became the district's youngest mayor in history when elected in 2006. Previously he was a Ward Four council member.

A Baptist minister and civil rights activist, Jesse Jackson founded Operation PUSH and the National Rainbow Coalition.

FEDERAL GOVERNMENT

What popular African Americans **sought the U.S. presidential nomination** in **recent years**?

In 1984 Jesse Louis Jackson (1941–) was the first black American to be a viable candidate for the presidential nomination. Jackson was born in South Carolina and educated at the University of Illinois and North Carolina Agricultural and Technical College (later University). He was ordained a Baptist minister in 1968, after studying at the Chicago Theological Seminary. He was a field director for the Congress of Racial Equality (CORE), and in 1967 was named by the Southern Christian Leadership Conference (SCLC) to head its Operation Breadbasket, which he had helped found. A close associate of Martin Luther King Jr., Jackson left the SCLC in 1971, and founded Operation PUSH (later called People United to Serve Humanity) in Chicago. He also founded the National Rainbow Coalition, a civil rights group. In 1983 Jackson launched a major voter-registration drive among black Americans and toward the end of the year declared his candidacy for the Democratic presidential nomination. Jackson ran in a large number of Democratic primary elections in 1984, finishing a strong third to former Vice President Walter Mondale and Senator Gary Hart. In 1987 Jackson again ran unsuccessfully for president. From 1991 to 1997 he served as a shadow senator for Washington, D.C.

Alan L. Keys (1950–), federal government official and diplomat, announced his candidacy for the U.S. presidency in 1995, and became the first Republican African American in the twentieth century to seek that office. His poor showing failed to deter him from a second run for the GOP nomination in 2000. Al Sharpton (1954–) religious leader and community activist, formed a new political party, the Freedom Party, in 1994. He had an unsuccessful run for the U.S. Senate, and in 2003 became a Democratic candidate for the presidential election. He ended his campaign the next year.

Who was the first **black presidential candidate** to run for office on a **minor party ticket**?

The first black to run for president of the United States on a minor party ticket was George Edwin Taylor (1857–1925). He ran in 1904 and represented the National Liberal Party.

What **black woman** first ran for the office of the **presidency**?

In 1972 Shirley Chisholm (1924–2005) became the first black to seek to run for U.S. president representing one of the major parties, and the first black woman to seek the office. She sought to become the nominee of the Democratic Party. Chisholm pulled together a coalition of blacks, feminists, and other minorities. During the campaign, she received little support from white women-led organizations or black male-led organizations. Male opponents never considered her as a serious challenger. Hubert H. Humphrey and other

A U.S. Representative from New York from 1969 to 1983, Shirley Chisholm was the first African American to run for the office of president of the United States.

271

candidates released 151 votes to Chisholm on the first ballot, but this was insufficient for her to win the nomination. Born Shirley Anita Saint Hill, she lived in Barbados for six years. She graduated from Brooklyn College and Columbia University. While at Columbia, Chisholm became involved with the local political organization, the Seventeenth Assembly District Democratic Club. It was through this experience that she learned the potential power of the black vote and women's vote.

What **black woman** was the first to appear on the **presidential ballot in all fifty states**?

In 1988 Lenora Fulani (1950–) was the first black American woman to qualify for federal matching funds in a presidential election and also the first African American (and woman) to appear on the presidential ballot in all fifty states. She was also the only black woman Marxist psychologist to run for president. A social psychologist, Fulani was running on the National Alliance Party ticket. She was on the ballot in forty-five states in 1992. Born Lenora Branch in Chester, Pennsylvania, she received her bachelor's degree from Hofstra University, master's degree from Teachers College, Columbia University, and her doctoral degree from City University of New York, Graduate Center.

How did **African-American participation** in national politics **improve under President Bill Clinton**?

A record number of African Americans joined President Bill Clinton's cabinet. Among such appointees were Jesse Brown, who headed the Veterans Affairs Department, and Ron Brown, who was named secretary of commerce. Clinton's cabinet included a number of African-American women. Hazel O'Leary was named secretary of energy. When Joycelyn Elders was appointed U.S. surgeon general, she stirred considerable controversy simply by advocating the use of condoms as a means of birth control; this advocacy caused her to lose the appointment. The position of secretary of agriculture went to Michael Espy, and Rodney Slater was named secretary of transportation. After serving as director of the White House Office of Public Liaison and one of Clinton's most trusted advisors, Alexis Herman was appointed secretary of labor. Deval Patrick, who in 2006 was elected governor of Massachusetts, headed the Civil Rights Division during Clinton's administration.

Presidential advisors hold important positions in that they help identify key people for federal positions. Vernon E. Jordan Jr. (1935–) served President Clinton, first as chair of his transition team in 1992, when Clinton was President-elect; he was the first and only black to serve in that capacity. Although Jordan refused to accept the position of U.S. attorney general in Clinton's administration, he helped Clinton select cabinet officers. During Clinton's tenure, Jordan remained an advisor to the President on domestic and foreign policies and became one of the most influential voices in the Clinton administration. Since the 1960s Jordan has been a high-profile figure in America. The Atlanta-born Jordan received his bachelor's degree from DePauw University in Greencastle, Indiana, and his law degree from Howard University's law school. He moved into civil rights work immediately, serving as law clerk in the office of civil rights attorney David Hollowell in Atlanta. He was a member of Hollowell's legal team that worked with Charlayne Hunter-Gault and Hamilton Holmes in their efforts to enroll in the all-white University of Georgia. When Hunter-Gault was finally admitted, Jordan used his body as a shield and forced a path through an angry white mob that tried to prevent her from entering the campus. From 1961 to 1963 Jordan was field secretary of the NAACP's Georgia branch. In 1964 he joined civil rights attorney Wiley A. Branton in Little Rock, who was counsel for the "Little Rock Nine," the group of African-American students who integrated Central High School. Jordan was also director of the Southern Regional Council's Voter Registration Project for four years. After a stint with the U.S. Office of Equal Opportunity in Atlanta and a year as fellow at Harvard University's John F. Kennedy School of Government, he became executive director of the United Negro College Fund. In 1972 he became executive director of the National Urban League, and served until the end of 1981. Then he became partner in the law firm of Akin Gump Strauss Hauer & Feld, in its Washington, D.C., office. His book, *Vernon Can Read* (2001), is a memoir of his life from his early years through winter 2001, when he received the NAACP's Spingarn Medal.

What African Americans held **top positions** during the **George W. Bush administration**?

Although President George W. Bush appointed fewer African Americans to top positions than his immediate predecessor, blacks held important posts during his presidency. Significant among his appointees were Colin L. Powell, Rodney Paige, Alphonso Jackson, and Condoleezza Rice. Colin Powell (1937–) was secretary of state from 2001 to 2005. He had already achieved acclaim as a four-star general in the U.S. Army, and in 1987 was named the first black national security advisor to President Ronald Reagan. President George H. W. Bush appointed him chairman of the Joint Chiefs of Staff in 1989. In 2001 he became the first African-American secretary of state. When the 2008 presidential campaign was under way, Powell, a Republican, endorsed Barack Obama for the presidency. Rodney Paige (1933–) was the first African American and first school superintendent to become U.S. secretary of education. He drafted important education reform legislation, the No Child Left Behind Act of 2001. Paige

Under the George W. Bush administration, Condoleezza Rice, a political scientist at Stanford University, became the country's first black woman to be named secretary of state.

volunteered during the Bush presidential campaign of 1980 and was a delegate to the Republican National Convention that summer. Condoleezza Rice (1954–), diplomat and educator, was confirmed on January 28, 2005, as U.S. secretary of state, the second woman and the first African-American woman to hold that position. This led some to call her the most powerful woman in the world. Although in 1987 she was senior director of Soviet and Eastern European Affairs under President George H. W. Bush, and foreign policy advisor to President George W. Bush, her political career was best known while she was national security advisor and secretary of state. Alphonso Jackson (1945–) served as deputy secretary and chief operating officer of the U.S. Department of Housing and Urban Development from 2001 to 2004, before his promotion to full secretary. Before his appointment, Jackson had worked with housing authorities in St. Louis, Dallas, and in the District of Columbia.

What visible **positions** did **Barack Obama** hold in **2004**?

In this year, Barack Obama handily won a seat in the U.S. Senate. He reached and favorably impressed a national audience when he gave the keynote address at the Democratic National Convention held in Boston in 2004.

Who became the **first African-American president of the United States**?

Barack Hussein Obama (1961–) won the nomination for the U.S. presidency and in 2008 became the first African American elected to the highest office in the nation. He was sworn in on January 20, 2009, and took the oath of office using the Bible that President Abraham Lincoln used when sworn in during his first inauguration in 1861, making Obama the first president sworn in using that Bible since its initial use. When the Democratic primary season for the presidency ended on June 3, 2008, Obama became the first African American to secure the nomination of any major national political party. His stirring keynote address before the Democratic National Convention in July 2004 catapulted Obama onto the national political scene. With a landslide victory in November, he was also elected U.S. senator from Illinois, becoming the third African American elected to the U.S. Senate since Reconstruction. In February 2007 he announced his intent to seek the Democratic Party's nomination for the U.S. Presidency. During his campaign, Obama garnered financial support from small donations solicited over the Internet and went on to amass a record-breaking $745 million. His use of the Internet, twenty-four-hour cable television programming, blogs, and other nontraditional media changed the way political campaigns are conducted. During his campaign, Obama frequently drew enormous crowds and was placed under Secret Service protection nine months before the election, earlier than any other candidate who ever ran for president. He defeated Senator John McCain (R-AZ) in the November 4 election and was sworn into office on January 20, 2009, as the 44th president. He was soon awarded a Nobel Peace Prize. His first one hundred days in office were consumed by a range of activities, including passage of a massive stimulus bill to help jumpstart the sagging economy, interventions in the housing and credit markets, a plan to bail out the automobile industry, strict regulations proposed for Wall Street, an overhaul of foreign policy, and a push for a national health insurance plan. During the 2012 presidential election, Obama defied predictions by sailing to re-election. This triggered a face-off with Republicans over averting a "fiscal cliff" that threatened to send the nation into a recession; the fiscal cliff was never realized.

Obama was born in Honolulu, Hawaii, the son of Barack Obama Sr., a native of Kenya, and Ann Dunham, a white woman and a native of Kansas; they divorced in 1964. Obama lived in Jakarta, Indonesia, with his mother and stepfather before resettling in Hawaii, where he lived with his maternal grandparents and attended an elite college preparatory school. In 1983 Obama graduated from Columbia University in New York City, and then worked as a researcher. Two years later he moved to Chicago and became a community organizer in several low-income neighborhoods. He entered Harvard Law School in 1988, and in 1990 was elected president of the prestigious and competitive *Harvard Law Review*—the first African American to hold that honor. While he is articulate, serious, and challenging, Obama's initial popularity at home and abroad, and, for a time, his continuing high approval rating among the American public led him to be regarded as a celebrity president.

Who became the **first black "First Lady"** of the United States?

When Barack Obama took office as President of the United States in 2009, Michelle Robinson Obama (1964–) became the first black First Lady of the United States. She filled her new role by extending her interests far beyond that of attending official

President Barack Obama is the first African American to hold the highest office in the country.

First Lady Michelle Obama is a graduate of Princeton and Harvard Law School. In addition to supporting the president, she has been an advocate of women's health issues and for better nutrition and exercise for children.

ceremonies and dinner parties. Her special concerns included the plight of military families, childhood obesity, and promoting healthier eating habits. Michelle Obama quickly became a fashion trendsetter as she selected styles from affordable dress lines rather than the high-end fashion designers. The Chicago native and former community organizer graduated from Princeton University and Harvard Law School. The Obamas have two daughters: Malia and Sasha.

WOMEN AND THE POLITICAL PROCESS

Were **slave women** involved in **political activities**?

Slave codes that states enacted during slavery denied all black people governed by the codes the right to hold meetings and engage in social activities unless sanctioned by their masters. This action effectively limited slave women in their ability to aid themselves and their families. Such laws, however, failed to prevent slave women from seeking redress and making bold political statements at secret meetings or from planning and participating in slave revolts.

How were **black women in free states** involved in **political action**?

Black women in the North and West faced racism and sexism, yet they were free to act without interference from state and federal governments. Thus they publicly involved themselves in alternative political activities. The strong female-centered communities that they built were in their churches, mutual aid societies, and women's organizations. Between 1830 and 1860, they worked through the convention movement at the local, state, and national level and promoted temperance, education, black self-reliance, and other concerns. Leadership positions in some of these organizations had not opened to them during this time, yet they combined their efforts with those of black men to advocate suffrage, protest slavery, and seek redress for discrimination.

How did the **Republican leadership** during **Reconstruction enable black women**?

Black women remained excluded from the political process during the Reconstruction period. While black men had been given voting privileges with the passage of the Fifteenth Amendment and could be—and were—elected to political office, the same was not true for black women. Radical Republicans had an agenda that black women found favorable; for example, their platform paved the way for black emancipation and equal rights under the law. Black women responded by once again working through their churches and organizations to push for reform laws and ensure programs for racial uplift. They practiced techniques important in organizational and political leadership, such as drawing up constitutions for their organizations, electing officers, holding formal meetings, keeping records (including financial), and practicing other business tech-

> ## How did anti-slavery societies empower black women?
>
> Increasingly, black women joined anti-slavery societies when they could, and some became powerful forces in these organizations. Here they honed their ability to shape group culture and explore solutions to black problems. These societies afforded black women crucial training to deal with the struggle for political equality. Many were aided by white suffragists as well.

niques. Their efforts were hampered, however, when the *Plessy v. Ferguson* decision became law in 1896, challenging all facets of black life and freedom. Even white women who had been sympathetic to the causes of black women, such as the various suffrage associations, grew hostile to blacks and opposed the black female ballot.

What role did the **African-American women's club movement** play in shaping **politics**?

After its founding in 1896, the National Association of Colored Women (NACW) soon began to agitate for the rights of black women. Among the leaders were Mary Church Terrell (1863–1954), educator, orator, writer, and civil and women's rights activist, who was also president of the organization. The Memphis native, who relocated to Washington, D.C., became known for her social activism on behalf of blacks and women in the United States and foreign countries. When the National American Suffrage Association met in 1898, Terrell spoke before the organization on behalf of women's right to vote. Joining Terrell in her women's activism were NACW presidents Ida B. Wells-Barnett and Mary McLeod Bethune. Wells-Barnett (1862–1931) was a crusader against lynching and founder of the first suffrage organization for black women. Bethune (1875–1955), educator, activist, and later advisor to four U. S. presidents, worked tirelessly to empower African-American women and sought civil rights for men and women of her race.

How did the **changed political landscape** in the **Midwest and Northeast** affect **black women** and the **ballot**?

The Midwestern and Northeastern states finally granted women limited access to the ballot. Black women knew the power of the ballot for social reform in their community and its ability to promote the political process in the community. Illinois was the first state east of the Mississippi to give women access to municipal politics. Thus, in Chicago elections, this resulted in almost twice as many black votes on Chicago's South Side. Black women then founded suffrage clubs, taught women the power of the political process, and taught them how to register and vote. Ida B. Wells-Barnett and a white colleague founded the Alpha Suffrage Club in Chicago, developed their own political platforms, and searched for the best candidate regardless of party affiliation. The suffrage clubs also made demands on political candidates and insisted on their presence at meet-

277

ings. Some claim that the effectiveness of the Alpha Suffrage Club was seen in the 1915 election of Oscar DePriest as Chicago's first black alderman.

Why have some **black women** been involved in **third-party politics**?

After Chicago empowered women to vote in 1913 and black women began to endorse candidates, they sought the best candidate and never hesitated to support a third-party candidate. Years later, Fannie Lou Hamer, a Mississippi sharecropper who became field secretary for the Student Nonviolent Coordinating Committee, became involved with third-party politics. In 1964 she was instrumental in the development of the Mississippi Freedom Democratic Party and worked tirelessly in the plight of the disenfranchised black voter and black women in political action. The MFDP's mission was to serve the political interest of the African-American commu-

Sharecropper Fannie Lou Hamer was instrumental in founding the Mississippi Freedom Democratic Party.

nity in that state. The MFDP was an alternative to the all-white Democratic Party. The MFDP also sought to be seated at the Democratic Presidential Convention in Atlantic City, and to be seated in place of the all-white Democratic delegates who supposedly represented Mississippi. Instead, the Democratic Party stated that two members of the MFDP could serve in place of the elected white delegates. This offer was rejected, and the MFDP challenged the appointments of five of Mississippi's U.S. congressmen. They claimed that those elected officially had not been elected fairly, since black citizens had not been allowed to register and vote. In 1964 Harner, representing the MFDP, ran unsuccessfully for the U.S. Congress.

What was the **impact** of the **Nineteenth Amendment** on **black women** and **politics**?

By 1918 support for women's suffrage was broad. That year Congress proposed a constitutional amendment stating that the vote should not be denied or abridged for any U.S. citizen because of his or her gender. The Nineteenth Amendment to the U.S. Constitution, ratified in 1920, granted women the right to vote. African-American women had long sought rights equal to men and to whites, and worked in a number of arenas to encourage black women to vote. The amendment would at least bring about a new freedom for them. Some joined the white organization, the League of Women Voters, and others formed their own black leagues. In the South, black women hung on to the Republican Party, while the Democrats now held sway among whites. Four decades would pass before Southern blacks overcame threats of violence and loss of economic opportunity if they voted.

Black women in other areas of the country fared better politically. For example, Seattle, the District of Columbia, and New Jersey elected black women to their school boards. Women were also involved in the Republican conventions and garnered support of black men who ran for political office. Urban centers like New York, Chicago, and Detroit took notice of the power of black women, especially their block vote.

FEDERAL COURTS

What is **black America's involvement** on the **U.S. Supreme Court**?

President Lyndon B. Johnson, in 1967, named Thurgood Marshall (1908–1993) as the first black associate justice of the U.S. Supreme Court. (In 1965 he had became the first black American U.S. solicitor general.) Baltimore-born Marshall graduated from Lincoln University in Pennsylvania and Howard University, and became one of the nation's foremost civil rights lawyers. From 1938 to 1961 he served as NAACP counsel. Marshall represented the plaintiff in the *Brown v. Board of Education of Topeka, Kansas* case before the Supreme Court, which ruled in 1954 that racial segregation in public schools was unconstitutional. In 1962 President John F. Kennedy appointed Marshall judge of the Second Circuit Court of Appeals. President Lyndon B. Johnson appointed him solicitor general—the highest law enforcement position held by an African American at the time. He was the recipient of the coveted NAACP Spingarn Medal in 1946.

Only two African Americans have served on the U.S. Supreme Court. After Thurgood Marshall, in 1991 Clarence Thomas (1948–) became the second black associate justice of the U.S. Supreme Court. President George H. W. Bush nominated him to replace Marshall; he was sworn into office on October 18.

Have African Americans served on the **appeals court**?

In 1966 Spottiswood Robinson (1916–1998) became the first black judge of the U.S. Court of Appeals in Washington, D.C. Robinson was born in Richmond, Virginia. He attended Virginia Union University in Richmond for a while, but entered Howard University School of Law, graduating *magna cum laude* in 1939. He taught for eight years at Howard in Washington, D.C., advancing from teaching fellow to associate professor. Robinson was admitted to the Virginia bar and practiced in Richmond during the struggle for civil rights. Immediately his work catapulted him to national prominence. He left Howard and became an attorney for the Legal Defense Fund of Virginia's NAACP. He joined his former mentor, Charles Hamilton Houston, in a successful Supreme Court case that outlawed restrictive covenants that prevented the sale of real estate to blacks.

Robinson was named southeast regional counsel for the NAACP's defense fund in 1951. Working with Thurgood Marshall and others, he was successful in his argument before the Supreme Court, resulting in the court's historic decision in *Brown v. Board of Education of Topeka, Kansas* to strike down the "separate but equal" doctrine in public education in the South. Other civil rights cases that Robinson won related to desegregation in interstate buses and in public parks. Robinson left his practice in 1960 and became dean of the law school at Howard University until 1963. President John F. Kennedy, in 1961, named him to the U.S. Commission on Civil Rights. In 1964 Robinson became the first black to serve as a judge of the U.S. District Court in Washington, D.C. He was named to the Court of Appeals in 1966, becoming chief judge of that court from 1981 to 1986. Robinson retired in 1992 and returned to Richmond where he died.

What African-American woman served the nation as the **first black woman federal judge**?

Constance Baker Motley (1921–2005), who received national acclaim for her civil rights work, became the first black woman federal judge on January 25, 1966. After receiving President Lyndon B. Johnson's nomination and Senate confirmation, she became a judge on the United States District Court, the Southern District of New York. She was elected to the New York state senate in 1964, and in 1965 she became president of the Borough of Manhattan. Her appointment as a judge of the Circuit Court of the Southern District of New York made her the highest paid black woman in government. The Connecticut-born jurist received her education at New York and Columbia Universities. Motley worked with the NAACP as legal assistant and associate counsel and won many difficult civil rights cases; her most famous victory was the case of James Meredith against the University of Mississippi. Working with the NAACP Legal Defense Fund, she and other attorneys represented demonstrators in the sit-in movement, including Martin Luther King Jr., Fred Shuttlesworth, and other protesters. Her numerous writings have been published in legal and professional journals.

Eric Holder is the first African American to hold the high office of U.S. attorney general.

U.S. DEPARTMENT OF JUSTICE

Who is the **top law enforcement officer** in the nation?

Eric Holder (1951–) was appointed U.S. attorney general in 2009, becoming the first

African American to hold that post. He became the highest-ranking black American law enforcement officer in history in 1997, when he was confirmed as deputy attorney general. He held the number-two post at the Justice Department. He resigned in 2001 and became a partner in the law firm of Covington & Burling in Washington, D.C. Holder was born in New York City and educated at Columbia University, earning a bachelor's degree in 1973 and a law degree in 1976. Holder was previously a trial attorney for the U.S. Department of Justice, Public Integrity Section, and associate justice of the Superior Court in Washington.

WOMEN IN THE U.S. SENATE

What **black woman** was the **first** to be **elected** to the **U.S. Senate**?

Carol E. Moseley Braun (1947–) became the nation's first black woman U.S. senator in 1992. She was elected on November 3 and served one term in the 103rd Congress, representing Illinois. She was also Illinois' first black senator. In 1995 she became the first woman named to a full term on the powerful Senate Finance Committee. The Chicago-born attorney was educated at the University of Illinois at Chicago (B.A., 1969) and the University of Chicago (J.D., 1972). She was active in Chicago legal circles and the state legislature, and served as Cook County (Illinois) recorder of deeds/registrar of titles. In 2000 she became ambassador to New Zealand and to the tiny South Pacific state of Samoa (formerly Western Samoa). In fall 2001 she became professor of politics at Morris Brown College in Atlanta. In 2011 she ran, unsuccessfully, in the Chicago mayoral race. She currently runs a private law firm in Chicago.

MAYORAL ELECTIONS

What African Americans have been elected **mayors** of **major cities**?

Many cities in the U.S., from small to large, have elected blacks as mayor, the first of their race to hold these posts. Carl Burton Stokes was elected mayor of Cleveland in 1967 and became the first black elected mayor of a major American city. Others included Walter E. Washington, District of Columbia, 1967; Kenneth Allen Gibson, Newark, 1970; Thomas Bradley, Los Angeles, 1973; Coleman Alexander Young, Detroit, 1973; Maynard Holbrook Jackson, Atlanta, 1973; Ernest Nathan "Dutch" Morial, New Orleans, 1977; Harold Washington, Chicago, 1983; Woodrow Wilson Goode, Philadelphia, 1984; Kurt Lidell Schmoke, Baltimore, 1987; David Norman Dinkins, New York City, 1989; Norman Blann Rice, Seattle, 1989; and Ron Kirk, Dallas, 1995.

The first black woman to be elected mayor of a major American city was Sharon Pratt Dixon Kelly (1944–) in 1990. The Washington, D.C., native was educated at Howard University where she received her bachelor's degree in 1965 and her law degree from the university's law school in 1968. She held a number of positions before becoming mayor of Washington, D.C. Her experiences include house counsel for the Joint Center for Political Studies, an associate with Pratt and Queen law firm, and attorney and professor at Antioch School of Law in Washington, D.C. Dixon joined Potomac Electric Power Company, serving as associate general counsel and later director of the office of consumer affairs (1979–1983), vice president of community relations (1983–1986), and vice president of public policy (1986–1989). While serving as mayor, she continued her involvement with the Democratic National Committee, where she has held such positions as acting general counsel, co-chair of the rules committee, and treasurer.

Other women have fared well in mayoral races, holding that office in Pasadena, California; Atlanta, Georgia; Hartford, Connecticut; Baltimore, Maryland; Houston, Texas; Dallas, Texas; Little Rock, Arkansas; Dayton, Ohio; Evanston, Illinois; East St. Louis, Missouri; Hampton, Virginia; and Newport News, Virginia.

RELIGION

AFRICAN–AMERICAN CHRISTIANS IN COLONIAL AMERICA

What was the **slave owners' attitude** toward **Christianizing** the bonds people?

In the mid-1600s, those who held slaves in Colonial America questioned the wisdom of Christianizing their bonds people, as some slaves who became Christians successfully sued for their emancipation. Then King Charles II asked the Council for Foreign Plantations to Christianize African slaves as well as Indians. George Fox, who founded the Quaker Movement, urged his followers to give slaves religious teachings and take them to Quaker meetings.

Who led sustained efforts to **convert slaves** to **Christianity**?

The Society for the Propagation of the Gospel in Foreign Parts (SPG), headquartered in London, was a missionary movement that systematically sought to evangelize and teach among slaves. The organization made the first sustained effort to convert African Americans to Christianity in 1701. Its success was largely due to Thomas Bray, who in 1695 became commissary in Maryland. The SPG was financially independent of churches in the colonies. In the eighteenth century, Maryland and Virginia saw the Anglican Church firmly established, and the SPG developed an overarching plan to influence the church's outreach to all colonies. These missionaries had little success among the Africans; many blacks mocked those who imitated the whites too closely, and thus resisted the missionaries. In addition, white slave masters often resented losing slaves' time to church services and feared that slaves would lay a claim to freedom through conversion.

What were the African influences on the slaves' religion in America?

The type of African spirituality that took root in North America merged elements from many African cultures. Since slave masters intentionally mixed Africans from many tribal backgrounds, no "pure" African religion preserving one tradition emerged and/or survived. Nevertheless, the long-standing scholarly controversy about the extent to which African traditions have been retained in African-based religions is gradually being resolved in favor of those who see extensive survivals. In addition to singing, church music, and preaching styles—aspects where an African influence has generally been conceded—scholars have made persuasive arguments for African influences in family structure, funeral practices, church organizations, and many other areas.

What were some of the successful efforts of **Baptists and Methodists** to **convert slaves** to Christianity?

Between 1742 and 1770 spellbinding orator George Whitefield led seven successful missionary tours throughout North America, leading to the conversions of large numbers of blacks and whites. By the end of the eighteenth century, Methodist circuit riders, such as Francis Asbury, were also well received by African Americans. Churches attracting the most black members were Baptist and Methodist. These churches allowed their ministers to function without an education, thus opening doors for many aspiring ministers, many of whom lived in states where teaching African Americans to read and write was legally forbidden. Baptists and Methodists were also less hostile to the passion of black preachers and congregations than the more staid denominations, such as Episcopalians. African Americans were also attracted to the anti-slavery stance of notable Methodist and Baptist leaders, such as John Wesley, Francis Asbury, and John Leland, and the greater degree of equality nurtured within many of their congregations.

Who was **Black Harry**?

The first known black Methodist preacher was Harry "Black Harry" Hosier (also spelled Hoosier, Hoshur, and Hossier; c. 1750–1806). He was so nicknamed because he was very black in complexion. His sermon, "Barren Fig Tree," was delivered at Adams Chapel, Fairfax County, Virginia, in 1781, and was the first preached by a black to a congregation of Methodists. His sermon in 1784 at Thomas Chapel in Chapeltown, Delaware, was the first preached by a black to a white congregation. Hosier was a circuit-riding preacher who traveled from the Carolinas to New England, where he brought the gospel to slaves, free blacks, and poor as well as affluent whites. Although he was uneducated, Hosier had a remarkable talent and was unusually intelligent. He had a great ability to retain information; since he was unable to read, he memorized the Bible, and became highly creative in his sermons. Some sources call him the most eloquent preacher of his time. Hosier was born a slave near Fayetteville, North Carolina. Except that they came from Africa and were enslaved, nothing is known about his parents. Hosier became a free man and was converted to Methodism; whether this occurred before or after he was freed is unknown.

What was **Black Harry's relationship** to **Francis Asbury**?

Harry Hosier, or "Black Harry," met Francis Asbury, the founder of American Methodism, around 1780, a meeting that Asbury called "providentially arranged." When Asbury went to Todd, North Carolina, near that time, he may have encountered Hosier. Hosier became a servant and guide to Asbury, while at the same time becoming a circuit-riding preacher. In 1784 and again in 1786, Asbury arranged a preaching tour through Delaware, Maryland, and Virginia to introduce Thomas Coke to the work of the Methodists. Coke came to America as John Wesley's representative. After hearing Hosier preach, Coke wrote in his journal that he believed Hosier was one of the best preachers in the world and that he was also one of the humblest people he ever saw. The first tour ended in time for the Christmas Conference in Baltimore's Lovely Lane Chapel from December 24 to January 2, 1785. It was here that the Methodist Episcopal Church was formally established in America. This also established a permanent relationship between black and white Methodists. Hosier was present at the historic conference. After being cleared of an erroneous charge against him in 1791, Hosier fell from grace in the church. He was then excluded from the group of black Methodist preachers, including Richard Allen, who were ordained around 1799.

What are **"hush harbors"**?

Attempts to maintain segregation in churches during the slavery period led to the establishment of formal black churches. However, informal black churches existed in slave communities in places called "hush harbors," or "bush harbors," which were hollows, or other remote and/or inconspicuous places. These places were also called cane breaks, hush arbors, and even praise houses, but certainly they were hidden, secret spots. So secret were these places, including their nature and function, that their true histories, rhetoric, and practices remain difficult to know. It is through oral histories, however, that the insights into hush harbor practices are at least partially known. Here they "broke the prescription against unsupervised or unauthorized meetings by holding their services in secret, well hidden areas." It is here that slaves met surreptitiously and worshipped God as they pleased, in a tradition of their own, and shared with each other the thoughts and beliefs that their masters never knew they had. Slave preachers led the services.

THE FOUNDING OF THE
BLACK CHURCH IN AMERICA

What led to the **establishment** of the **black church** in America?

During Colonial America blacks were only minimally touched by Christianity. Church membership was available only to "free Blacks, favored slaves, household servants, slave artisans, and urban slaves." Those who lived in rural areas might have been included in family prayer circles, Bible-reading groups, and other forms of religious instruction; however, they were generally afforded fewer opportunities to attend church. During The Great Awakening (1730–1780), a period of revivalism, slave owners did allow their servants to become Christianized. This period brought to black people an opportunity to hear narratives of Bible stories, and an opportunity to participate in worship through singing, praying, and testifying, resulting in some slaves claiming to have been born again. Revivalism brought sizeable numbers of blacks to Christianity, and these converts felt a need to found their own churches.

When was the **first black church established**?

The independent black churches founded in Colonial America were Baptist. The first black Baptist church known to have begun during this period was the African Baptist or "Bluestone" Church. It was organized in 1758 on William Byrd's plantation located near Bluestone River in Mecklenburg, Virginia. (A claim for priority is also advanced for a congregation known to exist at Lunenburg in 1756. The evidence is not clear-cut, but all substantiated claims so far refer to Virginia and the decade of the 1750s.) Later, other black Baptist churches were established in South Carolina, Virginia, and Georgia. The first black Baptist church under black leadership seems to have been formed in Silver Bluff, South Carolina. David George, a slave, became its first black pastor. George Liele (c. 1750–1820) and, less probably, Andrew Bryan (1737–1812) have also been associated

The First African Baptist Church and Parsonage in Waycross, Georgia, is part of the oldest black Christian church in America.

with the church. The congregation seems to have been founded between 1773 and 1775. The present church was remodeled in 1920, and a cornerstone with the founding date of 1750 was put in place. This date appears too early for most historians to accept. In 1793 the congregation of some sixty persons, led by Jesse Galpin, moved to Augusta, Georgia, about twenty miles away.

What was **Andrew Bryan's importance** as a plantation preacher and in the **Baptist Church**?

Andrew Bryan (1737–1812) began to erect the first African Baptist Church building in Savannah, Georgia. The first building built for the purpose of black worship in the city, it was finished in 1794. Bryan was a slave who refused to give up his mission in spite of whippings and imprisonment for preaching. He had formed his church on January 20, 1788. Bryan was born near Charleston, South Carolina, in Goose Creek. Sometime before 1790 Brown purchased his freedom. In 1773 or 1774 he may have come in contact with George Liele, when Liele preached on the Brampton Plantation where Bryan lived last before he became free. Bryan was baptized in 1782 and began preaching about nine months later. He also learned to read around this time. In 1788 a white minister from Georgia, Abraham Marshall, ordained him. Bryan and his supporters preached in cells on plantations, either in the open or clandestinely, depending on the disposition of the plantation owners.

How were **blacks affected** by the **revivals** of the **Methodist societies** during the **Colonial Period**?

In addition to the work of blacks in the Baptist church, they were attracted to the revivals that the Methodist societies held. Methodist churches had racially mixed memberships and attracted large numbers of blacks. The emotional revivals and meetings that white ministers led attracted both races, who considered themselves reborn in African-style celebrations. In an electrifying atmosphere, worshippers fell down as if they were dead, and hundreds of blacks were said to have cried when they heard sermons recounting Ezekiel's vision of dry bones.

BLACK PREACHERS
AND RELIGIOUS LEADERS

How were **early black preachers** able to spread the Gospel?

Early black Baptist and Methodist preachers, many of whom were unable to read or write, memorized massive portions of the Bible and then went out to teach. Men named Moses, Benjamin, Thomas Gardiner, and Farrell were slave preachers, and it is possible that John Michaels, a white Baptist preacher on the Byrd plantation in Virginia, or-

Richard Allen was a minister and educator who founded the African American Episcopal Church, the first independent black denomination in the United States.

dained them in 1774. George Liele and Andrew Bryan were called exhorters, or preaching assistants to white missionaries. After the Revolutionary War ended, white ministers began to license black preachers. Some of the earliest Christian preachers and exhorters were former African priests equipped with leadership and persuasive abilities. Their services were emotionally charged and filled with imagery. Their congregants participated in "shout songs," handclapping, and holy dancing, and a mourner's bench was usually maintained.

Why was religious leader **Richard Allen** important?

The African American Episcopal Church grew in response to the denial of full rights for and disrespectful treatment of black people and their right to worship as they pleased. Richard Allen (1760–1831) and Absalom Jones (1746–1818) left St. George's Methodist Episcopal Church, a white congregation in Philadelphia, and formed the Free African Society. Allen organized Philadelphia's Bethel African American Church on July 17, 1794, believing the Methodist practices were more compatible with black people. Today the church is called Mother Bethel Church and is the first black Methodist church in America. At a general convention in Philadelphia on April 9, 1816, ministers from several states met and officially formed the African Methodist Episcopal Church, the first black denomination in America. At the convention, Allen was elected the first black bishop. Under his leadership, the denomination, which was concerned with equality of access and treatment, quickly expanded geographically. The church was an advocate of equal rights and treatment for all. Allen sanctioned the inclusion of women in the ministry and authorized Jarena Lee to be an exhorter in the church. The church served as a forum for abolitionists and antilynching, allowing individuals to use its pulpits to address the issues. It has continued its mission work, educational opportunities, and political involvement in the fight for equality.

What **religious leader** first declared that **"God is a Negro"**?

Henry McNeal Turner (1834–1915) was the first prominent black churchman to declare that God is black. In 1898 he said: "We had rather believe in no God, or … believe that all nature is God than to believe in the personality of a God, and not to believe that He is a Negro." Turner was also the first black chaplain in the United States Army, in 1863. As a minister and bishop in the African Methodist Episcopal (AME) Church, Turner later advocated that blacks return to Africa. Born free in Newberry Court House, South Carolina, he worked in cotton fields along with slaves for a while, and then moved to Abbeville where he was a janitor in a lawyer's office and later a beginning carpenter. While working at the lawyer's office, he received instruction in elementary subjects, in violation of state law. Turner converted to Christianity in 1844 and joined the Baptist church. After hearing stirring messages from Methodist preachers at summer camp meetings, he was admitted to the Methodist church in 1848. He was licensed as an exhorter in 1851 and as a preacher in 1853. Turner became an evangelist and preached throughout the South, where he attracted blacks and

Henry McNeal Turner, the first Southern bishop of the African Methodist Episcopal Church, declared that God is black.

whites with his spellbinding sermons. He rose rapidly within the denomination, pastoring churches in the Baltimore conference while he supplemented his education. He later pastored Union Bethel in Baltimore and Israel Church in Washington, D.C. In 1860 he was ordained a deacon and in 1862 an elder. His work with the AME Book Concern and his writings for the *Christian Recorder* enhanced his reputation in the church. He was a chaplain for the First Regiment of the United States Colored Troops, receiving his commission on November 6, 1863.

Turner became involved in Reconstruction politics from 1867 to 1871 and used his church's resources to help organize the Republican Party in Georgia. In 1868 he served as a member of the Georgia legislature. Turner was elected bishop in 1880 and presided over various districts for four-year terms. He had doctrinal differences with the church that gradually led to his having a more liberal position on the Bible. In 1896 he called for a new translation of the Bible by and for blacks, and initiated some of the themes of a black theology. Around this time he declared that "The devil is white and never was black," and, by 1895, he proclaimed at a Baptist convention in Atlanta that "God is a Negro." Further, Turner believed that the first humans on earth were black. He advocated increased missionary activity and founded a women's auxiliary, the Women's Home and Foreign Missionary Society, to support his cause. In time he became unpopular for his stance on emigration to Africa and for encouraging blacks to keep guns in their homes during the rising tide of anti-black violence and lynchings in 1897. Turner is remembered, however, for his vigorous and effective leadership of the AME church in the South.

EVANGELISTS AND EVANGELISM

Who was the nation's **first black healing evangelist**?

Sarah Ann Freeman Mix (Mrs. Edward Mix; 1832–1884)), who had been healed of tuberculosis, became the nation's first black healing evangelist in the 1860s and 1870s. Mix was so well respected for her accomplishments that doctors sent their patients to her for prayer. She had been healed under the ministry of Ethan O. Allen who, in 1846, became the first American to associate Christian perfection with divine healing. He, too, had been healed of tuberculosis while in his late twenties, and later became the first American to practice faith healing ministry full time. On February 27, 1879, Mix offered prayer to Carrie Judd (Montgomery) (1858–1946), an invalid white woman from Buffalo, New York. Within a few months Judd was healed and told her story in the *Buffalo Commercial Advertiser* on October 20, 1880. Judd became a prominent Pentecostal as a minister-teacher, writer, and social worker in Oakland, California. Mix, who was a Baptist, married a Baptist minister and lived in Wolcottville (later called Torrington), Connecticut.

What well-known **evangelist** spread his **gospel on the radio**?

Known as the "Happy Am I Evangelist," Solomon Lightfoot Michaux (1885–1968) of the Gospel Spreading Church, Washington, D.C., began radio broadcasts in 1929. After the purchase of a local station by the CBS network, he was the first black to have a national and international audience on a regular basis. In 1934 he broadcast on Saturdays on the CBS radio network and internationally on shortwave radio, to reach an estimated audience of twenty-five million people. He preached a mixture of holiness themes and positive thinking, and his church was related to the Church of God, Holiness. By 1941 his radio broadcasts were heard only in a few cities where he had congregations, but the broadcasts continued until his death. Michaux once sold fish on the streets of Newport News, Virginia. A shrewd businessman, he became chief local purveyor of fish to the U.S. Navy during World War I. This brought him a fortune and he used his money to support needy black and white people. The Solomon Lightfoot Michaux Temple was located at the corner of Jefferson Avenue and Nineteenth Street in Newport News. Michaux had large congregations in New York, Philadelphia, and Washington, D.C., as well.

RACIAL SEGREGATION
AND THE BLACK CHURCH

How did **early black churches react** to racial **segregation**?

Resistance to discrimination in the church consistently has taken many forms. In the North, for example, Peter Spencer (1782–1843) in Wilmington, Delaware, Richard Allen (1760–1831) in Philadelphia, and James Varick (c. 1750–1827) in New York, led their black followers out of white Methodist churches and set up independent black congregations. In Allen's case, his departure was preceded by a dramatic confrontation over segregated seating in Philadelphia's white Methodist church. Each of these men then used his congregation as the nucleus of a new black Methodist denomination—Spencer formed the African Union Church in 1807, Allen the African Methodist Episcopal Church (AME) in 1816, and Varick a denomination eventually called the African Methodist Episcopal Zion Church (AME Zion) in 1821.

MUSIC AND THE BLACK CHURCH

What is the **importance of music** in the **black church**?

Second only to preaching as the focal point of black church worship is music, particularly singing. It is a magnet of attraction and serves as a vehicle of spiritual transport for the congregation. In a ritualistic cadence, black church preachers and deacons often sing their prayers. A successful ministry can often depend on good preaching as well as good music and good singing, whether the music is vocal or instrumental. Music in the church setting was seen in the religions of the West African diaspora and later introduced in the United States. Music in the church is said to reduce barriers that separate people in the church, such as those of different economic or social backgrounds. When members of a congregation sing together, they are united in joy, sorrow, love, despair, and hope. Some believe that when slaves were allowed to worship in white churches, they found no meaningful participation in the services because they were unable to express themselves or celebrate their sense of belonging through songs that emerged during a common experience. The use of African drums, for example, was once considered a heathen rite and generally forbidden from use in the church, despite the fact that drums have always been a part of the African cultural heritage. Early black churches mixed spirituals with preaching during worship service. The use of spirituals in the black church has been perpetuated; most churches never stopped singing spirituals after emancipation or manumission, and thus there has been a continuous flow of such singing. In addition to what

Sometimes called the "Prince of Preachers," Charles Tindley was a Methodist minister and gospel music composer known for songs like "Stand By Me" and "I'll Overcome Someday."

291

some scholars call use of black song, music in black churches popularly includes use of instruments and performances of groups of liturgical dancers.

Who were some **promoters of gospel music** in the black church?

Methodist minister Charles Tindley (1851–1933) began his work as an itinerant preacher, speaking and singing at camp meetings throughout Maryland. Later he became one of the most powerful leaders in Philadelphia's black community and a popular speaker before both black and white audiences. By the early 1900s he founded a church now known as Tindley Temple United Methodist Church, which became famous for concerts and new music, much of it he had written. In 1901 he published the first collection of many of the hymns that he wrote during his ministry, including "Stand By Me," and "We'll Understand It Better By and By." In 1916 he published *New Songs of Paradise,* which was intended for informal worship. Included in this collection was a song that would be known fifty years later as the signature piece of the Civil Rights Movement, "I'll Overcome Someday." His songs were the first black gospel songs ever published and were used in black churches regardless of denomination. They are meant to help the oppressed survive and speak to the "harvest to be reaped once the storms of this life have been successfully weathered."

Other gospel composers and arrangers who helped to spread the gospel are Sallie Martin, Roberta Martin, Lucie Campbell, Thomas Dorsey, Mahalia Jackson, and groups like the Five Blind Boys of Mississippi. At first the so-called "advanced" black churches disapproved of gospel singers and refused to permit them to sing in their churches or to allow gospel singing during their services. Gradually, however, these churches have become more tolerant and accepting of gospel singers and singing as a part of the black music and church tradition.

EARLY RELIGIOUS LEADERS
AND CIVIL RIGHTS

How was **Morris Brown** involved in **slave uprisings** or other acts of protest?

Among the major religious leaders and their work for civil rights was Morris Brown (1770–1850). Black Methodists in Charleston, South Carolina, secretly formed their own church when the separate black quarterly conference was abolished. Morris Brown was one of two people sent north to be ordained by Richard Allen. Brown became pastor of the first church. The church was suppressed, and the building demolished in 1822, because of the involvement of some of its members in the Denmark Vesey slave uprising. Brown escaped by being smuggled north. He settled in Philadelphia and continued his work in the AME church. In 1826 he took charge of the Bristol Circuit in Bucks County, Pennsylvania. He became the first to travel west and develop the church in western Pennsylvania and Ohio. In 1828 Brown was elected second bishop of the AME church and shared the burden of the older and weaker Allen. He was consecrated at Bethel

Church on May 25, 1828, and became sole bishop after Allen died in 1831. Brown was born free, of mixed parentage, and lived in Charleston, South Carolina. Although he had no schooling, he was successful in strengthening the AME church.

What **other religious leaders** were **abolitionists** or civil rights activists?

Henry Highland Garnet (1815–1882) was a leading abolitionist, an advocate of political action as a necessary alternative to ill treatment of African Americans, and an outspoken orator who sought remedies for the ill treatment that they received. Alexander Crummell (1819–1898), black nationalist, promoted emigration of blacks from the United States and became a lecturer for the American Colonization Society. James Theodore Holly (1829–1911) of the Protestant Episcopal Church strove to get support for the emigration of black people to Haiti, remained involved in fights for black rights, and believed that the only way to receive equality was for black people to separate themselves from whites. Francis J. Grimké (1852–1937) of the Fifteenth Street Presbyterian Church in Washington, D.C., was a leader among African Americans in Washington, D.C., and used his position to fight racism both within his denomination and in society at large. Reverdy C. Ransom (1861–1959) was a minister in the African Methodist Episcopal Church who had militant views about civil rights.

THE BLACK CHURCH IN THE MODERN CIVIL RIGHTS MOVEMENT

How did the **black church respond** to the **modern Civil Rights Movement**?

A key component in the success of the Civil Rights Movement, churches produced leadership and also provided spaces for organizing, strategizing, and training. They also served as places of refuge during various civil rights activities. Most black churches were not participants in the movement; instead, they provided much of the leadership needed, and the church as well as its leaders remained at the forefront of the movement. As well, some church leaders discouraged women from participating in the movement and warned them against receiving the civil rights workers in their homes or serving the movement in any way. The women, however, disregarded such directives. The Southern Christian Leadership Conference (SCLC) was organized in 1957, primarily with black Baptists, but ministers from other church affiliations were also members. Founding president Martin Luther King Jr. was joined by Ralph Abernathy, Andrew Young, Fred Shuttlesworth, C. T. Vivian, James Lawson, Joseph Lowery, Kelly Miller Smith, Jesse Jackson, and others. Will D. Campbell was one of the few white pastors to actively work for civil rights in the South during the early years of the movement. Some pastors and spiritual leaders from other parts of the country became directly or indirectly involved in the movement as it gained momentum, while others did not participate for a variety of reasons, including their own racial prejudices.

How did Martin Luther King Jr.'s **"Letter from the Birmingham Jail"** relate to the work of **spiritual leaders**?

Martin Luther King Jr.'s "Letter from the Birmingham Jail," written in 1963, included his critique of fellow spiritual leaders who were unwilling to address problems of discrimination inside and outside of the religious community. In nearly every African-American community, one or more churches provided tangible as well as moral and spiritual support to the movement as an extension of its traditional role of service. The majority of civil rights rallies and mass meetings were held in black churches, which were generally the largest facilities independently owned and operated by African Americans in any given location. Some churches encouraged participation and/or membership of their congregations in civil rights organizations and created support networks for students, civil rights workers, and volunteers. In Nashville, Tennessee, for example, plans for the local sit-in movement were made in Clark Memorial United Methodist Church. Black churches also continued civil rights initiatives after media coverage and publicity from major events ended. Designated offerings raised during regular church services and community mass meetings were used for direct financial support for various civil rights activities, such as helping jailed demonstrators to make bail and paying for fines. Many churches have now been designated as state and/or national historic landmarks as a result of their role in the Civil Rights Movement.

What is the significance of **Birmingham's Sixteenth Street Baptist Church** in the **Civil Rights Movement**?

The Sixteenth Street Baptist Church in Birmingham, Alabama, had served as the primary meeting place for the community and as an important part of the planning and events of the civil rights activities in the 1960s. The bombing of the church in 1963, which killed four little black girls, was the most tragic of the period. The Sixteenth Street Baptist Church was first constructed as the First Colored Baptist Church of Birmingham, Alabama, in 1873. In 1911 a new building with three stories was constructed. It was designed by black architect Wallace Rayfield.

With the Supreme Court ruling in *Brown v. Board of Education of Topeka, Kansas*, in 1954, the South was charged to desegregate its public schools. Sixteenth Street Baptist Church served as the meeting place for marches and protests to impress upon Alabama the need to implement the ruling. The 1955 Montgomery Bus Boycott also pushed the state toward confronting many of its racist and separatists laws and attitudes. The resistance to change was prevalent from the lowest to the highest level of government in Alabama. When two black students—Charlayne Hunter and Hamilton Holmes—tried to register to attend the University of Alabama, Governor George Wallace attempted to deny their entrance by placing himself in front of the doors. Tension continued to mount, and in the spring of 1963 white supremacist groups took an even more aggressive response.

The community of Birmingham had been demonstrating for the end of segregation with the hope that the court-ordered integration of public schools would be implemented. On September 15, 1963, a Sunday morning, three members of the Ku Klux Klan planted

During the 1960s, the Sixteenth Street Baptist Church in Birmingham, Alabama, was the hub of the Civil Rights Movement.

nineteen sticks of dynamite outside the basement of the Sixteenth Street Baptist Church. Four young girls dressed in their "Sunday best" were in the basement, as they planned to attend the adult service, at 11:00 A.M. As the other children entered the basement after an earlier youth service the dynamite exploded; Addie Mae Collins, Carole Robertson, Cynthia Wesley, and Denise McNair were killed and twenty-two others injured.

This act of violence marked a new low that was condemned by blacks and some whites. This tragic event, along with the assassination of President John F. Kennedy two months later, helped the nation to realize the importance of equal rights and finally pass the Civil Rights Act of 1964, which protected blacks' right to vote. The church was declared a national historic landmark on September 17, 1980.

POPES, SAINTS, ARCHBISHOPS, AND NUNS

Has there ever been a **black pope**?

About 186, Saint Victor I was the first pope identified as an African, although his racial identity is not clearly established. What was rare then, and now, is that he was a deacon when he became pope. It was Saint Victor who established a set date for the annual cel-

Who was the first black saint?

Saint Moses the Black is the first saint whose black identity is well established. A rebellious former slave who had become an outlaw in the Egyptian desert, he became a monk and priest and left writings on monastic life. Moses was martyred in 410.

ebration of Easter. He reigned until c. 197 and died in 199, a martyr for the faith. He was buried on Vatican Hill near St. Peter's tomb. Two other early popes, who, like Saint Victor I, became saints, are also of African origin—Saint Miltiades (311–314) and Saint Gelasius I (492–496). Saint Miltiades ended persecutions by signing the emperor Constantine's famous Edict of Milan in 313. Christianity then became the empire's established and legal religion. Highly regarded as pope, according to Saint Augustine, Saint Miltiades was called "a son of peace and father of Christians." He was the last pope to be buried in a catacomb. Saint Gelasius I was born in Rome and became well known for holiness, kindness, and scholarship. Although he upheld old traditions, he also made exceptions and modifications, including "his decree obliging the reception of the Holy Eucharist under both kinds." He is credited with saving Rome from famine, and he was recognized also for his concern for the poor. He composed a book of hymns for use in the church and also clarified the church's teaching on the Eucharist. He was ranked high as a writer. Many of his decrees were incorporated into the Canon Law.

Who was **America's first black Catholic archbishop**?

In 1988 Eugene Antonio Marino (1934–2000) became the first black Catholic archbishop in the United States and only the second black ordinary bishop (a bishop who heads a diocese). Marino, a native of Biloxi, Mississippi, was educated at Saint Joseph's Seminary in Washington, D.C. He was ordained to the priesthood on June 9, 1962. Marino taught at Epiphany College from 1962 to 1968. From 1968 to 1971 he was spiritual director of St. Joseph's Seminary. He was elected vicar of the Josephites in 1971 and assisted the society further by serving as director of spiritual and educational formation. In September 1974 he became auxiliary bishop in Washington, D.C. He became archbishop of the Diocese of Atlanta from 1988 to May 1990 and was the ranking black member of the Catholic hierarchy when he stepped aside because of exhaustion and stress. In August 1990, however, his inappropriate relationship with a single mother became public knowledge. He went into seclusion after he resigned and received spiritual direction as well as psychiatric and medical care for stress. Before his death, he spent his last five years as spiritual director in an outpatient program for clergy at St. Vincent's Hospital in Harrison, New York, while he lived at a Salesian Fathers home in New Rochelle.

Who were the **Oblate Sisters of Providence**?

On July 2, 1829, the first permanent order of black Catholic nuns, the Oblate Sisters of Providence, was founded in Baltimore, Maryland. The order was founded through the efforts of a French priest, James Joubert, and four women of Caribbean origin—Elizabeth Lange, Rosine Boegues, Mary Frances Balas, and Mary Theresa Duchemin. This teaching order was formally recognized on October 2, 1831. The sisters opened the first Catholic school for girls in 1843. The school survives today as Mount Providence Junior College, established in 1952. The second order founded was the Sisters of the Holy Family. Henriette Delille and Juliette Gaudin founded the order in New Orleans in 1842; that order was not officially recognized until after the Civil War. The third predominantly black order was the Franciscan Handmaids of the Most Pure Heart of Mary, founded in Savannah, Georgia, in 1916. At the invitation of Cardinal Patrick Hayes, the Handmaids moved to Harlem in 1924 at the time that many blacks were relocating there. The cardinal saw a need for a day nursery for the children of working parents and the Handmaids responded by opening the St. Benedict Day Nursery, now their primary charity. They also operate a summer sleep-away camp on Staten Island. The order is located on West 124th Street between Lenox and Fifth Avenues. In its heyday, over eighty Handmaids of Mary were members of the order. By 2001 the oldest member of the order was Sister Mary Joseph, who was 101 years old. In October 2001 the Handmaids celebrated their eighty-fifth anniversary.

MEGACHURCHES IN THE AFRICAN–AMERICAN COMMUNITY

Where are some of **African America's megachurches** and how do they operate?

During the last two decades of the twentieth century African-American ministers and congregations became a part of the megachurch phenomenon. Some belonged to the historically African-American denominations, yet others were developed independently. Their leaders were generally charismatic preachers and speakers, and included such popular people as T. D. Jakes, Creflo Dollar, Eddie Long, and Frederick K. C. Price. The televangelist, entrepreneur, and writer T.D. Jakes has been cited as perhaps "the best known of black megachurch ministers" and makes no apologies for his "prosperous lifestyle," his "celebrity status," or his "material success." Some of the larger sanctuaries that provide seating to support growing memberships are: Faithful Central Bible Church, in Inglewood, California; the Faith Dome of the Crenshaw Christian Center in Los Angeles; Jericho City of Praise Church in Landover, Michigan; The New Birth Missionary Baptist Church in Lithonia, Georgia (pastor Eddie Long); The Potter's House in Dallas (Bishop T.D. Jakes); and the Apostolic Church of God in Chicago. Some embraced newer approaches to worship that involved contemporary gospel music, dance, drama, and other art forms, along with preaching and teaching. In 1989 George A. Stallings, a former priest, left the Roman Catholic Church and formed the Imani Temple African American Catholic Congregation in Washington, D.C., as an African-centered alternative to existing Roman Catholicism. He was excommunicated from the Roman Catholic Church, became an archbishop, and also established Imani Temple locations across the United States and Nigeria. Some megachuch leaders remained within established denominations. Examples are Floyd Flake of Greater Allen AME Cathedral of New York; Kirbyjohn Caldwell of Windsor United Methodist Church in Houston; Charles Blake of West Angeles Church of God in Christ in Los Angeles; and Jeremiah A. Wright Jr. of Trinity United Church of Christ in Chicago.

BLACK JEWS

What are **Black Jews**?

Several different groups in the past century have been known as Black Jews. Included among these are the Commandment Keepers, founded in Harlem in 1919 by a Nigerian-born man known as "Rabbi Matthew"; the Church of God and Saints of Christ, founded in 1896 in Lawrence, Kansas, by William Crowdy; and the Church of God founded in Philadelphia by Prophet F. S. Cherry. In terms of doctrine, these groups share little more than a dislike of Christianity and affection for the Old Testament. Some Black Jews claim descent from the Falasha Jews of Ethiopia, who now reside in Israel. However, few Black Jews are recognized as such by orthodox rabbis. The Church of God and Saints of Christ is the largest of these groups. Many of this religion regard Ethiopian Emperor Haile Selassie, who died in 1977, as God.

PENTECOSTALISM IN THE BLACK COMMUNITY

What has been the **impact of Pentecostalism** on the black community?

Pentecostalism burst on the American scene in 1906 and has become a major religious force within the black community. The Church of God in Christ, a Pentecostal denomination, has become the second largest black denomination in the United States. Meanwhile, the charismatic, or Neo-Pentecostal, movement has revitalized many congregations within mainline black denominations. The Black Nationalism of Bishop Henry McNeal Turner helped achieve its full potential in the work of such men as Marcus Garvey (and his chaplain general, George A. McGuire), Elijah Muhammad, and Malcolm X. There has been a spectacular rise in storefront churches, some of which were led by flamboyant showmen such as Father Divine and "Sweet Daddy" Grace. Each of these trends has been significantly aided by the black migrations from the South to the North, which greatly strengthened Northern black communities.

Black nationalists like Malcolm X (shown here) were key in growing the movement begun by Bishop Henry McNeal Turner.

Who was influenced by Pentecostals and established a Peace Mission?

It was about 1914 that M. J. "Father" Divine (some sources indicate his real name was George Baker; 1879–1965) first proclaimed himself God as he established his movement, Father Divine's "Kingdom" and Peace Mission. His initials stood for Major Jealous, which was taken from Exodus 34:14, "for the Lord, whose name is Jealous, is a jealous god." His followers also believed that he was God. He was tried on a charge of insanity in a Valdosta, Georgia, court on February 27, 1914, on the grounds that his claim to be God was clearly aberrant. He was convicted but not incarcerated. Born in Rockville, Maryland, into a poor family, Baker learned the skills of a gardener and yard worker. He moved to Baltimore in 1899 and became interested in the storefront churches that were popular at that time. He became a preacher who developed his own ideas about religion, drawing on Methodist, Catholic, and popular black traditions; he was also influenced by the New Thought movement that preceded the Christian Science and modern New Age movements. Baker went South in 1902, where he sought to save souls. Then he moved to the West Coast, where William J. Seymour and his Azusa Street revival meetings and the traditions of the Pentecostal movements influenced him. As he heard blacks and white "speak in tongues" and did so himself, he began to reshape his religious thoughts.

When did Father Divine become the Messenger and the Son of Father Jehovia?

Father Divine (1879–1965), met the preacher Samuel Morris in 1907, and the two united in a ministry. After that, Morris called himself Father Jehovia, and Baker became the

299

Messenger and the Son. Reverend Bishop Saint John the Vine, or John A. Hickerson, joined them, and the three built up a following at their residence. They went their separate ways in 1912. The Messenger, or Father Divine, returned to the South and spread his message as he traveled. His pattern of worship consisted of preaching, singing, and lavish Holy Communion banquets. His following then was predominantly black women who found him liberating, as he denounced male chauvinism. Baker drew the ire of black ministers, and a confrontation in Savannah in 1913 led to his imprisonment and sixty days on a chain gang. By 1917 he had married a woman named Peninnah, who became known as Mother Divine, and spread his gospel to the North as well. He settled in Sayville, Long Island, New York, and widened his support to attract middle- and upper-class whites. Then he shifted his base to New York City, where he held a series of successful meetings at Harlem's Rockville Palace. Father Divine established a Peace Mission that included restaurants and other businesses that became the source of much of his revenue. His mission grew rapidly in 1937, but his entire institution declined after that. He moved his Peace Mission to Philadelphia around 1942, but the aging and frail Divine ceased public appearances in 1963 and died two years later.

RASTAFARIANISM

What is the **Rastafarian movement**?

In the early 1930s a religious movement known as Rastafarianism was founded in Jamaica. It is based on specific interpretations of the Bible and repatriation to Africa. It embraces rituals and practices such as *reasonings,* which are gatherings of members who come together to pray and smoke holy weed, or marijuana. It also embraces *binghi,* or all-night merriments to celebrate memorable dates and occasions, such as Marcus Garvey's birthday, the coronation of Emperor Haile Selassie I, and freedom from slavery. Rastas believe that they are descended from black Hebrews exiled in Babylon and therefore are true Israelites. They also believe that Haile Selassie (whose name before ascending the throne was Lij Ras Tafari Makonnen) is the direct descendant of Solomon and Sheba, and that God is black. Rastafarians consider dreadlocks as a symbol of wisdom and a priestly image. Around the world young blacks have popularized dreadlocks,

Ethiopia's Emperor Haile Selassie I was, according to Rastafarians, a direct descendant of King Solomon.

Rasta colors (red, green, and gold), and smoking marijuana more like a fashion trend, rather than a true statement of cultural and religious values.

MUSLIMS IN AMERICA

Why was **Wallace Fard** important among Muslims?

In 1930 W. D. Fard (1891–?) organized the group that became Temple No. 1 of the Nation of Islam in Detroit. Accounts of his life vary widely. He used several names, including Fred Dodd and Wallace Ford; by the time he arrived in Detroit, however, he had become W. D. Fard. He was known to his followers as Fard Muhammad. He was born to a white mother and a black father, or may have had Polynesian ancestry. Whatever his ethnic heritage, he was known to have passed for white when he was jailed later on. His birthplace was either New Zealand or Portland, Oregon. In the 1920s Fard operated a café in Los Angeles. After various encounters with the law he was jailed and spent three years in San Quentin Prison for selling narcotics. He was released from prison on May 27, 1929, and then settled in Detroit where he worked as a retail salesman in the black community. He began to organize the Nation of Islam in 1930. By some accounts, Fard thought of himself as the deity. "My name is Mahdi; I am God, I came to guide you into the right path that you may be successful and see the hereafter," he told Elijah Muhammad (Elijah Poole, Elijah Karriem; 1879–1975) when asked who he was and what was his real name. The Nation of Islam was considered radical and therefore a target for police harassment. In November 1932 Fard was arrested only because the police tied a murderer to the Nation of Islam. When it became known that Fard's persecution made him a martyr, he was ordered to leave Detroit. Fard instead went into hiding and prepared Elijah Karriem to head the organization, giving him the surname of Muhammad and making him chief minister of Islam. The fragile unity of the Nation of Islam was shattered, and fierce fighting followed. The police also accelerated their harassment. Meanwhile, Elijah Muhammad avoided the struggles and finally relocated the headquarters to Chicago. He met with Fard in June 1934—and after that Fard disappeared.

GENDER EQUALITY IN THE BLACK CHURCH

Who was the **first black woman bishop**?

Leontine Turpeau Current Kelly (1920–2012) became the first woman bishop of a major denomination, the United Methodist Church; she was consecrated on July 20, 1984. In addition, she was the first woman of any race to preach on the program National Radio Pulpit of the National Council of Churches. Born in Washington, D.C., Kelly's call to the ministry came after the death of her second husband. Made an elder in 1977, she had experience at both the local and the national levels. Upon the retirement of the first, and only, woman bishop in the church, she was elected and supervised the California and Nevada conferences until her retirement in 1988. Kelly was born in the parsonage of the church that her father pastored, Mount Zion Methodist Episcopal Church in Washington, D.C. She was the seventh of eight children. Later the family relocated to Pittsburgh and then settled in Cincinnati by the late 1920s. The basement of their Cincinnati parsonage had been used as a station on the Underground Railroad and connected the house to the church. Leontine Kelly interrupted her college education when she married and had children. After a divorce, she remarried and returned to school, receiving her bachelor's degree in 1960 from Virginia Union University in Richmond. After her second husband died, the congregation of Galilee United Methodist Church in Edwardsville, Virginia, where James Kelly was pastor, asked her to succeed him. Already she was active in the church and a popular speaker. By now she also felt a divine calling and served as layperson in charge of the church. She began theological study at Wesley Theological Seminary in Washington, D.C., and graduated in 1976 with a master of divinity degree. She was ordained as a minister and became a deacon in 1972. In 1977 she was ordained an elder. After holding several posts, she joined the national staff of the United Methodist Church, located in Nashville, from 1983 to 1984 and received the prominence she needed to become a candidate for bishop. In 2002 she received the Thomas Merton Award. She was also inducted into the National Women's Hall of Fame.

Did the **Anglican church** appoint a **black woman bishop**?

In 1989 Barbara Clementine Harris (1930–) became the first woman Anglican bishop in the world. Although she was elected on September 24, 1988, she took office the next year. On February 12, 1989, she was consecrated suffragan bishop (an auxiliary bishop who is given a special mission) in the Diocese of Massachusetts. As a woman, her election to a post held only by men from the time of Saint Peter, aroused the same controversy as the ordination of eleven women priests did in 1974. This earlier event encouraged Harris to prepare for the priesthood to which she herself was ordained in 1980. Harris felt a call to the church while she was a young child growing up in Philadelphia. While a teenager, she was baptized and confirmed at St. Barnabas Church in the Germantown section of Philadelphia. She completed college courses and special training for mid-career clergy recruits at Villanova University from 1977 to 1979, and received a doctor of sacred theology degree from Hobart and William Smith Colleges in 1981. She was ordained to the diaconate in 1979, and from 1979 to 1980 she served as deacon-in-training at the Church of the Advocate. She was ordained to the priesthood in 1980. From 1980 to 1984 Harris was priest-in-charge at St. Augustine-of-Hippo in Norristown, Pennsylvania, and interim rector at the Church of the Advocate, the position she held when she was elected as suffragan bishop of the Massachusetts diocese. Harris' election stirred controversy—she was divorced, female, an advocate of women's rights, and had a different educational background than suffragan bishops usually possessed. Harris survived the controversy, however, and became an effective religious leader and catalyst for social justice.

What is **Vashti McKenzie's relationship** to the **AME church?**

Vashti Murphy McKenzie (1947–) became the first woman elected bishop in the African Methodist Episcopal (AME) Church, in 2000. The election came during the church's quadrennial convention held in Cincinnati. McKenzie and the Reverend Carolyn Tyler Guidry, a presiding elder who supervised nineteen AME churches in the Los Angeles area, were the only women among forty-two candidates. McKenzie became bishop of the eighteenth Episcopal District in southeast Africa that includes Lesotho, Botswana, Swaziland, and Mozambique, where there were ten thousand members and two hundred churches. In September McKenzie left for her four-year assignment. The commanding preacher achieved a first in 1990 as well, when she was appointed pastor of Payne Memorial AME Church, a

The first time a woman was named a bishop in the AME Church was in 2000, when Vashti Murphy McKenzie was selected.

large church in Baltimore. Under her leadership, Payne instituted twenty-five new ministries and increased the size of its membership from 300 to over 1,700. McKenzie is a member of the Murphy family, founders of the *Afro-American* newspaper. The Baltimore native graduated from the University of Maryland at College Park and became a fashion model; she also followed her great-grandfather, John Murphy, into the field of journalism. After working as a journalist and as a broadcaster on a Christian radio station, she decided to enter the ministry. She received a master of divinity degree from Howard University and a doctor of divinity from the United Theological Seminary in Dayton, Ohio. McKenzie was national chaplain for the Delta Sigma Theta sorority; she is granddaughter of one of the sorority's founders, Vashti Turley Murphy. In 1997 *Ebony* magazine named McKenzie one of its "Fifteen Greatest African-American Preachers" and placed her at the top of the list. Among McKenzie's publications are the books *Not without a Struggle: Leadership Development for African-American Women in Ministry* (1996) and *Strength in the Struggle: Leadership Development for Women* (2002).

Who is the **first** black **woman bishop** in the **CME** church?

On June 30, 2010, Teresa Elaine Snorton became the first black woman and the fifty-ninth bishop in the Christian Methodist Episcopal (CME) Church. The CME church, founded in 1870, has approximately 850,000 members in 3,500 churches in the United States. Snorton was at first assigned as the presiding bishop of the new Eleventh Episcopal District, which includes eleven countries in Central, Southern, and Eastern Africa. In March 2011 she was assigned to the Fifth Episcopal District comprising of four regions in the states of Alabama and Florida; she remains in this position today. She received her bachelor's degree from Vanderbilt University, a master of divinity from Louisville Presbyterian Theological Seminary, a master of theology in pastoral care from Southern Baptist Theological Seminary, a post-graduate certificate in patient counseling from Virginia Commonwealth University, and the doctor of ministry from United Theological Seminary. Bishop Snorton is a fourth-generation, life-long CME. Her great-grandfather and uncle were CME pastors and her grandmother a missionary. Her two sisters are also CME ministers. She was ordained in the CME Church and formerly served as a pastor in Kentucky. Before moving to Atlanta, Snorton was a pastor, a psychiatric staff chaplain in Kentucky, an adjunct faculty member of the Louisville Presbyterian Theological Seminary, and on the faculties of the Patient Counseling Program at the Medical College of Virginia and the School of Theology of Virginia Union University. She has also served as executive director of the Emory Center for Pastoral Services in Atlanta, director of pastoral services at Atlanta's Crawford Long Hospital, and an adjunct instructor in pastoral care at Candler School of Theology at Emory University. Bishop Snorton has published several articles, chapters, and book reviews on pastoral care and ministry.

WOMEN OF RIGHTEOUS DISCONTENT

What are some contributions of **early black women ministers**?

The contributions of black women ministers are vital in the black community. Sometimes women served as traveling evangelists, especially within the black denominations. While Sojourner Truth's oratory has become appropriately famous, women like Maria Stewart, Jarena Lee, Zilpha Elaw, and other early nineteenth-century women also spoke eloquently and, in Lee's and Elaw's cases, traveled widely and labored diligently. Although these women were not ordained, Elizabeth (whose last name is unknown), a former slave from Maryland whose ministry began in 1796, spoke for many female preachers when she was accused of preaching without a license: "If the Lord has ordained me, I need nothing better." During the postbellum years, some black women sought and obtained formal ordination from their denominations. Many women exercised their ministry through para-ecclesiastical structures, such as women's temperance and missionary societies, while others, such as Anna Julia Cooper (1858–1964) and the African Methodist Episcopal Church's Frances Jackson Coppin (1837–1913), became renowned educators.

Who was **Jarena Lee**?

In 1817 Jarena Lee (1783–?) became the first woman to preach in the African Methodist Episcopal (AME) Church. Lee was born in Cape May, New Jersey. After hearing Richard

Allen preach, she experienced conversion and later felt a call to preach. In 1817 she rose in Bethel Church, Philadelphia, to give a spontaneous talk. Although never formally licensed to speak by the church, Lee began an extraordinary career as an evangelist. She began her work as leader of a predominantly female praying and singing band, later becoming an evangelist. Lee, and other women, like Juliann Jane Tillman, made a considerable impact on religious life as well as on the growth of their denominations. Although she had little formal education, Lee published two autobiographies: *The Life and Religious Experience of Jarena Lee* in 1836 and *Religious Experiences and Journal of Jarena Lee* in 1849. Both of these works are extant.

How was **Sojourner Truth** involved in **religious activities**?

Isabella Baumfree (1797–1883) took the name Sojourner Truth on June 1, 1843. Her decision came after one of her many religious visions. She was a member of the Zion Church in New York but had a mystical personality that could not be confined by a church structure, nor within a cult she joined for a brief period called the Mathias group. She set out on her own anti-slavery crusade, seeing it as "the secular counterpart of spiritual salvation." This was a period when many who spoke out against slavery were fine orators, such as Frederick Douglass. Yet, Truth could well match his wit, wisdom, and eloquence. A licensed deacon in the Zion Church, Douglass ended one of his despairing speeches, which prompted Sojourner Truth to stand and stun the meeting by asking, "Frederick, is God dead?" Yet the two had a common

bond: they linked abolitionism and the women's suffrage movement. Like Douglass, Truth was in great demand as a suffrage speaker and attracted crowds of listeners. Her classic speech, "Ain't I a Woman?", attacked the views of men as well as white women for their neglect of the black woman's plight. Although illiterate, Sojourner Truth captivated audiences with storytelling, singing of spirituals, and her remarkable knowledge of the Bible.

Who established the first largely black Shaker family in Philadelphia?

Rebecca Cox Jackson (1795–1871) established the first largely black Shaker family in Philadelphia. Its existence in Philadelphia can be traced back to at least 1908. A religious visionary, Jackson became an itinerant preacher and spiritual autobiog-

Born a slave, Sojourner Truth grew up to be an eloquent speaker against slavery, inspired by her religious visions and personal determination to end injustice.

rapher. She was free-born and lived in Philadelphia early on. When she was thirty-nine years old, she challenged the African Methodist Church that had nourished her until then. Jackson joined praying bands influenced by the Holiness movement within the Methodist church. Throughout the late 1830s and early 1840s she traveled in Pennsylvania, northern Delaware, New Jersey, southern New England, and New York, recounting her own experiences while also urging people to live free and celibate. In June 1847 Jackson and her friend and disciple, Rebecca Perot, joined the Shaker society; they lived in the Watervliet community, located near Albany, until June 1851 when they returned to Philadelphia. Jackson returned to Watervliet from 1858 to 1959 and negotiated with the Shakers about her right to establish a separate mission in Philadelphia. Jackson was known in the Shaker community as a very unusual speaker and one who gave impressive performances. Her spiritual writing survived; it traces her inner life and gives examples of her visionary dreams and various accounts of Shakerism.

Who was **Mary J. Small**?

In 1898 Mary J. Small (1850–1945), wife of Bishop John Bryant Small (1845–1905), became the first Methodist woman to be ordained an elder. Earlier, on May 19, 1895, Small became the second woman to be ordained as a deacon. Her status infuriated some of the male clergy, who thought it inappropriate for women to hold such status. There is no indication that Small ever pastored a church, but she was active in evangelistic activities. She was an officer in the Women's Home and Foreign Missionary Society and also belonged to the Women's Christian Temperance Union. Small was born in Murfreesboro, Tennessee. She joined her husband in his parish work in Connecticut, North Carolina, Washington, D.C., and elsewhere. She was licensed as an evangelist and missionary in 1892. Small died in McKeesport, Pennsylvania.

Who was the **first woman ordained a deacon** of the **AME Zion church**?

Julia A. J. Foote (1823–1901), of the African Methodist Episcopal Zion church, became the first woman ordained a deacon on May 20, 1894. Foote became the second black woman elder in 1900. Bishop Alexander Walters, whose family Foote lived with from 1884 to 1901, ordained two black women elders in the AME Zion church—Mary J. Small in 1898 and then Foote in 1900. They became the first women of any race in the Methodist denomination to achieve the full rights that ordination as an elder provided. Born in Schenectady, New York, Foote was the fourth child of former slaves. She went to live with a prominent white family in 1833, where she enrolled in an integrated school. In 1836 she moved with the family to Albany, New York. In 1838, when she was fifteen years old, Foote received a religious conversion. She married in 1839, moved to Boston, and joined the AME Zion Church. Like Foote, all members of the church had left the Methodist Episcopal Church in search of greater religious freedom and affiliation with a black denomination. Until her conversion, Foote made it known that she opposed women in the ministry; however, she said later that she had to preach in response to a call from God. For over fifty years Foote was an evangelist and a pioneering

What is the traditional role of black women in the church?

The membership of the black church is composed mainly of women. Even so, too few hold formal positions in ministerial and lay leadership. Ironically, even though the black church was established in response to discrimination in the larger culture, it has not fully ensured gender equality. Some studies say that "men occupy the pulpits while women are relegated to the pews." Women have worked through parallel and auxiliary organizations—some of them founded because of the denial of equal participation of women in the black church—to develop organizational and leadership skills. Women have filled roles that churches themselves claim to fill, such as advocacy work, work for social change, and social service work in the community. The megachurches are no exception, for they, too, have yet to give women equal access to formal positions of ministerial leadership. Some churches cite scriptures as justification for keeping women from the pulpit: "Let your women keep silent in the churches: for it is not permitted unto them to speak" (1 Corinthians 14:34). Although, traditionally, black women have protested their subordinate roles in the church, some writers conclude that "there is a strong tradition of patriarchy and discrimination in black churches and black megachurches."

black Methodist holiness preacher. She traveled and lectured widely, speaking at camp meetings, revivals, and churches in several states. Later she wrote about her experiences in her autobiography, *A Brand Plucked from the Fire*.

What is **womanist theology**?

Womanist theology is a denial of overreliance on male-centered traditions and preaching in the church. It calls for black preachers and theologians to relate the scriptures to black women's struggles and triumphs. Womanist theology uplifts and respects women of African descent in the Bible. Womanist theology upholds the plight of Hagar, an enslaved woman of Egyptian heritage, who was forced to have the child of her owners to give them an heir. Hagar ran away from the household, was later expelled from it, and lived in the wilderness where God took care of her. Womanist theologians see Hagar as a single mother who, despite her exploitation, obtained freedom.

Since the 1970s there has been considerable debate concerning black women and the rise of the feminist movement. Some say that there has been a continuing need for racial unity in a white society, and a concern that two few black women joined the feminist movement. Black women were the unrecognized backbone of the Civil Rights Movement as well as the black church, and for too long kept in the background of both the movement and the church. Women like Jacquelyn Grant and Delores Williams are among those who have organized units of advocacy and protest that they felt addressed the needs of black women, "womanist" theology. They derived the term "Womanist"

In the Bible, Hagar is an Egyptian slave and concubine to Abraham; she bears him a child, Ishmael, and is later exiled by the jealous Sarah, Abraham's wife; yet Hagar survives through God's grace. In Womanist theology, Hagar is used as an example of a single mother who obtains freedom.

from writer Alice Walker's view that the experiences of black women and white women are vastly different. "Womanist" also is considered a more accurate reflection of the needs and language of the black community. Theologian Grant believes that such theology emerges from the suffering and experiences of black women and brings to the forefront issues of race, sex, and class. It provides a broad and comprehensive base for liberation theology.

TOWARD A BLACK THEOLOGY

What is **black theology**?

Black theology has its roots in the period of slavery in the United States. Although not identified as such, it was fashioned out of the prevailing belief of that time, when white churches attempted to justify slavery, some saying that it was "ordained by God." Theology "is about the manner in which individuals seek to understand through spiritual eyes their relationship with the known and unknown aspects of the seen and unseen world that impacts their lives," according to the *Encyclopedia of African American Popular Culture*. It embraces the feeling, passion, and expressiveness of black Christianity and a systematic attempt to interpret the faith of the church. Black theology questions the black experience in American culture and acknowledges that God accepts blacks. Black people developed a sense of pride in their heritage, while their new theology saw them as people declared to be heirs of God. Black theology became "a theology of hope, liberation, and the sovereignty of God."

The period of black liberation theology influenced James Cone to publish *Black Theology and Black Power* in 1969. After that a host of other theologians and scholars elaborated their views on what should be included in a program of black theology. These scholars include Gayraud Wilmore, DeOtis Roberts, Major Jones, William Jones, Charles Long, Pauli Murray, Jacquelyn Grant, and Cornel West.

Who is recognized as one of the **best-known proponents** of **black theology**?

Alfred Buford Cleage (1911–2000) was one of the best-known proponents of black theology. Known as Jaramogi Abebe Agyeman since the 1970s, the Indianapolis native decided to enter the ministry, and after years of study became a minister with the Congregational and Christian Church. He was a vibrant proponent of black theology and builder of strong congregations. In 1951 he returned to Detroit as pastor of St. Mark's Community (Presbyterian) Church. Cleage, like his father, was an activist in his field, protesting a white Christianity that did not recognize his humanity. This, and other events of the 1950s, such as the Civil Rights Movement and the rise of Islam, as well as his reading from the works of black nationalists, led him to construct a black theology for the black community. Cleage argued that Jesus was a black Messiah born of a black Madonna and a black revolutionary. While preaching a sermon in 1967, he unveiled an eighteen-foot painting of a black Madonna and child and launched the Shrine of the Black Madonna and the Black Christian Nationalist Movement.

Why did **Jeremiah A. Wright Jr.** reach the national spotlight?

Reverend Jeremiah A. Wright Jr. (1941–), one of the most influential black ministers in America, reached the national spotlight during President Barack Obama's first run for the U.S. Presidency. The media often misunderstood and misinterpreted his messages and method of delivery. Wright speaks from the perspective of black liberation and transformative theology. Wright, already one of black America's most widely acclaimed preachers due to his political activism, concern with social issues, and a powerful and dynamic force in the pulpit, is a sought-after lecturer and preacher. He drew widespread attention, however, in March 2008, during the Democratic presidential race. He had been a close advisor to presidential candidate Barack Obama, and Obama and his family were among Wright's parishioners. Reporters who were following the race uncovered several of Wright's comments and took many out of context. For example, the reporters quoted Wright's comment "God damn America" and said that Wright accused America of bringing on the 9/11 terrorist attack upon itself. Negative reactions to Wright followed. Obama distanced himself from Wright and withdrew membership from his church. The entire controversy sparked national debate about religion in politics and the African American community.

SCIENCE, INVENTIONS, MEDICINE, AND AEROSPACE

SCIENCE

Who was **Benjamin Banneker**?

Benjamin Banneker (1731–1806) was the first African American to issue an almanac. His almanac series began in 1792 and continued until 1797. Because of his expertise in mathematics and astronomy, he is sometimes called the first African-American scientist. Banneker was born free in Maryland, where he became a tobacco farmer. As a result of his interest in mathematics and mechanics, he constructed a successful striking clock around 1752. His model for the clock was the mechanism of a watch someone lent to him. The clock was still running at the time of his death. In 1787 a Quaker neighbor lent Banneker some texts on astronomy and instruments, and he taught himself the skills necessary to produce his almanac. Banneker, one of the country's earliest civil engineers, also helped in surveying the national capital. Although Banneker was unwell and unable to work in the field, he served as an assistant to George Ellicott in the survey of the ten-mile-square District of Columbia from early February to the end of April 1791, when he returned to his farm.

What were George Washington **Carver's agricultural discoveries**?

American botanist and agricultural chemist George Washington Carver (c. 1864–1943) won international fame for his research, which included deriving some four hundred products from peanuts, sweet potatoes, and pecans. He also created face powder, butter, cheese, milk, creosote, soaps, and stains. By 1924 he had become firmly established as the "Peanut Man," and peanut growers and processors called on him for his expertise. The son of slave parents, Carver was born near Diamond Grove, Missouri, and through his own efforts obtained an education, earning a bachelor's degree in 1894, and his master of science in agriculture, in 1896, from Iowa State University. That year he joined the

Brilliant botanist and chemist George Washington Carver found hundreds of uses for peanuts, soybeans, pecans, and sweet potatoes. He received many honors, including being the first black man memorialized by a federal monument.

faculty of Alabama's Tuskegee Institute (now University) as director of agricultural research, remaining in this position until his death in 1943. His first research projects centered on soil conservation, crop diversification, and other agricultural practices. Carver gave lectures and made demonstrations to Southern farmers, particularly black farmers, to help them increase crop production. He followed the mission of Booker T. Washington, the school's president, of taking education to the people. He took his mule-drawn "movable school" on weekend visits to impoverished farmlands to teach poor farmers to raise, improve, and preserve foods. Then he turned his attention to finding new uses for two Southern staple crops: peanuts and sweet potatoes. Carver found that peanuts could be used to make a milk substitute, printer's ink, and soap. He found new uses for soybeans and devised products that could be made from cotton waste. His efforts were all intended to improve the economy in the American South and enhance the way of life of Southern black farmers. His scientific work improved the quality of life for millions of people. Carver was a cultural man as well—he was an accomplished pianist and a skilled painter.

Carver was lauded for his accomplishments: He was named a fellow of the Royal Society of Arts of London (1916); he was awarded the Spingarn Medal for distinguished service in agricultural chemistry (1923); and he was bestowed with the Theodore Roosevelt Medal for his valuable contributions to science (1939). He became the first black scientist memorialized by a federal monument in the United States. On July 14, 1953, the United States Congress authorized the establishment of the George Washington Carver National Monument; it was erected on his birth site and dedicated on July 17, 1960. In 1948 his photograph appeared on a commemorative stamp. His laboratory is the Carver Museum, a historic site on the campus of Tuskegee University.

INVENTIONS AND PATENTS

What are some of the **inventions of slaves**?

Much of the work of early black scientists and inventors is largely unknown, because of the fact that historians failed to record such accomplishments and slaves were forbidden from receiving patents. Instead, patents were assigned to their masters, for slaves were not considered citizens and were forbidden from entering into contracts with their owners or the government. Efforts of slaves were largely dismissed or, if accepted, credited entirely to their masters. It was not until 1790 that the federal government passed the U.S. Patent Act. This legislation gave inventors, including free blacks, the right to patent their inventions. For slaves, however, that right was delayed until the Fourteenth Amendment was passed. Some accounts of slaves as inventors emerged, as, for example, in the case of the McCormick harvester. It is said that Joe Anderson, a slave of grain harvester Cyrus McCormick, played a major role in the creation of the harvester, yet the degree of his involvement is undetermined. Benjamin Montgomery, one of President Jefferson Davis's slaves, is thought to have invented an improved boat propeller.

What are some early **inventions of free blacks**?

Unlike the restrictions on slave inventors, for free blacks, some recordings of their inventions do exist. Henry Blair (c. 1804–1860) of Glenross, Maryland, was long believed to be the first black to receive a patent, on October 14, 1834, for a corn (or seed) planter. The device was easier to operate than the crude planters that existed, and permitted seeds to be dropped in a checkerboard fashion. However, Thomas L. Jennings (1791–1859) is said to be the first black to *actually* receive a patent, for a dry-cleaning process, on March

2, 1821. He was a tailor and dry cleaner in New York City and an active abolitionist; he was the founder and president of the Legal Rights Association. Records fail historians, however, for the race of patent-seekers was rarely noted. There were many unheralded black inventors, including Augustus Jackson, who in 1832 perfected a better way to make ice cream, but his invention was not patented. Since the race of patent applicants was rarely recorded, the number of inventions that slaves or free blacks created cannot be determined with certainty.

Who was America's **first** known **black clockmaker**?

In 1781 the first known black clockmaker in America, and the only black clockmaker known to have worked in the late eighteenth and early nineteenth centuries, was Peter Hill (1767–1820). He was one of the few blacks who opened a

Enjoy ice cream? Thank African American Augustus Jackson, who perfected a way to make ice cream, and also invented new flavors.

small business. Other black entrepreneurs of this period were barbers, restaurateurs caterers, merchants, and tailors. Since Hill was not an inventor, his contribution to the art of clockmaking was minor, yet his historic achievement as America's first black clockmaker is significant. Born on July 19, 1767, probably on the property of Quaker clockmaker Joseph Hollinshead Jr., Peter Hill was the son of Hollinshead's slaves. To provide assistance in his shop, Hollinshead trained Hill in the craft of clockmaking. Hollinshead followed the custom of local Quakers, who dedicated themselves to enhancing the lives of blacks by teaching them certain skills. From the time he was fourteen until he was twenty-one, Hill served a form of an apprenticeship with his master. After that Hill may have been a salaried, skilled shop assistant or a journeyman clockmaker. Since Hill was paid for his work, he earned enough money to buy his freedom, and in 1794 the master freed his twenty-seven-year-old mulatto slave. Hill married Tina Lewis on September 9, 1795, four months after he was manumitted; he purchased her freedom as well. While the date on which he opened his first shop is unclear, it is known that Hill opened a shop before he was freed, some time before 1795. Records locating Hill's shop in different locations lead to confusion; however, he lived and worked in Burlington Township, New Jersey, and later in Mount Holly. He operated a clockmaking business in Burlington Township for twenty-three years. He bought land at various times between 1801 and 1811, and his prosperity increased during these years. By 1814, however, he and his wife may not have fared as well and sold some of their land. By 1820 the Hills had purchased a new house and several buildings, suggesting that the family prospered again. Hill enjoyed his new home and surroundings only briefly before he died in December 1820. His wife may have died around the same time. Hill was buried in the Society of Friends' Burial-Ground near the Friends Meeting House in Burlington Township, across the street from one of Hill's residences and shops. Five of Peter Hill's clocks are known to be extant; they contain eight-day striking movements. Hill's work and skill demonstrate a rare accomplishment for a black man in early American history.

Whose inventions were of value to the **sugar-refining industry**?

A native of New Orleans, Norbert Rillieux (1806–1894) was the son of Vincent Rillieux, a wealthy engineer, and Constance Vivant, a slave on his plantation. Young Rillieux's higher education was obtained in Paris, France, where his extraordinary aptitude for engineering led to his appointment, at the age of twenty-four, to instructor of applied mechanics at L'Ecole Centrale. Rillieux moved to Paris permanently in 1854, secured a scholarship and worked on the deciphering of hieroglyphics.

Rillieux's inventions were of great value to the sugar-refining industry. The method formerly used required gangs of slaves to ladle boiling sugarcane juice from one kettle to another—a primitive process known as "the Jamaica Train." In 1854 Rillieux invented a vacuum evaporating pan (a series of condensing coils in vacuum chambers) that reduced the industry's dependence on gang labor and helped manufacture a superior product at a greatly reduced cost. The first Rillieux evaporator was installed at Myrtle Grove

How did the phrase "the real McCoy" originate?

On July 2, 1872, Elijah McCoy (1843–1929) patented the first version of his lubricator for steam engines. This was the first in a series of forty-two patents, most of which were designed to facilitate machine lubrication. Numerous continuous industrial devices flooded the market soon after McCoy's. According to folk etymology, his devices were sought after and those in the know wanted "the real McCoy," nothing else. The claim that the phrase "the real McCoy" originated with his devices is not fully substantiated. Around 1920 McCoy opened his own business, the Elijah McCoy Manufacturing Company, where he made and sold a number of his inventions. McCoy was born in Colchester, Ontario, Canada, and after an apprenticeship in mechanical engineering in Edinburgh, Scotland, he moved to Michigan where his family had relocated after the Civil War erupted. His last patent was granted in 1920 for a graphite lubrication device.

Plantation, Louisiana, in 1845. In the following years, factories in Louisiana, Cuba, and Mexico converted to the Rillieux system.

When Rillieux's evaporator process was finally adopted in Europe, he returned to inventing with renewed interest and applied his process to the sugar beet. In so doing, he cut production and refining costs in half. Rillieux died in Paris on October 8, 1894, leaving behind a system that is universally used throughout the sugar industry and in the manufacture of soap, gelatin, glue, and many other products.

Who patented a cost-efficient method for use with electric lights?

Lewis Howard Latimer (1848–1928) patented the first cost-efficient method for producing carbon filaments for electric lights on June 17, 1882. Born in Chelsea, Massachusetts, his father, George, was an escaped slave whose capture precipitated the first of the highly publicized fugitive slave trials in 1842, and provoked Frederick Douglass's first appearance in print. During the Civil War, Lewis Latimer enlisted in the U.S. Navy as soon as he was old enough. He then became an office boy in a patent office and then a patent draftsman. Latimer made drawings for many of Alexander Graham Bell's telephone patents. He also worked for the United States Electric Lighting Company, where he made many significant innovations in the development of electric lighting and supervised the installation of electric light plants in New York and Philadelphia. In 1884 he began to work for the Edison Electric Light Company and entered its legal department in 1890. From 1896 to 1911 he was head draftsman for the Board of Patent Control and later worked as a patent consultant.

Who invented the shoe-lasting machine?

On March 20, 1883, Jan Matzeliger (1852–1889) patented the first successful shoe-lasting machine. Matzeliger was born in Surinam of a Dutch father, who was an engineer, and a black mother, who was Surinamese and probably came from West Africa. He left Surinam in 1871 and became a sailor on an East Indian ship. Matzeliger settled in Philadelphia for a while, holding odd jobs until he moved to Boston in 1876. The next year he settled in nearby Lynn, Massachusetts. There he developed his device while working in a shoe factory. The machine increased productivity as much as fourteen times over hand methods and led to concentration in the industry. Matzeliger continued to work on the machine to improve its quality. He invented a number of other devices, including a mechanism for distributing tacks and nails. On September 15, 1991, a Black Heritage postage stamp honoring Matzeliger was issued.

Who patented an **electric railway trolley**?

Inventor E. R. Robinson was the first person to receive a patent for an electric railway trolley on September 19, 1893. To propel the car, he used electricity that flowed from an overhead wire through a pole attached to the roof of the vehicle. It became the forerunner of the electric street railways and buses that continue to operate in some sections of the country.

Who was called the **"Black Edison"**?

Granville T. Woods (1856–1910) patented his first electric device, an improved telephone transmitter, on December 2, 1884. By 1900 Woods—often called the "Black Edison"—had received twenty-two patents, most dealing with electricity used in railway telegraphy systems and electric railways. He was born free in Columbus, Ohio, where he completed only three years of schooling. Woods was self-educated, however, and spent considerable time in public libraries reading about electricity. After an apprenticeship as a machinist and blacksmith, Woods worked principally on railroads, becoming a locomotive engineer before founding, around 1884, the Woods Electric Company in Cincinnati, Ohio. On January 3 of that year he patented a steam boiler furnace, and on December 2 he patented a telephone transmitter. Perhaps the most advanced devices among his inventions was the Synchronous Multiplex Railway Telegraph that he patented in 1887, allowing moving trains to communicate with each other and with railroad stations to avoid accidents. Woods moved to New York in 1890 and patented an automatic air brake, which was purchased by George Westinghouse in 1902. His inventions paved the way for the development of the electric streetcar.

Granville T. Woods's numerous electrical inventions earned him the nickname "the Black Edison."

Who invented the **wooden golf tee**?

George F. Grant (1846–1910), an avid golfer, invented the wooden golf tee, receiving a patent on February 16, 1899. His invention would revolutionize the way golfers swing at the ball. Grant was a Boston native and became the second black to graduate from the Dental School at Harvard University. He became the first black member of Harvard's faculty, where he was a "demonstrator" and instructor from 1878 to 1889. He became known for his dental bridgework. One of Grant's personal patients was Harvard University president Charles William Eliot.

When were **protective devices for smoke** patented?

Garrett A. Morgan (1875–1963) was the first person to receive a patent for a safety hood and smoke protector, in 1912. He demonstrated its worth in 1916 by rescuing workers trapped in a smoke-filled tunnel of the Cleveland, Ohio, waterworks. Born on a farm near Paris, Kentucky, Morgan was one of eleven children born to a part-Indian slave mother who was freed by the Emancipation Proclamation, and a father who was the son of a Confederate colonel. Morgan moved to Cincinnati and worked as a handyman for a prosperous landowner. He hired a tutor to help him improve his grammar. In 1895 he moved to Cleveland and worked for a clothing manufacturer, adjusting sewing machines. This led to one of several businesses that he began. First Morgan sold and repaired sewing machines, and in 1909 he established the Morgan Skirt Factory, a tailoring plant with thirty-two employees. In 1913 he founded the G. A. Morgan Hair Refining Company that offered a complete line of hair-care products bearing the Morgan label. Morgan was also the first to patent a three-way automatic traffic signal, in 1923; he sold the patent to General Electric. He became known as a very astute businessman and inventor.

Who invented a **manual coupler** for **railroad cars**?

On November 23, 1897, Andrew Jackson Beard (1849–1941), of Alabama, was the first black to patent a coupling device for railroad cars, called the Janney (sometimes misspelled "Jenny") Coupler. The coupler consisted of a knuckle joined to the end of a drawbar that fastened to a mechanism on the car. The knuckled end was also designed to prevent moving cars from derailing on curved track. To engage the coupler, it was necessary for a railroader to stand between the cars and drop a pin in place when the cars came together. This was a dangerous maneuver because misalignment in the knuckles when the cars came together could lead to the loss of an arm, hand, or even death. Although coupler devices were among the most popular subjects for patents—there were some 6,500 patents by 1897—Beard was able to sell his invention for some $50,000. Beard's invention was adopted nationally in 1916; his work was so impressive that he was elected an honorary member of the Master Car Builders Association. Beard's invention made him Alabama's first black millionaire. He was a prolific inventor, receiving patents for such items as a plow and a steam engine. Beard was born a slave in Mount Pinson (now Pinson) in Jefferson County, Alabama, and was freed at age fifteen. He never learned to read or write, or to recognize his name in print. After marrying, he became a farmer near Birmingham. He built a school on his farm for his tenants, and he later built a flour mill near Hardwick. After he became a millionaire, he organized Beard's Jitney Line (a taxi service) in Birmingham and made his fleet one of the best that existed. Unfortunately, he was a poor financial manager who, with failing health in later years, ruined his own career.

Who invented a **refrigeration system** for **trucks and railroad cars**?

Frederick McKinley Jones (1892–1961) was the inventor of a practical refrigeration system for trucks and railroad cars. He received the patent on July 12, 1940. Born in Cincinnati, Ohio, his parents died early on, after which he lived in Covington, Kentucky, with a Catholic priest, Father Ryan. His formal education ended in the sixth grade. His keen interest in machines and his obsession with automobiles led him to convert ordinary cars into mint-condition racers. Jones worked as an automobile mechanic and an automobile shop foreman, and later moved to hotel maintenance. While working in a hotel, Jones met a guest from Minnesota who recognized his skills and offered him a position repairing farm equipment and cars in Hallock, Minnesota. Jones became an automobile racer, driving on the dirt track circuit until 1925. He also became movie projectionist in Hallock. By 1930 his self-taught knowledge of movie technology was so effective that he was manufacturing movie sound equipment and later invented and patented a movie ticket dispensing machine. McKinley's development of the refrigerating device marked a new direction for his efforts, and its success revolutionized the transportation and marketing of fresh foods. In 1991 he was the first black to receive the National Medal of Technology (posthumously).

Who invented the **implantable heart pacemaker**?

Otis F. Boykin (1920–1982) invented the implantable heart pacemaker—a medical contraption used to prevent heart failures; it was the most popular item of the twenty-eight different electronic and mechanical devices that he invented. The pacemaker "has helped to save and lengthen the lives of thousands of men and women around the world," and helped to make Boykin one of the greatest inventors of his time. Variations of his resistor models are used worldwide in televisions, computers, guided missiles, and radios. He received his first patent in 1959—a wire precision resistor, followed by the 1961 inexpensive

The implantable heart pacemaker that keeps many people's hearts beating these days was invented by Otis F. Boykin.

electrical resistor (U.S. patent No. 2,972,726) with the ability to withstand great temperature changes, extreme accelerations, and shocks. Not all of his works were patented; however, eleven of his inventions were patented. His achievements attracted wide attention and led to his work as electronic consultant in the United States and abroad. Boykin was born in Dallas and attended Fisk University in Nashville. He worked for several electronic firms in Chicago and did graduate study at Illinois Institute of Technology. He died of heart failure in Chicago.

Who patented a device for **detecting electromagnetic radiation**?

George Robert Carruthers (1939–) was the first black to patent an image converter for detecting electromagnetic radiation, on November 11, 1969. Born in Cincinnati, Carruthers graduated from the University of Illinois with a bachelor's degree in 1961 and a master's in 1962. After earning a doctorate in physics from that university in 1964, Carruthers began working as a researcher for the U.S. Navy and later for the National Aeronautics and Space Agency. He received the NASA Exceptional Scientific Achievement medal for his work as one of the two people responsible for the development of the lunar surface ultraviolet camera/spectrograph, which was placed on the moon in April 1972 during the Apollo 16 mission.

Who invented the **world's smallest computer**?

Cleveland native Phil Davis (c. 1960–) invented, in 2008, the world's smallest patented, personal-sized, and portable microwave oven called the iWave Cube. Although the microwave was invented in 1947, its size required that it be placed on a kitchen counter, over the range, or on a cart or table. The iWave Cube is manufactured in China by Midea, weighs twelve pounds, and measures less than twelve cubic inches. It can be used to cook popcorn, heat meals, warm beverages, cook small pizzas or small frozen entrees, or cook any small or single-sized food item. When invented, the iWave Cube used 600 watts and was relatively quiet when in operation. An American, European, or Asian plug can accommodate the machine. Early on, "Phil" Davis invented a deodorant for children. He is a graduate of Stanford University and holds an MBA from the University of Virginia.

BLACK WOMEN INVENTORS

Who was the **first** known **black women inventor**?

The first known black woman inventor is Sarah E. Goode, who patented a folding cabinet bed on July 14, 1885. Since ethnic identity is not part of a patent application, it is impossible to be absolutely sure who was the first black female inventor. Another black woman might be the first, since Ellen F. Eglin of Washington, D.C., invented a clothes wringer before April 1890. While no patent was issued in her name, Eglin sold the idea to an agent for eighteen dollars, since she believed that it would be impossible for a black woman to exploit the device successfully. At the beginning of the twentieth century, Miriam E. Benjamin of Massachusetts, patented a gong signal system for summoning attendants on July 17, July 17, 1888; her invention was adopted by the U.S. House of Representatives to summon pages. By 1892, another black woman inventor emerged. In that year Sarah Boone received a patent for an ironing board. Her invention was a narrow board with a padded cover and collapsible legs, an improvement over the existing board that was placed across chairs for support.

Who discovered and invented a **device** for **cataract surgery**?

Patricia E. Bath (1942–) discovered and invented the laserphaco probe in 1986, a new device for cataract surgery. She is also the first black woman doctor to receive a patent for a medical purpose. An ophthalmologist and laser scientist, Bath advocates for blindness prevention, treatment, and cure. She now holds four patents. In 1974 Bath became the first woman ophthalmologist to be appointed to the faculty of the University of California at Los Angeles School of Medicine Jules Stein Eye Institute. In 1983 she was the first woman to chair an ophthalmology residency program in the United States. Born in Harlem, she graduated from Hunter College and received her M.D. degree from Howard University.

What **black woman** patented a **permanent wave machine**?

Marjorie Stewart Joyner (1896–1994) was the first black to patent a permanent waving machine for hairstyling, in 1928, and became one of the first black women to receive a patent for an invention. She later developed a hair straightening comb. Joyner was an employee of Madam C. J. Walker, to whose company the patent was assigned. She eventually became national supervisor of the Walker organization's chain of beauty schools. In 1916 Joyner, the first black graduate of A. B. Molar Beauty School in Chicago, opened her own salon. In 1945 she was a cofounder of the United Beauty School Owners and Teachers Association. (The graduates of these schools belong to the Alpha Phi Omega sorority and fraternity.) She organized the first Bud Billiken Parade in 1929—a benefit for delivery carriers of the black newspaper, the *Chicago Defender*. The granddaughter of slaves, Joyner was born in the Blue Ridge Mountains near the town of Monterey, Virginia. She was one of thirteen children, only four of whom lived beyond infancy. The family relocated to Dayton, Ohio, in 1904 and soon the parents divorced. Joyner lived with one family member and then another, finally settling in Chicago with her mother. Her high school education was interrupted until 1935, when she finally graduated. In the meantime, she received a music school certificate in 1924. It was not until 1973, when she was seventy-seven years old, that she received her bachelor's degree from Bethune-Cookman College (now University) in Florida. There she was often called the "Godmother of Bethune-Cookman College." She was also called the "Grand Dame of Black Beauty Culture." Among her various honors, in 1990 the city of Chicago honored

her by naming her birthday Marjorie Stewart Joyner Day

MEDICINE

Who were some **self-trained medical practitioners** during slavery?

There were many self-trained practitioners during the slavery period. As early as 1740, a fugitive slave named Simon was identified as a "doctor among his people." He was able "to bleed and draw teeth." Another, Joseph Ferguson, a barber in Richmond, Virginia, was a competent leecher and cupper, and later on studied and practiced medicine. Midwifery and folk cures, practiced in the slaves' former homeland of Africa, were common practices. There were also black pharmacists; for example, Wilcie Elfe of Charles, South Carolina, kept a prescription book dated 1853, which showed that he formulated many drug recipes. His drunkard master trained him and he became so proficient that he managed his master's drug store. Elfe's patented drugs were sold throughout South Carolina. While some slaves who were medical practitioners were so respected by their masters that the masters permitted them to buy their freedoms, others became so famous for their remedies that their masters actually granted them freedom. For example, Sir William Gooch of Virginia reported, in 1729, that a very old black man who performed "wondrous cures of diseases" sold his concoction of roots and bark in return for his freedom. Likewise, the General Assembly of South Carolina freed a black practitioner named Cesar, for discovering a remedy to cure rattlesnake bite. He was also granted an annual stipend of one hundred pounds of sterling for publishing his prescription in the *South Carolina Gazette* on February 25, 1751, so that the general public could benefit from his remedy. His cure was widely publicized beyond the state, appearing in the press in Philadelphia and in Massachusetts.

Who was America's **first black physician**?

By the 1780s James Durham (some sources say Derham; c. 1762–?) was the first regularly recognized black physician in the United States. Later he was recognized as "more than an ordinary physician." Born a slave in Philadelphia, his early masters taught him the fundamentals of reading and writing. After he was sold to John Kearsley Jr., a successful Philadelphia practitioner and an authority on sore throat distempers, his new master taught him medicine that was in line with medical training of that time, which primarily consisted of mixing drugs and handling patients. He was owned by a number of physicians, ending up in New Orleans with a Scottish physician, who hired him to perform many medical services. His master was so impressed with Durham's medical competence that he permitted him to buy his freedom in 1783. Durham built a flourishing practice in New Orleans and had both black and white patients. Durham also became a superb linguist and was fluent in both French and Spanish. He treated patients with diphtheria and was instrumental in helping to contain the yellow fever epidemic that ravaged New Orleans in 1796. His knowledge of medicine had deepened and he developed into an authority on the relationship of disease to climate. In 1801 the city council restricted him because he was unlicensed and untrained.

Did slaves practice medicine?

Issues of health and healing have helped to shape the African-American experience since the first Africans came to America. Inhuman conditions on slave ships, and later inadequate, crowded, and unsanitary living conditions caused slaves great concern. Enslaved Africans in the United States brought with them from their homeland knowledge of herbs, barks, and other items found in everyday life and successfully developed many useful medicines that black and white practitioners used early on. They knew that a wide variety of mineral, plant, and herbal concoctions had medicinal value. Although plantation rules were stringent, slaves chose self-treatment or medicine dispensed by herb or root healers. They believed that many of their illnesses were caused by demons and therefore sought such curative measures as charms, incantations, and rituals that required medicine men and "conjure women" to drive away evil spirits. To them, demons were the cause of many illnesses prevalent during that period.

What was the **general health status** of **slaves**?

Because of the living and working conditions of slaves, they needed constant medical care. They lived in poor housing, under unsanitary conditions, and had an inadequate diet. Their living quarters were wooden huts with leaky roofs, and their broken-down cabins consisted of a single room of about twenty feet square where entire families—sometimes several families—lived. Their cabins had little or no ventilation nor a privy for their most private needs. Diets were meager, consisting of hominy and bacon. Clothing was of poor quality, with trousers, jackets, and dresses made of coarse wool and cotton. Masters spent as little as possible on food and housing of their slaves. Thus, the overall living conditions of slaves had an adverse effect on the health of plantation hands, who had started their work as early as age eight or nine and reached their maximum efficiency by the time they were in their early youth. They worked from sunrise to sunset. Such conditions, however, at times prompted slaves to fake illnesses, engage in work slow-downs, break tools, engage in self-mutilation, or engage in other tactics in their struggle against slavery and the conditions imposed on them. Slaves did suffer from genuine illnesses, such as smallpox, measles, pleurisy, cholera, whooping cough, and other diseases that were of such virulence as to cause many to miss a number of work days. The overcrowded and unsanitary living quarters, a bare subsistence diet, inadequate health care, and long and arduous work resulted in a shorter life expectancy for slaves than for their white masters and their families. Even so, records of slave deaths were unreliable and often unreported, far more so than those of whites. Some say that "the disparity between slave and white death rates was greater and not less than recorded in the census returns."

What **free blacks practiced medicine** in the **antebellum North**?

A handful of free blacks practiced medicine in the antebellum North, yet they cannot be described as forming a professional class. In the tradition of the time, they were self-taught, apprentice-trained, or college educated. Those who were self-instructed included James Still (1812–1882) of New Jersey, whose contemporaries called him the "black doctor" and "doctor of the pines." He was born in Indian Mill (or Mills), Burlington County, New Jersey, the son of a former slave who had purchased his freedom from his master in Maryland; later the family moved to Lumberton, where Still spent the remainder of his life. His two brothers, William and Peter, were prominent abolitionists: William became an agent on the Underground Railroad while Peter became the author of *The Kidnapped and the Ransomed*. James Still had very little education but a desire to be a doctor. In 1843, when he was thirty-one, he began to make medicines to sell in his neighborhood. He bought his first medical books soon afterward, but began to practice medicine quite by accident when his medicine cured a neighbor's daughter of scrofula. Still's practice grew and so did his reputation as a successful practitioner. Even charges against him for practicing without a license were dropped. His practice grew large, consisting of both white and black patients who flocked to his office; he used his horse and buggy to visit others in the deep woods.

Who were some other **self-taught healers** of the **North**?

Among the self-taught healers of this period who had little medical background were John P. Reynolds, David Ruggles, and William Wells Brown. They "helped many and harmed few." Reynolds gained his knowledge in the late 1820s from an "Indian physician" and built a thriving practice in Zanesville, Ohio, and later in Vincennes, Indiana. He was held in high esteem, became quite wealthy, and had considerable local influence. He belonged to a group called the "eclectic" school of medicine, which comprised physicians in colonial America and those among the Native Americans. Like slave healers, they believed in native remedies such as in plants and herbs. They formed an organization in 1840, which became known as the Eclectic Medical Association; it existed for about thirty years.

One of the best-recognized names among self-taught healers of this period was David Ruggles (1810–1849), who became an ardent abolitionist. He was the first known black bookseller and sold anti-slavery works, among other items. Ruggles was born in Norwich, Connecticut, the son of free parents, and educated in schools founded by emancipation societies. He worked extremely hard as an abolitionist, but by age thirty-five his health began to fail. So impressed was Ruggles with German-born Robert Wesselhoeft, a hydrotherapist in Cambridge, that he decided to become a hydropathic doctor himself. Aided by some friends, in 1846 Ruggles opened a hydrotherapeutic institution in Northampton. Although he lacked a license and a medical degree, he became a highly successful practitioner. His business, "Dr. Ruggles' Water-Cure Establishment," attracted doctors, clergy, artisans, and abolitionists who sought his treatment. Among his clients was anti-slavery leader William Lloyd Garrison. Another abolitionist-turned medical practitioner was William Wells Brown (1814–1884), who is perhaps best known as the first black novelist. In 1853 his novel, *Clotel; or, The President's Daughter: A Narrative of Slave Life in the United States,* was published in England. Brown was born near Lexington, Kentucky, to slave parents. In 1816 he was taken to St. Louis where he was exposed to the rudiments of medicine. When he was eighteen years old, he escaped to Ohio and became active in the abolitionist movement as an agent of the Underground Railroad, and as lecturer and writer. His work took him to England in 1849, where he became friendly with distinguished ophthalmologist and anti-slavery advocate John Bishop Estlin. Estlin urged Brown to resume his study of medicine, and he did so when he returned to Boston. In 1865 he opened his office and established his practice. He, too, was a member of the "eclectic" school of medicine, but apparently never had a large or successful practice.

Who were some of the **early black physicians** trained by **apprenticeship** or in **schools**?

Among the early trained physicians were those who, in the fashion of the day, were educated by apprenticeship or in professional schools. These included Charles Dunbar of New York, who studied under a Dr. Childs, and Daniel Laing Jr. and Isaac Humphrey Snowden, who worked under a Dr. Clark in Boston. There was also a more familiar name, John Sweat Rock (1825–1866), who became an abolitionist, a lawyer, and the first black man admitted to practice before the U.S. Supreme Court. A native of Salem, New Jersey, Rock studied medicine under a Dr. Shaw and a Dr. Gibbon. He was denied admission to a medical school in Philadelphia because of his race; then he studied dentistry under a Dr. Hubbard and opened an office in 1850. In 1852 he was admitted to the American Medical College in Philadelphia. After graduating, he practiced dentistry as well as medicine but left his practice because of ill health. Martin Robison Delany (1812–1885), best known as editor and publisher of the newspaper *Mystery* and as an abolitionist, was born in Charlestown, Virginia; the family later moved to Chambersburg, Pennsylvania. Delany joined abolitionist Frederick Douglass as co-editor of the celebrated *North Star* newspaper. He studied medicine, serving as apprentice to several distinguished physicians in Pittsburgh. He was denied admission to several medical schools because of his race, despite the fact that he had studied under prominent physicians. Delany was finally admitted to the Harvard Medical School in 1850–1851 but apparently failed to return to complete his studies. He returned to Pittsburgh and distinguished himself as a medical practitioner during the 1854 cholera epidemic. He became known also for his book *Condition, Elevation, Emigration, and Destiny of the Colored People of the United States, Politically Considered.*

Other professionally trained physicians included David J. Peck, graduate in 1847 of Rush Medical College in Chicago; John V. De Grasse of New York and Thomas J. White of Brooklyn, who received medical degrees from Bowdoin in Maine; James J. Gould Bias, who in the early 1850s graduated from the Eclectic Medical College in Philadelphia; Robert B. Leach, graduate of the Homeopathic College in Cleveland in the early 1850s; James McCune Smith, who received his medical degree in 1837 from the University of Glasgow; and Alexander Thomas Augusta (1825–1890), who received a bachelor of medicine degree from Trinity Medical College in Toronto, Canada.

Who was the **first black doctor** to perform successful **open heart surgery**?

Daniel Hale Williams (1856–1931) performed the world's first successful open heart operation on July 9, 1893. The open heart surgery took place at Provident Hospital in Chicago, a hospital that Williams founded. He opened the chest of James Cornish, a laborer who had been stabbed, found the pericardial sac, emptied it of blood, and successfully sutured it. "Doctor Dan" was a founder and first vice president of the National Medical Association, and the first and only black invited to become a charter member of the American College of Surgeons in 1913. Born in Hollidays-

The first black doctor to perform open heart surgery was Daniel Hale Williams.

burg, Pennsylvania, Williams graduated in 1883 from the Chicago Medical College. He founded Provident Hospital in 1891, the nation's first interracial hospital. He was the first black on the Illinois State Board of Health in 1889, and in 1893 he was appointed surgeon-in-chief of Freedman's Hospital, where he reorganized the services and established a nursing school. Williams had two main interests: the NAACP and the construction of hospitals and training schools for African-American doctors and nurses.

Where was the **first black medical school**?

The establishment of black medical schools in the United States dates back to the period after the Civil War. Although they were established to train black physicians, these schools did not discriminate in enrollment by race or gender and admitted black and white women at a time when discriminatory practices were observed at most white medical schools. Howard University in Washington, D.C., was the first historically black institution to establish a medical school, in 1868, one year after the university was founded. Over the next four decades at least thirteen other black institutions followed. Notable among these is Meharry Medical College, founded in 1876; it is the oldest surviving black medical school in the South.

What was the **funding base** of the **early black medical schools**?

Early medical schools were either church-related schools affiliated with black colleges or proprietary, for-profit, schools. The First Congregational Church in Washington,

D.C., figured prominently in the beginning of Howard and its medical school. Presbyterians founded a medical school at Lincoln University in 1870, and Meharry Medical College began as a division of Central Tennessee College, which had been founded by the Freedman's Aid Society of the Methodist Episcopal Church. Shaw University in Raleigh, founded in 1865, was affiliated with the Baptist Church; its medical school, Leonard Medical School, began in 1882 and became the South's first four-year medical school. Proprietary institutions (which operated as for-profit organizations) were, for the most part, established by blacks. Medical schools in this group included Louisville National Medical College, established in 1888, and the University of West Tennessee College of Physicians, founded in 1891. Today the four existing historically black medical schools are Howard University College of Medicine, Meharry Medical College, Charles Drew University of Medicine and Science in Los Angeles, and Morehouse School of Medicine in Atlanta.

Who helped to strengthen **Howard University's medical school** early on?

Numa Pompilius Garfield Adams (1885–1940), a 1924 graduate of Rush Medical College in Chicago, became dean of Howard University's College of Medicine in 1929 and immediately played a leading role in its development. He assembled the first ever all-black medical faculty, upgraded salaries and professional opportunities of physicians associated with the school, and raised the level of medical instruction and departmental morale.

Who was called the **"Father of Blood Plasma"**?

Charles Richard Drew (1904–1950) was the first person to set up a blood bank, in 1940. His work made him internationally prominent and earned him the title "Father of Blood Plasma." Born in Washington, D.C., Drew graduated from Amherst College in 1926. He also coached and taught at Morgan State College (later University), received his medical degree from McGill University in 1933, and taught pathology at Howard University in 1935. Drew's research at the Columbia Medical Center in New York City led to the discovery that blood plasma could supplant whole blood in transfusions. He set up and administered the British blood bank from 1940 to 1941, then the American Red Cross project to collect and store blood. Drew was dropped from the American Red Cross project because he objected to the policy of refusing the blood of black donors. He asserted that there was no scientific difference between the blood of blacks and whites. His research was responsible for saving numerous lives during World War II. He was awarded the NAACP's Spingarn Medal, as well as other tributes. While accounts vary concerning his care after an automobile accident near Burlington, North Carolina, according to the *New York Times,* he died at a segregated hospital "that had no blood plasma that might have saved his life."

What was the **"Tuskegee Syphilis Experiment"**?

Historically, much medical experimentation has been enacted on poor people, both
black and white. Between 1932 and 1972 the Public Health Service conducted what

Dr. Charles Richard Drew (top right, sitting on a table) talks with colleagues at the Moorland-Spingarn Research Center. Dr. Drew invented the process that separates plasma from red blood cells, saving uncounted lives. Ironically, he died of blood loss after an automobile accident because he was sent to a segregated hospital that had no blood plasma that might have saved his life.

has been called "one of the most outrageous abuses of African Americans in this period"—a research project throughout Macon County, Alabama, that focused on patients with untreated syphilis. Participants included more than six hundred infected and uninfected black men. The men were primarily impoverished sharecroppers or day laborers. Treatment for syphilis was withheld even though penicillin was determined to be an effective drug for treatment of the disease. Participants were offered free medical care, free meals, expenses of burial, and other inducements that have been called unethical, but they were unaware of the risks, including possibility of death. There is no evidence to suggest that the men gave "informed consent." The Public Health Service sought continued cooperation from the groups and thus worked through Tuskegee Institute (now University) in Alabama and the Tuskegee Veterans Hospital. Some one hundred men died, forty wives were infected, and nineteen children were born infected. The project became known by different names: the Tuskegee Study, the Tuskegee Syphilis Experiment, the Tuskegee Experiment, and the Tuskegee Study of Untreated Syphilis in the Negro Male. By the 1970s, the study, previously kept silent, was made public, and it was discontinued in 1972. In 1974 the federal government initiated reparation payments to the few survivors. President Bill Clinton apologized to the eight who had survived until 1997, calling the actions of those responsible for the study "clearly racist."

This is a group of men who were test subjects in the now-infamous Tuskegee Syphilis Experiment. In the 1970s, the truth about how men and women were the victims of a deadly experiment was released to the public.

Who is **Benjamin Carson?**

Benjamin Solomon Carson (1951–) gained international acclaim when he separated seven-month-old West German twins who were conjoined at the backs of their heads. On September 6, 1987, Carson led a seventy-member surgical team in a twenty-two-hour operation at Johns Hopkins Hospital in Baltimore to perform the first successful operation of this kind. Carson was born in Detroit and raised in an inner city neighborhood. He received his bachelor's degree from Yale University in 1973 and his medical degree from the University of Michigan in 1977. After completing an internship at Johns Hopkins Hospital, Carson moved to Western Australia and became senior neurosurgical resident at the Sir Charles Gairdner Hospital, a leading center for brain surgery. In 1985 he returned to Johns Hopkins, became one of its leading surgeons, and, at age thirty-four, was promoted to director of pediatric neurosurgery, becoming one of the youngest such directors in the country. He became especially successful in performing high-risk operations. The life story of Carson, based on the best-selling book *Gifted Hands: The Ben Carson Story*, was made into a television movie and aired on TNT on February 7, 2009. President George W. Bush awarded Carson the Presidential Medal of Freedom in 2008 "for his skills as a surgeon, high moral standards and dedication to helping others."

Who was the **first** African American to receive a **medical degree?**

James McCune Smith (1811–1865) was the first black to obtain a medical degree, in 1837. Born in New York City, he studied at the African Free School in New York, where

What is black America's attitude toward medical experiments?

According to the book *Medical Apartheid* (2006), research was conducted on black prisoners between the 1950s and 1970s. By the 1970s, however, such research began to wane. In recent years there have been "medications marketed for 'genetically distinct' populations of African Americans." *Medical Apartheid* also notes that medical research "has not spared black children its very worse abuses in the name of scientific research." Black children have been recruited "primarily or exclusively" for medical experiments, focusing on such areas as violent behavior in families and experimental vaccines. A recent study revealed that medical experiments on the black poor continue. The book *The Immortal Life of Henrietta Lacks,* published in 2010, recounts the use of an African-American family's cells for research and profit. The study was conducted without informed consent. Some believe that the study, as well as documentation of early experiments, reinforces black America's lack of confidence in medical experimentation and treatment.

he was so gifted a student that when Lafayette visited the United States in 1824, the young Smith delivered the welcome address. Unable to pursue his education in the United States because no college was open to him, Smith studied at the University of Glasgow in Scotland, where he received his bachelor's, master's, and medical degrees. He was a very successful physician in New York, with a busy practice and two pharmacies where he trained several black pharmacists. Sometimes Smith was accused of elitism and snobbery because of his wealth and his mansion on Sixth Avenue. He served on the staff of the Free Negro Orphan Asylum for twenty years. An avid abolitionist, he supported the Underground Railroad and was especially involved in the movement for black manhood suffrage in the state. Smith and Henry Highland Garnet (1815–1882) argued before the state legislature in 1841, demanding the removal of restrictions to black manhood suffrage. Smith also supported women's suffrage, calling for a state women's rights convention to be held in Rochester. Prominent in education and journalism as well, in 1838 he assumed editorial responsibility for the *Colored American*. He resigned in June 1839 and became an unpaid columnist for Frederick Douglass' paper. In 1859 he launched the *Weekly Anglo-American,* a short-lived publication.

Who was the nation's **first black psychiatrist**?

Solomon Carter Fuller Jr. (1872–1953) became the nation's first black psychiatrist, in 1897. He was also one of the first black physicians to teach on the faculty of a multiracial medical school in the United States, the University of Boston School of Medicine. Fuller was born in Monrovia, Liberia, and received his bachelor's degree in 1893 from Livingstone College in Salisbury, North Carolina. He earned his medical degree from Boston University Medical School in 1897. That same year he was an intern in the pathology laboratory of Westborough State Hospital for the Insane. He was named head of pathology in 1899 and served in that position until 1919. Still with the hospital, he became a faculty member in the pathology department at Boston University's medical school in 1899, and in 1904 he took a sabbatical for one year of study at the University of Munich in Germany. There he studied psychiatry with influential neuropsychiatrist Emil Kraepelin. In 1919 Fuller taught full-time at the medical school but later retired because of racism. He was denied status as a full professor and, although he was the functioning head of the Department of Neurology, that title was never assigned to him. When the school promoted a white assistant professor to full professor and department head, Fuller had had enough. He retired in 1933 and worked in a succession of part-time posts. He had suffered from diabetes for some time, and beginning in 1942 his eyesight began to fail. Still, he accepted psychiatric patients and gave up all else except a positive attitude on life. In 1909 Fuller married Meta Vaux Warrick, a talented sculptor who had studied with Paul Rodin in Paris.

BLACK WOMEN IN MEDICINE

Who was the **first black woman** to receive a **medical degree** in the United States?

Rebecca Davis Lee Crumpler (1831–1895) was the first black woman awarded a medical degree in the United States. Born in Richmond, Virginia, she was raised in Philadelphia by an aunt. By 1852 she had moved to Charlestown, Massachusetts, and worked as a nurse until 1860. She completed the four-year medical program at the New England Female Medical College in Boston, and on March 11, 1864, she was awarded the doctress of medicine degree. She married, and at the end of the Civil War returned to Richmond to work with the Freedmen's Bureau, providing health care and treatment to newly freed blacks who had no medical provisions. After returning to Boston in 1869, she may have continued her practice; whatever the case, there is no indication that she was in active practice after 1883. Crumpler's interest in women and children led her to publish, in 1883, a two-part work of advice, *Book of Medical Discourses*. In honor of her pioneering work in the medical profession, the first medical society for black women was founded and named the Rebecca Lee Society.

Who was the **first black woman dentist**?

In 1890 Ida Gray Nelson Rollins (1867–1953) became the first black woman to earn a doctor of dental surgery degree in the United States. She graduated from the University of Michigan in June. Nelson Rollins was born in Clarksville, Tennessee. Her family arranged for her to live in Cincinnati with a relative, Caroline Gray. Around 1860 she worked in the office of Jonathan Taft, a local dentist of prominence who had supported women in the dental profession. When he became dean of the Dental Department at the University of Michigan, he maintained his office in Cincinnati and thus kept in touch with Nelson Rollins. Taft encouraged her to apply to the dental school, knowing that her experience in his office would help her to pass the entrance examinations. She enrolled in October 1887 and graduated in June 1890, then returned to Cincinnati where she established a dental practice. There she served all races and ages, women and men. After she married in 1895, she moved to Chicago and opened an office there. Although sources give conflicting information, she appears to be the first black woman to establish a dental practice in Chicago.

What **black women** were the first to receive the **doctoral degree in veterinary medicine**?

The first two black women to graduate from veterinary school and to receive the doctorate in veterinary medicine degree were Jane Hinton (c. 1920–) and Alfreda Johnson Webb (1923–1992); both graduated in 1949. Hinton received her degree from the University of Pennsylvania School of Veterinary Medicine. Her father was William Augustus Hinton, a medical researcher at Harvard who invented the Hinton Test (an accurate test for syphilis). After serving as a technician in Arizona during World War II, Jane Hinton pursued her degree in veterinary medicine. She graduated and returned to her home in Canton, Massachusetts, and worked in Framingham as a practitioner for small animals. She later became an inspector for the federal government, working in Framingham Center, Massachusetts. Alfreda Johnson Webb was born in Mobile, Alabama, and received her bachelor's degree from Tuskegee Institute (now University) in 1943. Tuskegee established its veterinary school that same year; it remains the only such school on a black college campus. The school was established specifically to train black veterinarians. After receiving her veterinary degree from Tuskegee, Webb completed her master's degree at Michigan State University in 1951 and went on to teach and conduct research. She moved to Greensboro, North Carolina, and taught at North Carolina Agricultural and Technical State College (now University). She also became a renowned anatomist.

AEROSPACE

Who were America's **early black pilots**?

Among the early black pilots in America were Eugene J. Bullard, who in 1917 flew for the French. In the late 1920s, A. David Porter and James Herman Banning obtained their licenses and became pilots as well. Banning and Thomas C. Allen made the first transcontinental flight by blacks, in 1932, when they flew from Los Angeles to New York. In 1933 C. Alfred Anderson and Albert E. Forsythe made a round-trip cross-country flight from New Jersey to Los Angeles.

Who was America's **first black female aviator**?

In 1921 Bessie Coleman (1893–1926) became the first black woman aviator to gain an international pilot's license from the Fédération Aéronautique Internationale.

American pilot Eugene J. Bullard flew for the French during World War I.

Coleman, who envisioned opening a flight school, was also the first black woman "barnstormer," or stunt pilot. In May 1922 she went to Europe for advanced training in stunt flying and parachute jumping, receiving training in France, Holland, Germany, and Switzerland. When she returned to Chicago, the *Chicago Defender* became her sponsor. On Labor Day 1922, Coleman gave her first exhibition in the United States, at Garden City, Long Island, New York. In October of that year she performed in the Chicago region and gave successful exhibitions throughout the Midwest. From 1922 to 1926 she lectured in Texas, Florida, and elsewhere, refusing to perform if the audiences were segregated. She prepared for a barnstorming show in Jacksonville, Florida, to be held on April 30, 1926, as a fundraiser for the Negro Welfare League. When Coleman and her co-pilot, William D. Wills, tried out their open-air plane in preparation for the exhibition, the equipment malfunctioned and both died as a result. Coleman was born in Atlanta, Texas, one of thirteen children. While Coleman was still a young child, the family relocated to Waxahachie, Texas. She loved to read biographies of black achievers. She spent one year at the Teacher's College in Langston, Oklahoma, but dropped out for financial reasons. Sometime between 1915 and 1917 Coleman moved to Chicago where her brothers John and Walter lived. There she studied at Burham's School of Beauty Culture where she learned the beauty trade. She worked as a manicurist at a barbershop near Comiskey Park, where the White Sox played baseball. She earned enough income to relocate her mother and other family members to Chicago in 1917. Coleman heard stories from the men in the barbershop about black aviators in the armed services and those serving with French units. She became so curious about their activities that she read as many articles about black aviators as she could find. After learning that there were women pilots in France and that some American women were pilots as well, she developed an interest in learning to fly. She was encouraged to study in France and entered the most famous flight school in that country. In 1995 the U.S. Postal Service issued a stamp in the Black Heritage Series honoring Coleman.

Daring pilot Bessie Coleman was a famous barnstormer in the 1920s.

Who was the **first black woman** to hold a **commercial pilot's license**?

In 1934 Willa Brown-Chappell (1906–1 992) became the first black woman in the United States to hold a commercial pilot's license, and the first black woman to gain officer rank (lieutenant) in the Civil Air Patrol Squadron. In 1937 Brown-Chappell and Cornelius R. Coffee, who was her flight instructor and also became her husband, formed the National Airmen's Association of America, the first black aviators' group. Its mission was to promote black aviation. In 1972 Brown-Chappell was the first black member of the Federal Aviation Agency's Women's Advisory Commission. Brown-Chappell was born in Glasgow, Kentucky, and relocated to Indianapolis with her family when she was about six years old. Still later the family moved to Terre Haute, Indiana. In 1927 she graduated from Indiana State Teachers College and then taught school in Gary, Indiana. Five years later she moved to Chicago and taught in the local schools. She began graduate study at Northwestern University in 1934, graduating three years later. While at Northwestern Brown-Chappell developed an interest in aviation and began to take flying lessons. Her friend, aviator Bessie Coleman, had inspired her. In 1935 she received a master mechanic's certificate from the Aeronautical University located in the Chicago Loop. After obtaining her private pilot's license, she became affiliated with a flight service at Harlem Airport and gave short entertainment jaunts for those who would pay one dollar for the ride. After Brown-Chappell, her husband Cornelius R. Coffee, and journalist Enoc P. Waters Jr. founded the National Airmen's Association of America in 1939, she was elected national secretary of the organization. She also began to teach aviation in the Works Progress Administration's Adult Education Program and worked to stimulate blacks to prepare for careers in aviation through the children's flight clubs that she founded. In the early 1940s Brown-Chappell taught aviation mechanics in the Chicago schools. In 1946 she was the first black woman to run for a congressional seat, but was unsuccessful in her bid.

Who were the **first blacks** appointed to the **space program**?

America's space program selected several blacks to be trained as astronauts. On March 3, 1963, Edward Joseph Dwight Jr. became the first black astronaut candidate. He was dropped from the program in 1965. Robert H. Lawrence Jr. (1935–1967) was named the first black astronaut in 1963 and assigned to the Manned Orbiting Laboratory. He died in a plane crash on December 8, 1967, never starting his mission. The Chicago native grew up on the city's South Side. He received his U.S. Air Force commission and a bachelor's degree in chemistry from Bradley University in 1956. He completed a doctorate in physical chemistry at The Ohio State University. He

Though Air Force Major Robert H. Lawrence Jr. was named America's first black astronaut, he perished in a plane crash in 1967 before he could go into space.

was officially recognized as an astronaut thirty years after his death. After a long bureaucratic dispute over the definition of an astronaut, in December 1997 Dwight's name was added to the astronaut's memorial at Kennedy Space Center. The space program had no other black astronauts until 1978, when Guion S. Bluford Jr., Frederick Drew Gregory, and Ronald E. McNair joined the program.

Who was **Ronald McNair**?

On January 20, 1986, Ronald McNair (1950–1986) was the first black astronaut killed during a space mission, when the space shuttle *Challenger* met disaster, exploding shortly after liftoff. He was also the nation's second black astronaut to travel in space. McNair was born in Lake City, South Carolina, and was able to read and write by age three. He received his bachelor's degree from North Carolina Agricultural and Technical State University in Greensboro in 1971 and received a scholarship to Massachusetts Institute of Technology where he received his doctorate magna cum laude in 1976. McNair then joined Hughes Research Laboratories in Malibu, California, as a researcher. He joined the space program on invitation from the National Aeronautics and Space Administration in 1978. McNair completed training and evaluation as a shuttle mission specialist and then worked at the Shuttle Avionics Integration Laboratory. He made three space flights in 1984. While these were rather routine flights, the mission flight scheduled for January 28, 1986, was a high-profile event—it would carry the first private citizen into space, teacher Christa McAuliffe. McNair was mission specialist. As millions of television viewers watched the rocket bearing the shuttle liftoff at 11:38 A.M. and climb nearly nine miles, a sudden explosion seventy-three seconds later killed all seven on board, devastated witnesses, and challenged the U.S. space program. Later, Morton Thiokol, manufacturer of the O-rings used in the shuttle, was charged with negligence for knowingly using a defective design and failing to advise astronauts of the problem.

Who was America's **first black astronaut** to make a **space flight**?

On August 30, 1983, Guion (Guy) Stewart Bluford Jr. (1942–) was the first black American astronaut to make a space flight. He made his maiden voyage into space on the STS-8, the shuttle's eighth mission. He worked the remote manipulator system,

The first black American astronaut to actually fly into space was Guy Bluford Jr. (above). The honor of first black man in the world to go into outer space, however, belongs to Arnaldo Tamayo Méndez, a Cuban cosmonaut who flew on a Soviet mission.

Spacelab-3 experiments, shuttle systems, Shuttle Avionics Integration Laboratory, and the Flight Systems Laboratory. He went on to make two more flights and spent 314 hours in space before retiring from the program in 1993. A native of Philadelphia, Pennsylvania, Bluford received his doctorate in aerospace engineering from the Air Force Institute of Technology in 1978. He had earned his wings in 1965. He was the second black in space; a black Cuban named Arnaldo Tamayo Méndez had previously flown on a Soviet mission.

Who was America's **first black woman astronaut**?

Mae C. Jemison (1956–) was named the first black woman astronaut in 1987. On September 12, 1992, she boarded the space shuttle *Endeavor* as science mission specialist on the historic eight-day flight. Jemison left the National Aeronautic and Space Administration in 1993 and founded a private firm, the Jemison Group. The firm specializes in projects that integrate science issues into the design, development, and implementation of technologies. She also became professor of environmental studies at Dartmouth College, from 1995 to 2002. She directs the Jemison Institute for Advancing Technology in Developing Countries. Jemison was born in Decatur, Alabama, and moved to Chicago with her family when she was three years old. She graduated from Stanford University in 1977 with a degree in chemical engineering and Afro-American studies. Jemison received her medical degree from Cornell Medical School in 1981. She worked as a staff physician for the Peace Corps for two and a half years in Sierra Leone. Jemison, who has received numerous awards and accolades, has also appeared on television multiple times, including a guest spot on *Star Trek: The Next Generation*. She is currently professor-at-large at Cornell University.

The first African American woman in space, Dr. Mae C. Jemison.

Who was the first black to **lead NASA's space program**?

The first in a series of joint ventures between the United States and Russian space programs began on February 3 and ended on April 11, 1994. Black commander Charles Frank Bolden Jr. (1946–) was the first black to lead the National Aeronautics and Space Administration's shuttle *Discovery* mission on such a joint venture. In 2009 Bolden became the first African American to lead the NASA space program. With that appointment, Bolden became America's leading voice for space exploration. He also became the twelfth administrator of the agency, with responsibility for managing NASA's resources as well as advancing its mission and goals. President Barack Obama appointed the highly decorated and highly regarded Bolden to the position, and on July 15 the Senate confirmed his appointment. Of his experiences in space, Bolden said "I never dreamed of being an astronaut," but admitted that astronaut Ronald McNair encouraged him to apply for the space program. "And had it not been for him, who knows what I would have been doing now, but I wouldn't have been sitting here as NASA administrator." NASA's manned space program ended in July 2011.

Born in Columbia, South Carolina, Bolden graduated from the U.S. Naval Academy in 1968, became a second lieutenant in the Marine Corps, and fought in Vietnam where he flew over one hundred combat missions. He received his master's degree from the University of Southern California in 1977. He was a candidate for the National Aeronautic and Space Administration (NASA) from 1980 to 1981 and did systems development group work for NASA. Bolden held several positions with NASA, including serving as special assistant to the director and pilot on the STS 61-C for Johnson Space Administration. He was commander for STS-60, the Russian/American Space Shuttle Mission. In May 2006 he was inducted into the Astronaut Hall of Fame.

SPORTS

AFRICAN–AMERICAN SPORTS HISTORY

Who was called the **"Father of Black Sport History"**?

Edwin Bancroft Henderson (1883–1977) was the first to initiate an examination of African Americans in sport. While teaching physical education in the segregated school system in Washington, D.C., in the 1920s, he also helped to form several African-American sports organizations. A prolific writer, numerous academicians have used his works to develop publications of their own. As result, for over half a century nearly every article, book chapter, or history about African-American athletes has been influenced by his work. His book, *The Negro in Sports,* published in 1939, is the first published survey on African Americans in sports. His writings aimed to foster pride among African Americans and alter white beliefs about race. His works centered on black athletes who played in both segregated and white organized sports during the late nineteenth and early twentieth centuries. Henderson's pioneering efforts earned him the much-deserved title "Father of Black Sport History." Because he introduced basketball in the black Washington, D.C., schools in 1904, he has also been given the moniker "Grandfather of Black Basketball." He was a civil rights activist as well.

EMERGENCE OF THE BLACK ATHLETE

How were **sports** practiced among **African warrior-athletes**?

Although the first European slavers came from the southern rim of Africa, they had little to do with the emergence and practice of sports in Africa, as sports were already well-woven into the social fabric of daily life. Every child in Africa participated in sports as a

337

part of their upbringing; thus, it is commonly assumed that Africans brought their athletic prowess with them when they came to the New World as slaves. Africans also enjoyed contests that were often connected to "religious ceremonies, fertility rites, rites of passage, or entertainment of visitors." They engaged in stick fighting, then a sport second only to wrestling. Some showed prowess with a bow and arrow—considered a prized military art and used also to kill animals for food. Above all of this, however, the most honored contestant was the champion wrestler. Africans also practiced gymnastics, and the sport was sometimes held at night under a full moon, where very intricate acts of physical contortion were demonstrated.

SPORTS IN THE TIME OF SLAVERY

What **legal regulations** impacted **slave sports**?

The religious beliefs of African slaves and indentured servants, who were the first to come to the United States, restricted their practice of sports. Some believe that slaves had more in common with Native Americans in their love and practice of sports than with white Europeans. Native Americans also had more free time on their hands than blacks, and their sports were not restricted by religious beliefs. As sports activities threatened to disrupt the daily life of the colonists, colonial governors allowed field days for whites only, in an effort to keep control of the sports activities. Slaves were allowed to train gamecocks and horses, and to work in taverns (then called "ordinaries"). Before the Revolutionary War, slaves ran races, swam, engaged in stick fights, wrestled, boxed, and played ball games—all activities that they knew from their motherland.

What **free black** left a **valuable account** of the **sporting life** of **slaves before the Civil War**?

William Tiler Johnson (1809–1851), a slave who had been freed, was a barber and slave owner who lived in Natchez, Mississippi. He kept a diary of his important business affairs; his writings from 1835 to 1851 are the first known account written by a black man and documents sports activities of himself and his peers. He writes about how he "negotiated a society of racial limitations and discrimination while embracing many white aristocratic values." His diaries are one of the few extant records that provide extensive insight into the social and economic history of slaves. He documented his wins and losses in business as well as in the games that he played, such as "shuffleboard, checkers, quoits, marbles, billiards, and cards." He was competitive in hunting, fishing, and horse racing, and also engaged in lotteries and raffles. Johnson documented his attendance at horse races, mule races, and cockfights. He practiced the sport of broad jumping against his sons. He and other free blacks of means were allowed to race their own horses, which were the slower, non-thoroughbred type. Whites who owed the race tracks often rented out their courses on weekdays for those who could pay the fee.

In **what sports** were blacks involved **before the Civil War**?

Before the Civil War, free blacks and slaves engaged in numerous sports. Horse racing, boat racing, and pedestrian events drew large numbers of crowds, both black and white, and the events were well-mixed by gender. Blacks were especially involved in horse racing, and the best jockeys and horse trainers were black. Most jockeys in the South around 1800 were diminutive slaves who had grown up around horses and knew how to handle them well. In the North, however, English jockeys were imported, or local whites were used as jockeys. Around 1806 "Monkey" Simon became the first known black jockey. He had been called the best jockey of his day, and he commanded more than a hundred dollars per ride for himself and his master. In 1814 General Andrew Jackson is said to have imported a crack black jockey named Dick to race his horse at a local event. The horse won, beating a favored racer.

HORSERACING

Who was the **first jockey** of any race to win the **Kentucky Derby**?

Oliver Lewis (1856–1924) was the first jockey of any race to win the Kentucky Derby. In 1875 he rode three-year-old Aristides in the first race in record time. Thirteen of the fifteen jockeys in the first race were black. African-American jockeys won fifteen of the first twenty-eight Kentucky Derby races, before the races were segregated. In 1921 Henry King was the last black jockey from the United States to ride in a derby until Marion St. Julien in 2000. Other black derby winners included William "Billy" Walker (1877), George Lewis (1880), Babe Hurd (1882), Isaac Murphy (1884, 1890, 1891), Erskine Henderson (1885), Alonzo Clayton (1892), James Perkins (1895), Willie Sims (1896, 1898), and Jimmie Winkfield (1901, 1902).

What **black jockey** won the **Kentucky Derby three times**?

Isaac Burns Murphy (1861–1896), the first jockey of any race to win the Kentucky Derby three times, was considered one of the greatest race riders in American history: He won

One of the most successful jockeys of all time was Isaac Burns Murphy, the first person to win the Kentucky Derby three times.

44 percent of all the races he rode. His Derby record held until 1930. Murphy won the first in 1884, the second in 1890, and the third in 1891, which made him the first jockey to capture Derby titles two years in a row. In 1884 he became the only jockey to win the Derby, the Kentucky Oaks, and the Clark Stakes in the same Churchill Downs meeting. In 1955 Murphy was the first jockey voted into the Jockey Hall of Fame at the National Museum of Racing, Saratoga Springs, New York. Born on the David Tanner farm in Fayette County, Kentucky, he took the name Murphy to honor his grandfather, Green Murphy, a well-known auctioneer in Lexington. He learned to ride at age fourteen and was one of the dominant figures in thoroughbred racing from the Civil War until 1891. Murphy won forty-nine of fifty-one starts in Saratoga in 1882 and had multiple wins in the Clark Handicap, the Latonia Derby, and the American Derby, during the 1880s. In the latter years of his racing career, he had a weight problem and once was suspended for being drunk while racing when, in reality, weakness from dieting caused him to fall from his horse. His participation in races declined, and he tried to change gears and become a horse trainer. He was a resident of Lexington, Kentucky, at the time of his death. His body was removed from its grave in a segregated cemetery in 1967, and his remains were reburied with a marker at Man O' War Memorial Park in Fayette County, Kentucky.

Why is **Willie Simms** important in horse racing?

The Kentucky Derby distance was trimmed from one and one-half miles to one and one-quarter miles in 1896. Willie (Willy) Simms (1870–?) of Augusta, Georgia, was the first winner of the race at that distance, in 1899. He won many of the best-known horse races in America, such as the Preakness Stakes (1898), Belmont Stakes (1893 and 1894), and the Champagne Stakes at Belmont (1895). He was also the first American jockey on an American horse to win on the English track, and he became the first black American jockey to win international fame.

BOXING

What role did free black **William Richmond** play in black boxing history?

Bill (William) Richmond (1763–1829), born free on Staten Island, New York, was the first black to become a prominent boxer in England, in 1805. A semi-professional boxer, by 1800 he had built an impressive list of wins and scored enough wins to earn a title berth against Tom Cribb, who held the title of champion. The thousands of spectators at the match included dukes and other nobility who appeared on horseback, and the bout was well covered by the *London Times*. Richmond lost the unequal match and Cribb would face Tom Molineaux in a match in 1810. Richmond remained active until 1810 and fought again in 1814 and 1818. He was also the first black to seek his living as a boxer, and the first American boxer to achieve a substantial measure of success. As a fifteen-year-old soldier for the British Army during the American Revolution, Richmond was the hangman at Nathan Hale's execution. He accompanied the British troops when they withdrew to England after the American Revolution.

How were blacks involved in **boxing** on **slave plantations**?

There are claims that boxing has had a more profound effect on the lives of African Americans than any other sport. During slavery one strong black man was often matched against a peer from a nearby plantation. An example was seen in the boxing feats of Tom Molineaux (1784–1818). Born a slave in the Georgetown section of Maryland (now a part of the District of Columbia) on March 23, 1784, Molineaux came from a family of boxers and "was forged into a pugilist of historical significance and acclaim." Algernon Molineaux, who owned Tom and his family, moved them to a plantation in Richmond, Virginia. There the master followed common practice of the day and arranged frequent bouts between his slaves and those on neighboring plantations. Healthy male fieldhand slaves were considered worthy of a hefty price. Since the Molineaux boys fit this description, they commanded a premium at every bout. By 1909 Tom Molineaux's master had won a considerable amount of

Boxer Tom Molineaux literally fought his way out of slavery in America to become a champion pugilist in England.

money and offered Tom his freedom if he won a final bout against "Black Abe," another slave. Tom defeated his opponent and won $100 for his master and his freedom. He moved to New York City, worked as a porter and later a stevedore, turned semi-professional in 1800, and continued his boxing career in England in 1809. Molineaux defeated the recently retired white boxer Tom Cribb to become the first black American boxing champion in England, in 1810. His victory was never acknowledged, however, because Londoners did not want the public to know that Cribb had lost to a black. Instead, they referred to Molineaux's race as "unknown." Molineaux astonished everyone as much by his extraordinary power of hitting and his gigantic strength as by his acquaintance with the science of boxing, which was far greater than any had credited him. The two fought again on September 11, 1811, and Molineaux defeated Cribb for the second time. By then, Molineaux had become a celebrated boxer in England but his success remained unrecorded in the American press.

Who was the **first black boxing champion**?

George "Little Chocolate" Dixon (1870–1909), born in Halifax, Nova Scotia, became the first black world champion in boxing on June 27, 1890, when he defeated Nunc Wallace to win the bantamweight title. On March 31, 1891, he knocked out Cal McCarthy and became the first black man to hold an American title in any sport. In that same year he won the featherweight title when he defeated reigning champion Fred Johnson. Dixon was also the first to regain the title and the first to win the paperweight world championship. When he began boxing professionally, the relatively diminutive Dixon stood five feet three and one-half inches tall and weighed eighty-seven pounds. In 1956 Dixon was elected to boxing's Hall of Fame.

What **boxers** achieved **success after the Civil War**?

After the Civil War ended, African Americans participated in baseball, horse racing, bicycling, and boxing. On scene by the end of the nineteenth-century was Peter Jackson (1861–1901), known as the "black prince" as well as the "Black Prince of the Ring." He was called "the most marvelous fighting man of his time." He was a quick, hard-hitting fighter who was claimed to have been found in San Francisco. Jackson was a sailor who was already known in some places; in 1886 he beat Tom Lees, the champion of Australia. He was a big and unspoiled fighter who became one of the "greatest and most scientific boxers in the world." In 1892 Jackson won the British Empire heavyweight title and became a public figure. He was an actor in *Uncle Tom's Cabin* and other plays, enjoyed a four-year tour, and fought boxing exhibitions. Johnson spent his final years in Australia, where he fought as late as 1899. He died in the Queensland province, where an impressive monument has been erected in his honor.

Why did boxing promoters seek a **"Great White Hope"**?

Boxer Jack Johnson was the first black heavyweight champion, winning the title in 1908. At that time racial segregation tightened its stranglehold on the American South; hence, Johnson's skill as an unrepentant black who dominated white boxers was cause for much concern. Jack (John Arthur) Johnson (1878–1946) knocked out Tommy Burns on December 26, 1908, in Sydney, Australia, in the fourteenth round to become the first black heavyweight boxing champion of the world. He lost only five of his first ninety-seven fights. Born in Galveston, Texas, Johnson was known as "Little Arthur" in his childhood. Because of his fearlessness, flamboyant style, and colorful life, he became one of the most reviled and hated men in America. Some experts called him the greatest fighter of the heavyweight class ever. His professional career, which included more than 125 fights, spanned more than thirty years; forty-four of his wins were by knockouts. Johnson did not have a blissful boxing career. He had difficulty getting a title fight despite an astounding record of 54 and 2 in official bouts. Once he did, and won, there was a hue and cry to find "The Great White Hope," a white boxer who could win the title back. Boxing promoters settled on former champion Jim Jeffries, who had retired unbeaten four years earlier. Johnson faced Jeffries on July 4, 1910, at Reno, Nevada, in a scheduled forty-five-rounder called the "Fight of the Century"; the one-sided fight ended in the fifteenth round, when Jeffries went down three times. As news spread around the country, racial nerves were hit and riots and unrest ignited. Johnson lost his title in Havana, Cuba, in 1915, and continued to wander until 1920, when he returned to his homeland and spent close to a year in prison. Once released, he boxed sporadically, winning some and losing others. He also continued to perform as a vaudevillian, which he had begun years earlier to supplement his boxing income. In 1954 Johnson was elected to the Boxing Hall of Fame. He was made a member of the International Boxing Hall of Fame in 1990. Johnson's story is told in the stage play and movie *The Great White Hope.*

How did **Joe Louis** impact boxing?

Heavyweight boxer Joe Louis (Joseph Louis Barrow; 1914–1981) became the first black of his rank to score a first-round knockout when he defeated Max Schmeling on June 22, 1938, immediately becoming the first black national sports hero. He was the first black to hold a boxing title ten years or more, maintaining the title of world champion for almost twelve years. He was also the first black heavyweight champion since Jack Johnson in 1908. Universally loved, Louis fought Max Baer in New York on September 24, 1935, and became the first black fighter to draw a million-dollar gate. The following year he was the first black to win *Ring* magazine's Fighter of the Year award. By 1949 Louis had become the first black to

Knocking out German Max Schmeling in a 1938 bout put Joe Louis in the spotlight as America's first national black sports hero.

defend his title successfully twenty-five times, and in 1954 he became the first black heavyweight and one of the first three boxers elected to Boxing's Hall of Fame. Born in Alabama, this son of a sharecropping cotton farmer fought often as a child. At the age of eight he knocked out four boyhood tormentors, and by 1934 he turned professional. A folk hero, his success broke down many barriers to black participation in athletics. Louis' personal integrity contributed to his popularity, and so did his service to the armed forces during World War II. He volunteered for the army in 1942, received the Legion of Merit medal when he was discharged in 1945, and had fought title matches for the benefit of army and navy relief funds. In his later years, problems with the Internal Revenue Service plagued him. He was charged with having an enormous unpaid tax bill but was eventually able to negotiate a settlement. After suffering an aneurysm in 1977, Louis was paralyzed and wheelchair-bound. There are many tributes to Louis's memory: The U.S. Mint struck a coin with his face on one side and victories on the other in 1982, and he was the subject of a Postal Service commemorative stamp in 1993.

What colorful prizefighter is self-proclaimed as **"The Greatest"**?

The first black prizefight to gross more than a five-million-dollar gate was the bout at the Louisiana Superdome in New Orleans on September 15, 1978. Muhammad Ali (1942–) won in a thirteen-round unanimous decision over Leon Spinks and became the first to win the heavyweight title three times. He held the title from 1964 to 1967, 1974 to 1978, and 1978 to 1979. Almost all of Ali's fights became events with enormous popular appeal. Ali was born Marcellus Cassius Clay in Louisville, Kentucky. He changed his name

"Float like a butterfly, sting like a bee," that was the style of Muhammad Ali, the first heavyweight boxing champion to win the title three times.

in 1963 when he became a Muslim. When he burst upon the boxing scene, he was articulate, outspoken, and given to writing poetry, sometimes in rhyme, sometimes in blank verse. Ali won an Olympic gold medal in Italy in 1960, six Kentucky Golden Gloves championships, and one National Golden Gloves title. He has, however, suffered both highs and lows in terms of public opinion. His lows became evident after he refused to serve in Vietnam because, as a Muslim, he was a conscientious objector. In 1967 the New York State Athletic Commission and the World Boxing Association suspended Ali's boxing license, and the heavyweight title was taken from him. He was sentenced to prison but released on appeal. His conviction was overturned three years later. Ali returned to winning boxing matches in November 1970, and after losing the championship to Joe Frazier in Manila in 1971, he won it back in their 1974 rematch. Personal health became a problem for Ali in 1980 when he was misdiagnosed as having a thyroid condition. He fought his sixty-first and last fight in a losing effort in 1981. In 1982 he began to be treated for Parkinson disease. As he neared the end of his boxing career, he became more active in politics, supporting Jimmy Carter for the presidency in 1980. In 1985 he worked unsuccessfully with his advisors to secure freedom for four Americans in Lebanon who had been kidnapped. Toward the end of the 1990s he seemed to become a beloved figure once more. He was chosen to light the Olympic torch in Atlanta in 1996. The young Ali became known as "The Greatest." His autobiography, *The Greatest—My Own Story,* was published in 1975.

Who are **other early black boxing greats**?

The first black fighter on record is Joe Lashley, who fought in England. His place of birth is unknown. In 1901, Joe Walcott (1873–1935) became the first black welterweight champion, defeating Rube Ferns and winning the title at Fort Erie, Ontario, on December 18. He also won the New England lightweight and middleweight wrestling titles on the same night. Born in Barbados, he was sometimes known as the "Barbados Demon." In 1926, Tiger (Theodore) Flowers (1895–1927) became the first black middleweight champion of the world, defeating Harry Greb in fifteen rounds to win the title in New York City on February 26. He had a habit of reading Bible verses, which earned him the nickname "Georgia Deacon." The sole person to hold three championships and world titles at once was Henry "Hammering Hank" Armstrong (1912–1981). During a ten-month period between 1937 and 1938, he won the featherweight, welterweight, and lightweight titles and challenged for the middleweight crown, fighting to a draw. Armstrong won twenty-seven fights in 1937 alone, twenty-six by knockout. He lost the last of his three titles, the welterweight, in 1940. In 1951, he became a minister. These men, and others of that era and later, were often taken advantage of by their white managers and cheated out of their earnings. "Imitation" friends took their earnings as well, and ignored them when the money was gone.

Who are the **boxing greats** of the **television era**?

The first televised heavyweight boxing championship bout was between Joe Louis and Jersey Joe Walcott (Arnold Raymond Cream; 1914–1994) from Madison Square Garden in 1947. In 1951 Walcott and Ezzard "Quiet Tiger" Charles (1921–1975) fought in the first heavyweight championship prizefight telecast coast-to-coast. In the fifteen-round bout held in Philadelphia's Municipal Stadium on June 5, Walcott outpointed Charles and then became the oldest person ever to win the heavyweight title. Sugar Ray (Walker Smith) Robinson Jr. (1921–1989) became the first black fighter to hold the middleweight title on five separate occasions. He lived like a champion, drove flashy cars, and enjoyed fun and nightlife. Floyd Patterson (1935–2006) became the first black to regain the heavyweight title, in 1960. Another boxing great, Archie Moore (1913–1998) set the record for the most knockouts in his twenty-seven-year career that ended in 1963. Joe Frazier (1944–2011) won the Olympic gold medal in Japan in 1964 and became the first

American Olympic heavyweight champion to win the heavyweight title of the world. The first black boxers to draw a multimillion dollar gate were Joe Frazier and Muhammad Ali (1942–). They fought at Madison Square Garden on March 8, 1971; Frazier won the match on points. Thomas "Hit Man" Hearns (1958–) became the first black to win boxing titles in five different weight classes, in 1987. George Edward Foreman (1948–), another popular fighter, knocked out Michael Moorer in the heavyweight championship fight in Los Angeles on November 5, 1994, and regained the title he had lost to Muhammad Ali twenty years earlier. In doing so, he became the oldest man to hold the world championship title. A minister, he named all of his five sons George: George H., George II, George III, George IV, and George V.

What **African-American women** have been **involved in boxing**?

Laila Ali (1978–) scored a majority decision in a fight with Jacqui Frazier-Lyde (1962–) on June 8, 2001, at the Tuning Stone Casino in Verona, New York. This was the first pay-per-view boxing match between two black women. By all accounts, the fight lived up to hopes and expectations, with both women slugging it out. Although both women are considered highly talented boxers, the pre-fight publicity and anticipation probably was due as much to their lineage as to their talent. Each is the daughter of a legendary boxer, Muhammad Ali and Joe Frazier, respectively, and the fathers had their own rivalry and contests. Joe Frazier was there to spur his daughter on; Muhammad Ali was not, but Laila

Ali's mother was present. Frazier-Lyde had hoped to run her string of consecutive knockouts to eight. Jacqui Frazier-Lyde beat Suzette Taylor at the Pennsylvania Convention Center in Philadelphia and won the Women's International Boxing Association (WIBA) light heavyweight belt. Her father, Joe Frazier, also won the bout during his career; thus, Frazier-Lyde's win marks the first time a father and daughter have held boxing championships.

BASEBALL

What was the **impact of Negro Leagues Baseball** on American **culture**?

Prior to 1947 professional baseball was segregated, and blacks played in their own Negro leagues, called Negro Leagues Base-

Laila Ali, daughter of Muhammad Ali, became a fine boxer in her own right.

ball. These leagues provided the only opportunities for several generations of extremely talented and dedicated minority ball players. Professional Negro baseball leagues were organized to showcase the talents of African-American players during segregation. Their organized efforts became a successful business enterprise generating millions of dollars in revenue and thousands of jobs for other blacks besides players, coaches, managers, and team owners. Andrew "Rube" Foster, a player, manager, and owner with the Chicago American Giants, developed the Negro National League in 1920 in Kansas City, Missouri. Similar efforts in southern and eastern regions produced the Southern Negro League, Eastern Colored League, East-West League, and other organizations, but the Negro National League (1920–1931; 1933–1948) and the Negro American League (1937–1960) had the most sustained success.

During the heyday of the Negro Leagues, their best teams included the Kansas City Monarchs and the Homestead Grays, with legendary players such as pitcher Leroy "Satchel" Paige and home run hitter Josh Gibson. Their all-star games sold out major league venues in Chicago, and the best black players outclassed white major league teams in unofficial exhibition games. Gibson was a strong, stoic catcher and was called "the best black baseball player white America did not see." Kansas City Monarch Buck O'Neil (1911-2006) became a folk hero as a character in Ken Burns's PBS documentary *Baseball,* which aired in the late 1990s. When Brooklyn Dodgers owner Branch Rickey broke the color line by signing Jackie Robinson from the Monarchs in 1945, his integration of the major leagues in 1947 ironically signaled the demise of the Negro Leagues. By 1960 top young black players such as Henry "Hank" Aaron and Willie Mays were part of major league teams. Many of the earlier players are now honored in both the Baseball Hall of Fame in Cooperstown, New York, and the Negro Leagues Baseball Museum in Kansas City.

What was the importance of **Andrew "Rube" Foster** in Negro Leagues Baseball?

Andrew "Rube" Foster (1879–1930), a former pitcher, organized the first successful black professional baseball league, the National Association of Professional Baseball Clubs, usually called the Negro National League, on February 13, 1920. He was known as the father of the Negro Leagues. (The International League of Independent Baseball Clubs, with four black and two white teams, lasted one season in 1906, and in 1910 the National Negro Baseball League collapsed before a single game had been played.) The Indianapolis ABCs played the Chicago Giants in the league's first game. Foster insisted that all teams in the league should be black-controlled, with the one exception being the Kansas City Monarchs. The league ran into difficulties in 1926 when Foster became ill, and it collapsed in 1931, a year after his death. A new Negro National League was organized in 1933, controlled by men in the numbers racket. Of the Negro National League meetings, some said that they were "enclaves of the most powerful black gangsters in the nation." Foster, who was born in Calvert, Texas, the son of a minister, showed promise as a baseball organizer early, managing a team while in grade school. He left for Fort Worth, Texas, when he was in the eighth grade to go further in baseball. His personal playing days included stints with several Negro teams, including the American Giants (so named by Foster), who have been called one of the greatest Negro baseball teams. Foster was a businessman as well as a baseball phenomenon; he owned a barbershop and an automobile service shop. An accident with a gas leak in his home in 1925 preceded declining health for Foster, both physically and mentally. He was in the state asylum in Illinois at the time of his death. He was elected to the National Baseball Hall of Fame in 1981. In 2001 a set of two U.S. postage stamps bearing the images of Negro Leagues Baseball and Rube Foster was issued.

Former pitcher "Rube" Foster organized the National Association of Professional Baseball Clubs (aka the Negro National League) in 1920.

Who was **"Cool Papa" Bell**?

An outfielder for the old Negro Leagues, James Thomas Bell (1903–1991), known as "Cool Papa Bell," was regarded as the fastest man in professional baseball and one of the most important figures in the Negro Leagues. Bell was born in Starkville, Mississippi, to a farmer named Jonas and his wife Mary Nicholas Bell. In 1920 Bell, like other blacks of that time, left the impoverished South for urban centers. He settled in St. Louis and became a knuckleball pitcher for a black semi-pro team, the Compton Hill Club. In August 1921 he joined the East St. Louis Cubs as a pitcher. Bell signed on with the St. Louis Stars in May 1922, a major powerhouse team in the National Negro League. After he struck out the best hitter in the league, his manager gave him the name that would stick with him for life—"Cool Papa." Bell's pitching career ended in 1924 because of an arm injury; he then became an outfielder. Over the course of his career, Bell played on three of the greatest teams in black baseball: the Stars, the Pittsburgh Crawfords, and the Homestead Grays.

Bell and other players in the Negro Leagues experienced hardships as they traveled in cramped buses or cars that often broke down. Seldom were they served in restaurants, and sleeping accommodations were poor as well. It was racial segregation that kept the star players of the Negro Leagues such as Bell from entering mainstream baseball; for many years their stellar records were therefore known only to a few.

Why was **Moses Fleetwood Walker** important?

Moses Fleetwood Walker (1857–1924), or "Fleet" Walker, as he was popularly known, became one of the first African Americans to play white intercollegiate baseball in 1881, when he was a catcher on Oberlin College's varsity team. His baseball career took him to the Toledo Blue Stockings in 1884, where he became the first African-American major leaguer. He felt the sting of racism throughout his baseball career, as racial antipathy and segregation flourished in the late 1800s. In 1887 only seven black players were in the league. Racist taunts, jeers, and threats were commonplace to Walker. The Chicago White Stockings' manager refused to plan an exhibition game in 1883 if Walker and another African-American player, George Washington Stovey, were allowed to play. The men were barred from the field, and on that same day the league voted to deny contracts with black players. Although Walker was never more than a mediocre player, he refused to extend his career by joining all-black teams that invited him to play. Walker, a mulatto, was born to racially mixed parents in Mount Pleasant, Ohio, grew up in Steubenville, and attended Oberlin College. His complexion was fair enough to allow him to move with ease in the white society that he seemed to favor later on, yet his race was well-known in the baseball world. In his 1908 booklet, *Our Home Colony: The Past, Present, and Future of the Negro Race,* he rejected racial mixing and called for African repatriation. In 1904 he purchased the Cadiz opera house in Steubenville and offered live entertainment and movies to a mostly white clientele. Blacks who attended were seated in the balcony. Although Walker remained bitter because of his treatment in baseball, he continued to mix with whites and to live in white communities.

When was professional **baseball racially integrated**?

A surge in the popularity of baseball after World War II helped pave the way for black participation in the formerly all-white major leagues. Brooklyn Dodger second baseman Jackie Robinson broke the color barrier in 1947. He and other early black major leaguers faced widespread hostility from fans and second-class treatment in the segregated South. Jackie (John Roosevelt) Robinson (1919–1972) joined the Brooklyn Dodgers as a third baseman to become the first black in the major leagues of the modern era. Robinson played his first game in this capacity against the Boston Braves at Ebbets Field in Brooklyn on April 15, 1947, and in 1948 shifted to second base. He was named Rookie of the Year in 1947. Robinson probably endured more racial insults in his career than any other person in history. In 1949 he became the first black batting champion and the first black to receive the National League's Most Valuable Player Award. Robinson was the first black enshrined in the Baseball Hall of Fame, in 1962. Robinson was actually the first black to play at any level in the major leagues. He played with the Montreal Royals, the Dodgers' top minor league farm club, in 1946, and proceeded to hit .800 with 4 runs batted in, 4 runs scored, and 2 stolen bases in his debut game.

Born in Cairo, Georgia, Robinson's mother moved the family to Pasadena, California, after her husband left them when Robinson was thirteen months old. There he became active in sports while in grade school, playing competitively for the first time in a fourth grade soccer game. In high school and at Pasadena Junior College, he lettered in football, baseball, basketball, and track. His excellence in athletics continued at the University of California, Los Angeles, but Robinson left there because of financial pressures in 1941, just shy of a degree. He was drafted in 1942, and after boxing champion Joe

Jackie Robinson broke the color barrier in American baseball when he joined the Brooklyn Dodgers in 1947. An outstanding player, he had a career batting average of .311, including 1,518 hits and 137 home runs before retiring from the sport in 1956. His jersey with the number 42 was retired not only for the Dodgers but for *all* major league teams, who still honor the man on "Jackie Robinson Day," when everyone wears the number 42.

Louis and other notables protested, he was allowed to enter Officers Candidate School and was commissioned as a lieutenant in the U.S. Army in 1943. Threatened with a court martial while in the army because he defied bus segregation laws in Fort Hood, Texas, he was exonerated.

Robinson's first professional baseball team, which he joined in 1945, was the Kansas City Monarchs of the Negro American League. He was with this team when he came to the attention of the Dodgers. Robinson's impact on baseball goes far beyond his baseball statistics. He had to excel not only athletically, but to comport himself well in the face of the opposition to him because of his race. He is recognized for the extent to which he succeeded in both regards and is widely credited with opening the door for other black aspirants to a career in major league baseball.

Facing a trade in 1956, Robinson retired from baseball and became an executive with the New York-based Chock Full O' Nuts restaurant chain. He combined this position with active community involvement on behalf of African-American businesses, but he was often at odds with other black leaders of the day. New York's Governor Nelson

Rockefeller named him special assistant for community affairs in 1946. Independent throughout his life, Robinson refused participation in a 1969 Old-Timers' Game to protest baseball's lack of African-American involvement in baseball management and front office positions. An ailing Robinson threw out the first ball at the 1972 World Series. He died in Stamford, Connecticut, nine days later. In 1997, fifty years after Robinson burst upon the baseball scene, major league baseball officials dedicated the 1997 season to the pioneer, honoring the fiftieth anniversary of his breaking the color barrier and entering major league baseball.

The treatment that Robinson and other black players who integrated baseball endured failed to deter them from their goals, as they began to stream into professional baseball, breaking records previously held by white superstars. By the 1970s blacks were on the rosters of every team in the league and were joined in increasing numbers by talented players from all parts of Latin America. In 2013, *42,* a biographical sports film about Robinson, was released.

Why was **Satchel Paige** important to integrated baseball?

Satchel (Leroy Robert) Paige (1900–1982) was the first black pitcher in the American League, in 1948, and the first black to actually pitch in a World Series game. One of the best known players in black baseball, he became the first black elected to the Baseball Hall of Fame for his career in the Negro Leagues, in 1971. During five seasons in the majors, 1948–1953, he won twenty-eight games and lost thirty-two. He appeared in one game in 1965 to pitch three innings for the Kansas City Athletics. At fifty-nine—the oldest man ever to pitch in the majors—Paige allowed one hit. A native of Mobile, Alabama, Paige grew up in a family with eleven children. He began work at the Mobile Train Depot at age seven and often skipped school, although he pitched for the school baseball team when he was ten years old. He further developed his baseball skills and also added to his formal education during the five and one-half years he spent while serving time in a juvenile correctional facility after a shoplifting offense at age twelve. When Paige was released, he joined the all-black semiprofessional team of the Mobile Tigers, and his career was launched. In 1926 he became a professional baseball player when the Chattanooga Black Lookouts, a Negro Southern League team, signed him. He continued to play with Negro League teams, and while he was with the Pittsburgh Crawfords in the 1930s, his teammates included five future Hall of Fame stars.

In between his two stints with the Crawfords, Paige took a step back to semiprofessional baseball when he played with the Bismarck (North Dakota) team. This marked his first experience with white teammates. He also played with an all-star team he formed and once faced famed pitcher Dizzy Dean's exhibition team in a series of six games; Paige's team won four of the six. A few more moves led him to the Kansas City Monarchs, where he was their ace pitcher in the early 1940s. He was with the Monarchs when he became a major league pitcher for the Cleveland Indians. He later played with other teams and continued to have a role as coach, pitcher, or in public relations until shortly before his death. He died three days after he threw out the first pitch in a Kansas City

Royals game. Paige's name is legend in the baseball world. *Sporting News* included him in its 1998 list of the 100 greatest baseball players of the twentieth century.

What **other black legendary players** helped to **integrate** major league baseball?

Other blacks who began playing in major league baseball included Larry Doby, Roy Campanella, and Don Newcombe. The first black player in the American League was Larry (Lawrence Eugene) Doby (1924–2003), who joined the Cleveland Indians on July 5, 1947. Joining the National League were Roy "Campy" Campanella (1921–1993), who signed with the Dodgers in 1946 as catcher; and Don (Donald) "Newk" Newcombe (1926–), pitcher with the Dodgers in 1949.

Who are some of the **recent African-American stars** in major league baseball?

Those who have risen to prominence in major league baseball include Hank Aaron, Willie Mays, Reggie Jackson ("Mr. October"), and Barry Bonds. Reginald "Reggie" Martinez Jackson (1946–), led his team to five world championships and eleven division titles. Ranked sixth in home runs (563) when he retired, he also led the league with 2,597 strikeouts in his twenty-year career. He became a cultural phenomenon as a New York Yankee player against the Los Angeles Dodgers in the World Series on October 18, 1977. In three consecutive times at bat, he hit three home runs, batted a .450 average, and afterward became affectionately known as "Mr. October." *Sporting News* placed him on its list of "The 100 Greatest Baseball Players." Playing for the Atlanta Braves, on April 8, 1974, Hank (Henry Louis) Aaron (1934–), "Hammering Hank," hit his 715th home run in a game with the Los Angeles Dodgers to beat Babe Ruth's major league record. He led the National League in runs batted in four times. Aaron retired in 1976 with 755 regular-season home runs to his credit, and became vice president of player personnel for the Braves. He was named senior vice president in 1989. In 1982 Aaron was elected to the Baseball Hall of Fame. In 1991 he published his autobiography, *I Had a Hammer,* which was on the *New York Times* best-seller list for ten weeks. Aaron's chase for the home-run record was one of the most dramatic stories in sports history, made all the more so because Aaron did not revel in his star-

Barry Bonds, who spent much of his career with the San Francisco Giants, is considered one of the greatest stars to have played the game. His honors include eight Golden Gloves, twelve Silver Sluggers, and three Hank Aaron Awards.

dom. Many, but not all, cheered as he inched toward dethroning the legendary Ruth; others sent death threats. He set many records, most of which he still holds. Aaron was a National League all-star twenty-three times between 1952 and 1976. Willie Mays (1931–) had a phenomenal home-run hitting record with the New York Giants and later the San Francisco Giants. Because he caught, hit, threw, and ran spectacularly, he has been called the greatest all-round baseball player ever. Big-league slugger Barry Bonds became a superstar, first with the Pittsburgh Pirates and later with the San Francisco Giants. In August 2007, Barry Bonds eclipsed Aaron's home run record with 756 homers.

BASKETBALL

Who were the **New York Rens**?

Ironically, the New York Rens, organized in 1923, became what many believed was the greatest basketball team of its time. Ranked alongside the Harlem Globetrotters, the New York Renaissance (or Rens), was one of the earliest organized basketball teams. So good was the team that the men never performed at their best for fear of driving away opponents. Like the Harlem Globetrotters, the Rens performed fancy tricks and ball-passing with machine-like precision.

Who are the **Harlem Globetrotters**?

In 1952 the Harlem Globetrotters, a Chicago-based team, was founded, owned, and coached by Abe Saperstein of Chicago. While based in Chicago, it was the first basketball club to make complete playing trips around the world, first in 1952 and again in winter 1960–1961. It was also the first professional basketball team to have its own fall training camp, in October 1940. The best known and best-loved team in the world, its finest decade was the 1950s. Mannie Jackson, a former Globetrotter, became the first black to own the team in 1993. The team was founded in Hinckley, Illinois, around 1923–1924 and played its first game there on January 7, 1927. Since then, there have been five hundred team members, who have played in 115 countries. Based in Phoenix, in 1999 the Globetrotters received the John W. Bunn Award in recognition of its contribution to the game of basketball. It was the first team in the history of the Basketball Hall of Fame to receive this prestigious award.

How has **basketball incorporated black players**?

Major league sports were slow to integrate. Professional basketball was integrated in 1951, when the Boston Celtics drafted Chuck Cooper and the New York Knicks hired Nat "Sweetwater" Clifton. By the late 1960s, most of the sport's biggest stars were minorities—men like Bill Russell, Wilt "Wilt the Stilt" Chamberlain, Kareem Abdul-Jabbar, Elvin Hayes, and Willis Reed. These and other talented athletes helped transform the game from a relatively polite and static affair to a fast-breaking, high-speed contest.

353

Black players won more and more roster positions as the 1970s progressed. Athletes such as Kareem Abdul-Jabbar, Julius "Dr. J." Erving, Moses Malone, Bob McAdoo, and Wes Unseld helped further the evolution of the modern professional basketball game. By the 1980s, black dominance of the sport was assured with the arrival of Earvin "Magic" Johnson, Patrick Ewing, Michael Jordan, Clyde Drexler, and Charles Barkley. In 1992 the celebrated "Dream Team"—the first American Olympic basketball team composed of professional players—had only two white players; the team won the gold medal handily. In recent years, men such as Shaquille O'Neal (1972-), Allen Iverson (1975–), Kobe B. Bryant, (1978–), and LeBron James (1984–), have dominated the basketball scene.

One of the greatest basketball players of all time was Wilt "The Stilt" Chamberlain, who played in the 1960s and early 1970s with teams such as the Philadelphia 76ers and the Los Angeles Lakers.

Why is **Michael Jordan** considered a major sports figure?

Michael Jeffrey Jordan (1963–) earned $30.1 million in endorsements of commercial products, becoming the highest paid athlete, in 1994. Jordan, whose exploits on the basketball court have made him a household name throughout the world, was born in Brooklyn, New York, but grew up in Wilmington, North Carolina. He played Little League baseball as a child and, at first, participated in almost every sport—except basketball—when he was in high school. He was cut from the basketball team during his sophomore year but emerged as a promising player as a junior, after growing four inches over the summer. When he entered the University of North Carolina at Chapel Hill in 1981, Jordan was six-feet six-inches tall. He was named Atlantic Coast Rookie of the Year for the 1981–1982 season and was a unanimous All-American

Michael Jordan enjoyed such an amazing career that even non-basketball fans were familiar with his success, mostly with the Chicago Bulls. He was on six NBA championship teams and two Olympic gold medal teams, and has won nearly every basketball award imaginable.

choice the following season. He was named College Player of the Year twice and was a member of the U.S. Olympic gold medal men's basketball team in 1984. Jordan joined the Chicago Bulls after his junior year in college and continued along the route to superstardom in the pros. The Bulls won three consecutive NBA titles (1991, 1992, and 1993) during the first Jordan years. Jordan himself was piling up statistics and individual championships and awards. He was also on the U.S. Olympic teams that won gold medals in basketball in 1992 and 1996. He took a brief respite from basketball in 1993, to try his hand at professional baseball. He announced his retirement shortly after his father was murdered in 1993. Jordan returned to the Bulls in 1995 and won his fourth NBA Finals Most Valuable Player award; a fifth such award followed in 1998. In 1997, during the All-Star Weekend, he became the first NBA player to make a triple-double in points, assists, and rebounds. It would be difficult to find a basketball honor that Jordan has not received. His sparkling play gave rise to a variety of nicknames: "Superman," "Last Shot," "Air Jordan." He retired again in 1998 after the Bulls won its sixth championship in eight years, but retirement did not signify departure from the world of basketball. In 2000 he became president and a minority owner of the Washington Wizards NBA team. He also became CEO of the special Nike branch that carries Air Jordan shoes. He returned to the NBA in the 2001–2002 season, playing with the Wizards, but donated his salary to charities associated with the September 11, 2001, terrorist attacks relief efforts.

Who is basketball's **"King James"**?

LeBron James (1984–) emerged as a high school basketball phenomenon in 2003. The Akron, Ohio, native and son of a single mother moved directly from high school to the National Basketball Association and exceeded the high expectations placed on him. He has been called the best basketball player in the world. His prime sponsor is Nike, which, like his adoring fans, adores his regal charm and prowess. He has been called "King James." When James left the Cleveland Cavaliers in 2012 to join the Miami Heat, his fans were so embittered that some burned his jersey in effigy. Some black leaders accused his owners of treating James like a runaway slave simply because he left the Cavaliers. James continues to excel, however, and took his new team to a world championship in 2012 and 2013. He also was a member of the successful U.S. team that played in the 2012 Olympics in London.

LeBron "King" James is currently a leader in the NBA, first for the Cleveland Cavaliers and then with the Miami Heat.

What **black coaches** are **legendary** in college and/or professional basketball?

By 2012 many black coaches had achieved as team leaders. These include Johnny (John B.) "Coach Mac" McLendon Jr. (1915–1999), the first black coach of a predominantly white professional team in modern times. John Chaney (1932–) became the first black basketball coach at Temple University in 1982, and the next year George Henry Raveling (1937–) became the University of Iowa's first black head basketball coach. John Robert Thompson Jr. (1941–) became a legend at Georgetown in 1984, when he was the first black coach to win the NCAA Division I championship. In 1995 Lenny (Leonard) R. Wilkens (1937–) coached for the Atlanta Hawks and became the winningest coach in NBA history. The University of Georgia named Tubby (Orlando) Smith (1951–) its first black head coach in 1995; in 1997 he became the first black men's basketball coach at the University of Kentucky. Others in the South included Nolan Richardson (1941–), who in 1986 became the first black coach at the University of Arkansas and the first in the Southwestern Conference, and Robert Oran Evans (1946–), who in 1992 was the first black head coach at the University of Mississippi. There was also Wade Houston, the first black head coach of a major sport in the Southeast Conference in 1989, when he was head basketball coach at the University of Tennessee.

Clarence Edward "Bighouse" Gaines Sr. (1923–2005) led the Winston-Salem Rams of Winston-Salem State University to national prominence when they became the first black college, and the first college in the entire South, to win the NCAA (National Collegiate Athletic Association) College Division Basketball championship in 1967. Gaines never had a losing season. His players, like many others in the black colleges, helped to strengthen professional basketball when the game was integrated.

How has the sport of **women's basketball** developed?

On the college scene, legendary C. Vivian Stringer (1948–) became the first woman's basketball coach to advance to the Final Four from two different colleges. She coached the women's team at historically black Cheyney State University in 1982 and led the team to the NCAA tournament in Philadelphia. In 1983, while at the University of Iowa, she led her Hawkeyes to a place in the NCAA Final Four. In 1995 she moved to Rutgers University and became the country's highest-paid head woman's basketball coach. She went on to record six hundred victories by 2000. In 1999 Carolyn Peck (1966–) became the first black woman to coach a team to the women's NCAA national championship. She coached the Purdue Boilermakers to a 62–45 win over Duke and to its first NCAA championship. Women have become referees as well; for example, in 1997 Violet Palmer became the first black woman referee in the NBA.

When were the **WNBA** and the **ABL established**?

In 1997 two professional basketball leagues were established for women players—the Women's National Basketball Association (WNBA) and the American Basketball League (ABL). Although the ABL folded after three seasons, the WNBA remained successful and, early on, showcased the talents of such black women players as Lisa Leslie, Sheryl Swoopes, Chamique Holdsclaw, and Cynthia Cooper.

FOOTBALL

Who were the **early black professional football players**?

As early as 1904, Charles W. Follis (1879–?) became the first black professional football player, for the Blues of Shelby, Ohio. Unlike other major American sports, professional football began as an integrated entertainment. Blacks played alongside whites on the gridiron until 1930; then for fifteen years the sport was all white. In 1945 a handful of black players were recruited, including Woodrow "Woody" Strode (1914–1994) and Kenneth "Kenny" Washington (1918–1971) of the Los Angeles Rams, and Benjamin "Ben" Willis (1921–2007) of the Cleveland Browns. Slowly, the number of black players on football rosters increased as the 1950s progressed. In 1957 Jim (James) Nathaniel Brown (1936–) arrived and became a superstar for the Cleveland Indians, leading the league in rushing for eight of his nine years in football and establishing a new career rushing record. Other blacks who joined the sport had emerged as stars by 1966; these included Chicago Bears running back Gale Sayers (1943–) and New York Giants safety Emlen "The Gremlin" Tunnell (1925–1975), who in 1965 became the first black coach in the National Football League. The last NFL team to be integrated was the Washington Redskins; in 1962 the team signed Bobby Mitchell (1935–).

Other black icons include Alan Cedric Page (1945–), with the Minnesota Vikings and the Chicago Bears; O. J. (Orenthal James) Simpson (1947–) of the Buffalo Bills; Herschel Walker (1962–), with the Dallas Cowboys and the Minnesota Vikings; Walter Jerry Payton (1954–1999), with the Chicago Bears; Doug Lee Williams (1955–) of the Washington Redskins (the first black quarterback to start a Super Bowl game); Warren Moon (1956–), quarterback for the Minnesota Vikings; Jerry Lee Rice (1962–), wide receiver with the San Francisco 49ers; Barry Sanders (1968–), Detroit Lions star running back; and Marcus Allen (1960–), all-time leader in rushing touchdowns, with the Kansas City Chiefs.

Who are the **modern-day African-American icons** in **professional football**?

Leaders in the New Millennium include Plaxico Burress, wide receiver for the Pittsburgh Steelers; Donald Driver, wide receiver for the Green Bay Packers; Donovan Jamal McNabb, quarterback for the Philadelphia Eagles; Charles Woodson, defensive back for the Green Bay Packers; and the newest iconic player, Robert Griffin III, known as "RG3", quarterback for the Washington Redskins.

What **black coaches broke** the **glass ceiling** in **collegiate football**?

On the college scene, pioneer coaches include Tyrone Willingham (1953–) of the University of Notre Dame; Norries Wilson (1965–), the first black head football coach in the

Ivy League (Columbia University), in 2005; and James Franklin (1972–) the first black coach to head a major sport at Vanderbilt.

What **black coaches** broke the **glass ceiling** in **professional football**?

In professional football, Arthur "Art" Shell Jr. (1946–) became the first black head coach in modern NFL history, as coach of the Los Angeles Raiders in 1989. Raymond "Ray" Earl Rhodes (1950–) became the Green Bay Packers' first black head coach, in 1999. The first black coach to lead his team to a Super Bowl championship was Anthony Kevin "Tony" Dungy (1955–), on February 4, 2007. When Super Bowl XLI was held in Miami, Florida, Dungy led the Indianapolis Colts, the AFC champions, to the win. Friends since their stint with the Tampa Bay Buccaneers, Dungy and his opponent Lovie Smith (1958–), the black coach of the Chicago Bears, became temporary foes on that day. They were also the

Robert Griffin III is an award-winning quarterback for the Washington Redskins.

first two black coaches to lead their teams to a Super Bowl. Tony Dungy is also the first coach to lead a team to the playoffs for ten consecutive years and the first NFL head coach to defeat all thirty-two NFL teams. After retiring from the Colts, he became an analyst for NBC's *Sunday Night Football*. Lovie Smith continued his head coaching post with the Bears. Mike Tomlin (1972–) of the Pittsburgh Steelers twice led a team to the Super Bowl and won the contest in 2009.

What black players became **icons** in **college football**?

As early as 1890, William Henry Lewis (1868–1949) and teammate William Tecumseh Sherman Jackson (1820–1891) became the first recorded black players on a white college football team. Lewis was captain of the Amherst team in 1891–1892 and the first black to win this distinction at an Ivy League school. Jackson also became the first black track star as a runner for Amherst. Blacks achieved at Brown University as well, when Frederick Douglass "Fritz" Pollard Sr. (1890–1986), a diminutive black, became the first black to play in the Rose Bowl, in 1916. He became the first black quarterback and head coach in professional football in 1919 when he served with the Akron Indians, a team in the American Professional Football Association (which later became the National Football League). In 1923 Pollard became the first black quarterback and head coach in

the National Football League. Legendary Buddy (Claude Henry Keystone) Young

(1926–1983) was the first black to score a Rose Bowl touchdown in the University of Illinois vs. UCLA New Year's Day game. Young also moved up into management, becoming the NFL's first director of player relations and the first black to hold an executive position with the league.

What are the **contributions of black colleges** to the **history of football**?

Black colleges built powerful teams and played in contests of their own. In 1892 Biddle University (now Johnson C. Smith University), played Livingstone College, both in North Carolina, in the first recorded black college football game on Thanksgiving day, winning by a 4–0 score. Two years later, Howard University, Lincoln University (Pennsylvania), and Atlanta University fielded football teams. In 1929 the Prairie View Bowl, played on January 1, was the first black college football bowl game. It was held in Houston, Texas, and Prairie View lost to Atlanta University by a 6–0 score. The bowl was discontinued in 1961. Among the recent contests in black college football are the Circle City Classic (held in Indianapolis), and the Bayou Classic between Grambling and Southern University (held in New Orleans). By 1949 professional football had begun to notice black college football teams and their star players. In 1949 Paul "Tank" Younger (1928–2001), of Grambling, became the first black professional player from an all-black college; he signed with the Los Angeles Rams as a free agent but was not drafted. He remained there until 1958 and then moved to the Pittsburgh Steelers.

Who are the **legendary coaches** in **black college football**?

Legendary coaches in black college football include Arnett W. "Ace" Mumford (1898–1962) of Southern University in Baton Rouge, Louisiana. In October 1957 he became the first black college coach to reach two hundred victories, when his team defeated Langston University of Oklahoma. Previously Mumford coached at Bishop College, Jarvis Christian College, and Texas College. Fred "Pop," "Pops," "Big" Long (1896–1966) followed him in reaching the two hundred victory mark. Although Alonzo Smith "Jake" Gaither (1906–1994) of Florida Agricultural and Mechanical University has been called the first to reach two hundred wins, it was not until 1969 that Gaither, or "the Papa Rattler," as he was known, achieved that level. Eddie G. Robinson (1919–2007) of Grambling State, in 1990 became the first college coach of any race to win 308 games in a career.

GOLF

Who **pioneered** in golf and **won major professional championships**?

Blacks first achieved success in golf in 1896, when John Shippen (1879–1968) became the first to play in the U.S. Open— he was only sixteen years old. The game grew in popularity among blacks, and by 1924 the black Riverside Golf Club was organized and stimulated more black participation in the sport. In 1926 the United Golf Association for blacks held its first national tournament. Founded in the 1920s, national tournaments for black golfers continued for a number of years. It was not until 1957 that Charlie (Charles) Sifford (1922–) won the Long Beach Open on November 10 and became the first black to win a major professional golf tournament. He was also the first black to gain membership in the PGA and the first to play in a major PGA tournament in the South, in Greensboro, North Carolina, in 1961. Lee Elder (1934–) gained popularity in the sport as well, becoming the first black American to compete against whites in South Africa, in the South African PGA Open, in 1971. He qualified for the Masters Tournament on April 10, 1975, and teed off in Augusta, as the Masters' first black entry. The first black multiple winner on the PGA tour was Calvin Peete (1943–), who in 1982 captured the Greater Milwaukee Open for the second time, the Anheuser-Busch Classic, the BC Open, and the Pensacola Open. Previously he had been denied access to the most prestigious tournaments.

Who is the **first black golfer** to win the **Masters** and achieve iconic status?

Arguably the most popular and accomplished black golfer is Eldrick "Tiger" Woods (1975–). At fifteen, Woods was the first black, and the youngest person, ever to win the U.S. Junior Amateur championship. With his participation in the Los Angeles Open in March 1992, he became also the youngest person ever to play in a Professional Golfers Association tour event. He became the first two-time winner of the United States Golf Association Junior Amateur crown when he successfully defended his title in 1992, at the championship in Milton, Massachusetts. Woods won his third consecutive U.S. Junior Amateur Golf Championship title in 1993, at the Waverly Golf Course and Country Club, in Portland, Oregon. He is the only golfer ever to win three straight junior amateur titles. Woods also won three U.S. Amateur championships, and when he won his first in 1994, he was the first black and the youngest person ever to do so.

He entered Stanford University in 1994, and continued to demonstrate his magic strokes and his overall golf know-how. The interests of Woods, the golfer, soon became paramount, and in 1996 he left Stanford to join the PGA Tour. It took little time for him to become a household name. He had been on the professional tour less than a year when he won the crown jewel of golf matches—the Masters, held at Augusta, Georgia. He was the youngest ever to win the prestigious event and the first black to win a major professional golf tournament—and he did it at 18 under par.

Woods was named PGA Player of the Year in his first year on the tour. That was just the beginning. He kept on winning, putting together seasons that made him the one to beat in almost every match. Woods's dominance of the tour was clearly evident by the year 2000. When he won the Mercedes Championship in Hawaii, it was the fifth consecutive championship he had won that season, the first time that had been done since 1953. In July 2000 he became the youngest player to complete golf's career grand slam: the Masters in 1997, the PGA Championship in 1999, the U.S. Open in 2000, and the British Open in the same year. He is one of only five golfers to have completed the golf grand slam. In winning the British Open at 19 under par, Woods set a record for strokes

Tiger Woods has won four Masters Championships (as of this printing)—the first black man to win the coveted green jacket—and numerous other championships, including the U.S. Open and PGA Championships.

under par in a major championship. The Associated Press named him Male Athlete of the Year for the third time in 2000. Twice in 2001 he experienced wins at the same golf course, and he was the first player to have three consecutive victories in the NEC Invitational at the Firestone Country Club (Akron, Ohio).

His crowning glory, however, came when he won the Masters championship for the second time in April 2001. This was his fourth major championship in a row. Woods became the first golfer ever to hold all four major titles at the same time. On his march to the Masters again, he became the youngest golfer with thirty wins on the PGA tour and the first to win three straight titles at three tournaments—the Bay Hill Invitational, the Firestone, and the Memorial Tournament. On April 10, 2005, he won the Masters for a fourth time; he had back-to-back wins in that tournament as well. He is only the third golfer to reach this milestone. In 2007 he was named Player of the Year for the eighth time.

There are very few superlatives that have not been used in describing Woods, the golfer, and very few records remaining that he has not set. He made a name for himself when he started hitting golf balls at age two, scoring 48 after 9 holes by the time he was three. He added to that name until late 2009, when he stepped away from golf to try to control his controversial and well-publicized personal life. Woods returned to golf in 2010, but continued to suffer a major slump until March 2012 when he ended his thirty-month losing skid and won the Arnold Palmer Invitational at Bay Hill. He became the first golfer to win over $100 million after winning the Deutsche Bank Championship on

September 3, 2012. In 2013 he won the Cadillac Championship, and on March 25, the Bay Hill Invitational and regained the world No. 1 ranking.

What **black woman** became the **first professional golfer?**

The first black professional woman golfer was Althea Gibson (1927–2003), who, in 1964, became the first black woman to play on the Ladies Professional Golf Association tour. She is best known, however, for her achievements in professional tennis. She played in several golf tournaments from 1963 to 1967. Black women, however, continue to demonstrate an interest in the sport. In 2001 Jackson State University's women's golf team became the first from a historically black college to receive an invitation to the NCAA regional championship. They played in the twenty-one-team NCAA East Regional in Chapel Hill, North Carolina.

GYMNASTICS

What **black gymnast** was the **first to compete** on a **U.S. Olympic team?**

Among black women gymnasts in the United States, the named Dominique Dawes is among the most prominent. Dominique Margaux Dawes (1976–) became the first black woman gymnast to compete on a United States Olympic team. She was joined by Elizabeth Anna (Betty) Okino (1975–) in the 1992 Olympic Games in Barcelona, Spain. Dawes won a bronze medal at the games and two silver medals at the World Gymnasts Championships Competition held in Birmingham, England. Okino, born in Uganda, won bronze at the 1992 games and a silver team medal and individual bronze at the World Championships held in Indianapolis in 1991. In 1994 Dawes swept all five events in the National Gymnastics Championships held in Nashville. She was the first black woman gymnast to win a national championship and the first woman to win a sweep since 1969. At the Olympic Games in Atlanta in 1996, Dawes helped the U.S. women's team win its first Olympic gold medal.

Gabrielle "Gabby" Douglas is the first black woman to win gold in the all-around gymnastics competition at the Olympics.

Why is **Gabrielle "Gabby" Douglas** important?

Gabrielle "Gabby" Christina Victoria Douglas (1995–), then a sixteen-year-old gymnastic phenomenon and a member of the U.S. Women's Gymnastics team at the 2012 Summer Olympics held in London, became the first African American to win a gold medal in the women's all-around final competition. She is also the third straight American to win gymnastics' biggest prize at the Olympics. Gabby came away with two gold medals as she and her "Fierce Five" teammates won team gold two nights earlier. The "Flying Squirrel," as she is also nicknamed, was allowed to leave her mother, two sisters, and brother in Virginia Beach, Virginia, to live with a host family and train with her new coach, Liang Chow, in Des Moines, Iowa.

TENNIS

Who championed the game of **tennis** to become **African-American icons** in that sport?

Several black athletes challenged segregation and broke racial barriers in tennis and at the same time became legends. Names such as Althea Gibson, Arthur Ashe, and sisters Venus and Serena Williams are popularly known in the sport, yet there are other pioneers. Arthur Ashe (1943–1993) was a pioneering sports hero and one of the most passionate and articulate sportsmen for minority athletes. He spent his entire career protesting unjust racial practices in the sporting world. In 1975 he became the first black man to win Wimbledon, the U.S. Open, and the Australian Open—three of tennis's Grand Slam events. Ashe was recognized as one of the world's great tennis players. He is known also for his pioneering writings on black sports, especially for his multivolume work *A Hard Road to Glory: A History of the African-American Athlete* (1993). A champion for social change, his untimely AIDS-related death raised the nation's consciousness about the disease.

Althea Gibson was both a talented tennis player and a gifted golfer. In tennis, she was the first African American to break the color barrier and to win the Grand Slam.

Women excelled in the sport of tennis as well. The first was Althea Gibson (1927–2003), who won her first title in 1956 when she won the French championship, and then triumphed in the women's singles at Wimbledon in 1957 and again in 1958. Gibson also won the

363

Wimbledon doubles in 1958. In 1957 and 1958, Gibson won the U.S. Open Women's Singles title. She also became the first black woman to play on the Ladies Professional Golf Association tour in 1964.

Before the Williams sisters—Serena and Venus—entered tennis competition, the world had already known Ora Washington (1898–1971), the first black woman to win seven consecutive titles in the American Tennis Association. Then in 1988, Zina Lynna Garrison (Jackson) (1963–), won gold in doubles and a bronze in singles in the Olympics held in Seoul, Korea, becoming the first black Olympic winner in tennis. Lori Michelle McNeil (1963–) defeated five-time Wimbledon champion and number-one ranked Steffi Graf in the first round of the Ladies Singles in 1994.

Why are the **Williams sisters** important?

Serena Williams (1981–) and sister Venus Ebony Starr Williams (1980–) became the first black women's team to succeed at the U.S. Open in 1999. That same year Serena became the first black woman to win the U.S. Open since 1958, when Althea Gibson won. In 2001 Venus won both Wimbledon and the U.S. Open. She also achieved the top spot at the Women's Tennis Association's world ranking in 2002, becoming the first black player with a number-one rating since 1975, when Arthur Ashe held that honor. Together and singularly, the Williams sisters continued to win champions and achieve fame. In 2012 Serena became a four-time winner of the U.S. Open and won gold in women's singles at the London Olympics. She recaptured the world's number-one ranking in women's tennis in February 2013, and became a five-time winner of the U.S. Open in September of that year.

TRACK AND FIELD AND THE OLYMPICS

Who are the **black stars** in **track and field**?

Black stars dominate in the sport of track and field, including sprints, relays, long jump, broad jump, triple jump, and much more. Icons in the sport include legendary Jesse Owens (1913–1980), who broke five world records in 1935, setting the stage for his greatest athletic achievement. In 1936, at the Berlin Olympics, he won four gold medals and disproved the rhetoric of black inferiority endorsed by Adolf Hitler, who refused to acknowledge his superiority or that of fellow black athletes. Ralph Boston (1939–) won three Olympic medals—gold in 1960, silver in 1964, and bronze in 1968. The first Olympic performer since Jesse Owens to win four track and field gold medals in one Olympiad was Carl Lewis (1961–), in 1984. Other stars were William DeHart Hubbard (1903–1976), Rafer Lewis Johnson (1935–), Edwin Corley Moses (1955–), Michael Duane Johnson (1967–), and Maurice Greene (1974–). Perhaps the brightest contemporary star is Jamaican sprinter—and five-time World and six-time Olympic gold medalist—Usain Bolt (1986–). He became the first black to hold simultaneous world and Olympic records in the 100-meter and 200-meter competitions, in 2008. When the London Olympics was held in 2012, Bolt became the first man in modern Olympic history to win gold in the 100-meter, 200-meter, and 4 x 100-meter relays in consecutive Olympics. He is popularly known as "Lightning Bolt."

What **black women** have achieved in **track and field**?

Black women have been record-setting athletes in track and field. High jumper Alice Coachman Davis (1923–) became the first black woman to win an Olympic gold medal, at the 1948 Olympics in London. She paved the way for generations of black American athletes to come, including legendary Wilma Rudolph (1940–1994), who overcame a serious disability to win three gold medals in the 1960 Olympics; Florence Delorez Griffith-Joyner (1959–1998), winner of three gold and one silver medal at the 1988 Olympics; and Jackie Joyner-Kersee (1962–), Olympic champion in the heptathlon in the 1988 Olympics.

Six-time Olympic gold medalist Usain Bolt is taking up the baton in track first carried by black track stars like Jesse Owens and Carl Lewis.

MISCELLANEOUS SPORTS

In **what other sports** have blacks achieved **celebrity status**?

Other sports in which blacks have reached stardom include automobile racing, hockey, ice skating, motocross, poker, and rodeo. In 1923 Rojo Jack became the first black to participate in automobile racing. Wendell Oliver Scott (1921–1990), became the first and only black driver to win a NASCAR Winston Cup (then the Grand National) race, in 1963. The 1977 film *Greased Lightning* was based on his life. Willie (William) Eldon O'Ree (1935–), of the National Hockey League's Boston Bruins, became the first black hockey player in the league, in 1958. It was not until 1981 that the league drafted its first black player, goaltender Grant Scott Fuhr (1962–); with multiple awards and Stanley Cup championships, he became the most celebrated of all black hockey players. Then in 2002, Canadian-born Jarome "Iggy" Iginla (1977–) became the first black to win the league's goal-scoring title. Ice skating saw skaters Debi Thomas and Shani Davis rise to fame. In 1984 Debi (Debra) Thomas (1967–) was the first black skater on a World Team, and in 1986 she became the first black woman to hold United States and world figure skating championships. Speed skater Shani Davis (1982–) became the first black to make a U.S. Olympic skating team, in 2002. He won an Olympic title in 2006, in Turin, Italy, and again in 2010, in Vancouver, becoming the first skater of any race to win two consecutive Olympic titles at the Winter Games.

Motocross recognizes James "Bubba" Stewart (1985–) as the first African American to dominate in that sport, in 2004. He racked up a record-breaking eleven American Motorcyclist Association Amateur National titles. The world of poker acknowledges professional player Phillip D. "Phil" Ivey (1976–) as one of the world's best all-round poker players. In 2002 Ivey won three World Series of Poker bracelets, the youngest player to do so. He had accumulated over $13.8 million in live tournament winnings by 2010.

Who was considered the **fastest bicycle rider** in the world in the **late 1800s**?

Marshall W. "Major" Taylor (1878–1932), of Indianapolis, Indiana, was the first native-born black American to win a major bicycle race, in 1898. He began as a trick rider for a local cycling shop and participated in a few amateur events. Taylor won his first professional start, a half-mile handicap held at Madison Square Garden, in spite of racism in cycling. Taylor was also the first black member of an integrated professional team. Toward the end of the year, he compiled twenty-one first-place victories, thirteen second-place berths, and eleven third-place showings. Taylor was known as the "fastest bicycle rider in the world" until his 1910 retirement. His father worked as a coachman for a wealthy white family. Taylor and the son of his father's employer became fast friends and it was through his friend that Taylor was tutored, learning to read and write, and became exposed to riding bicycles. Working for a bicycle shop, he rode in his first race as part of the shop team; he won the first prize gold medal at age thirteen. Taylor won more races but was also barred from the Indianapolis track after he broke a track record. By 1895 he was in Worcester, Massachusetts, having reached there by accompanying retired cyclist Louis "Birdie" Munger when he established a bicycle factory in that town. In Worcester, Taylor raced with a black club. In 1896 he raced against top amateurs in Middletown, Connecticut. Prejudice against him as a black rider continued after his 1898 win. He raced in Europe for a few months in 1901, winning twenty-one of twenty-five races; he became a celebrity after this performance. He had his last European season in 1909 and raced in Salt Lake City in 1910. After retiring, Taylor tried his hand at being an inventor, but his efforts to produce a more efficient wheel for cycling were unsuccessful. Several of his other business ventures also failed to catch fire. He resurfaced to race one more time in a 1917 old-timers' race and won. Taylor fell upon hard financial times and spent his last years in Chicago, where he had gone to push sales of his self-published autobiography. The book had been published in 1929. He was in the charity ward of a Chicago hospital when he died, and he was buried in a pauper's grave. In 1948 the owner of the Schwinn Bicycle Company had Taylor's body reburied in a more desirable section of the cemetery. At the dedication ceremony, a bronze plaque commemorating his importance to cycling was installed.

What blacks have become **icons in rodeo**?

One sport often forgotten as a field for black winners is rodeo. In 1876 Nat Love (1844–?), former slave, frontiersman, and cowboy, was the only black claimant to the title Deadwood Dick and so claimed to be the first known black rodeo champion. In 1905 Bill Pickett (1860–1932), rodeo cowboy and son of a former slave, is generally credited with being the first person to develop a way of bulldogging that made the act a spectacular performance. Pickett was honored in 1984 when the first Bill Pickett Rodeo was held; it continues as the only black rodeo. Other rodeo icons include Charles Sampson (1957–), the first black World Rodeo champion, in 1982; and Fred Whitfield (1967–), the first black American to win the world title in calf roping, in 1991. By 2000 Whitfield had won four World Calf Roping titles and was the first black rodeo performer to earn more than $1 million.References

References

Anderson, James D. *The Education of Blacks in the South, 1860–1935.* Chapel Hill: University of North Carolina Press, 1988.

Andrew, William, and Henry Louise Gates Jr., eds. *Slave Narratives: James Albert Ukawsaw Gronniosaw, Olaudah Equiano, Nat Turner, Frederick Douglass, William Wells Brown, Henry Bibb, Sojourner Truth, William & Ellen Craft, Harriett A. Jacobs, Jacob D. Green.* New York: Library of America, 2000.

Andrew, William L., Frances Smith Foster, and Trudier Harris, eds. *The Concise Oxford Companion to African American Literature.* New York: Oxford University Press, 2001.

Appiah, Kwame Anthony, and Henry Louis Gates Jr., eds. *Africana: The Encyclopedia of the African and African American Experience.* 5 vols. New York: Oxford University Press, 2005.

Arsenault, Raymond. *Freedom Rides: 1961 and the Struggle for Racial Justice.* New York: Oxford University Press, 2006.

Asante, Molefi Kete, and Ama Mazama, eds. *Encyclopedia of Black Studies.* Thousand Oaks, CA: Sage Publications, 2005.

Asante, Molefi Kete. *Afrocentricity.* Trenton, NJ: Africa World Press, 1988; Chicago: African American Images, 2003.

Ashe, Arthur R. Jr. *A Hard Road to Glory: A History of the African-American Athlete.* 4 vols. New York: John Wiley & Sons, 2005.

Astor, Gerald. *The Right to Fight: A History of African Americans in the Military.* Novato, CA: Presidio, 1998.

Baer, Hans, and Merrill Singer. *African-American Religion in the Twentieth Century: Varieties of Protest and Accommodation.* Knoxville: University of Tennessee Press, 1992.

Baraka, Amiri (LeRoi Jones). *Blues People: Negro Music in White America.* New York: Morrow, 1963.

Barlow, William. *The Making of Black Radio.* Philadelphia: Temple University Press, 1999.

Bearden, Romare, and Harry Henderson. *A History of African-American Artists from 1792 to the Present.* New York: Pantheon, 1993.

Bennett, Lerone Jr. *Before the Mayflower: A History of Black America.* 8th ed. Chicago: Johnson Publishing, 2007.

Black Americans in Congress, 1870–2007. Prepared under the Direction of the Committee on House Administration of the U.S. House of Representatives, by the Office of History and Preservation, Office of the Clerk, U.S. House of Representatives. Washington, DC: U.S. Government Printing Office, 2008.

Blassingame, John W. *The Slave Community*. New York: Oxford University Press, 1979.

Bogle, Donald. *Blacks in American Films and Television: An Encyclopedia*. New York: Garland Publishing, 1998.

Bogle, Donald. *Toms, Coons, Mulattoes, Mammies, and Bucks: An Interpretive History of Blacks in American Films*. Rev. ed. New York: Continuum, 1989.

Bontemps, Arna, ed. *The Harlem Renaissance Remembered*. New York: Dodd, Mead, 1972.

Borgman, Gerald, and Thomas S. Hischak, eds. *The Oxford Companion to American Theatre*. 3rd ed. New York: Oxford University Press, 2004.

Boyd, Todd, ed. *African Americans and Popular Culture*. 3 vols. Westport, CT: Praeger, 2008.

Bracks, Lean'tin. *African American Almanac: 400 Years of Triumph, Courage and Excellence*. Detroit: Visible Ink Press, 2012.

Branch, Taylor. *Parting the Waters: America in the King Years, 1954–1963*. New York: Simon & Schuster, 1988.

Branch, Taylor. *Pillar of Fire: America in the King Years, 1963–1965*. New York: Simon & Schuster, 1997.

Burnim, Mellonee V., and Portia K. Maultsby, eds. *African American Music: An Introduction*. New York: Routledge, 2006.

Bynoe, Yvonne, ed. *Encyclopedia of Rap and Hip Hop Culture*. Westport, CT: Greenwood Press, 2006.

Carpenter, Bill. *Uncloudy Days: The Gospel Music Encyclopedia*. San Francisco: Backbeat Books, 2005.

Chalk, Ocania. *Black College Sports*. New York: Dodd, Mead, 1975.

Christian, Charles M. *Black Saga: The African-American Experience*. Boston: Houghton Mifflin, 1995.

Collier-Thomas, Bettye, and V. P. Franklin, eds. *Sisters in the Struggle: African American Women in the Civil Rights-Black Power Movement*. New York: New York University Press, 2001.

Collins, Patricia Hill. *Black Feminist Thought: Knowledge, Consciousness, and the Politics of Empowerment*. New York: Routledge, 1990.

Cone, James H, and Gayraud S. Wilmore, eds. *Black Theology: A Documentary History*. 2 vols. New York: Orbis Books, 1993.

Crawford, Vicki L., Jacqueline Anne Rouse, and Barbara Woods. *Women in the Civil Rights Movement: Trailblazers and Torchbearers, 1941–1965*. Bloomington: Indiana University Press, 1993.

Cripps, Thomas. *Black Film as Genre*. Bloomington: University of Indiana Press, 1978.

Dates, Jeannette L., and William Barlow. *Split Image: African Americans in the Mass Media*. Washington, DC: Howard University Press, 1990.

Davis, Francis. *The History of the Blues: The Roots, the Music, the People*. Cambridge, MA: Da Capo Press, 2003.

Detweiler, Frederick G. *The Negro Press in the United States*. College Park, MD: McGrath, 1968.

Donaldson, Gary. *The History of African Americans in the Military; Double V*. Malabar, FL: Krieger, 1991.

Encyclopedia of African American Music. 3 vols. Santa Barbara: Greenwood, 2011.

Epstein, Dena J. Polacheck. *Sinful Tunes and Spirituals: Black Folk Music in the Civil War*. Rev. ed. Urbana: University of Illinois Press, 2003.

Field, Ron. *Civil Rights in America, 1865–1980*. Cambridge: Cambridge University Press, 2000.

Fine, Elizabeth C. *Soulstepping: African American Step Shows*. Urbana: University of Illinois Press, 2003.

Finkelman, Paul, ed. *Encyclopedia of African American History 1896 to the Present*. 2 vols. New York: Oxford University Press, 2009.

Finlayson, Reggie. *We Shall Overcome: The History of the Civil Rights Movement*. Minneapolis: Lerner Publications, 2003.

Foner, Eric. *Freedom's Lawmakers: A Directory of Black Officeholders during Reconstruction*. Rev. ed. New York: Baton Rouge: Louisiana State University Press, 1996.

Fouche, Rayvon. *Black Inventors in Age of Segregation*. Baltimore: Johns Hopkins University Press, 2003.

Franklin, John Hope, and Evelyn Brooks Higginbotham. *From Slavery to Freedom*. 9th ed. New York: McGraw-Hill, 2011.

Frazier, E. Franklin. *The Negro Church in America*. New York: Schocken, 1963.

Garrow, David J. *Bearing the Cross: Martin Luther King, Jr. and the Southern Christian Leadership Conference, a Personal Portrait*. New York: Morrow, 1986.

Gasman, Marybeth. *Envisioning Black Colleges: A History of the United Negro College Fund*. Baltimore: Johns Hopkins University Press, 2007.

Gates, Henry Louis Jr. *Life upon These Shores: Looking at African American History 1513–2008*. New York: Knopf, 2011.

Gates, Henry Louis Jr., and Cornel West. *The African-American Century: How Black Americans Have Shaped Our Country*. New York: Touchstone Simon & Schuster, 2000.

Gates, Henry Louis Jr., and Evelyn Brooks Higginbotham, eds. *African American National Biography*. 8 vols. New York: Oxford University Press, 2008.

Gay, Kathlyn. *African-American Holidays, Festivals, and Celebrations: The History, Customs, and Symbols Associated with Both Traditional and Contemporary Religious and Secular Events Observed by Americans of African Descent*. Detroit: Omnigraphics, 2007.

Gayle, Addison Jr., ed. *The Black Aesthetic*. New York: Anchor Books, 1971.

Glasrud, Bruce A., and Merline Pitre, eds. *Southern Black Women in the Modern Civil Rights Movement*. College Station, TX: Texas A&M University Press, 2013.

Glass, Barbara S. *African American Dance: An Illustrated History*. Jefferson, NC: McFarland, 2007.

Gubert, Betty Kaplan, Marian Sawyer, and Caroline M. Fanning. *Distinguished African Americans in Aviation and Space Science*. Westport, CT: Oryx Press, 2002.

Haines, Herbert H. *Black Radicals and the Civil Rights Movement, 1954–1970*. Knoxville: University of Tennessee Press, 1995.

Harris, Abram L. *The Negro as Capitalist*. College Park, MD: McGrath, 1936.

Harris, Cecil, and Larryette Kyle-DeBose. *Charging the Net: A History of Blacks in Tennis from Althea Gibson and Arthur Ashe to the Williams Sisters*. Chicago: Ivan R. Dee, 2007.

Harris, Othello, George Kirsch, and Claire Nolte. *Encyclopedia of Ethnicity in Sports in the United States*. Westport, CT: Greenwood Press, 2000.

Haskins, James. *Black Dance in America: A History through Its People*. New York: Crowell, 1990.

Haskins, Jim, and Kathleen Benson. *Black Stars: African American Religious Leaders*. San Francisco: Jossey-Bass, 1998.

Havranek, Carrie. *Women Icons of Popular Music: The Rebels, Rockers, and Renegades*. Westport, CT: Greenwood Press, 2009.

Hawkins, Billy. *The New Plantation: Black Athletes, College Sports, and Predominantly White NCAA Institutions*. New York: Palgrave Macmillan, 2010.

Henderson, Edwin B., and the editors of *Sport* Magazine. *The Black Athlete: Emergence and Arrival*. Washington, DC: Publishers Company, 1968.

Herkovits, Melville J. *The Myth of the Negro Past*. Boston: Beacon Press, 1958.

Hess, Mickey, ed. *Icons of Hip Hop: An Encyclopedia of the Movement, Music, and Culture*. Westport, CT: Greenwood Press, 2007.

Hill, Errol G., and James V. Hatch. *A History of African American Theater*. Cambridge: Cambridge University Press, 2003.

Hine, Darlene Clark, ed. *Black Women in America*. 2 vols. Brooklyn: Carlson Publishing, 1993.

Hine, Darlene Clark, ed. *Black Women in America*. 2nd ed. 3 vols. New York: Oxford University Press, 2005.

Hoatling, Edward. *The Great Black Jockeys: The Lives and Times of Men Who Dominated America's First National Sport*. Rockin, CA: Forum, 1999.

Hornsby, Alton Jr. *Chronology of African-American History*. Detroit: Gale, 1991.

Hornsby, Alton Jr. *Milestones in 20th-Century African-American History*. Detroit: Visible Ink Press, 1993.

Houck, Davis W., and David E. Dixon. *Women and the Civil Rights Movement, 1954–1965*. Jackson: University of Mississippi Press, 2009.

Huggins, Nathan, ed. *Harlem Renaissance*. Updated ed. New York: Oxford University Press, 2007.

Hutton, Frankie. *The Early Black Press in America, 1827–1860*. Westport, CT: Greenwood Press, 1993.

Ingham, John N., and Lynne B. Feldman, eds. *African-American Business Leaders: A Biographical Dictionary*. Westport, CT: Greenwood Press, 1994.

Iron, Richard. *In Search of the Black Fantastic: Politics & Popular Culture in the Post-Civil Rights Era*. New York: Oxford University Press, 2008.

Jaynes, Gerald D., general ed. *Encyclopedia of African American Society*. 2 vols. Thousand Oaks, CA: Sage Publications, 2005.

Johnson, Charles. *The Spirit of a Place Called Meharry*. Franklin, TN: Hillsboro Press, 2000.

Johnson, James Weldon. *Black Manhattan*. Reprint. New York: Da Capo. 1996.

Jones, James H. *Bad Blood: The Scandalous Story of the Tuskegee Experiment: When Government Doctors Played God and Science Went Mad*. New York: Free Press, 1981.

Jones, LeRoi (Amiri Baraka). *Blues People*. New York: Morrow, 1963.

Joseph, Peniel E., ed. *The Black Power Movement: Rethinking the Civil Rights-Black Power Era*. New York: Routledge, 2006.

Joyce, Donald Franklin. *Gatekeepers of Black Culture. Black-owned Book Publishing in the United States, 1817–1981*. Westport, CT: Greenwood Press, 1983.

Karenga, Maulana. *Kwanzaa: A Celebration of Family, Community and Culture*. Los Angeles: University of Sankore Press, 1998.

Katz, William Loren. *The Black West*. 3rd ed. Seattle: Open Hand Publishing, 1987.

Kellner, Bruce, ed. *The Harlem Renaissance: A Historical Dictionary for the Era*. New York: Methuen, 1987.

Knight, Gladys L. *Icons of African American Protest: Trailblazing Activists of the Civil Rights Movement*. 2 vols. Westport, CT: Greenwood Press, 2009.

Larkin, Colin, ed. *Encyclopedia of Popular Music*. 4th ed. New York: Oxford University Press, 2006.

Leab, Daniel I. *From Sambo to Superspade: The Black Experience in Motion Pictures*. Boston: Houghton Mifflin, 1975.

Leckie, William H., with Shirley A. Leckie. *The Buffalo Soldiers: A Narrative of the Negro Calvary in the West*. Rev. ed. Norman: University of Oklahoma Press, 2003.

Levy, Peter B. *Let Freedom Ring: A Documentary History of the Modern Civil Rights Movement*. Westport, CT: Praeger, 1992.

Levy, Peter B. *The Civil Rights Movement*. Westport, CT: Greenwood Press, 1998.

Lewis, Camella S. *African American Art and Artists*. Berkeley: University of California Press, 1994.

Lewis, David Levering. *When Harlem Was in Vogue*. New York: Alfred A. Knopf, 1981.

Lincoln, C. Eric, and Lawrence H. Mamiya. *The Black Church in the African American Experience*. Durham: Duke University Press, 1990.

Livingston, Ivor Lensworth, ed. *Praeger Handbook of Black American Health: Policies and Issues Behind Disparities*. 2nd ed. Westport, CT: Praeger, 2004.

Locke, Alain. *The Negro and His Music*. Washington, DC: The Associated Publishers, 1936.

Lomotey, Kofi, ed. *Encyclopedia of African American Education*. 2 vols. Los Angeles: Sage, 2010.

Lovell, John Jr. *Black Song: The Forge and the Flame*. New York: Macmillan, 1972.

Lowery, Charles D., and John F. Marszalek, eds. *The Greenwood Encyclopedia of African American Civil Rights: From Emancipation to the Twenty-first Century*. 2 vols. Westport, CT: Greenwood Press, 2003.

MacDonald, J. Fred. *Blacks and White TV: Afro-Americans in Television since 1948*. Chicago: Nelson-Hall, 1983.

Marable, Manning, ed. *The New Black Renaissance: The Souls Anthology of Critical African-American Studies*. Boulder, CO: Paradigm Publishers, 2005.

McElroy, Guy C. *Facing History: The Black Image in American Art, 1710–1940*. San Francisco: Bedford Arts, 1990.

Morais, Herbert M. *The History of the Negro in Medicine*. New York: Publishers Company, 1967.

Moss, Alfred A. Jr. *The American Negro Academy: Voice of the Talented Tenth*. Baton Rouge: Louisiana State University Press, 1981.

Murphy, Larry G., J. Gordon Melton, and Gary Ward, eds. *Encyclopedia of African American Religions*. New York: Garland Publishing, 1993.

Nalty, Bernard C. *Strength for the Fight: A History of Black Americans in the Military*. New York: Free Press, 1986.

Ostrom, Hans, and David Macey, eds. *The Greenwood Encyclopedia of African American Literature*. 5 vols. Westport, CT: Greenwood Press, 2005.

The Oxford Handbook of African American Citizenship, 1865–Present. Eds. Henry Louis Gates, Jr., Claude Stele, Lawrence D. Bobo, and others. New York: Oxford University Press, 2012.

Page, Yolanda Williams, ed. *Icons of African American Literature: The Black Literary World*. Santa Barbara, CA: Greenwood/ABC-CLIO, 2011.

Penial, Joseph E. *Waiting 'til the Midnight Hour: A Narrative History of Black Power in America*. New York: Henry Holt, 2006.

Pierce, Joseph A. *Negro Business and Business Education*. New York: Harper & Row, 1947.

Powell, Richard. *Black Art and Culture in the 20th Century*. New York: Thames and Hudson, 1997.

Powell, Richard, and David A. Bailey. *Rhapsodies in Black: Art of the Harlem Renaissance*. Berkeley: University of California Press, 1997.

Pride, Armistead Scott. *History of the Black Press*. Washington, DC: Howard University Press, 1997.

Quarles, Benjamin. *Black Abolitionists*. New York: Da Capo Press, 1991.

Raboteau, Albert J. *Canaan Land: A Religious History of African Americans*. New York: Oxford University Press, 2001.

Reagon, Bernice Johnson, ed. *We'll Understand It Better By and By*. Washington, DC: Smithsonian Institution Press, 1992.

Rhoden, William C. *Forty Million Slaves: The Rise, Fall, and Redemption of the Black Athlete*. New York: New York: Crown Publishers, 2006.

Riley, James. *The Biographical Encyclopedia of the Negro Leagues*. New York: Carroll & Graf, 1994.

Roberts, Deotis J. *Black Theology*. Philadelphia: Westminster Press, 2009.

Robinson, Jo Ann Gibson. *The Montgomery Bus Boycott and the Women Who Started It: The Memoir of Jo Ann Gibson Robinson*. Knoxville: University of Tennessee Press, 1987.

Ross, Charles K., ed. *Race and Sport: The Struggle for Equality On and Off the Field*. Jackson: University Press of Mississippi, 2004.

Ross, Rosetta E. *Witnessing and Testifying: Black Women, Religion and Civil Rights*. Minneapolis: Fortress Press, 2003.

Rucker, Walter, and James Nathaniel Upton, eds. *Encyclopedia of American Race Riots*. Westport, CT: Greenwood Press, 2007.

Salzman, Jack, Cornell West, and David Lionel Smith, eds. *Encyclopedia of African-American Culture and History*. 5 vols. New York: Simon & Schuster, 1996.

Sammons, Vivian O. *Blacks in Science and Medicine*. New York: Hemisphere Publishing, 1990.

Sampson, Henry T. *Swingin' on the Ether Waves: A Chronological History of African Americans in Radio and Television Broadcasting, 1925–1955*. Lanham, MD: Scarecrow Press, 2005.

Savitt, Todd L. *Medicine and Slavery: The Diseases and Health Care of Blacks in Antebellum Virginia*. Urbana: University of Illinois Press, 1978.

Scott, Emmett G. *Scott's Official History of the American Negro in the World War*. New York: Arno Press, 1996.

Smith, Earl. *Race, Sport, and the American Dream*. Durham: Carolina Academic Press, 2007.

Smith, Jessie Carney. *Black Firsts: 4,000 Ground-breaking and Pioneering Historical Events*. 3^d ed. Detroit: Visible Ink, 2013.

Smith, Jessie Carney, ed. *Encyclopedia of African American Business*. 2 vols. Westport, CT: Greenwood Press, 2006.

Smith, Jessie Carney, ed. *Encyclopedia of African American Popular Culture*. 4 vols. Santa Barbara, CA: Greenwood/ABC Clio, LLC, 2011.

Smith, Jessie Carney, ed. *Images of Blacks in American Culture: A Reference Guide to Information Sources*. Westport, CT: Greenwood Press, 1988.

Smith, Jessie Carney, and Linda T. Wynn, eds. *Freedom Facts and Firsts: 400 Years of the African American Civil Rights Experience*. Detroit: Visible Ink Press, 2009.

Southern, Eileen. *The Music of Black Americans: A History*. 3d ed. New York: Norton, 1997.

Stearns, Marshall, and Jean Stearns. *Jazz Dance: The Story of American Vernacular Dance*. New York: Schirmer, 1964.

Steward, T. G. *Buffalo Soldiers: The Colored Regulars in the United States Army*. New York: Humanity Books, 2003.

Stuckey, Sterling. *Slave Culture: Nationalist Theory and the Foundations of Black America.* New York: Oxford University Press, 1987.

Townes, Emilie M. *Womanist Justice, Womanist Hope.* Atlanta: Scholars Press, 1993.

Townes, Emilie M. *In a Blaze of Glory: Womanist Spirituality as Social Witness.* Nashville: Abingdon Press, 1995.

Trotter, James Monroe. *Music and Some Highly Musical People.* Boston: Lee & Shepard, 1878.

Tucker-Worgs, Tamelyn N. *The Black Mega-Church: Theology, Gender, and the Politics of Public Engagement.* Waco, TX: Baylor University Press, 2011.

Van Sertima, Ivan, ed. *Blacks in Science: Ancient and Modern.* New Brunswick, NJ: Transaction, 1983.

Walker, Juliet E. K. *The History of Black Business in America: Capitalism, Race, Entrepreneurship.* New York: Macmillan Reference Library USA, 1998.

Walker, Juliet E. K., ed. *Encyclopedia of African American Business History.* Westport, CT: Greenwood Press, 1999.

Webster, Raymond B., ed. *African American Firsts in Science and Technology.* Detroit: Gale, 1999.

Whitaker, Matthew C. *African American Icons of Sport: Triumphs, Courage and Excellence.* Westport, CT: Greenwood Press, 2008.

White, Deborah Gray. *Aren't I a Woman? Female Slaves in the Plantation South.* 2nd ed. New York: Norton, 2000.

Wilmore, Gayraud S. *Black Religion and Black Radicalism: An Examination of the Black Experience in Religion.* Garden City, NY: Anchor Press Doubleday, 1973.

Wilson, Dreck Spurlock, ed. *African American Architects: A Biographical Dictionary 1865–1945.* New York: Routledge, 2004.

Winbush, Raymond A., ed. *Should America Pay? Slavery and the Raging Debate on Reparations.* New York: Amistad/Harper Collins, 2003.

Wolseley, Roland E. *The Black Press, U.S.A.* 2nd ed. Ames: Iowa State University Press, 1990.

Woodson, Carter G. *The Education of the Negro Prior to 1861.* 1919. Reprint. New York: Arno, 1968.

Index

Note: (ill.) indicates photos and illustrations.

381

Joyner, Tom, 35
Joyner-Kersee, Jackie, 20, 365
Judd, Carrie, 290
Julien Rosenwald Rural Negro
    Schools project, 121–22
Julius Rosenwald Fund, 44, 112
Juneteenth, 3

K

Kansas, 77–78
Kappa Alpha Psi, 11
Karenga, Maulana, 130
Karriem, Elijah, 301
Kearsley, John, Jr., 321
Keeble, Sampson W., 264
Keister, George, 32
Kelly, James, 302
Kelly, Leontine T. C., 15, 301–2
Kelly, Sharon Pratt Dixon, 281–82
Kennedy, Adrienne, 177
Kennedy, Edward, 265
Kennedy, John F., 92, 132, 196, 250,
    279, 280
Kennedy, Robert, 145
Kentucky Derby, 17, 339, 340
Keppard, Freddie, 230
Kersands, Billy, 25
Keys, Alan L., 271
King, B. B., 6, 234 (ill.), 234–35
King, Charles, 49
King, Coretta Scott, 150, 253
King, Henry, 339
King, Jerry, 49
King, Martin Luther, Jr.
    Albany, Georgia, movement, 87
    Alpha Phi Alpha, 252
    assassination, 30, 94, 177
    biography, 182
    Black Arts Movement, 178
    Bloody Sunday, 88
    Civil Rights Movement, 3
    Height, Dorothy, 258
    Highlander Folk School, 92
    "I Have a Dream" speech,"
        89–90, 90 (ill.), 92
    Jackson, Jesse, 271
    Jackson, Mahalia, 221
    "Letter from Birmingham Jail,"
        89, 294
    March on Washington, 247
    Montgomery Bus Boycott, 86
    Morehouse College, 129
    Motley, Constance Baker, 280
    nonviolence movement, 86
    Sleet, Moneta, 150
    Southern Christian Leadership
        Conference, 14, 245, 293
    "We Shall Overcome," 229
    Withers, Ernest C., 150
King Charles Troupe, 49

King-Reeves, Hattie, 26
Kirk, Ron, 281
Knight, Etheridge, 177
Knight, Gladys, 64, 236
Knights of Peter Claver, 252
Knowles, Beyoncé Gisele, 226 (ill.),
    226–27
Komunyakaa, Yusef, 179
Kool DF Herc, 235
Korean War, 207–8
Kraepelin, Emil, 330
"Krazy Kat," 47

L

labor unions, 64–66
Lacks, Henrietta, 329
Lafayette, 329
Lafon, Thomy, 70
Laing, Daniel, Jr., 324
LaMothe, Ferdinand Joseph, 33
Land Grant Act of 1890, 106–7
land-grant colleges, 106, 107
Landrieu, Mary, 85
Lane, William Henry, 29
Laney, Lucy Craft, 110
Lange, Elizabeth, 297
Langston, John Mercer, 117, 240
Lankford, John A., 21–22, 22 (ill.)
Larsen, Nella, 6, 33, 171
Lashley, Joe, 18, 345
Latimer, Lewis Howard, 15, 315
Lautier, Louis, 144
law enforcement, 267–68
law schools, 117–18
Lawrence, Jacob, 6, 44, 46
Lawrence, Robert H., Jr., 17, 334,
    334 (ill.)
Lawson, Belford, 245, 246
Lawson, James, 88, 293
Lawson, Jennifer Karen, 38
Leach, Robert B., 324
Lee, Canada, 26
Lee, Don, 177, 178
Lee, Jarena, 13, 15, 165, 304–5
Lee, Mrs. Herbert, 92
Lee, Spike, 40 (ill.), 41
Lees, Tom, 342
Leftenant-Colon, Nancy, 202
Legal Defense and Educational
    Fund (LDEF), 242–43
Leidesdorff, William Alexander, 7
Leland, John, 284
Leslie, Lisa, 357
"Letter from Birmingham Jail"
    (King), 14, 294
Lew, Barzillai, 184
Lewis, Carl, 20, 364
Lewis, David Levering, 169, 182
Lewis, Edmonia, 6, 43
Lewis, George, 339

Lewis, John, 3, 60 (ill.), 88, 246
Lewis, Oliver, 17
Lewis, Reginald F., 57–58, 58–59
Lewis, William Henry, 358
Liberia, 76–77
Liberty Party, 261
Library of Congress, 174
Liele, George, 286, 287, 288
Lincoln, Abraham, 2, 79–80, 185,
    242, 274
Lincoln Motion Picture Company,
    40
Lincoln University, 104, 106, 129
Links, Inc., 11, 258–59
Lipinski, Ann Marie, 148
literature. *See also* Harlem Renais-
    sance; poetry; slave narratives
    acceptance of African Americans
        in, 181
    Black Aesthetic, 177
    Black Aesthetic Movement,
        178–79
    Black Arts Movement, 177–78,
        178–79
    Butler, Octavia, 175
    Civil Rights Movement, 176–77
    Delany, Samuel Ray, 175
    Ellison, Ralph, 179, 179 (ill.)
    Hammon, Briton, 161
    Lewis, David Levering, 182
    Morrison, Toni, 181–82, 182 (ill.)
    science fiction, 175
    Soyinka, Wole, 180
    Walcott, Derek, 180
    Walker, Alice, 179–80
"Little Rock Nine," 124–25
Locke, Alain
    Black Aesthetic, 177
    Harlem Renaissance, 6, 33–34,
        43, 114, 168, 169
    Hurston, Zora Neale, 172
Lomax, Louis, 150–51
Lomax, Michael L., 50
Lombard, Carole, 39
Long, Charles, 308
Long, Eddie, 14, 297
Long, Forest, 250
Long, Fred, 359
Louis, Joe, 18, 343 (ill.), 343–44,
    349
Love, Nat ("Deadwood Dick"), 20,
    367
Lowery, Joseph, 293
"Lucille," 234 (ill.), 234–35
Luckett, LeToya, 226
Lucy, Autherine Juanita, 117
L'Union, 136
Luper, Clara, 93
Lynch, John Roy, 265
lynching, 85, 97
Lyons, Maritcha, 256–57

N

X, Y, Z